Everyday Heroism

Victorian Constructions of the Heroic Civilian

John Price

B L O O M S B U R Y

LONDON • NEW DELHI • NEW YORK • SYDNEY

Bloomsbury Academic

An imprint of Bloomsbury Publishing Plc

50 Bedford Square	1385 Broadway
London	New York
WC1B 3DP	NY 10018
UK	USA

www.bloomsbury.com

Bloomsbury is a registered trade mark of Bloomsbury Publishing Plc

First published 2014

British Library Cataloguing-in-Publication Data
A catalogue record for this book is available from the British Library.

ISBN: HB: 978-1-4411-0665-0
ePDF: 978-1-4411-3037-2
ePub: 978-1-4411-3675-6

Library of Congress Cataloging-in-Publication Data
A catalog record for this book is available from the Library of Congress.

Typeset by Deanta Global Publishing Services, Chennai, India
Printed and bound in Great Britain

Paul C. Price
(1932–1996)

Contents

List of Tables   viii

List of Figures   x

Acknowledgements   xii

Introduction   'Capable of Splendid Deeds': Heroism and the Heroic in the
                Nineteenth and Early Twentieth Centuries   1

1   'Gallantry in Saving Life': The Albert Medal   31

2   'Heroism in Every-day Life': Alternative Approaches to Everyday
     Heroism   63

3   'Erected by Public Subscription': Monuments to Everyday Heroism   95

4   'Heroes for Hire': The Carnegie Hero Fund Trust   125

5   'Courage for a man is heroism for a girl': The Gendered Nature of Heroism   167

Conclusion   197

Appendix One   205

Appendix Two   207

Notes   215

Bibliography   241

Index   261

List of Tables

Table 1 Number and percentage of nominations for the Albert Medal
between 1866 and 1914 42

Table 2 Number and percentage of Albert Medals awarded and refused
between 1866 and 1914 44

Table 3 Number and percentage of Albert Medal nominations refused
between 1866 and 1914 and the reason given for refusal 48

Table 4 Number and percentage of Albert Medal nominations for men
awarded and refused between 1866 and 1914 57

Table 5 Number and percentage of men, women and minors who
received the Albert Medal (AM) or awards from the Carnegie
Hero Fund Trust (CHFT) or the Society for the Protection of Life
from Fire (SPLF) 138

Table 6 Occupations of men who received the Albert Medal (AM) or
awards from the Carnegie Hero Fund Trust (CHFT) and the
Society for the Protection of Life from Fire (SPLF) 139

Table 7 Occupations of women who received the Albert Medal (AM)
or awards from the Carnegie Hero Fund Trust (CHFT) and the
Society for the Protection of Life from Fire (SPLF) 144

Table 8 Number and percentage of awards given by the Society for the
Protection of Life from Fire (SPLF) between 1908 and 1914 and
the nature of the incident 146

Table 9 Number of awards made to minors by the Carnegie Hero Fund
Trust (CHFT) between 1908 and 1914 and the reason given for
making the award 147

Table 10 Nature of awards made to minors by the Carnegie Hero Fund
Trust (CHFT) and the Society for the Protection of Life from
Fire (SPLF) in comparison with awards of the Albert Medal (AM) 148

Table 11 Number and type of honorary awards given by the Carnegie
Hero Fund Trust (CHFT) between 1908 and 1914 154

Table 12 Number and percentage of the type of awards given by the
Carnegie Hero Fund Trust (CHFT) between 1908 and 1914 154

Table 13 Number of awards made by the Carnegie Hero Fund Trust
(CHFT) between 1908 and 1914 and the reason given for making
the award 155

Table 14   Number of one-off payments awarded to individuals by the
            Carnegie Hero Fund Trust (CHFT) between 1908 and 1914 and
            the reason given for making the award   156
Table 15   Number of one-off payments awarded to individuals by the
            Carnegie Hero Fund Trust (CHFT) between 1908 and 1914 and
            the reason given for making the award (with figures for cases
            adjusted to include honorary awards as recognition of action and
            percentages recalculated)   157
Table 16   Sum of money awarded by the Carnegie Hero Fund Trust
            (CHFT) in the case of a one-off payment to an individual and the
            number of times that sum was awarded between 1908 and 1914   158
Table 17   Number and percentage of married and unmarried women who
            received the Albert Medal (AM) or awards from the Carnegie
            Hero Fund Trust (CHFT) or the Society for the Protection of Life
            from Fire (SPLF)   172
Table 18   Occupations of women who received the Albert Medal (AM)
            or awards from the Carnegie Hero Fund Trust (CHFT) and the
            Society for the Protection of Life from Fire (SPLF)   173

List of Figures

Figure 1 The Watts Memorial to Heroic Self-Sacrifice, Postman's Park,
London EC1, 2004 (*John Price*, 2004)   19

Figure 2 An example of the ceramic tablets that form the Watts Memorial
(*John Price*, 2004)   20

Figure 3 Alice Ayres pictured with one of her sister's children to whom
she was nursemaid (*Illustrated London News, 1885*)   23

Figure 4 The interior of the Red Cross Hall, Southwark, 1893 (*English
Illustrated Magazine, June 1893*)   71

Figure 5 Illustration of the Walter Crane mural, 'Alice Ayres', erected in
the Red Cross Hall in 1890 (*English Illustrated Magazine, June 1893*)   73

Figure 6 Illustrations showing part of the planned panel layout for
the mural project in the Red Cross Hall (*English Illustrated
Magazine, June 1893*)   75

Figure 7 Study for 'Alice Ayres' for the Red Cross Hall, Southwark, c.1889
(*Royal Borough of Kensington and Chelsea Library and Arts Service*)   76

Figure 8 Illustration of the Walter Crane mural, 'Jamieson', erected in the
Red Cross Hall in 1892 (*English Illustrated Magazine, June 1893*)   78

Figure 9 Drinking fountain commemorating Ethel Harrison, Newark-on-
Trent, 2008 (*John Price*)   96

Figure 10 Monument to William Hunter in Townhill Cemetery,
Dunfermline, Scotland, 2008 (*John Price*)   101

Figure 11 Monument to Edgar George Wilson, Thames towpath, Osney
Lock, Oxford, 2008 (*John Price*)   102

Figure 12 Monument to William Walton, Town Hall Gardens, Ferryhill,
Durham, 2008 (*John Price*)   103

Figure 13 Monument to Mark Addy, Weaste Cemetery, Salford, 2008 (*John
Price*)   104

Figure 14 Bronze memorial plaque commemorating Percy Henry Gordon,
Rochester Esplanade, Kent, 2010 (*John Price*)   107

Figure 15 Memorial to Albert Lee, Queens Park, Heywood, Rochdale, 2008
(*John Price*)   109

Figure 16   Monument to Timothy Trow, London Road, Stoke on Trent,
            2008 (*John Price*)   111
Figure 17   Monument commemorating Mary Rogers, Western Esplanade,
            Southampton, 2008 (*John Price*)   114
Figure 18   Monument commemorating Alice Ayres, erected over her grave
            in Isleworth Cemetery, 2004 (*John Price*)   116
Figure 19   Illustration of the wreck of the SS Stella with an inset of
            Stewardess Mary Rogers (*Illustrated London News, 1900*)   184

Acknowledgements

The research for this book was funded by the Arts and Humanities Research Council (AHRC) under its Doctoral Awards Scheme and I would like to gratefully acknowledge its support.

This study employs a wide and varied range of source materials and locating and accessing these required the services of a number of archives whose services I would like to gratefully acknowledge: The British Library and Newspaper Archive; Dunfermline Carnegie Library, Fife; Durham County Record Office; Ferryhill Library, County Durham; The Guildhall Library and Manuscripts Department, London; Heinz Archive, National Portrait Gallery, London; Hounslow Local Studies Library, Middlesex; John Rylands University Library, Manchester; Liverpool Record Office and Local History Library; London Metropolitan Archives; The National Archives, Kew; Newark Local Studies Library, Nottinghamshire; Nottinghamshire County Archives; Rochdale Local Studies Centre, Lancashire; Salford Local History Library and City Archives Centre, Lancashire; Southampton Archives, Hampshire; Southwark Local History Library, London; Stoke on Trent City Archives, Staffordshire; Tower Hamlets Local History Library and Archives, London.

In addition to these archives, a number of organizations were invaluable for providing archival materials and I would like to thank the following for their support and assistance: Agnes Knoll at the Bankside Open Spaces Trust; Diana Coke, Mary Nayler and Dick Wilkinson at the Royal Humane Society; Morna O'Neill for correspondence and information regarding Walter Crane; Mark Bills and Desna Greenhow at the Watts Gallery; Heather Birchall at the Whitworth Art Gallery; Didy Graham at the Victoria Cross and George Cross Association and the Royal Borough of Kensington and Chelsea Library and Arts Service for permission to reproduce materials.

In June 2009, I had the pleasure of co-organizing an AHRC-funded symposium on non-military heroism, and I would like to thank all the delegates and speakers at that event, whose contributions helped me to develop my ideas on the nature of the idea, in particular, Craig Barclay; my co-organizer Michael Goodrum; Tanja Schult, Martha Vandrei and John Wilson.

The Department of History at King's College London, in particular Laura Clayton and Maddy Jessop, provided much assistance during the research for this book, and I owe an enormous debt and my sincere thanks to my two PhD supervisors, Ludmilla Jordanova and Paul Readman. Their advice and support was completely invaluable, both on an academic level where their expertise and knowledge was second to none and also pastorally where their guidance and reassurance was always forthcoming and generous. I would also like to thank Max Jones and Clare Pettitt for their valuable examination and analysis of my original thesis.

Finally, sincere thanks to my friends and family, in particular Tina and Carol, who have supported me every step of the way and without whom the journey would have been far more arduous and a lot less enjoyable.

Introduction

'Capable of Splendid Deeds':
Heroism and the Heroic in the Nineteenth
and Early Twentieth Centuries

The men whose bravery and great deeds are described in these pages have been selected not because they are faultless in character and life, but because they were brave, generous, self-forgetful, self-sacrificing and capable of splendid deeds. Men love and honour them . . . because they see in their heroes the kind of men they would like to be; for the possibilities of the heroic are in almost all men. This book is put forth in the faith that it will not only pass on the fame of the heroes of the past but help make heroes in the present.[1]

Heroes Every Child Should Know (1906)

Heroes and heroines in humble life might be as rewarding to study as Lord Kitchener or Lord Curzon. A history of carriage folk which ignored the horses' hooves, or a narrative of battles which only had eyes for the general staff, would be as airless as a bunker.[2]

Raphael Samuel (1989)

I think that the people on the plinths in the main square in our capital city should be identifiable to the generality of the population. I have not a clue who two of the generals there are or what they did.[3]

Ken Livingstone (2000)

Robert Baden-Powell (1857–1914); Field Marshal Sir Colin Campbell (1792–1863); Major-General Charles George Gordon (1833–85); Major-General Sir Henry Havelock (1795–1857); Field Marshal Horatio Kitchener (1850–1916); Lieutenant Colonel Thomas Edward Lawrence (1888–1935); David Livingstone (1813–1873); General Sir Charles James Napier (1782–1853); Vice Admiral Horatio Nelson (1758–1805); Sir James Outram (1803–63); Field Marshal Frederick Roberts (1832–1914); Captain Robert Falcon Scott (1868–1912); Field Marshal Garnet Joseph Wolseley (1833–1913); Field Marshal Arthur Wellesley (1769–1852).

When it comes to life-risking acts of bravery, the fourteen men listed above arguably represent some of the most important and notable figures to be recognized, celebrated and commemorated for their heroism in the period 1850–1914. At least that would be the conclusion most easily arrived at following a study of the historiography on the idea of heroism in the nineteenth and early twentieth centuries. Studies of female heroism have been relatively few and far between, and for men, a certain type of heroism has tended to dominate. As a result of these historiographical trends, the study of heroism during the period has become a subject which is largely viewed as synonymous with the military or with adventurism and involving events that most often took place in 'exotic' places, usually parts of the British Empire such as Africa or India. Furthermore, historians have tended to approach the subject of heroism by focusing on the actions of notable individuals and their real or metaphorical 'journey' to heroic status, which tends to privilege the study of 'the hero' over the study of heroism as an idea itself.

By contrast, this book establishes new avenues for the study of the idea of heroism in the period 1850–1914 and, by revealing, charting and examining the development of a distinct discourse of 'everyday' heroism, it will widen the focus beyond military heroes and the so-called Great Men of History. The term everyday heroism refers to acts of life-risking bravery, undertaken by otherwise ordinary individuals, largely in the course of their daily lives and within quotidian surroundings. This study shows that, rather than being overlooked or considered inconsequential by contemporaries, everyday heroism was a popular, widespread, prominent and influential idea, and individuals who undertook such acts were as celebrated, admired and commemorated as their military or imperial counterparts.

The timeframe of 1850–1914 has been chosen because it was in the late nineteenth and early twentieth centuries that powerful discourses of life-risking heroism, including everyday heroism, prominently emerged and developed. This is not to say that ideas of heroism and exemplary lives were not present or prevalent at other times. For example, as Peter Karsten has outlined, the lives and exploits of patriot heroes such as Oliver Cromwell, John Hampden and Charles I experienced fluctuating periods of acclaim up to and beyond the period under discussion in this thesis.[4] Also, as discussed below, high-profile and influential thinkers, such as Thomas Carlyle, as well as the authors of other volumes recounting stories of historical heroism, certainly contributed to a pre-1850 atmosphere in which ideas of heroism and exemplary lives were stimulated and could develop.[5] Notwithstanding this, it was not until after 1850 that a more distinct discourse of everyday heroism in particular began to emerge and develop, hence the focus on that period.

Thomas Carlyle's series of lectures entitled *On Heroes, Hero-Worship and the Heroic in History* (1841) is frequently cited as a precursor or early catalyst for the nineteenth-century idea of hero worship. Famously, Caryle's lectures opened with the bold claim that 'the history of what man has accomplished in this world, is at bottom the History of the Great Men who have worked here'.[6] *On Heroes* certainly motivated thought and discussion on the manner in which exemplary or heroic biographies could influence historical change and Carlyle's ideas were undoubtedly adopted by others, including, as Dinah Birch has shown, the writer and artist John Ruskin.[7] However, Carlyle is not discussed or examined at length in this book because his 'heroes' were the 'great men of history' – thinkers, politicians, statesmen and men of letters – rather than those who undertook single acts of life-risking bravery and certainly not the otherwise ordinary men and women who are the subject of this work.

Furthermore, although, as will be revealed, many of those who advocated and promoted the recognition or commemoration of everyday heroes had their own social or political motivations, Carlyle was employing historical heroic exemplarity to promote a higher philosophical agenda about, among other things, the nature of historical change, the limits of democracy and the failings of utilitarianism. As Birch put it, 'Carlyle's rather fevered celebration of the heroes of history . . . is as political as it is literary.'[8] Carlyle was effectively discussing heroes more as notional models rather than real people and the heroism he was advocating was characterized by dedication, inspiration and admiration rather than the risking of life to save others. Consequently, his work on heroes and hero worship, while undeniably an important foundation for wider Victorian attitudes towards heroism, had less direct impact or influence on the development of the idea of everyday heroism.

Studying civilian acts of life-risking bravery in a historical context has, until now, attracted little attention from scholars and this invites the question, why?[9] The relative absence of critical engagement with the subject of everyday heroism may be purely and simply because it has been overlooked. Historians may not, perhaps, have realized that a parallel strand of heroism existed alongside the military and imperial model and that the everyday variety was a prominent and influential idea within the more general discourse on the subject. It is undoubtedly the case that the examination of military heroes and imperial adventure heroes has predominated in studies that engage with acts of life-risking heroism during the Victorian and early Edwardian periods.[10] Furthermore, because this dominance has, in turn, had an impact on how the subject of heroism itself has come to be viewed and approached, it is important to explain how and why historians have largely approached the idea in this manner.

One explanation can be found by examining the methodology of historical research. Researching and writing history relies upon questioning things; asking who, what, when, where and why is the historian's *raison d'être*. Perhaps, then, one reason why everyday heroism has not been examined is because historians have not asked the kinds of questions that necessitate an engagement with the idea. When a historian selects a subject for investigation, they take a number of factors into consideration, including the type of history that they study, the type and nature of the discourses taking place during the period that concerns them and the currents of existing historiography. For example, military history is a distinct branch of the discipline and consequently there is a body of scholars who start from a position of examining ideas within a military context. Therefore, when approaching heroism, they have been largely unconcerned with studying the non-military varieties.[11] Similarly, cultural historians interested in the British Empire and popular imperialism have, when examining heroism, largely focused upon imperial subjects or conflicts.[12] This is not to suggest that there is anything wrong with researching military and imperial heroism in order to gain a greater understanding of military history and popular imperialism. However, one issue with studies such as these is that they have a tendency to suggest conclusions about heroism in general, without recognizing or acknowledging that they are only dealing with one particular strand or construction of the idea. In turn, they create or perpetuate assumptions and conclusions that the military and/or imperial model was dominant in the general discourse on heroism which, as this study will demonstrate, was not the case.

One example of this tendency is a study by C. I. Hamilton in which he proposed to discover 'what kind of men . . . the Victorians accepted as their heroes [and] what did the Victorians mean when they used the word hero'.[13] However, in seeking to answer these general questions about heroism, Hamilton chose to examine how the idea was constructed in the biographies of senior naval officers and how such biographies were received by junior recruits. From his evidence, Hamilton concluded that Christianity, and the model of the highly moral Christian warrior, formed the basis for the Victorian idea of heroism. His conclusion is convincing and useful, but only in relation to the very specific type of individuals that he examined and for understanding the equally specific naval or military construction of heroism. Furthermore, Hamilton reached the general conclusion that 'heroes were welcome not so much because they inspired but because they comforted', but he did so solely on the basis of how military hagiographic biographies were received by young naval officers.[14] Such a conclusion may well be correct for those examples, but it was certainly not the case with regard to everyday heroes. So while Hamilton's approach does, as he has argued, allow the reader to 'discover something of what the Victorians meant when they said *hero*', that 'something' is limited to the construction and reception of heroism solely within a naval context, which leaves a great deal still to be discovered and questions to be answered.[15]

So, military historians seeking to further their understanding of the military is one possible explanation for a historiographical tendency towards military heroism. Likewise, cultural historians examining popular imperialism through studies of heroism may account for the drift in that direction. Another explanation is related to how the ideas of a given society were being articulated in public at a given time and the manner in which that subsequently influences the approaches adopted by historians. To give an example, Hansard is the official report of the debates that took place in Parliament and as such it represents a key source for identifying prominent issues in the political discourse of the modern period. In these debates, for the period 1857 to 1914, the subject of the Victoria Cross, the highest decoration for military gallantry, was raised or discussed on around 150 occasions.[16] In comparison, the Albert Medal, the highest award for civilian gallantry, was only mentioned around twenty times between its introduction in 1866 and 1914. Other organizations recognizing civilian heroism did not fare any better; the Royal Humane Society was mentioned eighteen times between 1850 and 1915, the Society for the Protection of Life from Fire just twice in the same period and the Carnegie Hero Fund Trust was not mentioned at all. Clearly, this particular exercise only gives a rough indication of public prominence and subjects could be raised in Parliament within negative contexts as well as within positive ones. However, what these rough approximations show is that everyday heroism was not being discussed as often or featuring as strongly as the military variety in the high political discourse of the period. Consequently, historians seeking answers regarding the nature and construction of heroism within this particular type of setting or context would be more likely to encounter the military rather than the everyday strand of the idea.

A similar argument can be made with regard to other forms of public discourse. Take, for example, one that features later in this book, the creation of public monuments. Terry Cavanagh, writing about the lack of Victorian monuments to women in Liverpool, has provided an excellent summary of how prominent discourses could determine the type of people who were commemorated:

During the nineteenth century women did not have the vote, could not serve in the armed forces, were excluded by and large from public life, and, once married, rarely had independent wealth. Therefore they could not become politicians or soldiers and only in exceptional circumstances could run businesses or become public benefactors – which cover most of the principal spheres in which public commemoration was likely to occur.[17]

Political and military themes were, then, important driving forces behind the processes of Victorian civic commemoration and, consequently, these were the discourses that featured most often in public memorial schemes and the discussions regarding them.[18] So, once again, historians of the Victorian period who have chosen to investigate the idea of heroism by examining public monuments will have been far more likely to settle upon military examples, or those of notable individuals such as politicians, then the civilian heroes and heroines of everyday life.

A third possible explanation for a historiographical emphasis on military heroism can be identified by considering the position of militarism – the idea of a strong and guiding military spirit in society which was praised and celebrated – within the historiography for the period 1850–1914. There have certainly been many studies which have argued that militarism was a potent and influential discourse, although revisionist historians have challenged certain aspects of these arguments, especially with regard to the Edwardian period.[19] Vigorous historiographical debate tends to stimulate further interest in a subject and in turn this encourages historians to engage with those particular topics so as to contribute to the discussion. Consequently, militarism has become a significant area for historical investigation and military heroism has provided a rich and convenient seam of evidence. For example, cultural historians in particular have focused upon literary portrayals of subjects such as Henry Havelock and General Gordon and the suffusion of military heroism in juvenile literature and school textbooks, as convincing evidence for the militaristic nature of Victorian society.[20] Once again, employing military heroism to substantiate a hypothesis regarding militarism is fine, but the problem is, as before, that these studies have tended to lead to narrow conclusions regarding the idea of heroism, such as that the last quarter of the nineteenth century represented 'an age steeped in heroic military imagery'.[21] It was more the case that the period was steeped in heroic imagery and, although the military idea was a significant part of that landscape, so too was everyday heroism.

For example, militaristic ideology was, indeed, often pervasive within didactic and juvenile literature, but it is short-sighted to conclude that it was completely dominant in the genre. In fact, everyday heroism was equally well represented, with titles including *Heroes of Everyday Life* (1888), *Everyday Heroes: Stories of Bravery during the Queen's Reign* (1889), *Ballads of Brave Deeds* (1896), *Beneath the Banner* (1894) and *Deeds of Daring: Stories of Heroism in Every Day Life* (1900), focusing almost exclusively on the subject.[22] Furthermore, even when books documented military heroes alongside everyday examples, the latter were certainly not considered to be inferior, as in the case of *Heroism of Boyhood* (1865) in which the author, William Martin, stated 'the greatness of a nation does not consist so much in armies, in fleets, in extended conquests, or unbounded wealth, as in the exercise of the high virtue of our nature, in deeds of love, gentleness, honour, honesty and truth'.[23] Also, the existence of volumes recounting heroic acts undertaken by women and aimed at girls is further evidence that heroism was not limited to military subjects. Books such as *Brave little Women, Tales of the Heroism of Girls* (1888), *Heroines of Daily Life* (1896), *Noble Deeds of the World's Heroines* (1903) and *Heroines: True Tales of Brave Women – A Book for British Girls* (1904) were aimed at fostering the spirit of heroism in women and dealt with true stories of heroic acts undertaken by female civilians.[24] Clearly, military heroism was not the only strand that attracted the authors of didactic literature.

The three factors outlined above offer possible explanations for the propensity of historians to focus on military heroism. However, another possible reason, not directly related to militarism, why historians may have tended to overlook everyday heroism has been highlighted by Geoffrey Cubitt. 'The significance of great men', he has suggested, 'lies in their perceived prominence and effectiveness as historical agents: it is a dynamic rather than a passive significance, a significance less of what they are than of what they bring about'.[25] Essentially, Cubitt was asserting that great or notable individuals have enduringly been considered important because they could be conceived as agents within the development and progress of history.[26]

For example, from the perspective of the German philosopher Hegel, heroes were the individuals who emerged to assert leadership or to direct movements at key and decisive moments. Alternatively, heroes could be those who were regarded as the worthies who drove historical change by benefiting humanity and contributing to human development; a key idea in Auguste Comte's Positivist religion of Humanity. Then again, heroes were also characterized as the movers of history, men who should be worshipped for the influential power of their thought, as put forward by Thomas Carlyle in 1841.[27] So, on one level, there were the influential thinkers of the nineteenth century asserting and promoting, albeit in different ways, the idea that great or notable individuals should be exalted and celebrated for their influence upon history, thus reinforcing an emphasis and focus upon the actions of such individuals.

Cubitt also examines the focus upon the 'exemplary life' aspect of heroic reputation and, having identified the overlapping nature of discourses of exemplarity and heroism, he persuasively reveals the tensions and ambiguities between the two. Heroes, according to Cubitt, are both 'representative', in that they embody values with which others can identify, and 'exceptional', in that they live or behave outside of normal rules or conventions. This, it is argued, is a particular problem in the use or construction of 'great heroic' individuals as exemplars. Such individuals are largely admired for their role in historical change (what they bring about rather than who they are) whereas exemplarity relies upon the moral or ethical standards of the individual and the character and qualities that make them educationally useful rather than upon their achievements or role in historical processes. It is ambiguities such as these that Cubitt has suggested create tensions and contestation between heroism and exemplarity.[28]

Cubitt's outline of the relationship between heroism and exemplarity is particularly useful with regard to studying everyday heroism as it demonstrates that discourses of heroism *can* be seen as providing moral instruction but that the examples must represent not only excellence but also, more importantly, must be *relevant* if they are to perform any social function. This symbiosis was clearly understood by the groups and individuals, some of which feature in this study, who sought to employ acts of everyday heroism as didactic examples of model behaviour for the working classes. Furthermore, acts of everyday heroism were undertaken by those who, by and large, inhabited the same environment and were subject to the same rules and conventions as those at which the didactic examples were aimed. Therefore, the heroic individual might have been viewed as less 'exceptional' than the 'great individual' type of hero, thus reducing the sense of tension highlighted by Cubitt and allowing for a greater sense of exemplarity for certain audiences.

An excellent supporting example of this proposition is the work and ideas of the nineteenth-century writer and autodidact Samuel Smiles. In his prescriptively titled book, *Self-Help*, Smiles referred to exemplary biographies as 'most instructive and useful, as helps, guides and incentives to others. Some of the best are almost equivalent to gospels teaching high living, high thinking, and energetic action for their own and the world's good.'[29] Smiles employed such biographies in *Self-Help*, and in his later studies entitled *Character* (1871) and *Duty* (1880), as examples of how moral character, perseverance and responsibility were personal attributes to be adopted and promoted.[30] However, as Asa Briggs has noted, 'Smiles always broadened the range to include the humble as well as the great' and 'maintained that living examples were far more potent as influences than examples on paper.'[31] There was much, then, in the work of Samuel Smiles that was also prevalent in the discourse on everyday heroism. Many of the character traits that Smiles was advocating could be perceived in those who undertook acts of everyday heroism. Furthermore, according to Smiles, not only were the lives and actions of the morally sound members of the working classes suitable subject matter for exemplary biography, but also they were ideal as they would more directly appeal to the other less conscientious members of that class who were in need of moral education.

Great or notable individuals have also continued to be considered important to study because of their perceived role or function in the wider processes of historical change. For instance, it is possible to see how military commanders such as Nelson or Wellington might be studied, in relation to historical change, through recourse to Hegel's ideas about decisive leadership, while many of the prominent nineteenth-century military and imperial heroes, not to mention scientists, explorers, politicians and women such as Florence Nightingale or Elizabeth Fry, could conveniently be examined within Comte's Positivist model. Furthermore, Carlyle not only provided a basis for studying historical change, but also cited specific examples, such as Shakespeare, Cromwell and Samuel Johnson, essentially providing historians with suitable candidates for further examination.[32] Given these ideas that great and notable individuals could have profound effects on how pivotal events were shaped and history developed, it stands to reason that they would attract significant attention from historians seeking answers to broader questions about the processes of historical change and movement.

There is, however, a further level upon which historians can study great individuals as agents of influence in the process of historical change. Not only can a particular individual be examined in the context of the period in which they existed, but they can also be studied in relation to how groups or people in later periods approached and constructed them as great, or heroic, historical characters for their own time. So, for example, some historians may study the life and works of William Shakespeare to gain insights into his influence upon Elizabethan popular culture or examine the religious views of Oliver Cromwell to further their understanding of how he shaped early modern British politics.[33] However, historians interested in the nineteenth century have also been able to focus on the continuing influence of these same individuals by examining how they were represented, celebrated, commemorated and appropriated during that period. Thus, it has been argued, Shakespeare was reconstructed by London radicals as an icon of the common man rather than as an emblem of high culture, while the births, deaths and notable events in the lives of great men including Cromwell and Shakespeare were enthusiastically marked throughout the nineteenth century.[34] Even figures from much earlier periods about whom little personal information was known, such as Alfred the Great, were culturally and politically resurrected during the nineteenth century as exemplars.[35] Consider also, for example, the substantial *Calendar of Great Men* (1892) compiled and edited by an advocate of positivism, Frederic Harrison, which comprised 558 short biographical studies of men, including Alfred, Cromwell and Shakespeare, alongside others such as Charles V, Charlemagne and Milton.[36] Great men could not only be considered as great by their contemporaries, but the idea of their greatness could also be continually recreated and refreshed by later generations. As such, notable individuals, and later mediations of them, represent a valuable source which has been heavily drawn upon, especially by historians interested in the creation and reception of identity and exemplarity.

However, one consequence of this is that the great individuals in history have come to be seen as hero figures and the study of them, and the things they did, have been interpreted as the study of heroism. Once again, there is not necessarily anything wrong with this approach on its own terms, but it has a similar effect to the focus on military and imperial heroes in that it has led to a narrowing of the views and definitions of heroism as a subject for scholarly study. Max Jones, among others, has highlighted how the study of heroic individuals, great or otherwise, *can* be valuable for understanding the idea of heroism if approached correctly, and this is not by seeking to determine whether or not the person was correctly judged to have been a hero, but asking instead why people believed them to be heroic and, importantly, how did those people show their appreciation.[37] Crucially, by examining how particular models of heroism were constructed, rather than just identifying that certain individuals were viewed as heroic in certain contexts, this technique actually increases knowledge about the subject of heroism itself. Essentially, if historians go looking for the processes whereby heroes are constructed, they are likely to find the great men of history, whereas if they seek to understand how heroism is constructed, a wider and more inclusive field of individuals, from all walks of life, could become available to them, as this study demonstrates.

In addition to these subject-orientated elements that have influenced how historians have approached heroism, another factor, largely related to the focus on studying those perceived to be great or influential, has also shaped a specific methodological approach. In many cases, historians have tended to start from a position that the nineteenth century was 'a time when the classical and medieval heroic cults were recreated, modified and adapted for a new age'.[38] Arthurian legends and chivalric myths have been taken to be the building blocks of the Victorian construction of heroism and this has, in turn, led a few scholars to draw heavily upon Joseph Campbell's seminal 1949 study *The Hero with a Thousand Faces* and the theoretical framework it outlined.[39] Campbell examined the construction of mythical heroes in ancient religious texts and, drawing upon psychoanalytical and anthropological theory, suggested that a three-stage journey – consisting of a separation or departure, the trials and victories of initiation, and the return and reintegration with society – was required of all those who were deemed to be heroes.[40] While it is an excellent analysis of the subject of myth and mythical hero narratives, it can be argued that there has been a tendency to rely too heavily on Campbell's framework when approaching heroism more generally.

Campbell offers a structure of analysis which focuses on the personal journey, be it physical or metaphorical, of an individual and such an approach immediately shifts the focus of investigation onto the study of the hero figure, rather than the wider study of heroism. Consequently, any historian wishing to use Campbell's framework must seek a particular individual to study and are likely to start by looking for a recognized hero figure to test within it. Furthermore, the structure of a departure, followed by a trial or a period of adversity and finally a victorious return and reintegration, is ideally suited to the trajectory of the military or imperial hero figure and thus, those are the types of individuals most easily accommodated and often selected. Also, the explorer hero, the hero of science or medicine and even the political hero could, it can be argued, all be located relatively easily within this 'journey of discovery' system of analysis. Campbell's framework essentially comes pre-packaged with a firm and ahistorical construction of heroism already in place, and while this might be suitable for exploring or determining whether a certain type of individual underwent the required trial or adventure to qualify as a hero, it is far less applicable to single acts of everyday heroism or to examining alternative constructions of the idea.

To give one example, John MacKenzie, in a study which drew heavily upon Campbell in order to examine four prominent military and imperial heroes, concluded that 'nineteenth century heroism derived particular potency from exotic backgrounds' rather than from the 'mundane' environment of everyday life.[41] It could be argued that Campbell's framework, with its emphasis on the hero's challenging journey of discovery into the unknown, encourages the investigation of those who inhabited exotic backgrounds, rather than those in everyday life, and if these are the type of individuals that a historian seeks to identify, it is not particularly surprising that they find them. The military heroes of imperial Africa and India that MacKenzie, and others such as Michael Lieven, have set out to study, may well have derived particular potency from their exotic backgrounds, but they are far from being the sole representatives of nineteenth-century heroism.[42]

This study is concerned throughout with revealing and examining everyday heroism: it discusses otherwise ordinary civilian men and women who undertook life-risking heroic acts in the course of their everyday lives. These acts were not, by and large, undertaken in exotic locations, nor were they performed by military or imperial adventurers as a part of a challenging voyage of discovery and conquest. Instead, everyday heroism took place in and around the homes and streets where people lived and worked, and it occurred as part of the fabric of otherwise ordinary life. Unlike imperial adventurers, everyday heroes did not necessarily place themselves into situations where they would expect to encounter danger or to put their own life at risk. Heroism was something they undertook unselfconsciously because it was thrust upon them suddenly, when it was largely unexpected, rather than them seeking out situations which might offer the opportunity to perform it. For the imperial adventurer, heroism was something which, arguably, was actively sought out and indeed 'performed', as it provided an inevitable and desirable part of their endeavours and one that represented a necessary accomplishment on their ascendency to greatness. On the contrary, heroism tended to be an unusual occurrence in the everyday life of a previously average individual, an experience that rendered them notable or extraordinary for a short period of time before public interest moved on and they returned to relative obscurity. Heroism was, to some extent, an expectation in the life and career of the imperial adventurer, whereas everyday heroism was exceptional in the common lives of ordinary people.

It is these otherwise ordinary people that populate this book; the military men and imperial pioneers being set aside so as to reveal the miners, labourers, factory workers, train drivers, domestic servants, stewardesses, housewives and schoolchildren who also risked and gave their own lives for others and, more importantly, were recognized and commemorated for doing so. Seeking to identify and examine the otherwise ordinary people in the records of history is certainly not new; the French historian Jules Michelet widened his 1847 *History of the French Revolution* to include the actions of the common people or the 'simples' as he called them.[43] However, the approaches and techniques employed in this study owe a greater debt to more recent developments and, in particular, the emergence and development of what is known as 'the New History'.[44] Early antecedents of this movement can be seen in the work of Arnold Toynbee or the 'Webbs' and the 'Hammonds' in the late nineteenth and early twentieth centuries.[45] It was, though, the founding of the Annales School in 1929, the brainchild of French historians Marc Bloch and Lucien Febvre, which really laid the foundations. These were built upon, in the 1960s, by the work of groups including the Cambridge Group for the Study of Population and Social Structure and the highly influential History Workshop movement and, in the 1970s, by a third generation of the Annales School who incorporated the history of mentalities, more commonly defined as cultural history.[46]

The term 'New History' encompasses a wide range of social and cultural elements and, as such, it represents something of a complex nest of ideas. One of the best and most concise definitions was formulated by Peter Burke, who suggested that the concept was broadly characterized by the key ways in which it differed from the so-called 'old' history which it was challenging.[47] So, rather than focusing solely on politics, New History is effectively 'total history', the idea that every element is valid and all subjects and topics are open for consideration. New History largely eschews broad narratives in favour of analyses of structures and tends to regard 'reality' as a social and cultural construction instead of purely a series of events. Instead of approaching history 'from above' and concentrating on the actions of great men, New History approaches 'from below' and focuses more on the common people. Source materials also differ and the empirical privileging of official and governmental documents is replaced by an interdisciplinary or multidisciplinary approach in which everything is regarded as potential historical evidence.

This study of everyday heroism, while not an attempt at total history, certainly looks beyond politics and seeks to engage with a far wider cross-section of history. Every chapter is populated with examples of otherwise ordinary, and largely working-class, individuals who were, in most cases, simply going about their average and everyday activities. Other than becoming statistics in the studies of historical demographers, these individuals would, as far as historical enquiry is concerned, have remained unremarkable and unrecoverable, were it not for their acts of life-risking bravery. At that moment they briefly became the focus of public attention, other people discussed them or perhaps they featured in a newspaper report, and consequently they left an indelible and identifiable mark in the records of that time, a historical fingerprint, if you like. This is one reason why the study of everyday heroism fits well with a New History approach and is a useful and important tool for historical enquiry, as it provides access to the actions and activities of otherwise anonymous individuals.

This work, however, seeks not only to reveal these actions and activities but also to employ them to gain a greater understanding of the societal structures in which they took place and this, again, situates it squarely in New History territory. To give a very basic example, the relative frequency of acts of everyday heroism demonstrates the hazardous and precarious nature of daily life in Victorian and Edwardian Britain. The majority of cases derive from incidents or accidents in and around homes and workplaces, industrial accidents, house fires, incidents of drowning in inland waterways and encounters with public transport, such as runaway horses, trains or tramcars. Episodes of everyday heroism also reveal how people spent their time, be it working or leisure time. The reports of heroism at incidents in mines, in factories, at sea or on the railways, shed light upon the working conditions of those industries and, in some cases, the regulations or legislation that was introduced as a result of people losing their lives.

Furthermore, heroism undertaken at skating accidents on frozen lakes, at drowning incidents during swimming or boating activities, at fires or during evacuation crushes in crowded theatres, all illuminate our understanding of the activities that people undertook when not at work. It is true to say that any or all of these issues could conceivably be studied or examined independently of the study of heroism; for example, not every mining accident involved heroic acts. Nonetheless, in many cases, the presence of an act of everyday heroism raised the public profile of an incident, enlarged the press and media coverage of it, increased public pressure on policy-makers to prevent repetition or simply led to a focus that would not have otherwise been given. Everyday heroism took place in and was a part of everyday life, and as such it helps to shine a contextual light upon our historical understanding of that landscape.

In addition to illuminating the physical fabric and structure of daily life in which these everyday heroes existed, it is equally important to gain an understanding of the people, groups and society that surrounded them. Their heroic acts may have led them to be noted in the records of history, but this noteworthiness was a product of the opinions and attitudes of those who decided to record them. An act of life-risking bravery arguably requires two key elements in order for it to become an act of heroism; spectatorship and appreciation. If nobody is present to witness an act, it is less likely to be recorded, often because of the modesty of the rescuer or the lack of verifiable details. However, even if an act is witnessed, those who see it have to think highly enough of it and the person who has undertaken it, to take practical steps so that it receives the praise they believe it deserves. Consequently, exploring why certain individuals or acts were accorded the status of being 'heroic' provides insights into the society that recognized them. This is because heroism is not a single, static or rigidly understood notion, but rather a flexible and malleable constellation of ideas which can be shaped or constructed along different lines by different groups or people. Furthermore, the constructions of heroism employed represent and mediate the beliefs and opinions of those people and this is another reason why the study of everyday heroism provides valuable and revealing evidence for historians. If you want to identify the characteristics of a group or society, much can be learnt by studying its heroes.

With regard to another component of New History, the term 'history from below' has, in recent years, come to be regarded as somewhat anachronistic. This is partly because the principle of inclusiveness has become so central to the work of most historians that there is little need to isolate it, but also because history from below arguably became too closely associated with a particular political agenda. Raphael Samuel, one of the founders of the History Workshop movement, described the Marxist approach to history from below as stemming from claims that 'the people are constituted by relations of exploitation' and that it represents 'a history of the oppressed'.[48] Critics have argued that this inclined history from below to seek out conflict and struggle in history and focus more on the revolutionary than the everyday. This may well have sometimes been the case, but a more nuanced evaluation of the idea demonstrates how and why it still forms an important part of the New History approach. History from below, according to Samuel, also represented 'a gravitational shift in scholarly interest from the national to the local or regional study, from public institutions to domestic life [and] from the study of statecraft to that of popular culture' and, on these terms, this study is very much in accordance with that approach.[49]

Everyday heroism, although an idea that enjoyed national prominence, most often originated and was best understood by people on a local or regional level, and consequently, this is how it is best examined. It was local communities that most often instigated mechanisms for recognition or remembrance and even in the case of nationwide schemes, such as the Albert Medal, it was local people or communities that nominated individuals. Heroic individuals were often referred to as the hero or heroine of a particular area, such as Mark Addy, the 'Salford Hero' or Jane Whyte, the 'Aberdour Heroine'. Studies of everyday heroism, then, can provide historians with helpful evidence for understanding local or regional consciousness or identity. Furthermore, this study engages far less with public institutions and statecraft and much more with domestic life and popular culture. It sheds light on how the working classes lived, the beliefs and values that they held and the manner in which they expressed themselves, not just how the elites deemed they should live. As Eric Hobsbawm has concluded, one of the values of history from below is that it shows 'that what people wanted and needed was not always what their betters, or those who were cleverer or more influential, thought they ought to have'.[50]

The study of everyday heroism is wholly dependent on an engagement with the otherwise ordinary and often overlooked people who tended to represent the majority of society. Therefore, the practice of history from below, in the widest sense of the phrase and encompassing all of its variants, is a necessity for any study of everyday heroism, and this book is no exception. However, as Hobsbawm, Samuel and Thompson, among others, have demonstrated, the study of the working classes is at its most successful when it contributes not only to knowledge about those people as individuals or groups, but also to the wider understanding of how they functioned as a motive power or force within society and the effect or influence they had on the machinery of change and progress.

With regard to this purpose, this book reveals that, in relation to everyday heroism, the working classes in the period under examination were not necessarily or solely passive or acquiescent receptors of an idea of heroism that was created by the elites and handed down to them to accept. Instead, they could be autonomous in their thinking on the subject and not only did constructions of heroism originate from within the working classes as readily as those outside of them, but also constructions that did not equate with theirs were rejected or at least less enthusiastically embraced. For social and cultural historians, the study of everyday heroism is valuable and important because it involves seeking answers to questions about how, why and, most importantly, from where, ideas and attitudes originate. Heroism informs us about the beliefs and opinions of those who construct and use it, and everyday heroism is particularly valuable as it offers the opportunity to explore the constructions of not only the elites, but of all classes and indeed all sections of a society.

Max Jones has rightly concluded that 'work to date has been stronger on the representation of heroic icons, than on their reception' and that, 'the extent of the working classes' collective emotional investment in many of the most famous heroes remains unclear.'[51] Jones has made a major contribution to correcting this tendency, for example in his 2003 study of the Antarctic explorer Captain Robert F. Scott.[52] By examining not only the origins but also, more crucially, the reception of the representations and commemorations of Scott following his death, Jones has revealed the prevalence and centrality of grass roots agitation and organization based upon the requirements of the parties involved, as opposed to governmental or elite orchestration.[53] Furthermore, Jones has clearly exposed the contested nature of the construction of heroism by demonstrating the interaction between the views from above and those from below. Similar to Jones, this study attempts throughout to uncover and deliver the statements and opinions of the working classes regarding everyday heroes and heroism, alongside the more often recorded opinions of middle- and upper-class commentators. It also seeks to discover whether fault lines exist between working-class conceptions and constructions of heroism and those of the middle classes and if so, where they lie.

Acknowledging that constructions can originate from within both the upper sections of society and those lower down, as well as identifying whether such constructions were actually viewed and understood by the public, and any influences they had, involves analysing the reception of the ideas, arguably one of the biggest challenges to historians. Scarcity of source material might at first appear to be the key problem but, as both Jones and Peter Karsten have highlighted, the range of 'indicators of collective emotional investment' or 'soft evidence', from which to determine popular interest in and engagement with a subject is wide and varied.[54] Another potential problem, highlighted by Karsten, is that although there is much readily available evidence, it was often the 'product of the articulate', namely those who 'led a movement, spoke to an audience, wrote a poem or history, edited a newspaper [or] left any other deliberate record of their views'.[55] Thus, historians must work to scratch through the veneer of this commentary to gain a greater understanding of popular beliefs and the actions of the working classes which lie beneath the surface. Crucially, though, what is required of the historian is not only an awareness of the evidence and the willingness and skills to employ it effectively, but also the flexibility and foresight to structure an enquiry so as to facilitate discussions of both the diffusion and reception of ideas.

Several specific mechanisms of engagement with everyday heroism are returned to throughout this study, these being recognition, commemoration and construction, and all of these are particularly useful in terms of understanding the reception of the idea in addition to the projection or promotion of it. Furthermore, these mechanisms take place in or rely upon public attention or engagement to fuel them, and thus they further encourage and allow an engagement with the receiving audience. Recognition requires both a party to suggest it and a body of people to acknowledge it; commemoration relies upon a desire to undertake it, but also the funds and support to realize it; and if constructions or representations are to be successful, they need to be skilfully assembled with a mind to how they will be received. These areas were specifically selected for this study because they represent the occasions or points where there was the greatest level of public engagement with an act of everyday heroism, and consequently, they also provide the best opportunities for uncovering evidence. Even so, this was still not a straightforward exercise.

As Hobsbawm has correctly concluded, getting to the roots of what the working classes may have thought is a particularly difficult task for the historian because 'there simply is not a ready made body of material about it' and as a result the scholar 'finds only what he is looking for, not what is already waiting for him'.[56] Hobsbawm's conclusion certainly applies to this study which, rather than drawing upon the resources of a single archive or one particular type of evidence, has instead had to employ a wide range of different sources and methods in an attempt to get as close as possible to the authentic voice of the working classes. With regard to recognition, the Home Office records do provide a rich and wide vein of evidence, but largely for understanding the construction of heroism by a select and elite group of individuals. Consequently, this has been countered, partly by examining mechanisms other than state recognition, but also by using the available Home Office material to try and ascertain the general public's response and engagement with the awards, for example, by considering the volume of nominations rather than simply the number of awards given.

It is true to say that in the case of many of the public memorial schemes and the erection of civic monuments, the sources tend to privilege the opinions of those who conceived or administered the activities and these were usually members of the upper or middle classes. However, the memorials and monuments all occupied relatively prominent public positions where they were open and available for all to view and engage with. Furthermore, most of them were entirely reliant upon public cooperation, finance and support and the arrangements for them were, by and large, undertaken in public. So too were the ceremonies to unveil them and these, as well as other forms of public address such as meetings or lectures, are particularly useful as they represent oral communication which is not dependent on an audience's levels of literacy in order to be received and understood. The same can be said of visual or audio sources, such as the music hall songs mentioned at the end of this chapter or the Walter Crane murals discussed in Chapter 2, and employing these is necessary if an understanding of not only the social but also the cultural landscape of the working classes is to be sought.

There are clearly many important and useful reasons for historians to study everyday heroism, not only to gain a wider and more detailed understanding of the idea itself but also as a window onto the society and culture in which it existed. However, one of the major reasons to study it is its great significance to people at the time. The State and numerous charitable organizations created medals and awards to honour it, authors wrote books and poems about it, artists created paintings illustrating it, communities erected monuments to commemorate it, intellectuals discussed and debated the merits of it, groups sought to control or appropriate it and, most importantly, people from all walks of life embraced and championed it. It is surprising that, for an idea that was so pervasive, everyday heroism has not received more attention from historians, not only those interested in the idea of heroism, but also those, for example, seeking insights into the lives of working-class people in the Victorian period. Perhaps this has been, as Hobsbawm has concluded of people's history, because 'there is generally no material until our questions have revealed it' and historians have not, until now, been sufficiently inquisitive about heroism as a subject in its own right.[57] So perhaps heroism is, after all, a lens through which other ideas and subjects can be studied, but if that is the case, it needs to become not only a wide-angle lens, but also one that can be refocused and repositioned so as to provide the fullest and most accurate of pictures. In essence, that is the primary purpose of this book: to establish a new approach to the study of heroism and lay the foundations for the widening of the subject to encompass all of society rather than simply the great men of history.

The chronology and development of the idea of everyday heroism

The remainder of this chapter provides a broadly chronological outline of the emergence and growth of the idea of everyday heroism in the period 1850–1914 and introduces the initiatives, organizations and individuals that conceived and shaped it. Central to this overview is providing an initial understanding of the development of the idea of heroism over the course of the period and the ways in which it became more inclusive and egalitarian, in fact more 'everyday', in nature. Prior to 1850, there was little or no recognition or reward for the heroism of the working-class man or woman and yet by the early twentieth century, everyday heroism was almost entirely integrated into wider discourses. The process of change was relatively slow and distinctly incremental but, by looking at it chronologically, it becomes clear that the widening of the sphere of heroism was reflective of broader changes and reforms in Victorian and Edwardian society.

It can be argued that the Crimean War (1854–56) heralded an era in which a new and particularly vivid picture of military heroism and the sufferings of the common soldier were revealed and brought home to the general public. The expansion of the press, such as the increase in lower-priced, mass-circulation newspapers, coupled with technological advances in communications, including the introduction of new railway and steamship routes and telegraph networks, led to wider and more immediate reporting of events. Furthermore, within this so-called 'communications revolution' the important figure of the war correspondent emerged, with William Howard Russell for *The Times* being a notable example for the Crimean War.[58] His reports depicting events such as the forming of the 'thin red line' at Balaklava or the charge of the light brigade had a great impact on the British public and 'by arousing public, especially middle-class, indignation, contributed to the demand for military and administrative reform'.[59] Keen to capitalize upon this heightened and popular public awareness of the bravery and courage being displayed by British servicemen in the Crimea, some MPs began to call for changes in the system of recognition for servicemen. In December 1854, the Liberal MP Austen Layard gave a speech in the House of Commons in which he recalled returning home from a visit to the area on a ship full of allied servicemen and feeling regretful that while the French soldiers were already proudly wearing their Legion d' Honneur medals upon their chests, the British soldiers had nothing to show for their efforts. He then went on to suggest that, 'It occurred to him that there were men in our army who, though but its rank and file, would feel as proud of orders of merit, if given to them, as the officers who commanded them could be.'[60]

At that time, the highest award for honour in the British Army was the Order of the Bath, but this was only awarded to senior officers and it was felt that a more inclusive award, specifically for individual acts of gallantry in the face of the enemy, was required. Later in December 1854, George Scobell, MP for Bath, put forward a motion in the Commons calling upon the Queen, 'to institute an "Order of Merit" to be bestowed upon persons serving in the Army or Navy for distinguished and prominent personal gallantry during the present war, and to which every grade and individual, from the highest to the lowest . . . may be admissible'. He argued that the Order of the Bath was 'vastly too exclusive' and that 'if some such an Order as that referred to in his Motion were immediately instituted it would be tantamount to reinforcing our army of the Crimea, so great would be its effect on the spirits and temper of the troops'.[61] Scobell ultimately withdrew his motion but the point had been made and after further approaches from the Duke of Newcastle in 1855 and Lord Panmure in 1856, a Royal Warrant dated 29 January 1856 was eventually created to institute the new decoration to be known as the Victoria Cross. Cast in Bronze, the medal was in the form of a Maltese Cross, with the Royal crest in the centre and a scroll beneath inscribed with the words 'for Valour'.[62] The key regulation in the Royal Warrant was clause six, which ordained that,

> With a view to place all persons on a perfectly equal footing in relation to eligibility for the Decoration, that neither rank, nor long service, nor wounds, nor any other circumstance or condition whatsoever, save the merit of conspicuous bravery shall be held to establish a sufficient claim to the honour.[63]

Although a military rather than civilian decoration, it can be argued that the Victoria Cross, with its emphasis on inclusion and its willingness to recognize that acts of heroism were performed by men of all classes and ranks, represented one of the earliest steps in the development of the recognition everyday heroism.

The next significant State contribution to the recognition of everyday heroism came in 1866 with the introduction of the Albert Medal, which is discussed in detail in Chapter 1. However, the Albert Medal was initially restricted to seaman who had attempted to save life during shipwrecks or 'other perils of the sea'. Consequently, although in 1866 it represented the first Crown-sanctioned award for civilian heroism, a significant step towards the idea of everyday heroism, the qualification for recognition was still relatively narrow, this being male mariners undertaking acts of bravery at sea. The Albert Medal was introduced in response to State concerns about the alarmingly high losses of life at sea and the reporting of such losses to the public through the popular press. So in much the same way as the Victoria Cross, the Albert Medal was, to some extent, initially introduced in response to public opinion. Furthermore, this was certainly the case when, in 1877, qualification for the Albert Medal was extended to include acts undertaken on land as well as at sea.

The events that influenced this change took place between 11 and 22 April 1877, in a small and otherwise insignificant mining town in the Rhondda Valley in South Wales. Tynewydd colliery was situated four miles from Pontypridd and around a hundred men were employed by the Troedyrhiw Colliery Company to mine the Rhonda No.3 seam. Around 4 p.m. on 11 April, the fourteen men working in the pit were preparing to finish for the day when suddenly a powerful gust of air swept through the shaft accompanied by a low and ominous rumbling. Unbeknown to the miners, flood water from the nearby disused Cymmer pit had broken through and within seconds the Tynewyyd shaft was inundated, drowning several of the men and trapping the remainder.[64] In many ways, the disaster at Tynewydd was, by the standards of the time when single mining accidents often claimed hundreds of lives, relatively unremarkable.[65] However, over the following ten days, an enthralling saga of the determined, dangerous and stoic rescue of the surviving colliers was dramatically and episodically reported in the press and captured the imagination of the public. In accounting for this, one correspondent to the *Merthyr Press* in May 1877 concluded that, 'the great manual labour, the skill and ingenuity that was shown, the great despatch that was made in order to release the living men and the dauntless heroism of the workmen were the main features that aroused the attention of the country'.[66]

In the days after the rescue, suggestions began to circulate in the press about the best way to recognize the heroic actions of those who had undertaken it. In addition to pecuniary awards from the subscription funds, a recurring suggestion was put forward, as in the case of one correspondent to the *Western Mail*,

> Permit me to offer the suggestion of raising a small fund and forming a committee for the purpose of presenting commemorative medals in bronze or silver to those who so gallantly, at the peril of their lives, were instrumental in rescuing the five entombed colliers from the wretched death which would have been certain but for the untiring zeal of the generous-hearted men . . . who so courageously fought the elements.[67]

Public interest in the rescue had extended as far as the House of Commons and the circumstances of the 'entombed colliers' were even the subject of a parliamentary question to the Secretary of State.[68] Unfortunately, no Home Office file for the Tynewydd case appears to have survived and so the discussions regarding the matter and the extent to which public opinion swayed the decision cannot be ascertained. However, in a statement released from Windsor Castle on 25 April 1877, it was announced that 'the Albert Medal, hitherto only bestowed for gallantry in saving life at sea, shall be extended for similar actions on land, and that the first medals struck for this purpose shall be conferred on the heroic rescuers of the Welsh miners.'[69] This statement implies that it was the heroism of the Tynewydd miners and the desire to accord State recognition to them that prompted the extension of the decoration. Widening the field to include acts undertaken 'in mines, on railways and at fires' may not have substantially increased opportunities for awards to women or children, but it did represent State recognition of a broader definition of everyday heroism and thus it marked a significant development of the idea. Furthermore, this significant move to include and involve the working classes in the mechanisms for commemorating everyday heroes also provides valuable evidence for how state recognition of the idea was received by such individuals.

The Albert Medal may not have attracted the widespread popular interest and appeal hoped for by the State, but there is evidence that it was admired and coveted by those who were awarded it and the communities in which those individuals lived. In one 1908 case, that of Tram Driver Wilton who prevented his vehicle from crashing, the letter of application, from an Alderman Cutler, made the appeal that 'if his majesty would see his way to give some token of his appreciation of the bravery displayed . . . it would be much esteemed, especially by the working classes'.[70] In another case, in 1911, one unidentified letter in support of the application, for ten-year-old Jack Hewitt who rescued his nine-year-old playmate from drowning, reported that 'I have been inundated with letters asking me to press you to award him the King's medal. There is a very strong feeling in the town.'[71] When a Lancashire Schoolmistress, Hannah Rosbotham, was honoured in 1880, the letter sent by the local MP to the Home Office stated that 'the award of the Albert medal of the second class . . . has given sincere gratification throughout this district as a great honour conferred on a young woman whose bravery and presence of mind under very trying circumstances have won her the respect and regard of her neighbours'.[72] Of course, it could be argued that Aldermen and Members of Parliament had their own agenda for putting forward working-class individuals for awards such as the Albert Medal, including attempting to placate the working classes or even advancing their own careers through association. However, the standing of these types of individuals was such that, even if it was not the case, they might well have believed that their opinion alone would count, and the fact that they chose to mention public feeling suggests that it was probably more likely to have actually been the case than not.

On a couple of occasions, any ambiguity regarding how a recipient felt was entirely removed as it was the awardees themselves who wrote to the Home Office to express their feelings:

> I am sure you will believe me when I say that I feel exceedingly proud of the great honour that Her Majesty has thus done me, and I beg, if that is proper, that I may be allowed to express my grateful thanks through you for this great distinction.[73]

How kind of Mr Gladstone to appreciate me for my gallant conduct in saving Mrs O'Connor last year. Believe in my earnest gratitude for all his words. I am proud of being a British man and I will always stand for the king. I have the honour to be, sir, your most obedient servant, John McCandless.[74]

What is particularly interesting here is that McCandless wrote his letter to the Home Office after his nomination was refused. So to some individuals, it would appear that even to be considered for an Albert Medal for their heroism was a considerable honour, even if they did not ultimately receive it. This goes some way to demonstrating that the introduction of the Albert Medal did much to increase the general awareness, importance and regard for acts of civilian heroism in the mid-nineteenth century. In just twenty years, the endorsement had shifted from being seen as the preserve of senior officers in the armed forces, to an awareness and acceptance that it also encompassed working-class men. Furthermore, it was not just those in state or government service who were conscious of this shift.

When considering the formation and promotion of the idea of everyday heroism, the Victorian artist George Frederic Watts (1817–1904) must be seen as a highly significant figure. Although it is important not to over-elevate Watts, his influence upon the development of the discourse of everyday heroism was such that he warrants focused investigation; if for no other reason than, it can be argued, her was one of the first people to articulate and attempt to promulgate a distinctly 'everyday' strand of heroism. In 1866, he wrote to his patron, Charles Rickards, expressing his desire to 'get subscriptions to carry out a project I have long had which is to erect a great statue to Unknown Worth'.[75] Later, and more publically, he wrote a letter to *The Times* in 1887 suggesting the creation of a monument to commemorate 'heroism in daily life' and this letter inspired other projects that helped to publicize the general idea.[76] Finally, in 1900, Watts did indeed create his Memorial to Heroic Self-Sacrifice in Postman's Park, London (see Figure 1). This monument took the form of a sturdy wooden

Figure 1 The Watts Memorial to Heroic Self-Sacrifice, Postman's Park, London EC1, 2004 (*John Price*, 2004).

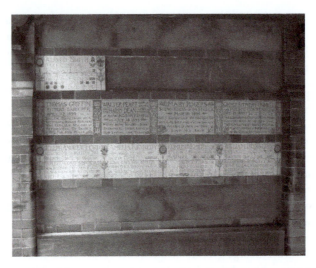

Figure 2 An example of the ceramic tablets that form the Watts Memorial (*John Price*, 2004).

cloister, constructed to shelter a series of glazed ceramic tablets, each documenting the heroic actions of civilians who had lost their own life while attempting to save another (see Figure 2). In all, fifty-four memorial tablets commemorating sixty-two individuals were erected on the monument which was, and has remained, one of the most important and enduring symbols of everyday heroism in Britain.[77]

It must be recognized, though, that, as important as he was, Watts was simply part of a larger, broadly left-leaning, liberal-radical circle whose projects and contributions fed the growth of the overall idea and helped to establish and legitimize a more non-establishment idea of everyday heroism alongside that being promoted by the State through its decorations. This circle encompassed authors such as Laura Lane and Frank Mundell, reformers including Octavia Hill and Walter Crane and associates of Watts such as Emilie Barrington and Hardwicke Rawnsley. This is not to say that a radical idea of everyday heroism would not have developed and become established without this circle; the work of organizations such as the Royal Humane Society and Carnegie Hero Fund as well as radical newspapers such as Reynolds News would certainly have stimulated it. However, it would not have developed as quickly without their projects, which played a central role, nor would it have developed along the lines that it did, with art and literature being so important to its shaping and disseminating. The discourse of everyday heroism that this study identifies owes much of its character to Watts and the circle of people who appear to have crystallized around him and thus he strands as an ideal spokesperson for that wider movement.

That said, for an individual who was so central to the idea and provided such stimulation to how it was shaped, Watts himself could sometimes be frustratingly vague and contradictory about what he believed constituted everyday heroism. On one occasion, the artist indignantly replied to a question on who should feature on the memorial by saying, 'there should be no classification. How could there be. Life is life . . . there could be no question of selection'. Yet a month later, he explained to another interviewer that 'the scheme would be limited to those who had sacrificed their lives without hope of fee or award, for in that instance the action is so much nobler'.[78] When asked outright, during one interview in 1898, 'but what is heroism?' Watts replied, 'heroic deeds which result in loss of life, absolute loss. It is where loss of life has been incurred to save another that I would erect permanent memorials'.[79] Following yet another interview, one newspaper summed up Watts' idea of everyday heroism thus: 'the root idea is that the heroism of humble men is no less worthy of being held in memory than the services (too often far from heroic) of those who happen to be highly placed'.[80] The risking of life in order to save life and the encompassing of all classes within the scope of commemoration were clearly fundamental parts of Watts' idea of everyday heroism, as was his opinion as to who should qualify.

While Watts may not have always been absolutely clear about who *would* feature on the monument, he was adamant about who *would not*: 'The scheme will not include the heroes of war, or of the battle field or the warship,' he told one interviewer.[81] When challenged about whether he was disparaging the heroism of the battlefield, the artist defended his idea, saying, 'Nothing of the kind; those who do brave deeds in battle get their reward'; what he desired was, 'honour to be done to those, equally brave, who neither expect it nor get it'.[82] Watts viewed heroic self-sacrifice in battle as laudable, but considered it to be a professional risk that was understood and accepted by servicemen; it was, in his words, risk 'incurred in the way of business'.[83] Conversely, the workmen who died at the East Ham sewage works in 1895, were, according to the artist, suitable for inclusion precisely because 'There was no rushing to their deaths amid the flourish of trumpets or the trappings of war . . . the impulse of the moment prompted the heroic action and man's best nature triumphed'.[84] This type of selfless action motivated by nothing other than a desire to save and protect life, rather than by a duty of service driven by authority and with the objective of taking life, was Watts' idea of everyday heroism and it was also one that ran more generally through all the various projects and organizations which took the more radical approach to the idea.

Everyday heroes were defined, it would seem, as civilians who while going about their usual business undertook an act of heroism when they had no professional responsibility to do so. Yet, even on these points, Watts struggled with his own conception of the project, as his attitude towards the heroism of lifeboat men demonstrates. The artist clearly believed that they should be eligible and on several occasions reported that he intended to include them. He was, however, challenged on this and asked why lifeboat men should qualify when surely they willingly accepted the same professional risks as servicemen. In reply, Watts accounted for their admission, stating that 'these brave men again and again venture out to save life when winds and waves are combined against the chances of a safe return . . . they do more, far more, than duty demands'.[85] Given that lifeboat men were volunteers and consequently the risks they incurred were not, in the strictest sense, 'professional', it is interesting that Watts chose not to offer this as a justification. Instead, the artist suggested that although those with a perceived duty to be heroic, such as servicemen, should not strictly be included on the monument, those who had that duty but on some occasions had gone well beyond it should be allowed. This was very much in keeping with the implicit message of the monument, discussed further in Chapter 2, which was that the individuals commemorated should stand out as possessing an ideal and exemplary character, with persistence and dedication beyond duty being two such characteristics. Ultimately, no lifeboat men came to feature on the monument, but it did include many individuals from relatively lowly occupations, and this prompted further confusion over what exactly everyday heroism was.

One newspaper, when reporting on Watts' plan to erect a monument to everyday heroism, referred to 'the heroism of ordinary life [being] the quiet sacrifice of himself by the working man to save his "mate"', and this idea was repeated by the Lord Mayor who, when unveiling the cloister in 1900, remarked that it was 'intended to perpetuate the acts of heroism which belonged to the working classes'.[86] This suggestion, that the monument was dedicated to working-class heroism, was put forward quite often, but it was not something that Watts publicly agreed with. He stated that the monument should not be limited to any class and after his death his widow also maintained that, 'there was never any thought in his [Watts'] mind of limiting the roll of names to any grade or position of life'.[87] In one way, it is possible to see how and why the confusion originated. Watts was simply proposing that heroism was a characteristic that could be present in all people, of any class, and consequently nobody should be excluded from the honour accorded to heroes and heroic acts. However, because the idea of heroism prior to this had generally been associated with military officers or imperial adventurers, this widening of the boundary was seen as something unusual and radical. Furthermore, it is clear, when examining the memorial and the manner in which it was conceived and implemented, that Watts, and his wider circle, were very concerned with ensuring that everyday heroism had a class element to it.

As discussed in Chapter 2, the radical approach to everyday heroism certainly focused closely on working-class individuals so as to try and increase the impact and influence of its messages of exemplarity upon working-class audiences. For Watts and the others who undertook similar projects recognizing and commemorating everyday heroism, one particular figure stood out – this being Alice Ayres, the Southwark nursemaid who died in 1885 while attempting to save her three nieces from a house fire (see Figure 3). But what impact, if any, did the heroism of Ayres have upon this working-class audience and how did they respond to the didactic projects offered to them?

To begin with, Alice's funeral was most certainly a public affair and was widely reported in both national and local newspapers. One such report, representative of the majority, described how 'amidst many local manifestations of sorrow . . . the coffin was carried [through the streets from her parents' house] to the grave by 16 firemen, who relieved each other in sets of four'.[88] The cortège was also followed by twenty local schoolgirls, dressed in white, who were to sing at the graveside, a performance that was curtailed by a sudden and inexplicable storm of hailstones. On 10 May 1885, a memorial service for Alice was held at St Saviour's church in Southwark and 'long before the service commenced the church was crowded and many were obliged to turn away having been unable to find standing room'.[89] The sheer numbers in attendance is substantiated by the collection that took place, which although amounting to a little over £7, consisted of around 950 coins.[90] Not only does this suggest that a considerable number of people wanted to attend, but also points towards a more working-class

Figure 3 Alice Ayres, pictured with one of her sister's children to whom she was nursemaid (*Illustrated London News, 1885*).

composition, as a small amount of money was given by many, rather than large amounts by a few.

A potent image of working-class Southwark, and indeed the effect that Ayres's heroism was perceived to have had upon it, was evoked by Laura Lane, who visited the area around Union Street where the fire took place to speak to people about Alice for her book, *Heroes of Every-day Life* (1888):

> As I looked around on the dull, commonplace streets, the grimy house-fronts, the dingy windows, where a missing pane was not unfrequently (sic) replaced by a square of whity-brown paper; as I beheld the toil-worn, toil-grimed faces of men and women hurrying to and fro, the prematurely-sharpened countenances of the ragged children who gazed wistfully into the windows of an eating house where the odours of fried black-puddings and suet dumplings provoked the hungry appetite, and the miserable pasty-faced babes wrapped in tattered shawls and carried in the arms of nurses scarcely out of babyhood themselves; as my eyes took in these squalid surroundings, the whole place became suddenly transfigured by the halo of a splendid action whose glory yet lingers upon Union Street, just as the Alpine sunset continues to flood the grey plains with the rosy warmth of after-glow.[91]

Lane's account was littered with quotations apparently taken directly from the working-class inhabitants of Southwark and, unsurprisingly, nobody had a bad word to say about the recently deceased heroine. However, Lane also highlighted the emotion that the incident had provoked in people and the manner in which it had touched them; 'I have seen the cheeks and lips of strong men grow pale as ashes; I have heard rough voices falter; I have seen tears spring to hard eyes, as the story of Alice Ayres' magnificent daring was poured into my ears.'[92] Even allowing for the middle-class mediation and the dramatic license liberally employed by Lane, it is clear throughout her account that the everyday heroism of Ayres was significantly admired by those within the community and that it had a profound and moving effect upon them.

Middle-class reporting or paraphrasing of the statements and opinions of the working classes may not always provide the most reliable or desirable method of ascertaining popular or grassroots emotional investment in a heroic individual, but it often represents the only insight available and if approached critically, provides the next best option. This is the case with regard to the murals depicting scenes of everyday heroism which were created by Walter Crane and erected in the Red Cross Hall in Southwark between 1890 and 1894. The creation and purpose of these murals is fully examined in Chapter 2, but evidence for how they were actually received can be usefully examined here. The first mural to be erected illustrated the everyday heroism of Alice Ayres and with it being installed in a community hall, a very short distance from the incident in which she died, and frequented by people who had possibly known her or certainly would have been familiar with her act, it would have represented a powerful and affecting image. Evidence for this is provided by Octavia Hill, the founder of the Red Cross hall, who in recalling a particular Sunday afternoon gathering in 1893 made reference to comments made by members of the audience.

> The other Sunday a gentleman recited a beautiful ballad about a heroic rescue from fire. The hall was hushed in breathless attention while the words re-echoed through it. As I passed down among the audience just afterwards I was twice stopped. One man said "did you see how every eye was turned to her" pointing to the Alice Ayres. A woman said "I couldn't but think of Alice Ayres". 'Did you know her?' I asked. "Yes, I always dealt there" she said "and I was glad when they put up the panel there."[93]

Although limited, this is compelling evidence that the audience at the Red Cross Hall, a space located within a predominantly working-class area, appreciated the murals and, more importantly, the everyday heroic individuals who were depicted within them. Interestingly, in this particular case, it is quite possible that those present in the hall or questioned by Laura lane may have had some personal contact with Alice or, at the very least, would have known people who had personally known her or witnessed the event. However, this was not the manner in which most people came to reach an understanding about the merits or bravery of a heroic individual.

By and large, Watts collected his accounts of heroism and made his selections on the basis of newspaper reports that he read or press cuttings that were passed on to him. He did not personally know any of the people involved nor was he an eyewitness to any of the incidents and this stimulates a discussion of one important aspect of examining heroes and heroism. Heroic acts do, of course, take place in the 'here and now' of real time, but aside from a few witnesses, most people perceive such acts through a process of imaginative reconstruction, stimulated and informed by narrative retelling and representation. People do not, then, necessarily reach their conclusions about heroes and heroism from the actual heroic act itself, but rather from the heroic narratives and reputations that were created out of it. Furthermore, it can be argued that an act is not considered heroic, nor therefore is the individual, unless or until people recognize it or the person to be so, and one key component in this is the construction of a heroic reputation.

The reputation and exemplarity of heroic individuals was an important consideration for the many writers of didactic or prescriptive literature during this period; as one compiler of a volume of heroic narratives wrote,

> It cannot be too often or too strongly urged that the reading of well-authenticated stories of heroism is bound to have a good influence, particularly on young people and his [the author's] object will have been attained if this book serves to emphasise the fact that there is a nobility of daring which all may emulate with advantage to themselves and others.[94]

Consequently, the development and increasing influence of the idea of everyday heroism can be usefully charted through a brief examination of the development of the genre of didactic literature. It is noticeable that from around 1880 onwards, the field begins to alter and volumes dedicated to everyday heroism appear alongside the more traditional collections of military and adventure narratives. Examples include *Heroes of Every Day Life* by Laura Lane (1888); *Everyday Heroes: Stories of Bravery during the Queen's Reign* (1889); *Beneath the Banner* by F. J. Cross (1895) and *Heroines of Daily Life* by Frank Mundell (1896). Books such as these, particularly the introductions and prefaces, provide valuable insights into how everyday heroism was viewed and the qualities that it was thought to exemplify. For example, one gives an idea of the prevalence of everyday heroism by stating that 'the Victorian age is full of examples of self-sacrificing devotion to our common race. Our heroes are all around us. They have saved life when jeopardized in the bowels of the earth; they have snatched it from the jaws of fiery death; they have rescued it from the grasp of the angry ocean.'[95] These final three categories would appear, judging from some of the twenty-two accounts given in the volume, to equate to miners, fireman and lifeboat men, usual suspects in the case of stories of everyday heroism.

Another example, albeit a less embellished summation of everyday heroes, appears in another introduction: 'Many a story can be told of our everyday heroes to show that, in our mining districts, along our seaboard, on our railways and boats, among the men and women quietly working around us, there needs but the occasion to develop in a moment the unselfish courage which is ready to risk life for life.'[96] A final example is provided by Charles Michael, who was unstinting in his praise for everyday heroes: 'how infinitely nobler is the daring of the man who walks the top of the tottering wall of some burning house, or plunges into the unplumbed ocean depths to rescue man or woman or child from threatened death! These, and such as these, are the deeds that win the world's sincerest admiration.'[97] So, it would seem that by the end of the nineteenth century, not only had these authors ceased to refer to ideas of everyday heroism in terms of being unusual or remarkable, but they were also embracing the idea and promoting it through their work.

Often, although it is not always possible to get beneath the surface of sources or ascertain the exact nature of their reception within a popular audience, they nonetheless offer tantalizing evidence for the possibility of a collective or popular emotional investment in an act of everyday heroism. For example, the *Dyer Brothers Illustrated Penny Library of Deeds Worth Recording* which featured, in volume three, *Working-Men Heroes: a roll of heroic actions in humble life* (1879). Given the subject matter and the low cost, it can be imagined that this volume was squarely aimed at a perceived working-class market, but whether or not they purchased or read it remains uncertain.[98] Occasionally, there is evidence of postcards being produced which depicted the heroic individual, most notably as a means to raise funds for commemorative projects. However, while it is clear that these postcards were purchased, and in some cases in reasonable quantities, it is less clear precisely who was purchasing them and whether it was simply as means of donating rather than because of a strong emotional investment.[99] Of course, donating to a memorial fund in itself represented something of an emotional, as well as a financial, investment but once again, the class origins of contributors are not always clear, as discussed in Chapter 3.

In 1892, the popular and prolific song-writing duo, George Horncastle and Felix McGlennon, composed a music hall-style song entitled *Heroes of Everyday Life*.[100] A jaunty piece, it told four separate stories of everyday heroes: a policeman who rescued a woman from a rabid dog, but was himself bitten and consequently died; a ship's captain who rescued the cabin boy before voluntarily going down with his sinking ship; a fireman who rescued three children from the top floor of a burning lodging house; and a 'labouring man, very poor' who rescued a young woman who had tried to commit suicide from drowning. Whether this song was ever performed and if so when and where is difficult to establish. Furthermore, the social composition of a music hall audience, it has been argued, was 'too mixed to be easily characterised' and 'the reception of material was bound to vary from hall to hall.'[101] Nevertheless, Horncastle and McGlennon were professional songwriters, producing a commercial product and as such their focus on everyday heroism as a subject for one of their compositions suggests a degree of popular interest and engagement. The choice to engage with the idea of everyday heroism, in a medium that was intended for a popular audience, demonstrates not only that it was considered to be a recognizable and widespread idea, but also one that was perceived to be of popular public interest.

This is also substantiated by the continued growth, particularly in the middle of the nineteenth century, of the numerous organizations that recognized or acknowledged everyday heroism as part of their work. These included the Order of St John of Jerusalem (1874), the Royal Humane Society (1776), the Royal National Lifeboat Institution (1824) and the Society for the Protection of Life from Fire (1836).[102] Commemoration of everyday heroism was also on the increase, with a number of everyday heroes who had died while undertaking their act being recognized publically through the erection of a monument. However, in 1908, an organization was founded that stimulated and reinvigorated debate about the nature of everyday heroism, and this was partly due to the controversial manner in which it sought to recognize the idea.

This organization, examined fully in Chapter 4, was the Carnegie Hero Fund Trust, founded by the Scottish-born steel magnate and philanthropist Andrew Carnegie. In the context of its position in the development of the idea of everyday heroism, some key points can usefully be introduced here. First, Carnegie was similar to Watts in that his understanding and awareness of everyday heroism originated many years before his scheme was launched. In 1886, the philanthropist donated £100 towards a monument to a young man who had drowned in a loch in Townhill, just outside Carnegie's hometown of Dunfermline in Scotland and an associate of Carnegie's recalls having conversations with him about the subject some time prior to the founding of the first hero fund in the United States in 1904. Secondly, when the scheme was announced the suggestion of recognizing everyday heroes barely raised a comment, and certainly no surprise or criticism, so embedded was the acceptance and belief in the idea. Thirdly, Carnegie intended to provide pensions or pecuniary awards to heroes who had been injured or the families of those who lost their lives, and it was this form of recognition that caused alarm. Newspapers were filled with both editorials and letters which bemoaned the vulgarization and denegation of something as pure and noble as everyday heroism through associating it with monetary award. The thought that Carnegie might create a system of 'heroes for hire' out of everyday heroism was viewed by many as a travesty, but it also suggests that, by 1908, much of the general public had embraced the idea of everyday heroism to the extent that they wanted to protect the supposed sanctity of it from corruption.

In August 1914, Britain declared war on Germany, and in the four years that followed, an estimated nine million servicemen were killed and a further fifteen million were severely injured. It can be argued that nineteenth-century ideas of heroism died along with them. As Bernard Bergonzi has suggested, 'after the mechanised large-scale slaughter of the Somme . . . the traditional mythology of heroism and the hero . . . had ceased to be viable.'[103] Melvin Smith has also strongly argued from this perspective and asserted, numerous times throughout his study of the Victoria Cross, that 'the Victorian army died in the mud of Flanders . . . with it died the Victorian ideals of heroism.'[104] Others have taken issue with such conclusions, in particular, Graham Dawson who has instead contended that the nineteenth century was marked with its fair share of anti-heroic imagery from various conflicts and that the dividing line should actually be drawn between adventurous and non-adventurous narratives rather than the pre- and post-World War I periods.[105] It is yet to be established whether or not everyday heroism was tarnished by the conflict. However, as it fell outside this paradigm, representing neither the military nor the imperial adventurer strands of the idea, it is possible, or indeed likely, that it was not affected in the same way as the military variety.

In that context, it is worth considering any long-term influence or legacy and, in the case of everyday heroism, there is evidence that the idea continues to produce strong and enduring feelings and emotions in those who encounter it. For example, the Royal Humane Society continues to receive a considerable number of enquiries from the relatives of people who were given awards, requesting further information regarding their ancestor or in many cases asking whether a duplicate medal can be reproduced to replace a lost or stolen original. Furthermore, there are also a significant number of requests for the reconsideration of cases in which an ancestor was unsuccessful in their nomination for a RHS medal, suggesting the importance and honour associated with the award.[106] This is also occasionally the case with the Albert Medal. Abraham

Dodd was one for the rescue party involved in the Tynewydd colliery accident; in fact, he was the man who finally broke through the wall of coal to liberate the trapped men. However, while all the other men involved were awarded the Albert Medal, Dodd was overlooked and this has been attributed to the fact that some months earlier he had been scalded as a result of an accident in another mine and had been perceived to have spoken out against the owners of the mine for their negligence.[107] In 2009, a relative of Dodd's contacted the Royal Humane Society asking if it could advise on how they might go about getting the original decision overturned and also commented that, 'Local people to this day still think Abraham (Abby) Dodd should have received the Albert Medal along with all the other miners who were part of this very brave action. I agree with them but I have no idea how to even begin my efforts to put this right.'[108] Dodd's actions are extremely unlikely to be recognized now, but the strength of feeling in the local community appears to remain strong, more than a hundred years later.

This is also the case with regard to the Watts Memorial in Postman's Park, both for the ancestors of those who feature upon it and the contemporary audience who view it. Police Constable Edward Greenoff was killed in January 1917 while trying to warn passers-by of the dangers posed by the fire and explosions at the Brunner Mond TNT factory in Silvertown, East London. His act of heroism is commemorated on the Watts memorial, much to the pride of his granddaughter, Barbra Hird; 'it makes me incredibly proud to think that my Grandfather did something so brave, so selfless.'[109] Her understanding of the memorial and her opinion of the everyday heroes who feature is that 'most of those remembered were just ordinary people who sacrificed their own lives. It's very poignant and I'm proud that Edward is up there too.' Similar sentiments have been expressed by Rob Jeffries, the great nephew of Alfred Smith, who was killed during an air raid on London in June 1913. Smith was trying to keep people off the streets but was killed when a shell exploded nearby, and he too is commemorated on the Watts Memorial. Jeffries, a City of London Heritage Guide, has undertaken some research on his great uncle and believes there is 'little doubt that Alfred's actions were highly regarded at the time, even if he didn't get a medal'.[110] As with Hird, Jeffries is immensely proud not only that his ancestor was commemorated, but that it was on the Watts Memorial, 'his bravery is remembered among some incredibly poignant stories at Postman's Park. . . . I'm just pleased that Alf has his place there'.[111]

One final, and most recent, example of a collective and public emotional investment with the idea of everyday heroism concerns a young print worker named Leigh Pitt who in 2007 jumped into a canal in Thamesmead in an attempt to save a nine-year-old boy who had fallen in. The boy was rescued but Pitt was unable to keep himself afloat and he drowned.[112] Pitt worked as a subcontractor in the offices of Merrill Lynch, located a short distance from Postman's Park, and staff members were familiar with the memorial. A campaign was undertaken and two years later, on 11 June 2009, a tablet commemorating Pitt was unveiled on the Watts Memorial. Pitt's fiancé, Hema Shah, spoke of her pride that Leigh had been recognized: 'It is a huge honour. In my eyes Leigh will always be a hero, but this is an opportunity for people to become aware of his actions, too.'[113] A spokesman for the Diocese of London added, 'Watts created the memorial to pay tribute to unsung heroes and it is appropriate that Mr Pitt should be commemorated in this way. The Diocese welcomes the renewed interest in this important part of London's heritage.'[114] The Watts memorial and the everyday heroes who feature on it have clearly remained an inspiration to others. Furthermore, the commemoration of Pitt, over eighty years after the last tablet was installed, demonstrates that the idea of everyday heroism, which originated in the latter half of the nineteenth century, has endured and is still relevant over a century later.

Fuller and more detailed examination of all these aspects of the development of the idea of everyday heroism will be undertaken in the chapters that follow, but this short chronology has set an agenda. Everyday heroism, in the definition adopted for this study, related to actions undertaken by civilian individuals which were considered, by their contemporaries, to be heroic. The definitions and classifications for how and why these acts, and consequently those who undertook them, were considered to be heroic varied and this variety will be discussed. By and large, however, it can be said that everyday heroes were individuals who risked their own life while attempting to save the life of another, and that their acts of heroism usually took place in or around the places where they lived and worked. Furthermore, it cannot be overstressed that acts of everyday heroism occurred relatively frequently, that the general public understood and were familiar with them and, most crucially, that people appear to have had great respect and admiration for those who undertook them. The Victorian and Edwardian periods are generally regarded and accepted as being suffused with a widespread and popular discourse on heroism and heroic individuals. What this book reveals for the first time is that the everyday heroism of otherwise ordinary civilians was just a prominent, important and influential within that discourse as the more well-known and exotic exploits of the great military and imperial men of British history.

1

'Gallantry in Saving Life': The Albert Medal

The 23rd March 1866 was a rough and stormy night. Off the coast of Devon, the cargo ship *Spirit of the Ocean* lost its battle with the force eleven gales and was torn apart as it was swept onto the notorious Start Point rocks. In complete darkness and battered by the wash and the wind, the situation was grave for all those on board and indeed, only four of the forty-two passengers and crew survived.[1] Those four were saved by Samuel Popplestone, the tenant of a nearby farm, who having witnessed the accident paused only to raise the alarm before setting off alone for the wreck, armed with just a small coil of rope. Popplestone clambered out onto the rocks and although swept off several times, he eventually managed to lift four men out of the water and drag them up the cliff to safety. He then conveyed them to his farm where he fed them, provided them with dry clothes and housed them overnight until the Coastguard arrived to assist them. As the story of Popplestone's bravery became known through the press, he was universally and understandably hailed as a hero and as a result of his heroism he became the first recipient of a brand new award for civilian gallantry.

This award was the Albert Medal, the first Crown-sanctioned decoration for civilian gallantry, and this chapter will investigate why the State was concerned with recognizing acts of heroism undertaken by civilian members of the public and how this recognition was administered. The Albert Medal was introduced with the explicit intention of increasing the public profile and awareness of the State's recognition of acts of everyday heroism and to act as an inducement to others to emulate the behaviour of those who undertook such acts. This desire to encourage emulation stemmed from a belief, on the part of the government, that acts of everyday heroism could be seen to represent an individual's allegiance and loyalty to the Crown and the nation in a similar way to acts of military heroism. However, what will be shown is that the civil servants charged with administering the medal based their decisions on the personal qualities and character displayed by the nominated individual and that only those who measured up to a set of strict criteria were considered worthy of reward. By examining what these criteria were and the prevailing ideas that influenced them, it is possible to construct a model of what constituted everyday heroism from an elite State-sanctioned perspective.

The Albert Medal was regulated under the Royal Sign Manual and therefore was undoubtedly an award of the Crown. Consequently, it will be referred to throughout this chapter as a Crown medal. However, evidence suggests that the monarch's role in the process was purely to approve the cases that were presented to them by the Secretary of State. Furthermore, the introduction of the Albert Medal originated from within the Board of Trade and those making the judgements and decisions on which individuals should be rewarded were, for the major part of the period under consideration, clerks and secretaries within the Home Office. In this respect, the important players in the practical administration of the medal were government ministers and civil servants and it is, therefore, more appropriate to class the medal as an award of the Government. Consequently, the term 'State', when used in this study in relation to the administration of the Albert Medal, refers to actions taken by the government but under the prerogative powers of the Crown. The term is not intended to imply any homogenization of the ruling body but is used purely for convenience to refer to the two institutions cooperatively involved in the awarding of the decoration. Finally, as will be shown, the core elements in the decision-making process were carried out by Home Office officials who ranged in social class from the middle to the upper. Once again, describing this group as 'Elites' is not intended to overlook or disregard these subtle social distinctions but simply provides a convenient shorthand for its general social position in relation to the majority of the general public.

'Daring and heroic actions': A brief administrative history of the Albert Medal

The Albert Medal is one of the lesser known awards for civilian gallantry, being overshadowed by the Victoria Cross and later superseded by the George Medal and George Cross. It therefore seems appropriate to offer a brief synopsis of the Albert Medal's history. In March 1866, *The London Gazette* published details of a Royal warrant instituting a new single-class decoration to be known as the Albert Medal. The warrant drew attention to the 'great loss of life . . . sustained by reason of shipwrecks and other perils of the sea' and set out regulations to reward 'the many daring and heroic actions performed by mariners and others to prevent such loss and to save the lives of those who are in danger of perishing'.[2] The medal derived its name from an understanding that 'The late Prince Consort was master of the Trinity House and took great interest in these matters'.[3] The decoration was to consist of a medal, described in the Royal warrant as,

> A gold oval-shaped badge or decoration enamelled in dark blue, with a monogram composed of the letters "V" and "A", interlaced with an Anchor erect in gold, surrounded by a Garter in Bronze, inscribed in raised letters of Gold "for Gallantry in Saving Life at Sea" and surmounted by a representation of the crown of His Royal Highness the lamented Prince Consort, and suspended from a dark blue riband of five-eighths of an inch in width with two white longitudinal stripes.[4]

As previously mentioned, the first award of the Albert Medal was made to Samuel Popplestone, and his medal was presented to him on 12 June 1866.[5]

The single-class Albert Medal awarded to Samuel Popplestone was, however, to be the only one of its kind. On 12 April 1867, a second Royal warrant was published which replaced the original single-class medal with two medals to be known as the Albert Medal of the First Class and the Albert Medal of the Second Class. The construction and decoration of the first-class medal was almost identical to the original single class, the only change being the introduction of a wider inch and three-eighths riband with four white longitudinal stripes instead of two. The new second-class medal differed in that it was to be 'entirely worked in bronze instead of gold and bronze' and also retained the original width two striped riband. The explanation given in the Royal warrant for the introduction of a second class of medal was that 'it has been represented to us that mariners and others perform many acts in preventing the loss of life from shipwreck and other perils of the sea, that are not of a character sufficiently daring and heroic to bring them under our warrant above cited, and are yet worthy of some distinguishing mark of our royal favour.'[6]

Although split into two classes, the medal was still awarded solely for acts undertaken at sea. This was to continue until 1877, when a Royal warrant of 30 April extended the scope of the decoration to cover 'cases of Gallantry in Saving Life on Land'. As with the sea award, the land medal consisted of a first- and second-class distinction and was introduced in recognition that 'many heroic acts are performed on land within our dominions, in preventing loss of life from accidents, on railways, and at fires, and other perils of the shore.'[7] The construction of the medal was essentially the same as with the sea medal, but with crimson enamelling instead of blue and with a crimson riband. With regard to decoration, the anchor motif was removed from the monogram and the words 'For Gallantry in Saving Life on Land' replaced the reference to the sea.

Over the next ninety-four years, the Albert Medal was subject to a number of Royal warrants that altered various components of its administration, its coverage and its title. In 1881, the responsibility for investigating and assessing proposed cases and keeping a register of awards was shifted from the Board of Trade to the Home Office.[8] Ten years later, in 1891, another Royal warrant allowed for the Admiralty to assume responsibility for administering cases involving the Royal Navy or Royal Marines, although the Home Secretary was still required to make the final submission to the monarch.[9] In 1904, changes were made to the riband for the second-class medal bringing it into line with that of the first class, and in 1905 the qualification for the land medal was extended to cover acts undertaken outside of the United Kingdom.[10] In 1917, it was decided that the use of the phrase 'second class' with regard to acts of heroism was no longer appropriate and demeaned both the act and the decoration. Consequently, the bronze second-class award was renamed, the Albert Medal, while the first-class award became the Albert Medal in Gold.[11]

The introduction of the George Medal and George Cross, both civilian decorations for gallantry, in 1940, complicated the decision-making process for rewarding civilian heroism. As a result, in 1949 it was decided that the Albert Medal in Gold would no longer be awarded and that the bronze Albert Medal would only be awarded posthumously as the George Medal was not given in such cases. This arrangement lasted a further twenty-two years until, on 15 December 1971, a Royal Warrant revoked the Albert Medal and with effect from 21 October 1971, all holders of the Albert Medal, of all types and classes, living on that day were regarded as holders of the George Cross and eligible to exchange their medal accordingly. The majority of surviving medal holders did exactly this, and the Albert Medal, originally intended to be 'highly prized and eagerly sought after', passed into relative obscurity.

An inducement to acts of gallantry: The reasoning behind the medal

Documentary evidence demonstrates that the Albert Medal was explicitly introduced to encourage the emulation of certain types of behaviour and attitudes that the State believed were exemplified by civilians who undertook acts of heroism in their everyday life. This objective was to be achieved in a number of ways. First, the awarding of the medal and details of the heroic act were made highly public so as to reach the widest possible audience. Second, the medal was promoted as being an award of the Crown which not only increased its prominence but also ensured that it represented official State endorsement of certain behaviour. Finally, the medal was administered so as to ensure that not only would it remain highly sought after but also that it was only awarded to those people whom the government could be certain were suitable models for emulation. Each of these claims will now be examined in more detail.

That the Albert Medal was introduced specifically with publicity in mind is substantiated by the fact that there was already a medal in place which rewarded civilian heroism but which was relatively unknown. In 1854, following the passing of the Merchant Shipping Act, the Board of Trade began to reward mariners who had saved or attempted to save lives from shipwreck. In cases of 'especial gallantry involving risk of life or other peculiar merit', the Board of Trade awarded a medal which was to become known as the Board of Trade Medal for Saving Life at Sea. Issued in both bronze and silver, the medal was 2.25in (57mm) in diameter. On one side it carried the head of the sovereign and the other was pressed with two different inscriptions. 'Awarded by the Board of Trade for Gallantry in Saving Life' was used in cases where the recipient had risked their own life in saving another, whereas 'Awarded by the Board of Trade for saving life at sea' applied to those who had assisted in saving life but who had not risked their own.[12]

In October 1864, Thomas Milner-Gibson, Cabinet Minister and President of the Board of Trade, wrote to the Queen highlighting the considerable number of Board of Trade Gallantry Medals awarded since its introduction. Gibson stated, unequivocally, that the purpose of the Board of Trade medal was to act as an 'inducement' to the undertaking of acts of gallantry. However, one particular characteristic of the medal was hampering this objective, as Gibson went on to explain in his letter;

> The medal is, however, too large to be worn and the Board of Trade are satisfied by the representations they receive that a decoration which could be worn upon the person, as the Victoria Cross is worn, would be prized much more highly

and would be much more useful as an inducement to those acts of gallantry and humanity which it has been the object of these rewards to encourage.[13]

Gibson's solution to this problem was to substitute the Board of Trade medal with one of a more suitable size to be worn and his suggestion met with general approval among his cabinet colleagues. The then Colonial Secretary Lord Carnarvon commented that 'What is coveted is something that can be worn on the coat' and another cabinet member added, 'it seems to me that the essential thing in an order of merit is the medal, riband or other outward mark which indicates to others at a glance the worth, ability and bravery of the holder.'[14] Although it is not completely clear as to when and where such medals would be worn by civilian individuals, the wearing of a medal, as opposed to the keeping of one in a presentation case, was a public act and one which would have undoubtedly promoted the cause for which it had been awarded.[15] Had the only consideration been that of rewarding civilian heroism, rather than increasing publicity around such recognition, there would have been little need to introduce the Albert Medal as the Board of Trade Sea Gallantry Medal already fulfilled that criterion, especially considering that the Albert Medal was initially introduced to reward mariners.

Another aspect of the award that supports the publicity claim is the manner in which the awarding of it was directly publicized. The original 1866 warrant stated that 'the names of those upon whom we may be pleased to confer the decoration shall be published in the London Gazette,' and this was carried out throughout the lifespan of the medal. Although the *London Gazette* had a limited, and to a great extent 'establishment' circulation, the award notices were reproduced in national newspapers such as *The Times* and regional or local papers related to the area of the original incident. Consequently, the announcements would have reached a far wider and more socially diverse audience.

A public presentation ceremony for the recipient also played a large part in increasing the publicity surrounding the award. In one note from the Board of Trade to the Home Office, it was stated, 'it is rather the object of the Board of Trade to make the bestowal as public and of as much importance as possible.'[16] This intention is also frequently echoed throughout the paperwork on individual cases, whereby it is stipulated that a ceremony should be held and a local dignitary procured if the monarch was unavailable. Only when assurances were given that the bestowal of the medal would be sufficiently publicized was the public presentation waived. In one such case, that of Miss Hannah Roabotham who rescued a number of children from a collapsed schoolhouse in St Helens, Lancashire, the local MP wrote to the Home Office;

> The notice of the award to Miss Roabotham in the Gazette has been copied into all the local newspapers and in that way full publicity has been given to the honour she has received. A presentation of the medal in public could hardly make it more generally recorded and I think would be trying to her as she is a very quiet and retiring girl and in other respects I question if it would be beneficial to her.[17]

Such was the prominence of publicizing the award that the public ceremony had to be detrimental to the well-being of the recipient before it would be discounted.

It would appear clear, from the evidence, that increasing the public awareness of the rewarding of everyday heroism and disseminating the concept to the widest possible audience was behind the government's decision to introduce the Albert Medal.

The government also sought to ensure that the award would not only be prominent in society but would also be accorded the same level of national influence and importance as military medals such as The Victoria Cross. In his 1864 letter to the Queen, Milner-Gibson stated, with regard to introducing the Albert Medal as a replacement for the Board of Trade Medal:

> The Board of Trade are also satisfied that these decorations would be more prized if they were awarded and recorded with the same degree of solemnity which attends the giving of other decorations of like kind.[18]

This, it was suggested, could partly be achieved by regulating the new award under the Royal Sign Manual, as with the Victoria Cross, which would effectively make the medal an award of the Crown as opposed to the Board of Trade. The importance of this is confirmed by a comment written by a member of the War Office in 1866, 'the bestowal of a medal in these cases by the Crown would of course be far more appreciated than a medal granted by a private society.'[19] The manner in which the medal was presented also greatly reinforced the fact that the medal was an award of the Crown. In a letter to Milner-Gibson dated 18 January 1866, the Queen's private secretary wrote, 'The Queen directs me further to state that she proposes to confer the medals first given with her own hand.'[20] This arrangement continued under Edward VII, who in 1902 wrote to the Home Office and asked them to give him as much notice as possible of an award ceremony in order that he would be more able to attend and present the medal.[21] Presentation by the monarch would not only have been a great honour for the recipient, but would also have reinforced the message that this was a Crown bestowed medal.

Aside from the added publicity and kudos, making the medal an award of the Crown also served another important function in that it reinforced the connection between Royal benevolence and loyalty to the throne.[22] Military heroism, occurring as it did within the context of serving the country, could easily be promoted and interpreted as heroism on behalf of the nation and thus underline a serviceman's allegiance to the Crown.[23] However, providing national State recognition and endorsement of everyday heroism widened the idea of heroism from the battlefield into the domain of the civilian. This meant that, potentially, every one of the monarch's subjects, and not just those in the military, could now receive a State reward for heroism and thus become a national hero representing allegiance to the Crown and service to the nation. Furthermore, instituting a decoration for acts of civilian heroism promoted an idea that every citizen in the country was capable of performing a heroic act and consequently the admirable qualities of a heroic individual could be perceived as national characteristics. By administering the medal under the Royal Sign Manual, the State was able to encourage allegiance to Crown and country while also promoting the idea that the nation was supported upon foundations of the highest ideals.

'Considerable difficulties' and
the measures to guard against them

Publicizing and endorsing acts of civilian heroism in order to encourage certain behaviour was, however, something that had to be approached with great care. First, it involved maintaining the number of awards at the right level; too few and the overall effect would be limited, too many and the medal would become worthless. Some did not view this as a particularly pertinent issue, as with one cabinet MP who wrote, 'There is a gap here which should be filled. I have no fear of decorations losing their value. The appetite for them is ravenous and is whetted rather than satisfied by food.'[24] However, the general feeling was that restraint had to be exercised to ensure that the Albert Medal remained 'highly prized'. One comment made in 1885 was that 'it is certainly desirable that these medals should not be awarded too easily,' while another in 1895 stated that 'a decoration like the Albert Medal would lose half its value if it were granted on mere impulse.'[25] Publicizing and encouraging acts of civilian heroism while not cheapening or devaluing them was clearly a delicate balancing act and one, it would seem, that was not always entirely achieved. In 1908, for example, one correspondent wrote, 'formerly it was almost impossible to obtain the decoration, [but] it seems better to be too generous in recommending the medal than to be too parsimonious' and also that 'a more liberal view is now taken in deciding whether cases shall be recommended for the medal.'[26] These comments suggest that the balance had, at times, been too greatly weighted against granting the award.

The second and potentially more damaging reason why the bestowal of medals for civilian heroism had to be approached with care was that if individuals were to receive highly publicized State endorsement of their behaviour, it was vital that only those who represented the correct qualities were promoted as worthy of emulation. It is apparent that even from the earliest government suggestion the Crown had explicit concerns about sanctioning the reward of civilian heroism. In December 1864, in response to Milner-Gibson's letter, the Queen's private secretary wrote that Her Majesty saw 'considerable difficulties in the establishment of a new decoration, as an order of merit for gallant acts performed in private life.'[27] Victoria's concern was that such an award was in opposition to the two principles on which the Crown had previously granted honours and in particular the Victoria Cross. These were that medals were currently only 'bestowed upon persons in the Queen's service or for acts performed in the Royal service' and consequently were 'recommended by officers of the service in which the recipient was employed and the grant was founded upon a chain of official responsible testimony.'[28] Effectively, there was a sense that under these principles the crown could make awards safe in the knowledge that the recipient was of good character, appropriately motivated, that the act undertaken was honestly and officially reported and that the presentation of the medal would reflect favourably upon the Crown.

The Queen's concern was that this would not be the case if the range of possible recipients was extended to all of her subjects. In the same letter of December 1864, the Queen made two very specific concerns explicitly clear; first that 'it might frequently happen that these daring acts might be performed by men of irregular life and immoral habits' and second that 'the present proposal would give decorations to men for gallant acts performed as citizens, in their ordinary life, and would be vouched for by people of their own class, probably their friends and neighbours.'[29] In the view of the Queen, there was a distinct possibility or even probability that awards given for everyday heroism could subsequently be discredited either due to the character of the recipient or to the validity of the act. Whereas this might not have been such a problem for the Board of Trade in awarding a largely unknown decoration, it was vitally important to the Crown if it were to sanction and endorse what was intended to be a high profile public encouragement of certain behaviour. In the light of the Queen's concerns, the matter was put to one side but discussions about how the medal could be regulated continued within the government. In 1866, Milner-Gibson once again wrote to the Queen but this time assuring her that the government had secured the necessary conditions by which the medal could be successfully administered. The reply stated, 'the Queen thinks that, as you have arranged and guarded it, in the order in council, there can be no further objection to the decoration to be called the Albert Medal, and her Majesty admires and approves the design.'[30] It would appear then that measures had been put in place to address and protect against the Queen's two concerns.

With regard to the Queen's first concern, that medals would be awarded to people of immoral habits, a clause within the Royal warrant ensured that the government could take action against anyone who brought the award into disrepute.[31] The recipient of the medal was also required to sign a declaration agreeing to forfeit and return their medal should they be considered to have infringed this clause. During the entire period that the medal was awarded not a single individual actually had their medal revoked and this might appear to suggest that people took the award very seriously, that they felt honoured by it and that the clause in the warrant deterred them from doing anything that might cause them to lose it. However, Home Office archives do record that three cases were considered for forfeiture but none were deemed to warrant such action.[32] Having gone to some lengths to ensure that it could take action against such people, the fact that the government chose not to do so is interesting enough to warrant further examination.

Of the three cases considered, the most interesting is that of sixteen-year-old Thomas Lewis. On 2 July 1909, following the collapse of a trench at Alexandra Dock, Newport, Lewis volunteered to enter a narrow passageway and worked for two hours to free a trapped man, who was later pulled out alive. The doctor at the works described Lewis as 'a boy of pluck and courage [who] well deserves the highest honour awarded for such brave conduct' and in the opinion of one Newport Police Inspector, 'Lewis displayed conspicuous bravery and rare pluck, and is undoubtedly worthy of the highest commendation.'[33] On 13 December 1909, at Buckingham Palace, the King awarded Lewis the Albert Medal of the Second Class in recognition of his bravery. However, in 1911, the *Daily Mail* reported that Lewis, described as 'the boy hero of the Newport disaster', had been fined for street fighting, expelled from a Church Army home, refused to work and had served a fourteen-day prison sentence for vagrancy.[34] This was brought to the attention of the Home Office which considered the situation serious enough to warrant contacting the Newport Police for a full report on Lewis' behaviour.

The opinion of the Newport superintendent was that Lewis had 'been giving considerable trouble by his general bad conduct in the streets'.[35] The report also listed three convictions since the medal was awarded, for sleeping out, street fighting and trespass and a further six convictions dating from 1904 through to 1909. The Home Office response to this report was, however, significantly more lenient than might have been expected and to some extent it sought to excuse Lewis' actions and seek rehabilitation rather than punishment,

> The great distinction connected with the award of the Albert Medal and the laudations showered on this boy seem to have had an unfortunate effect on him. The authorities seem to have done all in their power to get the boy away from his companions and find him honest work. He is evidently on the high road to serious crime but perhaps a serious caution by the police that on the next occasion of his being brought before the magistrate, forfeiture of his medal will be considered, may have some effect on him.[36]

Although cautioned, Lewis was back before the magistrate in 1912, charged with theft and defaulting on a fine, for which he received a one month prison sentence. Again, the Home Office response was more one of benevolence than of criticism,

> This seems a hopeless case. Every effort has been made to keep the boy straight – an attempt to send him to Australia failed, the army will not take him and yet there must be some good in the lad.[37]

Finally, in 1913 a request was received at the Home Office from Lewis Haslam, the MP for Monmouth, who originally nominated Lewis for the Albert Medal and appears to have taken a continued interest in his welfare, asking if the department could do anything to smooth Lewis' way into the regular army. It also came to light that Lewis no longer had his medal and it had been taken into the charge of *The Argus* newspaper for safe keeping and to prevent Lewis from 'exhibiting it on the music hall stage'. The Home Office's response that 'it was certainly safer in their custody than in Lewis' own' brought a sad close to the case.[38]

From an initial reading, it is perhaps difficult to account for the decision not to revoke; however, a number of reasons can be suggested. First, once it emerged that Lewis had six convictions *prior* to the award, the initial decision itself could have come into question along with the integrity of the Home Office and its policy on investigation. Although it was stated by the Home Office that 'the Newport police, however, no doubt with a mistaken notion of kindness did not inform S of S [Secretary of State] of the fact,' the force was never specifically asked to comment on Lewis' character or conduct prior to the award and therefore the Home Office would have received much of the criticism. A further reason for not revoking the medal was that it would have attracted a certain amount of bad publicity and could have called into question the whole matter of rewarding civilian heroism. Lewis' conviction for street fighting would have hardly been newsworthy at the time, were it not for him being an Albert Medal holder, and the fact that the *Daily Mail* picked up on it could suggest that there was perhaps some questioning of the policy of rewarding civilian heroism. Revoking Lewis' medal would have only fuelled such fire and consequently the matter was managed quietly within the Home Office until the point where it died away from the public interest.

The Home Office response to Lewis is, however, also very revealing with regard to the attitudes and ideas about heroism that were held by those who administered the medal.

In the first instance, Lewis' behaviour is attributed to the effects of the award itself and the adulation and acclaim resulting from it simply going to the young man's head. The fact that the Home Office used the threat of revoking rather than actually taking action shows that it genuinely believed that the Albert Medal could have an influential and beneficial effect on behaviour and that it was viewed as a tool to reward and instil good character. Moreover, it shows that the perceived presence of heroic capabilities and qualities in an individual instilled a sense that the person was, at their core, a decent citizen despite any minor failings in their behaviour. This is further substantiated by the slightly exasperated comment that 'there must be some good in the lad'. Despite all the negative evidence to the contrary, a belief was maintained that because he had been capable of heroism on one occasion Lewis must essentially be a person of good character. It became a question of how best to harness that character and keep it on the straight and narrow, but it can be imagined that had he not been an Albert Medal winner, an individual such as Lewis would have felt the full force of state punishment for his behaviour. For those in the Home Office, the capacity for heroism was, it would appear, viewed as an indication of inherently good character; 'once a hero, always a hero' might have been their motto.

In order to address the Queen's second concern, that individuals would be nominated and vouched for by their friends and neighbours, the Board of Trade was charged with thoroughly investigating each case that was put forward to ensure its validity and that it was based upon true facts before it was recommended to the Queen. In 1881, this responsibility was transferred to the Home Office and the final decision to recommend each case rested with the Secretary of State in consultation with his undersecretaries.[39] However, although there were official channels by which the recommendation was made to the Queen herself, there was no official procedure by which individuals could be put forward for consideration for the Albert Medal. Private societies, such as the Royal Humane Society, had a standard application form for nominating an individual to the society for its consideration. In this way, there was a clear procedure by which members of the general public could suggest individuals who they considered deserving of recognition. The Albert Medal procedure was quite different.

'Pestering . . . the Home Office': The process and influence of nomination

With the Albert Medal, the mechanism by which acts of heroism came to the attention of those empowered to recommend the award was far from clear-cut. In the first instance, as a medal given for gallantry at sea resulting largely from shipwreck, the Board of Trade itself would be aware of heroic acts as a result of investigating the incident. However, with the introduction of the land medal in 1877 and the transferring of the administration of the medal to the Home Office in 1881, the submission of cases for consideration became less regimented. It has already been shown that the Albert Medal was specifically introduced to increase the public profile of State rewarding of everyday heroism, yet there was no attempt to directly encourage or even engage the public in putting individuals forward for consideration. Perhaps this was a conscious decision intended to ensure that only the most notable cases or those that people felt most strongly about would be pursued with the necessary zeal to identify where and how they might be considered. Or perhaps the lack of publicity about how to put someone forward for the medal was an attempt, with the Queen's concern in mind, to ensure that cases only came through the right channels, namely those that were reliable, verifiable and most importantly trustworthy.

Whichever the case, it appears that people were not over enthusiastic about putting forward individuals for consideration. In the forty-eight years between March 1866 and May 1914, just 398 individuals were put forward to the Home Office as possible candidates for the Albert Medal.[40] Of course, it could be the case that other individuals were nominated locally and did not make it to the government office concerned or that files have been subsequently lost or destroyed. Nevertheless, the existing records are extensive enough to produce a statistical analysis of how the cases were being brought to the attention of the government. Between 1866 and 1881, cases were handled by the Board of Trade and unfortunately very few detailed case files for individuals were compiled or have survived. The number of medals awarded during this fifteen-year period can be calculated by reference to the *London Gazette* but this does not give any information about who nominated the individual and therefore substantial data for this initial period is unavailable. However, in the Home Office records kept between 1881 and 1914, each case considered has a detailed file of correspondence regarding the application and as this usually included details of the origin of the claim for the medal, these files provide the evidence for the following analysis.

Upon examination of the files it was found that certain general and recurring categories could be determined with regard to the nominating party (see Table 1). However, before proceeding to analyse these figures, it is necessary to address some of the possible objections to the arbitrary partitioning of such a variable quantity into a set of apparently convenient groupings. One of these could be that the selection is simply subjective and that such distinctions are not always black and white. However, where possible the title used by the nominating individual themselves has been used to establish their role (i.e. they signed their letter Dr, Rev or MP etc.) and where information such as this was not available, all the additional material within the file has been taken into consideration. There could still be semantic queries with regard to exactly how some individuals have been classified, so the process used has been outlined below the table so as to ensure transparency. Furthermore, for the purposes of this study all that is required is a broad overview of the general position held by the nominating party, particularly in relation to the proposed recipient, rather than an exact definition of their status. Another objection could be that although the final approach to the government department may have come through someone such as a clergyman or MP, they could actually have been acting on behalf of another individual, a collection of individuals or the community at large. In the vast majority of cases, the nominating party wrote in some detail about why they were proposing an individual and where it is clear that they were acting on behalf of someone else, this has been taken into consideration and attributed accordingly. However, it must be conceded that it will never be possible to know the exact motivation behind every individual nomination, if not explicitly stated, but that once again, for the purposes of this study such anomalies do not substantially distort the figures.

There are two ways of approaching this evidence: one, simply ascertaining which parties supplied the most nominations and two, examining the relationship between the nominating party and whether the medal was awarded. The first of these gives an

Table 1 Number and percentage of nominations for the Albert Medal between 1866 and 1914

Nominating party	Individuals nominated	%
Foreign/colonial state department [1]	50	17.1
Senior officer [2]	36	12.3
British state department [3]	36	12.3
Local government [4]	29	9.9
MP [5]	27	9.2
Local individual [6]	27	9.2
Employer	20	6.8
Local organization [7]	20	6.8
Clergy [8]	15	5.1
Coroner	9	3.1
Proposed recipient	7	2.4
Relative of the proposed recipient	6	2.0
Inspector [9]	6	2.0
General individual [10]	3	1.0
Local petition	1	0.3
The individual rescued	1	0.3
Subtotal	**293**	
Unknown	105	
Total	**398**	

[1] Consists of departments such as the Colonial Office, India Office and foreign governments
[2] Any person who was a hierarchical superior of the proposed recipient, for example military, police, fire service or coastguard
[3] Consists of departments such as the War Office, Board of Trade and the Admiralty
[4] Consists of the local council, mayor or any other local official acting in an official capacity, such as a JP
[5] Any MP and not necessarily or specifically the proposed recipient's constituency MP
[6] Those persons apparently acting entirely on their own initiative and living locally to the incident
[7] Any collected body working locally such as a labour union or service association
[8] Any individual describing themselves as working within the Church, regardless of denomination or location
[9] Government inspectors of mines or factories acting in an official capacity
[10] Those persons apparently acting entirely on their own initiative and living outside of the local area

Source: Home Office (HO) and Board of Trade (BT) documents, The National Archives.

insight into how cases came to be nominated whereas the second provides evidence of the influence that the nominating party had on the government department that was considering the award. In the case of the first approach, it is clear that the majority of cases were put forward through what can be loosely termed 'official' channels (see Table 1). Out of the 293 cases where data is available, only thirty-four (12%) can be classed as originating from an individual who had no stated connection to an official body.[41] So it would appear that it was not especially the case that people were nominated or vouched for specifically by their friends or neighbours.

By taking the second approach and examining the nominating party data in relation to the number of cases awarded, an interesting picture emerges (see Table 2). It is immediately clear that not only were cases more likely to be received through official channels, but such cases had a higher success rate with regard to medals awarded. Nominating parties that can be considered to have been acting in an official capacity have the highest success rates for the award of the medal.[42] This is perhaps only to be expected as not only were these parties perceived to be trustworthy and reliable, but in most cases they were able to obtain and provide extensive, detailed and verifiable testimonies as to the facts of the incident. The next major block of success comes from those cases proposed on a local basis.[43] Again, with local government there is a perception of official reliability and local individuals and organizations were especially well placed to provide detailed, albeit less verifiable, reports about the incident. Interestingly, MPs do not feature highly with regard to successful proposals and this could suggest that their opinion or influence was not particularly important. However, it could also suggest that, although not explicitly stated, they were simply acting as an advocate for the case and took no further involvement in the proposal thus reducing their influence. There is no distinct relationship between cases nominated by MPs and the reason given for refusing the award, so a definitive explanation for the statistics remains elusive. The same can be said of the clergy, who also appear lower on the scale than perhaps might be expected.

Given the concerns of the Queen and the Home Office, it is not surprising to find the cases nominated by those who were perceived to have a possible connection to the individual concerned, close to the bottom of the table for medals awarded. It would seem that the government was highly suspicious and sceptical about cases nominated by a relative of the proposed recipient and even to some extent nomination from the person who had been saved. It was most certainly not thought correct for any individual to request the medal for an act they themselves had undertaken and where that was the case the comments speak for themselves. One example of this is the case of James Hodges who in 1906 applied for the land medal for an act undertaken in 1876 when he had attempted to save a fellow big-game hunter who was being attacked by a tiger. His case was officially refused due to the land medal not existing when the act was undertaken. However, with one undersecretary having commented, 'the way that Mr Hodges is pestering the King, the Home Office and every body for the medal shows that he does not have that modesty which is usually supplied to accompany valour', it is clear that the method of nomination had a significant influence.[44] Moreover, it is evident that the fear that partisan nomination of individuals could lead to awards being made to those of poor character was acted upon and such nominations rarely resulted in success.

Table 2 Number and percentage of Albert Medals awarded and refused between 1866 and 1914

Nominating party	Individuals nominated	Medals awarded	%	Medals refused	%
Foreign/colonial state department [1]	50	39	78.0	11	22.0
Senior officer [2]	36	24	66.6	12	33.3
British state department [3]	36	24	66.6	12	33.3
Inspector [9]	6	4	66.6	2	33.3
Local government [4]	29	17	58.6	12	41.3
Local individual [6]	27	12	44.4	15	55.5
Local organization [7]	20	8	40.0	12	60.0
MP [5]	27	9	33.3	18	66.6
Coroner	9	3	33.3	6	66.6
Clergy [8]	15	4	26.6	11	73.3
Employer	20	4	20.0	16	80.0
Proposed recipient	7	0		7	100
Relative of the proposed recipient	6	0		6	100
General individual [10]	3	0		3	100
Local petition	1	0		1	100
The individual rescued	1	0		1	100
Unknown	105	90	85.7	15	14.2
Total	**398**	**238**	**60.0**	**160**	**40.0**

[1] Consists of departments such as the Colonial Office, India Office and foreign governments
[2] Any person who was a hierarchical superior of the proposed recipient, for example military, police, fire service or coastguard
[3] Consists of departments such as the War Office, Board of Trade and the Admiralty
[4] Consists of the local council, mayor or any other local official acting in an official capacity, such as a JP
[5] Any MP and not necessarily or specifically the proposed recipient's constituency MP
[6] Those persons apparently acting entirely on their own initiative and living locally to the incident
[7] Any collected body working locally such as a labour union or service association
[8] Any individual describing themselves as working within the Church, regardless of denomination or location
[9] Government inspectors of mines or factories acting in an official capacity
[10] Those persons apparently acting entirely on their own initiative and living outside of the local area

Source: Home Office (HO) and Board of Trade (BT) documents, The National Archives.

'Some rules to guide us': The decision-making process and those who undertook it

Before proceeding to examine the specific qualifications upon which the State based its judgement of which individuals should be considered worthy of reward and emulation, it is worth making clear exactly what it was encouraging people to emulate. When the medal was introduced, it was stated that the award was intended to act as 'an inducement to those acts of gallantry and humanity which it has been the object of these rewards to encourage'.[45] However, to interpret this as meaning that people were to be encouraged to go out and actively seek to commit acts of heroism is implausible, not least on purely practical grounds. Furthermore, as will be discussed below, one of the central qualifications for attaining the medal was that in the course of the act of heroism the recipient had to have placed themselves in a position where they were more likely than not to lose their life. Given this, it is even more improbable that the government was encouraging people to directly emulate the act of heroism itself. What they were actually seeking to encourage, through the rewarding of everyday heroism, was the type of behaviour that they believed was implicit in such acts rather than the act itself. The message was that you should strive to be the type of person who would lay down your life for another, but not that you should go out and actively seek to do so; emulate the qualities and character of the hero, not necessarily their act.

In addition to recognizing what was being rewarded, to fully understand how the decisions were reached it is vital to gain an understanding of how the award was administered and the social standing of those involved. As previously explained, there was no formal public application procedure for nominating an individual. However, once the matter had reached the relevant department there was generally a written discussion regarding the details, merits and eligibility of the case with regard to recommending the individual for the award. Although ultimately and officially the final decision rested with the Crown, it would appear that no case put before the monarch by the Secretary of State was declined. Therefore, it was essentially the government department who considered the case that made the judgement as to whether or not the individual deserved to receive the award. Between 1866 and 1881, this responsibility rested with the Board of Trade and cases were most often brought to their attention by the Marine Department of the Department of Transport.[46] After an amendment to the Royal warrant in 1881, the official responsibility for examining cases moved to the Home Office; however, it is clear from the surviving files that the Board of Trade did continue to initially examine cases that directly came to their attention and then pass their opinions and judgements on to the Home Office for a final recommendation. In the majority of these cases, the Home Office did not question any further the decision of the Board of Trade. Notwithstanding this, the majority of cases between 1866 and 1914, for which records survive and are of any substance, were considered by the Home Office. Although after 1891 the Admiralty were authorized to consider and directly recommend cases to the monarch, no individual case files appear to exist or have survived. It is, then, to the Home Office that we should look when ascertaining how decisions were reached.

The Home Office documents clearly demonstrate the procedure by which cases came to be recommended to the monarch for the award. Upon receipt of any communication in which an individual was put forward for the Albert Medal, an upper-division clerk would compose a memo in which he briefly outlined the factual details of the incident and made his own suggestions as to how the matter should be handled. Often, this would entail the collection of further details or evidence such as witness or police statements, but once all of these had been supplied the clerk would indicate his opinion as to whether or not the individual should be considered. This memo and all the documents were then circulated to other upper-division clerks and to the private and parliamentary undersecretaries who added their own opinions and judgements as to the suitability of the individual. Finally, the file was sent to the Secretary of State who, with regard to the comments entered on the memo, made the final decision. On some occasions, recommendations were made against the majority view and on other occasions cases were refused even though the majority of comments were in favour. On the whole, though, the Secretary of State appears to have followed the consensus of opinion given by the civil servants when making his decisions.

In 1880, the Home Office underwent what was perceived to be a radical reform with open competition replacing nomination as the basis for recruitment into the civil service.[47] However, as Jill Pellew has outlined, 'on the whole the social backgrounds of the upper-division Home Office Clerks did not change dramatically as the result of open competitive entry'. Between 1880 and 1896, nine out of the twelve graduates who entered the Home Office had degrees from Oxford, and between 1896 and 1914, every entrant came from either Oxford or Cambridge. A large proportion of these entrants had also been schooled at good public day or boarding schools reflecting an income group who could afford such education.[48] Although open competition led to the recruitment of fewer sons of public officials, the Home Office during the period under consideration was still staffed by the sons of professional upper-middle-class men. It was upon the judgements and perceptions of these elite individuals that the awarding of the Albert Medal was administered.

With regard to this administration, it might be imagined that some rules or guidelines would have been set in place to assist the government department in making its decisions. The Royal warrant itself gave little indication of exactly what constituted an act worthy of recognition. In the course of a lengthy discussion regarding the case of Charles Sprankling, who rescued five crew members of a fishing boat when it ran aground near Button Bradstock, Dorset in 1866, it was suggested that 'if we had some rules to guide us . . . it would prevent these present discussions'.[49] In reply to this suggestion, one undersecretary stated, 'it would be well if we could draw up some rules for the Albert Medal; but I suppose it will be rather difficult', while another lamented, 'I am in despair about drawing up rules . . . each case stands on its own grounds'.[50] The general view, that every case should be considered independently, is exemplified by one comment that 'every application for the Albert Medal is carefully considered on its own merits'.[51]

Despite these measures, it is abundantly and clearly stated throughout the case files that previous cases should be and were called upon as precedents for either awarding or refusing the medal. Indeed, in the case of eight refusals, 'it would go against the precedent' was explicitly cited as the primary reason for the decision.[52] This is perhaps only to be expected as the civil servants struggled to decide who should and should not be recommended to receive the award. Without any real guidance, the departments were left to adopt their own sets of standards, qualifications and judgements as to what constituted an act worthy of recognition and consequently what did not. It is an awareness of this that is absolutely essential to understanding why the Albert Medal was awarded in the manner that is was.

To reward or not to reward: The judgements behind the decisions

Given the decision not to implement any firm rules or guidelines, it would appear that the Home Office personnel administering the medal believed it would be reasonably straightforward to make judgements upon the relative heroism of an act. They would consider the facts of the matter and apply their collective knowledge and reasoning to reach an informed consensus. Similar presumptions appear to have underpinned the administration of the Victoria Cross, as highlighted by Melvin Smith who has suggested that 'There was . . . no definition of heroism, only the admonition that the act be self-evidently worthy of recognition'.[53] However, their judgements were based solely upon their own personal opinions regarding the nature of heroic behaviour and they essentially projected those assumptions onto the cases they passed judgement upon. In doing so, they unwittingly shaped a construction of everyday heroism around their perception of the underlying qualities and character of the individual person, rather than judging the award on the facts of the case. The Albert Medal was intended to encourage and endorse a specific type of behaviour, believed by the State to be exemplified by civilian heroes, and when Home Office staff felt they had seen it displayed, they awarded the Albert Medal.

In order to substantiate such a claim, it is necessary to identify and account for the judgements that were made and the qualities upon which they were based. Whereas with the Victoria Cross and other gallantry medals what most often exists or survives are the registers or details of those who were awarded the medal, what makes the Albert Medal documentation particularly interesting is that case files for refusals are also available. Refusing a nomination was effectively saying that the individual did not qualify for the award, and therefore reasons for refusal can be interpreted as inverse qualifications. For example, if an individual was refused because their rescue attempt was unsuccessful and the victim perished, then saving the victim could be taken to be a qualification for the award.[54]

From a total of 398 individuals considered for the medal in the period under examination, 160 (40%) were refused. This is, it might be argued, lower than expected given that the medal was intended to be restricted only to outstanding acts of bravery. However, the number of Albert Medals awarded between 1866 and 1914 was as follows: original single-class sea medal, 1; first-class sea medal, 16; second-class sea medal, 70; and between 1877 and 1914: first-class land medal, 25;

second-class land medal, 126. Consequently, an examination of the awarded cases shows that out of the 238 medals awarded, only forty-one (17%) were first-class medals, the rest being the slightly more attainable second class and therefore the amount of refusals does not suggest a cheapening of the decoration. In the majority of refused cases, the discussion does not reach the point where any particular grade of medal is considered, so it is not possible to ascertain which class of medal was being denied. However, in most cases considered by the Home Office there is a reasonably full discussion among the undersecretaries as to the details and merits of the case, and from this it is possible to get a significant impression as to how decisions were shaped.

By far, the most common reason given for refusal (just under 30%) was that the rescuer did not incur a sufficient amount of risk to their own life in undertaking the act (see Table 3). One example of this judgement is the case of Charles Putnam and Arthur Ruben, who both jumped into the River Thames off Victoria Embankment, during a fast running tide to rescue a semi-conscious woman who had attempted to commit suicide. The decision of the Home Office was that,

> This was a gallant action and both men seem to have jumped into the river without hesitation. They were, however, good swimmers and it seems doubtful if the risk run by them quite reaches the Albert Medal standard.[55]

Table 3 Number and percentage of Albert Medal nominations refused between 1866 and 1914 and the reason given for refusal

Reason given for refusal	Cases refused	%
Insufficient risk to life	47	29.4
Professional duty	20	12.5
Not up to the standard	17	10.6
Outside of warrant conditions	16	10.0
Multiple acts at same incident	14	8.8
Would go against the precedents	8	5.0
Insufficient evidence	7	4.4
Act not necessary	6	3.8
Act occurred too long ago	6	3.8
Individual already sufficiently rewarded	5	3.1
Act too common	5	3.1
Use of safety equipment	5	3.1
Accumulated acts of heroism	2	1.3
No discussion of case	2	1.3
Total	**160**	

Source: Home Office (HO) and Board of Trade (BT) documents, The National Archives.

There can be little doubt that Putnam and Ruben undertook a singularly brave act and one that was subsequently recognized by the Royal Humane Society. However, the fact that they themselves were not perceived to have been in any great danger led to the refusal of the Albert Medal.

This element of risk to life was also an important consideration with regard to successful cases when deciding which class of medal to award. The major distinction between the first- and second-class medal was the level of risk to life. The decision to apply this particular qualification may have grown out of the original Board of Trade Medal, which was awarded at a bronze and silver level respectively 'for saving life at sea' or 'risking life to save life at sea'. It could also be a result of a letter from the Board of Trade to the Royal National Lifeboat Institution asking for advice on how it decided upon its medals. In reply to this letter, the RNLI stated that,

> In our wreck forum the following question is put – "was there any risk of life incurred by the sailors?" if the reply corresponds with the other reports in our possession on the case and is "great risk of life" then the committee vote the silver medal of the institute. But when the reply to the question is "yes" then the thanks of the institute is cited on vellum.[56]

There was clearly a 'risk to life' distinction in place with the RNLI and it would appear that the Board of Trade, and subsequently the Home Office, chose to adopt a similar approach.

The matter of how much risk to life was sufficient to warrant an award and if so, which class, was, nevertheless, much debated within the Home Office throughout the period under investigation. The criteria can be best summed up thus; the second class was to be awarded when 'risk to life was not only great but exceeded the chances of safety' and the first class was reserved for acts where the risk to life 'was so overpoweringly great that there was practically no chance of safety'.[57] In short, to receive a medal at all you had to stand a good chance of losing your own life and to receive the first-class medal, it had to be almost certain that you would perish. These were, indeed, exacting standards and the use of 'risk to life' as a deciding factor for refusal was not universally approved of. As one undersecretary commented, 'It is very difficult to compare the amount of risk in cases where the circumstances differ widely'. Another made his feelings completely clear, writing, 'it does not seem right to estimate the heroism of an act exclusively by the consideration whether, on a subsequent cold blooded calculation, the risk to life was or was not in fact greater than the chances of safety'.[58] Notwithstanding these reservations, the willingness of the rescuer to place themselves voluntarily in considerable or near fatal danger in order to save another remained one of the principal qualifications for awarding the medal.

Another key aspect concerned with the risk to life was that life not only had to be risked, but it had to be *knowingly* risked at the time of the incident. In the case of Edward Battersby who saved a woman from the path of an oncoming train, the fact that 'he undoubtedly saved the woman's life; but the medal is given on account of risks knowingly incurred in taking certain actions, not on account of the results of such actions' led to his case being refused.[59] The inference here appears to be that had Battersby known the extent to which he was putting his life in danger he may not have undertaken the action. Furthermore, it was not only prior knowledge of the risk involved that was taken into consideration, but also the circumstances in which such risk was incurred. In the case of Francis Ward, who in 1908 assisted in saving his fellow workmen while trapped with them in a well, the decision to refuse the award rested on the fact that,

> The rule is to give the Albert Medal only to a person who to save life, voluntarily puts himself in a position of extreme danger. In this case, Mr Ward found himself involuntarily in the position of danger, though he showed in that position a presence of mind and endurance that saved his companion's life.[60]

Once again, there would appear to be the inference that Ward may not have committed the act if he had been given the choice not to. In another case where one hunter saved the life of another who was being attacked by a tiger, the medal was refused on the grounds that,

> It was a fairly brave act to rush forward, drive a bayonet into the tiger and shoot her but as they were out on a tiger hunt, the act was no more than constantly happens. There was no devotion in it. It is the sort of thing that people do who go tiger hunting.[61]

All these cases suggest that there were to be no 'accidental heroes' with regard to this decoration. The risking of life had to be a conscious decision and one that was positively entered into as opposed to simply being in the wrong place at wrong time.

The second most often-cited reason for refusing the medal (12.5% of refused cases) was that individuals in certain civilian positions had a professional duty or responsibility to undertake acts of heroism. As with the case of PC William Wootton who saved five people from a fire at South Molton workhouse in Devon but whose case was refused on the grounds that, 'it was more or less in the discharge of his duty that the risk was encountered – bravery is so constantly exhibited at fires that it is necessary to consider the merits of each case very carefully.'[62] Awards to fireman were also refused on similar grounds of professional duty and the fear of frequent applications based on such cases.[63] Much of the reservation about awarding medals in these cases stemmed from concerns about undermining the prestige of the medal by subsequently having to award it too frequently. Furthermore, it was perhaps only to be expected that those, such as policemen and firemen, who were professionally paid to undertake risks to save or protect life would be excluded.

However, 'professional duty' in the very widest sense of the word had a significant bearing on the decision to award or refuse a claim for the medal. Transport workers, such as tram drivers, railway guards and station porters, were all viewed as having a duty to protect the life of the general public. The fact that Railway Guard Sullivan, who pulled a man out of the way of an approaching goods train, was 'a railway servant and not an ordinary member of the public' appears to have counted against him being awarded the medal. The refusal letter stated that, 'in removing the passenger in question he was merely carrying out his duty.'[64] The burden of professional duty also took its toll in the case of Tram Driver Wilton, who stayed with his vehicle and attempted to stop it after it careered out of control on a hill in Bournemouth, Dorset. Following a Board of Trade enquiry into the incident, the investigating officer absolved Wilton from any blame and credited him for remaining at his post. However, in a separate memo relating more specifically to the award, he wrote,

> I have no wish to belittle driver Wilton's behaviour under trying circumstances. He remained at his post until the car left the rails as was his duty. But I have no doubt that 99 per cent of tramcar drivers would have done the same. Two other tramway employees were on the car throughout and though not responsible for the control displayed equal coolness.[65]

It would appear that undertaking an act of civilian gallantry within a working role where you were presumed to have a professional responsibility to save life was unlikely to win you the Albert Medal.

It is possible to see a picture developing of the qualities required to be considered worthy of an Albert Medal. An individual had to be prepared to substantially risk their own life to save another by consciously and voluntarily performing an act for which they had no professional duty or responsibility to undertake. Further to this, the qualities of self-control, sound judgement and presence of mind can be added to the portrait. One area that illustrates the rewarding of such characteristics is that of the medical treatment of diphtheria patients following tracheotomy. Following this procedure, it was not uncommon for poisoned mucus to collect and block the breathing tube, leading to suffocation if not removed. One means of clearing the poison was to apply suction to the breathing pipe in order to remove the blockage and this could be undertaken by a doctor or nurse sucking on the pipe. However, the danger in doing this was that the disease could be communicated from the patient to the practitioner via the poisoned matter.

In 1885, Dr Edward Thompson was awarded a second-class Albert Medal for undertaking just such an operation to save the life of a child patient. Unfortunately, the majority of paperwork relating to Thompson's case has been missing since 1905 and all that remains is a memo regarding the presentation.[66] It is not therefore possible to gain any insight into how the decision to award was made. However, as a direct result of the publicity surrounding the award to Thompson, three more nominations for exactly the same act were received within the space of a few months.[67] It was decided that awarding to one would mean awarding to all and that as it was not an uncommon act it would probably lead to numerous further awards. As one comment, regarding the case of Dr Malcolmson suggested, 'at this rate the manufacture of Albert Medals will be a brisk one – for there is no want of medical men ready to perform these brave acts and no lack of opportunity in many hospitals for their performance'.[68] The result of the discussions was that all three cases should be refused and act as precedent in any further cases of a similar nature.

However, further to these usual concerns about the number of medals being awarded, another highly public element came to light that influenced the decisions. In 1884, a young doctor, Samuel Rabbeth, died after sucking poisonous matter from a breathing pipe. His actions were generally applauded but there was an undercurrent in the medical profession that was critical of his behaviour. Several letters were written to *The Times* suggesting that in the vast majority of cases the operation could be undertaken using an air pump, a syringe or a pipette and that there was seldom any need for a practitioner to risk his life.[69] This professional opinion appears to have had some bearing on the decision not to award the Albert Medal in such cases. In considering the case of Dr Saunders, the opinion of the eminent naval surgeon and naturalist Dr George Busk was sought, and his reply substantiated the general impression,

> As to the advisability of bestowing any honorary award of the kind for professional services for the performance of which every properly qualified practitioner ought under ordinary circumstances to be well equipped and prepared for as for any other emergency. I am myself well aware that the universal voice of the profession is opposed to the system altogether; and in the recent case of Dr S Rabbeth (a devoted young practitioner who lately fell victim to his professional zeal) which was brought before the Senate of the London University, the unanimous opinion of that body was entirely concurrent with the voice of the profession at large.[70]

It is clear from this that, to some extent, the awards to doctors in these cases were refused partly because it was viewed that, although heroic, their actions were ill-conceived, unnecessary or foolhardy. Furthermore, these were not the only cases in which this judgement informed the decision.

In the case of a Mrs Connolly, who was severely burned as she tried to carry a leaking paraffin lamp out of an Edinburgh tenement building, the general feeling was that this was simply not an Albert Medal case, but one undersecretary was particularly critical, writing 'this is not an act up to the Albert Medal standard and though courageous was probably a very foolish thing to do. The sensible thing would have been to throw a rug or mat on it.'[71] It would appear that actions perceived to have been undertaken impetuously or through a hurried or ill-prepared course of action negated any genuine or innate heroic reaction in the eyes of those making the awards. Furthermore, contributing to the circumstances under which the act of heroism became necessary was also viewed harshly with regard to awards, as this quotation illustrates 'it seems proper that . . . the medal should not be bestowed on a person who is responsible for, or has contributed by his neglect to, the occurrence of the accident.'[72] As might be expected, being a maker of your own, or more importantly anyone else's misfortune, despite any subsequent bravery went against the awarding of the decoration.

To award or not to award II: The influences behind the judgements

It can be conceded that in some cases, the decision to refuse the Albert Medal was based on reasoning other than the personal qualities displayed by the individual. In some cases, although the Home Office appear to have investigated each case thoroughly and called upon the local police, government inspectors or eyewitnesses, there was simply insufficient evidence available or obtainable to ascertain the exact nature of the incident or the degree of risk incurred. This further demonstrates the Government's fear of making awards that might later be discredited. Sometimes it was judged that the case had happened too long ago in relation to the nomination being made and it was also decided that awards would not be made retrospectively, especially in the case of the land medal. Such refusals can be accounted for when it is remembered that the awarding of the Albert Medal was intended to serve a publicity purpose. Once an incident had dropped out of the public interest, the publicity value of bestowing a medal was significantly reduced and would therefore have had a lesser influence. Awards were also refused, as in the case of Captain Andrews, because it was 'not customary to award the Albert Medal in recognition of merit represented by a series of acts of bravery'.[73] This was partly because these acts were usually minor in nature and only significant when considered together, partly because they attracted less publicity and also because those nominated in such circumstances were often people with a working duty to save life, such as lifeguards.

However, although the Home Office secretaries were concerned with maintaining the exclusivity of the decoration and excluding individuals whose behaviour might bring the award into disrepute, it is clear that the majority of decisions to refuse the medal were based upon judgements relating to the personal character of the individual and their perceived suitability as an exemplary role model. For example, in the words of one undersecretary, 'he behaved very well: but medals must be reserved for those who go toward the danger promptly without stopping to find means of rescue which will involve less risk to themselves'.[74] Being unaware of the full danger, acting impetuously, seeking to minimize the risk involved or using safety equipment were all regarded, by those at the Home Office, as legitimate reasons for refusal and yet none of these altered the fact that, ultimately, the individual risked their own life while attempting to save another. The reason such judgements were applied was because the Home Office viewed behaviour such as facing danger, being in control, standing firm, acting independently, relying on your own abilities and making informed decisions as indicators of sound and exemplary personal character and these were the type of heroes that that they were seeking to recognize. For the decision-makers in the Home Office, the manner in which the heroic act was undertaken, and the personal characteristics displayed by the individual during that act, were crucial to determining whether or not the rescuer was suitably 'heroic' to receive the Albert Medal.

Although the government officials were working to their own standards and basing the qualification for the medal upon their own judgements and opinions of what constituted everyday heroism, they were not operating in isolation. If, as has been suggested, they did bring their own set of preconceptions to the table with them, it should be possible, by surveying some of the prevailing concepts of the time, to identify where such ideas could have originated from.

Stefan Collini has suggested that the concept of character 'enjoyed a prominence in the political thought of the Victorian period that it had apparently not known before and that it has, arguably, not experienced since'.[75] In 1871, Samuel Smiles's *Character* described the idea as 'that which dignifies [man], which elevates him in the scale of manhood, which forms the conscience of society, and creates and forms its best motive powers'.[76] The book extolled values such as courage, self-control, duty and truthfulness. Smiles also wrote in his preface, 'it will be found in the following pages that Character requires the exercise of many supreme qualities; such as truthfulness, chasteness, mercifulness; and with these integrity, courage, virtue and goodness in all its phases.[77] It is clear that many of the qualities that Smiles identified within the concept of character were present in the decision-making process for the Albert Medal. Furthermore, much of the way in which the medal was administered suggests that establishing and verifying the moral character of the individual was a key factor in the decision-making process.

As shown above, the Queen was so concerned about medals being awarded to people of 'immoral habits' that a specific clause in the Royal warrant was introduced to guard against it. It can be argued that clause six was solely concerned with the character of the individual and that 'disgraceful conduct' can only have related to the behaviour of the individual concerned as opposed to any consideration of the heroic act itself. In the three cases considered for forfeiture, explicit references were made to the good character of the individual at the time of the award and it was suspected lapses of that character that led to the cases being investigated rather than any discrediting of the act they had undertaken. With Lewis, the continued refusal to revoke the medal, even in the face of persistent re-offending and disregard for prior warnings, demonstrates the unswerving belief on the part of the Home Office that because Lewis had once undertaken an act of heroism then he must fundamentally be of good character. If the Albert Medal had been solely about rewarding heroic acts, then the habits of the person involved, whether immoral or not, would have been irrelevant and would not have detracted from the heroism that they had shown on that particular occasion. Furthermore, if it was simply the act that was being rewarded, it would not have mattered if the report came from a relative or from an independent party as the facts of the incident itself would have been verified by the departmental investigation. One reason why partisan nominations were approached with scepticism may have been because the nominating party was considered to have a predisposed bias or blind spot with regard to the personal qualities of the individual. Their nomination therefore represented an increased risk for the government of unwittingly rewarding a flawed character.

The importance of character is also demonstrated with regard to refusing awards to individuals who were perceived to have been carrying out a professional duty. Professionalism and duty *were* important concepts during this period but they were not what the Albert Medal was intended to reward. Had Albert Medals been awarded in such cases, it would have endorsed the view that heroism was undertaken simply because an individual had a professional paid responsibility to do so and not because they possessed the required qualities. Consequently, heroism would become a vehicle for the promotion of professionalism at work or adherence to professional duty which was not the intention. This is substantiated by the fact that in the small number of cases where an individual with a perceived duty was rewarded, the reasoning was because the individual had behaved far and beyond any professional responsibility. To put it another way, there were elements in the incident that could be conceived as demonstrating the application of character in addition to professional duty.

In asserting that certain definable qualities were essential for good character, Smiles was demonstrating that any construction of character brings with it certain assumptions and judgements. As Collini has argued, 'the constant invocations of the virtues of character in fact presuppose an agreed moral code'.[78] This understanding that character and morality were linked was being promulgated by writers such as Alexander Bain and Henry Maudsley in volumes of their psychological and physiological studies aimed at the general reader.[79] The suggestion was that a well-formed character was seen to be indicative of a well-formed will or, to put it another way, indicative of pure motive. In turn, the presence of pure motive indicated that such an individual possessed sound moral judgement. This suggestion has interesting implications with regard to the awarding of the Albert Medal. It could be argued that one reason why the Albert Medal was administered with a focus on the character of the individual was because the decision-makers considered true heroism to be the preserve of the morally sound. Therefore, in evaluating each case it was necessary to ensure the purity of motive behind the act which is why character was largely given priority over anything else. Smiles' work was largely didactic in nature, and he was attempting to establish his own moral code of conduct through the concept of character in order to offer a means of self-improvement.[80] What is less clear is if the ministers were acting unwittingly and in relation to what they themselves believed or wittingly in order to promote a specific moral code of conduct. This question will be examined in more detail towards the end of this chapter.

Character, morality and motivation were also at the centre of another concept that influenced the intellectuals of this period. As Collini has observed, 'the texture of moral response among the most prominent Victorian intellectuals was marked . . . by an obsession with the role of altruism and a concern for the cultivation of feelings'.[81] Collini has suggested that selfishness was viewed by many as being one of the primary moral failings and therefore the antithesis of it, altruism, was deemed to be characteristic of a morally healthy individual. Furthermore, it is suggested that altruism was connected to promoting 'enduring motives to noble action' which would in turn stimulate the will of individuals to 'overcome the enervating impasse of selfishness'.[82] With their primary qualification for the award being the unselfish willingness of an individual to give their life for another and their focus upon only those acts which were deemed to be noble and purely motivated, it could be argued that the concept of altruism had an influencing effect on those administering the Albert Medal. However, Collini has also asserted that there was some distortion in the understanding of altruism by stating that, 'the corresponding distinction is between positively directing our actions so that they benefit others rather than ourselves . . . and simply taking the interests of others into account when framing our actions'.[83] He goes on to suggest that Victorian moralists tended to group these two definitions together or at the least, blur the edges between the two ideas. However, it is absolutely clear that this was not the case with those who administered the Albert Medal.

In numerous cases, there was much debate as to whether the individual had placed themselves in danger to save another's life or whether the attempt to save life had been merely a by-product consequence of the individual attempting to save their own. This has already been partly illustrated by the case of Francis Ward who was refused the medal as a result of such a judgement. But perhaps a better example is that of John Barber, who was awarded a second-class medal for his actions during the shipwreck of the gunboat *Lilly* off the Newfoundland coast in September 1889.[84] Barber volunteered to swim ashore in rough seas and dense fog carrying a rope that would allow communication with the sinking ship. Although eventually rewarded, the lengthy debate centred on whether or not Barber had volunteered simply in order to leave the sinking ship and if he would have dropped the rope and swum ashore had he got into difficulties. It is clear from the discussion that saving the life of another as a by-product of saving your own, however perilous the pursuit, did not qualify you for the Albert Medal. This suggests that although those administering the medal may have been influenced by the concept of altruism, it was a more sharply defined concept than the more widely perceived version suggested by Collini. Once again, the reason for this comes down to character. Saving another life while saving your own may have been viewed as unselfish and therefore altruistic, but it did not demonstrate the pureness of motive that was sought by those administering the medal. Only those individuals who chose to risk their own life when there was no requirement to do so and for the sole benefit of others were seen as truly altruistic and therefore deserving of reward.

Taken together, the subjects of moral conduct, pure motive and unselfish gallantry do arguably suggest one very specific realm of possible influence: the nineteenth-century revival of chivalry. In what is widely regarded as a seminal work on the subject, Mark Girouard has summarized the qualities embodied by a chivalric individual, 'they must be brave, show no signs of panic or cowardice, be courteous and protective to women and children, be loyal to their comrades and meet death without flinching.'[85] Furthermore, Girouard quotes Kenelm Henry Digby, whose novel *The Broad Stone of Honour* was taken as a handbook for chivalric behaviour, who wrote 'chivalry is only a name for that general spirit or state of mind which disposes men to heroic and generous actions'.[86] Given these statements, it is certainly tempting to consider the revival of chivalry as an influencing factor. However, a more in-depth analysis of the concept reveals that the link may not be as strong as first thought.

First, one of the key concepts in the revival of chivalry was the protection of and gallantry towards women and children by men.[87] If the revival of chivalry was a notable influence upon those making the decision, it would be expected to find a preference for acts where a man had attempted to rescue women or children. However, this was distinctly not the case (see Table 4). The diversity of incidents and the nature of the case files mean that in some cases it is not possible to satisfactorily classify the gendered aspect of the rescue attempt. This may be because a group of men and women participate in a rescue attempt together or because both male and female individuals are the subject of the rescue. However, in the fifty-six cases where it is possible to determine that a solo man was attempting to save either a woman or a child (rows H and I on Table 4), only twenty-four medals (42%) were awarded. In contrast, out of the 131 cases of a solo man saving another man (rows F and G on Table 4), the number awarded was eighty-two (63%). This demonstrates that the Albert Medal was not awarded on the basis of men attempting to save women and therefore suggests that there was, to some extent, only limited influence from chivalric ideas.

Further to this, another central aspect of chivalry was that gallantry was something driven from the heart and not the head. The act of heroism itself was more important than any intelligent forethought that might have prevented it being necessary. This was certainly not the case with the award of the Albert Medal and, as demonstrated above,

Table 4 Number and percentage of Albert Medal nominations for men awarded and refused between 1866 and 1914

Type of attempted rescue by a man	Cases	Awarded	%	Refused	%
Group rescues					
(A) Group rescue of multiple men	119	96	81	23	19
(B) Group rescue of solo man	15	12	80	3	20
(C) Group rescue of multiple women and/or children	4	4	100	0	0
(D) Group rescue of solo woman and/or child	9	0	0	9	100
(E) Group rescue of multiple individuals	24	7	29	17	71
Solo rescues					
(F) Solo rescue of multiple men	45	36	80	9	20
(G) Solo rescue of solo man	86	46	53	40	47
(H) Solo rescue of multiple women and/or children	11	4	36	7	64
(I) Solo rescue of solo woman and/or child	45	20	44	25	56
(J) Solo rescue of multiple individuals	13	5	38	8	62
Variable rescues					
(K) Multiple acts of a long period	8	2	25	6	75
Total	**379**	**232**		**147**	

Source: Home Office (HO) and Board of Trade (BT) documents, The National Archives.

impetuous or ill-conceived actions were extremely unlikely to be rewarded. Finally, when considering the influence of the revival of chivalry, the purpose of such a revival has to be taken into consideration. As Girouard has summarized, 'the aim of the revival of the chivalric tradition was to produce a ruling class which deserved to rule because it possessed the moral qualities necessary to rulers.'[88] The Albert Medal was explicitly intended to induce and encourage a certain type of behaviour and to instil sound morals but it was clearly not aimed at producing 'gentlemen' or training any future ruling class. The Albert Medal was instituted to be available to all, and although it may have been administered through specific qualifications, there was no specific class distinction as there was within the concept of chivalry. It would be wrong to conclude that the concept of chivalry had absolutely no influence upon those administering the medal, especially allowing for a more simplistic contemporary understanding of the concept rather than a more modern interpretation. However, it is clear from the evidence that the actions of those administering the medal were not overwhelmingly influenced by the idea.

All those who judged qualification for the Albert Medal were men, and it appears that beliefs and ideas about gender had a significant bearing on their attitudes and decisions, as discussed in Chapter 5. Moreover, they were not just men, but they were exclusively, white British men, and consequently they also had fixed ideas about race and nationality. During discussions in 1875, it was stated that there was no reason why the medal could not be awarded to a 'foreigner' and that there was 'nothing in the principles or the rules of the medal to confine it to British subjects'.[89] However, the draft 1866 warrant included the phrase, 'sustained by reason of the wrecks of the ships of all nations on the coasts of the United Kingdom and by reason of the wrecks of British ships happening elsewhere', but was amended to 'sustained by reason of shipwrecks and other perils of the sea' because it was felt that this left the award open, 'to reward any act of this kind done by British seaman anywhere'.[90] The 1877 warrant stated that the award should be open to 'our faithful subjects and others' who undertook acts, 'within our dominions' as those who were eligible for the award. Further to this, it was stated in 1895 that 'British Nationality' rather than any territorial boundary was the distinction by which the medal was awarded.[91] This evidence suggests that there was some disagreement as to whether the medal was or was not 'officially' restricted by nationality.

In practice, however, things appear clearer as there were no awards to non-British subjects during the period under consideration. Furthermore, it is clear that those administering the medal had very fixed ideas about non-white British subjects who were nominated for the medal. In one 1911 case, that of an Australian aborigine who saved his police escort from drowning, one undersecretary stated, 'it seems clear that the native prisoner Neighboni did save the life of his police escort and, coming from an Australian aboriginal, the action was a remarkable one', while another commented that, 'the blacks are generally, and I fear justly, regarded as among the most degraded of the dark races. This fact makes the nobility of this particular subject of the King all the more remarkable'.[92] That a native was capable of displaying the necessary character to undertake an act of heroism was clearly a revelation to those assessing the case. Further to this, when considering the award to a native Indian seaman aboard a British ship who had dived in to save a slave boy from a shark attack, it was stated that,

> We should ascertain how far the rescuer would value an Albert Medal. If, as would appear, he was a seaman on board the "wild swan" it is possible that he may be sufficiently civilised to do so; but if he would prefer some other kind of reward [a pecuniary award was suggested] I think we would give it[93]

Despite such comments, which suggest than non-white individuals were not regarded as civilized enough to understand the concept of heroism, medals were awarded in both of these cases.

What is interesting is that the distinction was British subjects and not those born British. This suggests that you did not have to be British to possess the necessary qualities to undertake an act of heroism but you did have to have felt the influencing hand of British rule. Speaking at the presentation ceremony for the Aborigine 'Neighboni',

Professor Spencer, the Special Commissioner of Aboriginals, informed the audience that, 'to those who are endeavouring to uplift the aboriginals it was a matter of great satisfaction that the natives had proved themselves capable of acts, which amongst white people were regarded as heroic'. Following Spencer, Judge Bevan gave his views about the award: 'I trust that that this memorable occasion will mark the beginning of a new era when the native will follow the virtues of our race.'[94] What is implicit in both of these statements is the belief that the character required for heroic acts was inherent in the British race and that through contact with their colonial rulers it was possible for the native race to learn and adopt such characteristics.

This sense of influence is also illustrated by comments made in relation to an incident in India in 1898, when three Bengal sappers assisted their commanding officer in rescuing those trapped by an avalanche. In his assessment, one undersecretary commented that it was hardly a case for the medal but, 'it may perhaps be considered desirable from an Indian point of view to encourage the Chitralis of the natives engaged upon in those parts, by showing them that the government is prepared to reward bravery on the part of natives when they are under the orders of an English officer'.[95] In another Indian case, the view was that, 'It is no doubt desirable to reward bravery on the part of natives in India . . . it appears not improbable that the Indian Government therefore wish to make a striking example of men who are courageous and stick within duty'.[96]

It would appear that to qualify for the Albert Medal, it was not necessary to be British by birth, but it was a requirement to demonstrate the same level of character as somebody who was. This suggests that such characteristics were seen as being distinctly British, or to put it another way, inherent in the British national character. Given that such character traits were also viewed as indicators of moral purity or correctness, this has interesting implications with regard to colonial rule. Demonstrating that the influence of the British national character upon the natives of any given colony was making them more morally sound or more 'civilised' added legitimacy to the British presence in the country. Furthermore, reporting these and all other Albert Medal cases at home further substantiated the idea of a superior national character. In basing their decisions upon the character of the individual, those administering the Albert Medal were not only applying notions of individual character but were also constructing a national character which was then promoted through the bestowal of the award.

Conclusions

In concluding this examination of the Albert Medal, it is useful to return to the question of whether the decision-makers were consciously attempting to promote a specific moral code of conduct or were acting unconsciously and in relation to what they themselves perceived and believed. Jeffrey Richards has suggested that 'Empire was one of the major component elements of British national identity and its principal justification was the superiority of British character.' Good conduct and sound character were the basis of the 'Empire's raison d'être'.[97] School textbooks and juvenile literature were areas where the direct promotion of codes of conduct was clearly illustrated and on which considerable work has been undertaken. With regard to school textbooks, John MacKenzie has highlighted, 'there was a congruence between the imperial world view and the use of personalities in "moral training"'.[98] Furthermore, the work of Stephen Heathorn has identified the teaching of good citizenship through the endorsement of characteristics such as honour, duty and character and the promotion of such behaviour through the actions of national heroes such as General Gordon.[99] Heroes as exemplars of good character and heroism as a model of correct moral behaviour were also prominent themes in juvenile literature.[100] The mainstays of such literature were the lives and actions of so-called 'great men' largely from fields such as the military, science, engineering or exploration. Christian allegories of self-sacrifice were also common as was the combination of the two themes in the shape of 'muscular Christians' such as General Gordon. However, it has been shown that some authors were moving away from the great men approach and towards one that promoted characteristics other than a life of action or recourse to violence in order to be considered heroic.[101]

Born into this climate, it could be argued that the introduction and promotion of everyday heroism through the awarding of the Albert Medal was another State-controlled tool explicitly intended to promote a specific code of conduct and citizenship. There can be little doubt that the medal was introduced to act as an inducement to the public to behave in a particular fashion under certain circumstances and that the idea behind this was to instil a shared sense of moral correctness and conviction. However, on a day-to-day basis, the administration of the medal appears to have been a surprisingly 'ad-hoc' arrangement and those involved in the process were provided with little or no official guidance from which to reach their decisions. This partly stemmed from an initial elite perspective that heroism was a straightforward and uncontested concept for which there was a clearly understood definition.

It very soon became apparent to those administering the medal that this was not the case and as they struggled to pass judgement upon the individuals presented to them they inevitably drew upon their own understanding of the concept and applied what they believed were justifiable qualifications. From this, an elite State-sanctioned definition of everyday heroism worthy of Crown recognition emerged. Once again, there are parallels here with the Victoria Cross, as highlighted by Smith, 'the operative clauses were quite vague . . . and offered no exact definition of what was to be considered heroic and worthy of award . . . the vagueness of these instructions insured the masters of the military would have ample opportunity to define the form of heroism they wished to institutionalise'.[102] The Albert Medal was not intended to establish an official or legislative formula for judging and rewarding everyday heroism and consequently it does not really represent an attempt at State control. It can, however, be argued that in seeking to instil particular moral virtues by rewarding certain characteristics or types of behaviour, the administrators of the Albert Medal were attempting or engaging in a more subtle form of socialization.[103]

The State did, nevertheless, have political intentions and sought to promote and endorse everyday heroism so as to instil in the civilian public the same sense of loyalty and service to the nation that it instilled in its servicemen. In attempting to ensure that they only rewarded those individuals who were worthy of State recognition and, to a lesser extent, to maintain the exclusivity of the decoration, the administrators in the Home Office produced a strand of everyday heroism that derived its construction from a focus on the personal character and moral integrity of the individual. Consequently, to qualify for the decoration the individual had to have freely, knowingly and willingly entered into circumstances where their own life was at considerable risk in order to save the life of another, without any professional or personal duty to do so and without any outside assistance. These characteristics became the benchmarks against which the Home Office judged acts of everyday heroism and, as a result, a very particular construction of State-sanctioned recognition emerged into the public domain.

Restricting the Albert Medal to only those acts that represented the very pinnacle of sound moral character meant that actual awards were relatively few and far between which, in turn, limited the publicity element of the decoration. More crucially, though, the strand of everyday heroism constructed by the white, British, middle-class men in the Home Office very much reflected establishment ideas and did little to challenge the status quo. Character, altruism, pure motive, integrity and the triumphant or civilizing nature of British national identity were all implicitly, or sometime explicitly, deemed to be represented by those who were awarded the decoration. The Albert Medal was a Crown-sanctioned award of the State, designed to reflect the qualities that, it was believed, put the great into Great Britain and would communicate that pre-eminence throughout the nation, the empire and beyond.

It was, however, underpinned by a relatively narrow construction of everyday heroism, one that was judged against a set of exacting standards and largely limited to a particular type of individual, exhibiting specific characteristic, under certain circumstances. It appeared to be, by and large, somewhat out of reach to the average working-class man in the street, not to mention the average women or child, and it lacked the radical reforming edge that was increasingly informing popular politics and discourse in the latter half of the nineteenth century. It was, though, just one construction of civilian heroism one among many, all of which were jockeying for position and seeking to garner the hearts and minds of the public.

'Heroism in Every-day Life': Alternative Approaches to Everyday Heroism

He has the chivalrous spirit, the free hearted, open handed generosity which belongs to the typical English gentleman. The motive of his life has been self-sacrifice; not the promotion of his own interests, wealth or reputation, but the interest and advancement of others.[1]

George Frederic Watts was born in Marylebone, Middlesex in 1817. The son of a pianoforte maker, Watts was raised in reasonably modest circumstances where he soon displayed an aptitude for sketching and drawing. After a short spell working in the studio of a family friend, the sculptor William Behnes, the young Watts entered the Royal Academy School of Art in 1835. Watts progressed well with his studies and in 1842 he entered the Fine Arts Commission competition for large-scale historical paintings to decorate the new Palace of Westminster. Watts' submission *Caractacus Led in Triumph through the Streets of Rome* impressed the judges and the artist was awarded the highest prize of £300. Watts used this money to travel and spent several years living and painting in France and Italy before returning to Britain in 1847.

In 1850, through a connection he had made in Italy, Watts persuaded Lord and Lady Holland to lease Little Holland House in Kensington to Thoby and Sara Prinsep, neighbours of Watts when he had lived in Mayfair. Shortly after, Watts moved in as a kind of artist in residence thus beginning a twenty-five-year association during which Watts established many important, long-standing and influential acquaintances. These included the social reformer Samuel Barnett and his wife Henrietta; the poet Alfred Lord Tennyson; a number of pre-Raphaelite artists including Hunt, Burne-Jones, Leighton, Millais and Rossetti; other artists including Ruskin and Whistler; and politicians such as William Gladstone and Lord Rosebery. Partly influenced by some of his artist associates, Watts found much work as a portrait painter, but he always had his mind on grander projects. Notwithstanding this, Watts went on to become widely regarded as one of the greatest English portrait painters, with many of his best works being bequeathed to the nation and now making up the so-called Hall of Fame series.

Following his well-intentioned but unsuccessful marriage in 1864 to the young actress Ellen Terry, who was thirty years his junior, Watts eventually settled down with Mary Seton Fraser-Tytler whom he married in 1886. Although, once again, far younger than Watts, Mary had a mature character and as an artist of some renown in her own right, the two were well matched. Social concerns had always occupied Watts on some level, and in later life, he worked closely with Samuel and Henrietta Barnett who through their East-end church, St Jude's in Whitechapel, were actively engaged with trying to help the poor through settlement and education. In 1891, Watts moved to his newly built house in the village of Compton, just outside Guildford in Surrey, in the hope that the clean air would improve his ever-precarious health. In 1902, a further plot of land across the road from the house was purchased for the purposes of building a picture gallery which duly opened in April 1904. Watts did not live long beyond this, however, dying from bronchitis and a weakened heart on 1 July 1904, aged eighty-seven. As one biographer has written of him,

> Watts is essentially important as an artist who, in the course of the century, transformed the ideals of 'high art' which he inherited in the 1830s into an original visual language of universals for a range of genres. Equally important is the way Watts's life and career epitomized the modern notion of the artist as celebrity and hero.[2]

George Frederic Watts is undoubtedly a key figure in the history and development of the idea of 'everyday' heroism. His Memorial to Heroic Self-Sacrifice in Postman's Park, London, still stands as the most significant monument to everyday heroism in Britain. However, albeit highly influential, Watts was actually part of a wider social network of broadly liberal-minded reformers and radicals, all of whom were working to highlight and promote the heroism of ordinary everyday individuals and, in particular, the working classes. As far as Watts and those in this network were concerned, acts of everyday heroism were generally undertaken by honourable people of good moral fibre, who led conscientious and dutiful lives, and had fruitful contributions to make to society. As a result, working-class heroes could provide models of exemplary character and the commemoration of everyday heroism, rather than simply being straightforward recognition or remembrance of an individual, could be utilized as a mechanism to promote and encourage more 'respectable' behaviour among the working classes as a whole.

In some ways, this was similar to the motives underpinning the Albert Medal, the recognition and promotion of civilian heroism as a vehicle to modify the ideas and actions of the masses. However, the approach of the State was essentially to try and encompass civilian heroism within an existing establishment or ruling-class model which equated heroic acts with loyalty to the Crown or the nation-state. Furthermore, this establishment model extended into other areas. As John Gillis has demonstrated, nineteenth-century public commemoration of individuals was almost exclusively limited to those who were leading figures in public life, such as military leaders and politicians.[3] Also, as outlined earlier in the introduction, mechanisms of official or public discourse tended to privilege discussion and celebration of the 'great men of history' or the military heroes of imperial conflicts rather than the achievements of otherwise ordinary people.

Thus, the network of reformers, philanthropists, artists, writers and other public figures who acted, in various ways, to recognize and commemorate everyday heroism outside of State mechanisms, were adopting something of an alternative and radical position. Rather than simply seeking to encompass or accommodate civilian heroes, they were championing them and utilizing them to raise awareness that there was more to the working classes than the lurid and sensationalized claims of social explorers or the judgemental conclusions of government inspectors. For some, including Watts, Emilie Barrington and Octavia Hill, the goal was to improve the lives and outlook of the working classes by providing them with respectable and exemplary role models who would demonstrate the 'correct' way to behave. For others, like Walter Crane and fellow socialists including Laura Lane, there was a more political agenda, designed to inspire the working classes to take more control of their lives and to foster a sense of class consciousness and, ultimately, class conflict.

From a modern perspective, it is all too easy to view endeavours such as these as manipulative projects of social control or defensive ploys to maintain public order. No doubt some were motivated in these directions, but a careful examination of those who feature in this chapter suggests that their actions were generally well-intentioned attempts at genuine social improvement rather than cynical social engineering for their own benefit. They all had strong opinions about the shape and structure of society, firm beliefs about the nature of social change and a keen desire to promote the virtues of those they considered to be the respectable working classes. Recognizing and commemorating everyday heroism provided them with an ideal platform for expressing these radical ideas and they promoted them through a wide and varied range of projects. What is particularly interesting about these projects is the way in which they interweaved with one another, involved many of the same people and drew their inspiration from a shared network of ideas and case studies. Within this network, a particular and radical strand of everyday heroism was fostered which, in turn, filtered into and informed a growing and widening social and cultural discourse on civilian heroism that was developing through other initiatives. These will be discussed later in the chapter, but first an examination of one project which involved many of the key figures in the network.

The Red Cross Hall murals

At a meeting on 25 November 1886, the Ecclesiastical Commissioners of England agreed to a 999-year lease, at a peppercorn rent of a farthing a year, on a third of an acre plot of land in the south London borough of Southwark.[4] This plot, the site of a derelict paper factory, was sandwiched between White Cross Street and Red Cross Street opposite a new and vast development of model dwellings. The one condition attached to this lease was that the plot must be developed into and maintained as a garden and playground to serve the 500 families who occupied those dwellings and the other residents of Southwark. This was no problem at all as the new tenant was completely in tune with this idea and a strong and passionate believer in the necessity and benefits of recreational open spaces in poor urban environments. She was Miss Octavia Hill.

Octavia Hill was born in 1838 in Wisbech, Cambridgeshire, but following family bankruptcy, which led to the nervous breakdown of her father, she and her four sisters moved with her mother to London in 1852.[5] The move was motivated by an offer of work in a cooperative craft workshop administered by the Ladies' Guild and before long the fourteen-year-old Octavia was assisting her mother in managing the ragged-school girls who were employed there making toys. It was contact with such girls, and the homes in which they lived, that inspired Hill to found her scheme for developing, improving and managing social housing for the poor. In her youth, Hill worked for some time as a copyist for the artist John Ruskin and when the latter's father died in 1864, leaving his son a substantial inheritance, Hill persuaded Ruskin to fund her scheme for a five per cent return on his investment. In the years that followed, Hill became one of the foremost campaigners for implementing and improving social housing and eventually, although reluctantly, accepted a policy-making position on the London County Council.

However, in addition to ardently subscribing to the viewpoint that better housing would improve the lives of the poor, Hill also strongly believed that 'man ceases to be man if he lives only for creature comforts; there is no one so forlorn or degraded.'[6] Hill was part of a Liberal philanthropic movement that believed, especially following the extension of the franchise in 1884, that the lower and working classes needed to be culturally and spiritually educated if they were to fully participate in modern society. Essentially, this movement was intent on trying to make the working classes socially and culturally more like the middle classes. There was certainly a modicum of self-protection motivating this, driven by concerns over social or revolutionary disorder and a belief that societies which shared similar values and ideas were less susceptible to internal conflict. However, although it is easy, from a modern perspective, to view these ideas as paternalistic or even condescending, it should be noted that movements such as this were, more often than not, concerned with the 'raising-up' of people rather than the repressing of them and as such those who participated genuinely believed they were helping, rather than dictating or oppressing.

One of Hill's most passionate interests was the provision of open spaces and fresh air and it was one that she shared with her sister Miranda. In 1875, Miranda spoke at a meeting of the National Health Society and advocated, among other things, converting disused burial grounds into public gardens.[7] These ideas progressed and in 1887 developed into the formation of the Kyrle Society. Named after the Herefordshire philanthropist John Kyrle, the primary aim of the Society was 'bringing beauty into the lives of the poor'. In addition to Miranda, the inaugural committee of the Society included the artist and writer William Morris, journalist George Sala and G. F. Watts. Octavia acted as treasurer, although it is clear from the work of the society that she took a much more driving role than that. Hill was an active member of the Commons Preservation Society but whereas she saw its role as preserving wild and wide-open spaces, she saw the role of the Kyrle society as protecting and developing small patches in cities into public gardens. Partly as a result of Kyrle Society lobbying, the Metropolitan Open Spaces Act was passed in 1881 and in 1882 the Metropolitan Public Gardens Association was formed. Although the remit of the Kyrle Society was far wider and more diverse than open spaces alone, the creation of managed public gardens for 'rational recreation' by the working classes was, thanks to Octavia, high up on its list of priorities.

Consequently, in 1886 when Hill persuaded the Ecclesiastical Commissioners to lease the derelict paper factory to her, she called upon Kyrle Society members for financial assistance to develop it into an 'outdoor sitting room' for the poor of Southwark. This support was provided by Julia Reynolds-Moreton, Lady Ducie, who gave £1000 towards the laying out of the garden and others, including Robert Hunter with whom Hill would later collaborate in founding The National Trust, who supplied the goldfish for the ornamental pond.[8] Prior to Lady Ducie's donation, Hill had planned to canvas the wider Kyrle membership and the public at large for donations towards the garden. So, instead of abandoning such an appeal, she employed it as an opportunity to secure funds to purchase a plot of land adjacent to the garden, formerly a hop warehouse, which she persuaded the Commissioners to set aside for her. Her plan, as outlined in her letter published in The Times of 14 March 1887, was to build six workers' cottages and a community hall which would act as part 'parish parlour', part library and part reading room.[9] Hill estimated that the construction of the Hall would require £2000 and this was donated in full by Henry Cowper, former MP for Hertford. £1300 was the estimated cost of the six cottages and this was given by Lady Jane Dundas.[10] Work soon began and by December 1887, Hill was able to excitedly inform her friends and patrons that 'the walls of my hall begin to rise, and three of my cottages are getting their roofs on'.[11]

The Red Cross Hall and Gardens were officially opened on 2 June 1888 by Edward White Benson, the Archbishop of Canterbury. There were songs sung by the Kyrle Choir and Canon Hardwicke Rawnsley recited a sonnet especially composed to mark the occasion.[12] The cottages had already been completed earlier in the year and were, according to Hill, forming comfortable homes for families. The hall and cottages were designed by the architect Elijah Hoole and the architectural essence of them was mock-Tudor. The Times described the view thus, 'beyond the garden the eye rests, not on tall warehouses or mean and grimy dwelling houses, but on gables and red bricks, lattice windows and brightly painted paintwork' while The Graphic was of the opinion that Hill had created, 'a cheerful little oasis'.[13] The gardens would provide the open space so desired by Octavia Hill while the Hall was the perfect environment for exactly the forms of entertainment advocated by the Kyrle Society, plays, readings, music recitals and art exhibitions, as well as providing warm and dry communal space for those in the dwellings. One particularly fervent member of the Kyrle Society, however, had a further idea for how it could employ the interior of the hall to both 'bring beauty into the lives of the poor' and explicitly educate them as to correct modes of behaviour.

Mrs Barrington and 'A Suggestion for the Kyrle Society'

In 1876, Mrs Emilie Isabel Barrington became closely acquainted with G. F. Watts when she moved in next door to him in Kensington. Barrington, an amateur artist and writer on art, took on the role of agent for Watts, who, it is said, lacked the skills to promote and market his own work. Although their relationship cooled when Watts married his second wife Mary, they remained important figures in one another's lives. Shortly after Watts' death in 1904, Barrington published a biography of the artist in the form of her *Reminiscences*; a publication that, by all accounts, Mary Watts disapproved of and disputed much of its content.[14] In late September 1887, Watts wrote a letter to *The Times* highlighting what he described as 'heroism in every-day life', this being events in which otherwise 'ordinary' members of the general public lost their life while attempting to save another.[15] Less than a month later, a letter from Barrington appeared in *The Spectator*.[16] Her letter was entitled 'A Suggestion for the Kyrle Society' and began with a verbatim transcript of Watts' letter before going on to suggest that 'there has never arisen a better opportunity for carrying out such an idea as is afforded by the opening of the People's Palace.' The People's Palace was an impressive public hall in East London, opened by Queen Victoria on 14 May 1887 and used for meetings, plays, concerts and other cultural activities.[17] After outlining at some length her opinions regarding the nature of heroism and those who undertook heroic acts, which will be discussed in more detail below, Barrington concluded her letter by suggesting that 'if any art could be created which would recall such emotions, the Kyrle Society would have found a work to do worthy of all possible labour and skill. The "if", doubtless, is a very big one.'[18]

One artist who certainly believed that the 'if' was not only big but virtually insurmountable was Frederick Leighton. Barrington had sent Leighton copies of her *Spectator* letter and Watts' letter to *The Times* to seek his opinion on the project and he was far from reticent in expressing it. Although he reassured her that he was 'not seeking to throw cold water or to be what is called a wet blanket' he felt he should remind her of the complexity of the problem.[19] Yes, he agreed that Watts' idea was an excellent one and he 'sympathise[d] warmly with the thought of keeping the memory of heroic deeds alive in our people'. He also stated that, as he hardly need say, he wished to see good art spread among the masses. However, he did see problems with Barrington's plan to use public decorative art, and painting in particular, as a platform for communicating such ideas and these problems were twofold. First, he was not sure 'how far the idea of purely and directly didactic painting . . . is compatible with the *adornment* of spaces with a view to training the eye of the people to a sense of *beauty*' [emphasis in original] and second, he asked, could art satisfactorily communicate what was truly impressive within these cases? This, according to Leighton, was the determination and perseverance required by these heroic individuals and he drew upon the case of the Southwark nursemaid Alice Ayres, highlighted by Watts, as an example,

> her refusal to save herself, the successive journeys backward and forward, the spirit of self-sacrifice sustaining her throughout; that is the subject and it is not expressible in Art which requires one poignant moment. No one moment out of that drama could convey its meaning or its greatness.

Leighton concluded his letter by asserting that 'you may paint a picture (perhaps) of one moment in that drama, but you could not in a picture even hint at what makes it sublime'. It would appear that Barrington disagreed with Leighton and, more importantly, so did the artist who she later commissioned to undertake the task and who was actually a close associate of Leighton's.

Walter Crane, decorative artist and art theorist, was a major figure in the Victorian art establishment and the aesthetic movement. In addition to Leighton, he was associated with, among others, William Morris, Ford Madox Brown, Edward Burne-Jones and, once again, G. F. Watts. It is not entirely clear exactly how or at what point Crane became involved with Barrington's plans for the Red Cross Hall, or indeed when the plans were first put forward. According to Barrington, late in 1887, following her letter to *The Spectator* and presumably after Leighton's disapproval of the People's Palace scheme, she met with Hill, Crane and Lady Wentworth to formulate a plan to decorate the Red Cross Hall.[20] Following this, in March 1888, Barrington wrote to *The Times* and publicly announced the commencement of the scheme, with Crane in place as designer, and sought donations towards the costs involved.[21] It is singularly unsurprising to find Crane at the heart of this project, not least because he was heavily involved with the Kyrle Society and closely acquainted with many of its most influential supporters. However, there were a number of other elements in the life and work of Crane which would have made the scheme particularly attractive to him.

Although, as Clare Willsdon has argued in her comprehensive study of the subject, 'mural painting in Britain did not have an unbroken, firmly established tradition', it did enjoy something of a renaissance in the early part of the nineteenth century, as summarized thus by Morna O'Neill, 'the placement of painting within a public interior had formed a national preoccupation since the scheme for the new Palace of Westminster in the 1840s'.[22] According to Willsdon, this preoccupation represented, albeit in a 'piecemeal' fashion, a 'British mural revival' which enjoyed popularity for around another hundred years.[23] Crane was certainly an advocate of the importance and value of mural painting, stating in 1897 that, 'the decoration of public buildings should be the highest form of popular art'.[24] Furthermore, in his proposal for a course for designers at the Royal College of Art in 1899, the artist suggested that mural painting represented the apex of decorative art and the ultimate destination towards which all students should progress.[25] Crane later summarized his views on the medium, stating that 'it is in decorative mural painting alone that any comprehensive view of human life and history can be effectively symbolically treated, as its intellectual range may be said to be practically unlimited, while its methods and conditions are strictly so'.[26]

Mural painting was, however, intended to be more than just aesthetic or artistic in nature and as Willsdon has perceptively and concisely noted, 'Mural painting was an art with things to say'.[27] Crane, it would seem, would have agreed with this statement as in his view, 'the mural painter is not only a painter, but a poet, historian, dramatist, philosopher'.[28] Crane believed that public art, and especially large-scale murals, could serve as powerful tools for attempting to inform or educate those who viewed them. The artist lamented that 'the modern world has grown too accustomed to the idea that art is a luxury to be passively enjoyed . . . to realise its active and stimulating powers, its moral and educative function, its positive and practical side'.[29] Instead, Crane highlighted examples from ancient and medieval cities where, he argued, 'patriotism and citizenship was stimulated by pictured parables of heroic deeds of local saints and heroes'.[30] He saw ideas such as these being transposed to the modern world through new projects which would place public art in relevant places, as he outlined in his 1905 study *Ideals in Art*, 'if education was considered . . . might we not, from the storehouse of history and folklore, picture our school and college walls with great and typical figures of heroes'.[31] For Walter Crane, then, mural painting was not only about effectively communicating didactic messages, but also ensuring that they reached and were understood by relevant audiences.

In seeking to achieve this aim, Crane effectively employed two approaches, the first of which was the development of what Greg Smith has termed a 'secular language of public art'.[32] Smith argues that Crane, in attempting to create public art that could speak to everyone about matters relevant to all, encountered two principal problems. First, 'how to evolve a language which was generally intelligible but not dependent either on overtly religious symbols or on conventions discredited by a complicity with capitalism' and second, 'how to find subject-matter which, though it eschewed religion and the Christian virtues, did not abandon morality as its foundation'.[33] Crane certainly took some inspiration from the series of twelve murals created by Ford Madox Brown to decorate Manchester Town Hall which depicted Brown's interpretation of scenes from the city's history.[34] Furthermore, Brown also elucidated upon the reasoning and possibility of developing a so-called 'secular language of art', writing in 1893, 'I have noticed that subjects that interest infallibly all classes, educated or illiterate, are religious subjects. It is not a question of piety – but comes from the simple breadth of poetry and humanity usually involved in that class of subject'.[35] Thus, Brown argued, in art which depicted religious subjects, it was not necessarily the 'religion' which appealed to people, but more the morality and humanity that such subjects were perceived as projecting. Consequently, it would have been possible for Crane to communicate his didactic messages through secular imagery as long as it maintained its moral grounding. As Isobel Spencer has concluded, 'Crane believed than an artist's aim in depicting ordinary life should be to infuse it with improving factors like dignity, devotion and heroism.'[36]

The second approach that Crane employed was exploiting one of the unique elements of large-scale public murals, this being the link between their message and their location. Once again, to cite Willsdon, 'in public buildings, churches or schools, murals might offer a focus for ritual and remembrance, or provide propaganda and instruction'. Murals were, by their very nature, conceived and designed in relation to a given and specific space as opposed to hung paintings or pictures in books which could be viewed in variable spaces. For example, Brown's murals for Manchester Town Hall featured depictions of notable events in the City's history. Likewise, William Bell Scott's series of eight murals depicting scenes from Northumbrian history, created between 1855 and 1861 for Sir Walter and Lady Trevelyan of Wallington Hall, Northumberland.[37] This approach certainly chimed with Crane who wrote, 'the true place for the decorative perpetuation of local history and legend is the Town Hall.'[38] However, as already highlighted, it was not only strictly municipal buildings that Crane viewed as suitable locations for public murals. In fact, the artist believed that any public space, for example, schools, colleges or hospitals, was suitable as long as the message was designed to fit the audience. As O'Neill has concluded, 'as the "Drawing Room" of Southwark, the Red Cross Hall functioned as an open book for moral education, and the murals of Walter Crane depicting the everyday heroic deeds of the worker would provide the lessons'.[39] Before moving on to examine how Crane attempted to teach those lessons and the part everyday heroism played, it is useful to gain an overview of how the project itself was implemented and developed.

Walter Crane and the Red Cross Hall murals

Elijah Hoole's design for the interior of the Red Cross Hall included a vaulted hammerbeam ceiling, reminiscent of Westminster Hall, and the use of arches and leaded windows added to the mock-Tudor feel of the building. The design also included a number of large mural spaces, 11ft 6in high by 6ft wide which lined both long sides of the hall. According to Hill, during the building works, these spaces had been left bare so as to accommodate the decoratively painted plaster panels being designed by Crane (see Figure 4). In total, there were nine spaces, five along one wall and the remaining

Figure 4 The interior of the Red Cross Hall, Southwark, 1893 (*English Illustrated Magazine, June 1893*).

four on the wall opposite. It was envisaged that Crane would design and create quarter-size versions of the murals and these would then be scaled-up and painted directly onto plaster panels by other artists under the close supervision of Crane. The panels would then be delivered to the Hall and erected into the spaces on the wall. This was a method that Crane had advocated some years earlier in an essay about decorative painting and design, 'by a method of working in ordinary oil colours on a ground of fibrous plaster . . . much of the quality of fresco or tempera may be obtained, with the advantage that the plaster ground may be a movable panel'.[40] According to a feature in the *Pall Mall Gazette* on 8 October 1890, Crane had, by that time, completed all nine preparatory sketches and work was just getting underway on the first of the full-scale panels.[41] It was also reported that the designs had been exhibited at the 1890 Arts and Crafts Exhibition Society show, which was not exactly surprising as Crane was the Society's founding president.

Crane stated simply that the particulars of the heroic acts he depicted were supplied to him but he does not say by whom and Barrington also makes no mention of it in any of her reports on the project. Consequently, ascertaining exactly the factual act that the mural depicts is not always possible. There are, however, descriptions of the panels and the scenes that they portray and in some cases the details are alluded to. In the series of five panels, the scheme was to feature 'An Explosion in a Mine', 'Rescue from Drowning by a Youth', 'Rescue from fire: a man holding a ladder while his arms are exposed to a dropping of melted lead', 'A Sister of Mercy holding back a dog from attacking her school-children' and 'the rescue of a boat's crew from the rocks'. On the opposite wall, the planned panels were reported as depicting 'Rescue from a well', 'Alice Ayres', 'Jamieson' and 'the man who took the bull by the horns'.[42] Ultimately, only three of these designs, those depicting 'rescue from a well', 'Alice Ayres' and 'Jamieson', were translated into full-size versions and erected in the hall.

The first design undertaken by Crane was that for the panel commemorating Alice Ayres and it was erected in the hall in 1890 (see Figure 5). In the finished panel, Ayres is depicted standing on the ledge of the open window, wearing a long flowing gown or nightdress and holding a small child in her arms while another cowers behind her. In the foreground, two figures have ascended a ladder to assist Ayres, one being a fireman and the other a seaman. The fireman, depicted in vivid and well-crafted detail by Crane, holds his arms wide to receive Ayres and the child, while the seaman is shown cradling a third child. A single arm is shown reaching up from below so as to suggest the presence of further assistance below. The expression on Ayres' face suggests that she is calm and collected as she waits to be drawn into the arms of her gallant rescuers. As will be discussed below, in relation to contemporary reports of the incident Crane's depiction is hugely imaginative – a carefully idealized and highly symbolic design as the facts of the case were greatly different and far more tragic.

Witnesses to the terrible fire at 194 Union St, Borough, in 1885 spoke of how a young female figure, Alice Ayres, clad only in her nightdress and carrying a small crying child, appeared suddenly at an upper-storey window. Having successfully thrown a feather bed out of the window to help cushion the fall, the young woman carefully dropped the small child down to the waiting crowd who then implored her to save herself. When she disappeared back into the smoke, the crowd presumably feared

Figure 5 Illustration of the Walter Crane mural, 'Alice Ayres', erected in the Red Cross Hall in 1890 (*English Illustrated Magazine, June 1893*).

the worst, but Ayres appeared with a second child, whom she also deposited into the waiting arms of the crowd. Once more she disappeared and once again reappeared clutching yet another child, whom she also dropped from the window to the crowd below. This time she heeded the calls to save herself, but apparently overcome by smoke and exhaustion, she fell limply from the window and striking part of the shop front in her fall, hit the pavement below. Conveyed to Guy's hospital with severe spinal injuries, Alice's condition deteriorated and two days later she died.[43]

Alice was employed as a general assistant and nursemaid by her older sister, Mary Ann Chandler. After herself working as a domestic servant, Mary Ann had married Henry Chandler in December 1877, and at some point after 1881, Alice moved in with the family above Henry's paint and oil shop in Union Street. The Ayres were a large family, with Mary Ann, aged thirty-six in 1885 being the eldest of ten, and her sister Alice, eleven years younger. On the night of the fire, Mary Ann and her husband were sleeping in one bedroom with their six-year-old son Henry, while Alice slept in a room across the landing with the other children: Edith, aged five, Ellen, aged four, and Elizabeth, aged three. From her hospital bed, Alice related how, when the fire broke out, she had attempted to reach her sister but fearing there would not be time, set about rescuing the children. The first two that were dropped, Edith and Ellen, the latter of whom clung to her aunt and begged not to be released, were safely caught by the crowd below. Elizabeth, however, suffered terrible burns to her legs, and although she too was caught and transported to hospital, she died a few days later.

The quantities of stored paint and oil fuelled a ferocious blaze, and when the firemen eventually managed to extinguish it and enter the house, they discovered a dreadful scene. The badly charred body of Mary Ann was found near to a first-floor window with her young son Henry dead by her side. The body of her husband, also badly burnt, was lying on the staircase with a locked money box clutched in his hand; apparently he died trying to protect his valuables, while his wife and sister-in-law perished in attempting to save his children. Alice was laid to rest in Isleworth cemetery, while Mary Ann and her family were buried in Lambeth cemetery, Tooting. John and Mary Ayres, their parents, were left to mourn the loss of two daughters as well as two young grandchildren.

Unlike Crane's depiction, there was no ladder, no fireman, no seaman and Alice, although relatively calm and calculated given the circumstances, certainly did not stand serenely on the window ledge and await her rescue. Perhaps Leighton's assertion was correct and Crane had been unable to capture the full heroic drama of the event without also depicting the terror and tragedy. So instead, Crane chose to create a symbolic image that would allow him to communicate the messages he considered to be important. The fireman and the seaman, both traditionally working-class occupations, were perhaps added so as to emphasize and reinforce the heroism of that class. The image suggests that all three children were safely rescued and there is no reference to the tragic loss of life, either Alice's or of the other family members. This overlooking or misdirecting with regard to the outcome of the incident ensures that it was more the positive and exemplary ideal of heroism that was communicated and commemorated, rather than the negative connotations of a failed attempt to save life. Furthermore, these assertions, that Crane developed a highly idealized and symbolic image, are further substantiated through an examination of how the design evolved.

It would appear that Crane substantially changed the design at least twice before settling on the final image that was erected in the Hall. Crane's first design is undoubtedly the most realistic, but unfortunately the original preparatory sketches for it do not appear to have survived. Fortunately, an early sketch for the entire scheme was reproduced by Mrs Barrington in a feature for the *English Illustrated Magazine* in 1893, and that showed the original design for the Ayres panel (see Figure 6, top right hand corner). This design was also described by a *Times* reporter in a feature in the 6 June edition of the newspaper, 'Mr Walter Crane has represented her [Ayres] holding one child in her arms, and below another being lifted out of the sheet, the flames rising towards the window.'[44] Ayres was shown sitting on the window ledge and supporting herself with an outstretched arm while waiting to drop the child in her arms into the sheet below. This design would appear to closely and accurately depict the events of the fire and Alice's attempt to rescue the children, as it was related and reported by eyewitnesses, with no fireman, seaman or ladders. Given that the Red Cross Hall was situated no more than a few streets away from the site of the fire, many of those who

Figure 6 Illustration showing part of the planned panel layout for the mural project in the Red Cross Hall (*English Illustrated Magazine, June 1893*).

used the venue and viewed the mural would have been very familiar with the facts of the case and consequently would have been aware of the heroism that lay behind Crane's realistic depiction of the incident. Furthermore, descriptive panels beneath the images describing the details of each case were also planned for the mural scheme. Despite all this, it was clearly felt that this realistic image did not sufficiently communicate the messages that were desired, either by Crane and/or Hill and Barrington, and so the artist set about altering the design to achieve this objective.

Crane's second version of the design, for which the original quarter-size preparatory sketch has survived, was very different from the first and moved sharply away from realistically depicting the facts of the case (see Figure 7). Gone are the people below who held the sheets into which the children were deposited and instead, a fireman is depicted atop a ladder, his arms outstretched to safely rescue Ayres and the child that she holds in her arms. At the base of the ladder, another figure, far more resembling an otherwise ordinary young woman, wearing a dress and with a bow in her tied-back hair, rather than a seaman, grasps another child, apparently already rescued from the flames. Unlike the more realistic first design, in which Ayres and the child she holds are still in a precarious and possibly tragic position, the second one gave the impression that 'heroism', in the guise of the fireman, was set to save the day and that all would be well. Even so, there are still hints of tragedy in the second design. Ayres was still pictured sitting on the window ledge, apparently in her nightdress, supporting herself with her arm and her expression was one of uncertainty or concern as she looked down to the fireman. The child she holds is unclothed, suggesting an urgency to escape. In the window beside Ayres, Crane has sketched a pair of small, disembodied arms, reaching upwards, suggestive of a third child who remains in the burning building and is desperate to be saved. Maybe this was intended to be three-year-old Elizabeth Chandler who would later perish from the burns she received before being dropped from the window. Although highly imagined and symbolic with regard to

Figure 7 Study for 'Alice Ayres' for the Red Cross Hall, Southwark, c.1889 (With permission from the *Royal Borough of Kensington and Chelsea Library and Arts Service*).

actual incident, Crane's second design did still contain some more realistic elements that hinted at the actual outcome.

These elements were, however, more or less completely absent from the final design which, as far as can be ascertained, was finally erected in the interior of the Red Cross Hall (see Figure 5). The fireman remained, but the ambiguous female figure at the base of the ladder became a male, working-class seaman. No longer seated, Ayres was depicted upright with her right foot apparently resting on the shop sign while kneeling on the window ledge with her left leg. This is more difficult to see than before because her attire was drawn as being more akin to a classical robe than a simple nightdress. She no longer holds on for safety, instead wrapping both arms around the child, and her expression is calm, with almost a serene smile upon her lips. Rather than just a disembodied pair of arms, the third child was actually shown beside Ayres in the window giving the impression of being completely uninjured and simply awaiting their inevitable rescue. Both Ayres and the seaman look out from the picture, addressing and engaging the imagined viewer, rather than realistically inward at the other characters. All sense of urgency has disappeared, the children all being clothed, and other than the flames that lick around the window frame, there is little sense that this was a scene of impending tragedy. Rather, it was a scene of great heroism, largely on the part of the fireman who was affecting the rescue and the seaman who was assisting him, but also Ayres herself who has calmly and responsibly gathered up the children and is delivering them safely into their care. The design had developed from being a relatively realistic depiction of the event itself into an imagined or symbolically stylized image which downplayed the tragic loss of life that had resulted and instead emphasized everyday heroic actions, regardless of whether they had occurred in that way or not.

A similar approach can be seen with regard to the second panel, which was erected in the hall in 1892.[45] This full-size mural was painted by Crane himself from his initial quarter-size design as a copy artist was not forthcoming. Unfortunately, no preparatory sketches for this design appear to have survived, but an illustration of the final panel was, once again, reproduced in the *English Illustrated Magazine* in 1893 (see Figure 8). Crane's design depicted two railwaymen working on the line while in the distance an express train can be seen bearing down on them. Their fellow workers were shown beside the track, attempting to alert both the workmen and the train to the impending disaster. However, a closer examination of the design in relation to the facts of the case suggests that this was far from being simply a realistic portrayal of the incident. The event being related was the heroism of two Scottish railway workers, Alex Jamieson and his nephew Alexander, who lost their lives on 8 July 1874 while working on the Glasgow and Paisley joint line. Around 8.15 a.m., the Glasgow express was approaching and, not seeing the workmen, the driver continued at his usual speed.[46] A number of the men were in the process of moving a sleeper but when they saw the speeding train, they dropped it and ran in fear of their lives. The sleeper was obstructing the line and would have derailed the train had Jamieson and his nephew not rushed to the spot and moved it. Unfortunately, they were unable themselves to get clear of the line, and the express struck them, killing both men outright.

In Crane's depiction, there is absolutely no indication of any complicity on the part of the workmen in causing the initial problem which the Jamiesons were trying to correct. Instead, the two heroes are pictured apparently just working on the track as the train approaches, bent over and labouring hard while their fellow workers look on but do nothing to assist them with the problem or pull them out of the way. The other workmen appear almost resigned to the fate of the Jamiesons and perhaps Crane was making an allusion to the 'heroism' routinely displayed by labouring men on a daily basis simply in the course of their working day. This idea is further emphasized by the fact that the Jamiesons appear to be about to lose their lives while undertaking a job of work and in particular, labouring work; the tools of their trade still in their hands or lying on the track. Note also the relatively small but important addition of a traditional workman's pipe, apparently dropped on the track by one of the Jamiesons (central bottom of image). This item may have been inserted by Crane to represent the discarding or sacrificing of something personal on the part of the labouring man for the greater good of others. These symbols, it could be argued, alluded to the idea of the

Figure 8 Illustration of the Walter Crane mural, 'Jamieson', erected in the Red Cross Hall in 1892 (*English Illustrated Magazine, June 1893*).

'nobility of labour', propounded by, among others, Thomas Carlyle and illustrated by contemporaries of Crane's such as Ford Madox Brown in *Work* (1852–65) and James Sharples in *The Forge* (1859).[47] One of the fellow workers is shown waving a warning towards the train, but the other two are facing and waving at the Jamiesons, almost as if they are waving farewell to them. Equally, Crane could have intended them to be waving outwards at the viewer, suggesting that they were appealing or trying to call wider attention to the plight of working men in such conditions. Whichever the case, as with the Ayres panel Crane's design depicting the heroism of the Paisley Platelayers, bears only a passing resemblance to the facts of the actual incident. Instead, the artist sought to communicate a wider set of exemplary and educative messages through an idealized and symbolic image.

In 1894, the third full-size panel, once again painted by Crane himself in his studio, was erected in the hall, on the same wall and adjacent to the previous two. This portrayed the rescue of a child from a well but very few details were provided in the press regarding the incident behind this design and so the full details are relatively unknown.[48] Likewise, neither Crane's original design or sketches, nor a satisfactory reproduction of the panel appear to have survived, so it is difficult to speculate on its conception or development. Nevertheless, considering the nature of the previous two designs, it can be imagined that Crane would have adopted a similar approach of idealized symbolism over graphic realism. Although nine murals were proposed and initially designed by Crane, this was the last panel to actually be erected in the hall itself. Despite an initial contribution of £35 by Mrs Barrington herself in 1888, and a later donation of £5 from the Working Men's Club in 1892, it appears that the project had problems raising the funds to erect any more panels.[49] Perhaps the long delay between the original publicity surrounding the conception of the project and the completion of the initial panels or the piecemeal way in which the project was progressing lessened public engagement with the endeavour. Crane himself hints at this in his autobiography, writing, 'the work had to be largely a labour of love, as very little money was available for such a purpose, and as other work had to be attended to . . . the scheme is still incomplete'. Crane was also, it would appear, somewhat disillusioned after he had discovered that 'the hall is not all one could wish for such a work and I fear that the use of gas has injured the paintings.'[50] This fear was confirmed by Hill in a 1911 report when she noted that 'I am glad to say we have had electric lights installed, partly for the sake of better preserving the Walter Crane panels.'[51] This, it can be suggested, provides the best explanation as to why Crane did not complete the project.

The Red Cross Hall project and everyday heroism

This decorative scheme at the Red Cross Hall is valuable for gaining a greater understanding of everyday heroism because in the course of formulating and undertaking the project, the main protagonists in the extended network outlined their views and opinions about the subject. Consequently, it is possible to build a picture of what everyday heroism meant to these people, what attributes or characteristics it had, and why they saw it as being important and valuable in society. There were essentially two primary and interconnected motives at work with regard to the decorative scheme planned for the Red Cross Hall: one was concerned with art and beautification, the other with moral and social education. What is more, acts of everyday heroism were viewed as ideal vehicles for addressing both.

Clearly, with her interests in art and her close involvement with the Kyrle Society, it stands to reason that the beautification of spaces through public art would have been high on Mrs Barrington's agenda; in one letter to *The Times,* she described public murals as 'a treasure worthy of the best and healthiest times of art growth'.[52] Furthermore, Barrington perceived a reciprocal relationship between heroism and art whereby each would provide a 'lasting testimony' for the other. For years to come, people who looked upon the murals as works of art would also see 'a lasting testimony to the heroism of Englishmen and women who have displayed virtues [of] courage, fortitude and an unquestioning sense of duty', while those who came looking for educational or inspirational tales of heroism would also gain access to first-rate and enduring works of art.[53] Crane, as his involvement with the Kyrle Society and the Arts and Crafts movement attests, was also an advocate of the power of art to enrich and improve lives and the acts of everyday heroism at the heart of the murals provided an ideal subject. As Crane wrote in 1897 regarding the decoration of public buildings, 'a people without art, collectively speaking, is inarticulate, and that, after all, the highest, most vital art is the expression of character'.[54] Not only did everyday heroism provide the secular subject matter that Crane desired, but it also provided an honourable and noble subject worthy of the honourable and noble medium through which it was to be communicated.

The purpose of inspiration and particularly moral instruction or education formed the second, and more important, motivation behind the project. Barrington made this quite clear when setting out the purpose of the scheme in her letter to *The Spectator* in 1887. Her intention was 'to try and use such a record as a lever to raise the standard of good and excite admiration in many a nature which might otherwise remain unconscious and indifferent'.[55] However, there was something else at work in Barrington's sense of how and why this education would occur and it has a significant bearing on the understanding of everyday heroism. In 1888, Barrington wrote, with regard to the Red Cross Hall, that she believed, 'no place is more worthy or more appropriate in which to commemorate the heroic deeds of the poor', yet a year earlier, she had claimed, in *The Spectator,* that the People's Palace in Mile End provided the best location for the murals.[56] The reasoning, however, was the same for both locations and it was because the sites were conceived as places to be heavily used by the working or lower classes.

Clearly, Barrington's reasoning made sense as these were the people that she regarded as most in need of moral and social education. However, she went on to write that certain types of act, specifically acts of everyday heroism, were particularly useful for educating the working classes because they represented 'the heroism displayed by people of their own way of living'. Barrington was essentially suggesting that, in her opinion, the exemplary potential of heroic individuals was increased and strengthened if those individuals originated from, or were perceived to originate from, the same social class as their intended audience. Consequently, the project was shaped so as to offer working-class examples of heroism to the largely working-class audience. Furthermore, this link between audience and subject was not lost on the scheme's artist.

As already mentioned, murals were intrinsically tied to their location in a way that other forms of 'portable' art were not, and although the Red Cross Hall murals were technically created on movable panels, they were not designed to be removed once installed and, furthermore, they were certainly conceived with the specific site in mind. In his autobiography, Crane claimed that deeds of everyday heroism appealed to him because they were 'proof of the strength of the social bond and feeling of solidarity of the community when it is a question of life and death' and this was closely related to his political beliefs.[57] Initially Crane was influenced by his association with the radical polemicist and ardent Chartist, William James Linton, to whom Crane was apprenticed as an Engraver's Draughtsman in 1859. Through his later friendship with William Morris, Crane would develop into an active and passionate socialist, following in Morris' political footprints as the latter moved from party to party. Crane created designs and illustrations for a number of socialist and trade union organizations, many with different agendas but always in support of the broader ideals of liberty and equality. Crane drew for the Social Democratic Federation, including illustrations for its newspaper *Justice*. After following Morris and joining the Socialist League, Crane produced designs and again contributed material to its journal, *Commonweal*. Crane also produced designs for, among others, the Fabian Society, the General Federation of Trade Unions and Robert Blatchford's Socialist newspaper, *The Clarion*. Crane undoubtedly believed that his art and designs, especially when communicating through an appropriate medium to a relevant audience, were powerful tools in promoting his social and political beliefs and this informed his approach to the Red Cross Hall Murals.

In the Alice Ayres mural, Crane amended his original and most factually accurate design which depicted Ayres acting largely alone, to one in which a fireman and seaman, both solidly working-class occupations, were symbolically included and promoted as the heroes of the occasion. Likewise, in the design for the Paisley railway accident, the heroic individuals are unmistakably identified as labouring, working-class men; their clothing, tools and activities marking them out from supervisors or foreman. Both designs certainly refer to specific acts of individual heroism and the stories behind them would have been explained on the narrative plaques beneath. However, Crane's designs also attempted to communicate a broader message, which celebrated and championed the enduring, everyday heroism of the labouring man who undertook his work with diligence and responsibility, even at the risk or sacrifice of his own life. Furthermore, Crane recognized that this 'Parish Parlour' created by Hill for the benefit of the poorest members of the community was particularly fertile ground upon which to cast his seeds of socialism. Heroic figures that appeared to emanate from or were viewed as representing the working classes would provide, Crane believed, more relevant and therefore influential examples in the eyes of the working-class audience that would predominantly view them. In the same way that Barrington viewed everyday heroism as appropriate to a working-class audience because it represented 'the heroism displayed by people of their own way of living', Crane also believed that depictions of overtly working-class heroes would have a greater impact than heroes from other walks of life.

The scheme to erect decorative panels in the Red Cross Hall is extremely valuable with regard to forming conclusions regarding the conception and perception of a more radical idea of everyday heroism than that upheld by the State. Crucially, the scheme reveals a view that exemplarity through heroism was seen very much in class terms by those orchestrating the project. The nine panels could very easily have contained designs showing Nelson at Trafalgar, Wellington at Waterloo, Gordon at Khartoum, Florence Nightingale, Henry Havelock or Charles Napier, all of whom, it has been concluded by historians, were generally viewed as tremendously heroic individuals and would have acquainted well with establishment ideas of the heroic exemplar. However, Barrington, Crane, Hill and Watts were all part of a network that took the more radical approach of adopting everyday heroes as their subjects. They did this because they recognized and believed that such individuals would have a greater potential as exemplars for a working-class audience and this suggests they believed there was an important class element to the construction of heroism. For them, working-class everyday heroes were viewed as being more recognizable to, more highly regarded by and having more influence within and upon the working classes than those from other classes, which is why they were selected as educational and instruction examples for the working-class audience at the Red Cross Hall. Furthermore, they were the subject of other works and projects undertaken separately but all by individuals within the same extended network and with similar radical perspectives.

'Heroes of Everyday Life' and 'Ballads of Brave Deeds'

Less than a year later after Watts had written his initial letter to *The Times*, in which he referred to 'heroism in every-day life', Cassell and co. of London published a handsome hardback book entitled *Heroes of Every-day Life*.[58] Within its 225 pages were contained twenty dramatically embellished narratives of heroic acts which had been undertaken by individuals largely in the course of their everyday life. The author of this book was Lauretta Caroline Maria Lane, or Laura M. Lane as she was better known to the readers of the twelve novels she had written since 1875. These were predominantly semi-didactic advice stories, many of which had young independent working women as their central characters and carried subtitles such as 'a story for girls'.[59]

Lane was an interesting and somewhat non-establishment figure with a philan-thropic spirit and a concern for the oppressed or overlooked. Born in England in 1846, by her mid-twenties she was helping her sister to run a charity school and collecting evidence about women in sweated labour on behalf of the feminist and trades unionist Clementina Black.[60] In 1893, Lane met the writer and horticulturist Carl Luffman and two years later she moved to Melbourne, where he was working as an advisor for the Australian government, and they married. The marriage was, however, short lived and when it abruptly ended in 1902, Lane moved to Sydney where she took up journalism. In 1903, she met Hilma Molyneux Parkes, the founder of the Women's Liberal League of New South Wales, and began to contribute to and edit the league's various publications. During World War I, Lane campaigned vigorously for conscription, worked for the Australian Red Cross Society and served on the Australian League of Honour for Women and Girls. After the war, she served on the executive of the State branch of the League of Nations Union and continued to write short stories and novels until her death in 1929.[61]

There does not appear to have been any correspondence between Lane and Watts regarding the book and the artist does not feature in the list of individuals thanked by Lane in her preface. Nevertheless, it is clear that the discourse on everyday heroism being fostered in liberal-radical circles was the catalyst for the author. In her preface to *Heroes of Every-day Life*, she provided a lengthy quotation from Watts' letter and asserted that 'these words mark an epoch. They are the legend of the Victorian era.'[62] Lane's book also heavily featured the case of Alice Ayres, the Southwark nursemaid who, as we have seen, was an iconic figure for those seeking to promote acts of civilian, working-class heroism. In addition to press reports and other studies, Lane contacted numerous organizations, including the Royal Humane Society and the Society for the Protection of Life from Fire in search of cases to document, leading her to conclude that it would be impossible for a complete record of heroism in every-day life to be collected, as Watts had suggested, because of the 'overwhelming mass of material'.

Instead, she declared, she had chosen to focus on the cases which provided the most detail or material for her narrative recreation of the circumstances, but defended this by writing, 'the cases which I have described are not isolated instances of courage and self-sacrifice; they are but sheaves from that rich harvest of golden deeds which yet remains to be gathered in.'[63] The narratives that Lane offered were accounts of actual events and appear to have been well researched, although she did confess to a certain amount of dramatic license in her stories, arguing that this was intentional and necessary so as to appeal to readers accustomed to the 'sensational fiction, sensational journalism [and] sensational speechmaking' of the times.[64] In this way, Lane's approach is similar to that of Barrington and Crane, in that she knew who her target audience was and how to tailor her material to be in accord with it.

Lane was reasonably candid with regard to her purposes and objectives for documenting tales of everyday heroism. She started out by dedicating the stories to the working men and boys of Great Britain whom, unsurprising for someone with her socialist outlook, she declared she had great love for and sympathy with. However, a few sentences later she went on to add that 'no material advantages can prove of lasting benefit unless they are accompanied by the growth and development of the higher nature', thus suggesting that the working classes required more than simply financial assistance to lift them out of their lives of poverty.[65] What they required, according to Lane, was moral and social guidance as well as political and financial assistance and this could be achieved through the use of exemplary role models of correct behaviour. Her cases of heroism, then, were not solely selected on the basis of sufficient and suitable material, but also with one eye on which cases best served this purpose. Furthermore, Lane was not the only writer from within the growing field of radical discourse to compile and publish narratives of everyday heroism.

In 1889, the 'Committee of General Literature and Education appointed by the Society for Promoting Christian Knowledge' (SPCK) published a volume entitled *Everyday Heroes: Stories of Bravery During the Queen's Reign 1837–1888*.[66] Although published by the SPCK, the book was more intended as general education in good and proper behaviour rather than specifically communicating Christian ideas, although, of course, its authors would have believed in some considerable overlap between the two. As with Lane's, the short preface claims that 'the names we have mentioned . . . are only representative of thousands of noble lives. The Victorian age is full of examples of self-sacrificing devotion. Our heroes are all around us'.[67] There is no overt or explicit Christian message in the preface which interestingly opens with the line 'the true glory of a nation is not enshrined in its martial deeds' which is remarkably similar to the closing line of Watts' 1887 letter which read, 'the material prosperity of a nation is not an abiding possession; the deeds of its people are'.[68] One purpose of books such as these, as with many others produced by the SPCK, was that they could be given as prizes or gifts to young boys and girls so as to instruct them in the correct way to conduct themselves. This assertion is substantiated by many editions of these books containing dedications or citations inside their front covers stating that they were given in this way. For example, a copy obtained by this writer has a handwritten inscription stating, 'for our grandson Frank with fondest love Grandfather and Ma, hoping he may grow up a good and useful man', conveying similar objectives to Laura Lane.[69]

In 1896, seven years after the publication of the SPCK's *Everyday Heroes*, another book was published which again drew from the same well, being entitled *Heroines of Daily Life*.[70] The book was written by Frank Mundell and was part of a series of books by the same author which formed a 'Heroines Library' published by the Sunday School Union. These included *Heroines of History, Heroines of Travel* and *Heroines of Mercy*.[71] Once more, the book referred to the supposedly well-known fact that acts such as these, even undertaken by women, were commonplace; 'they crowd the world as daisies dot the summer fields'.[72] The qualification for a 'heroine of daily life', described as, 'one who, forgetting self, has, in the ordinary course of her everyday existence, performed some heroic action', was very close to that for 'everyday' heroism outlined by Watts.[73] In addition to this, the case of Alice Ayres was once again quoted in the preface as a shining example of female heroism, and a chapter dedicated to the tale of a young woman who rescued several children from a fire was entitled 'a Sheffield Alice Ayres'.[74] Chapter 5 will explore, in more detail, the non-establishment credentials of the recognition of heroism undertaken by women, but it is also important to note how the subject matter of this literature represented a radical challenge to the model constructed by the State. In the lifespan of the Albert Medal, only nineteen awards were made to women, just six of which were made prior to 1916, and not a single woman ever received the first-class decoration. From a Home Office perspective, civilian heroism was very much the pursuit of adult men and everyday heroism, with its wider focus encompassing women and children, provided another element in the radical and contentious discourse being promoted by Watts and his associates, including an influential clergyman, Canon H. D. Rawnsley.

In 1896, Canon Hardwicke Rawnsley published a collection of verse entitled *Ballads of Brave Deeds*.[75] The book contained thirty-eight poems, the subjects of which were, by and large, examples of everyday heroism and it is patently clear that Rawnsley was yet another part of the wider network discussed in this chapter. The book was dedicated to 'my dear friends G. F. Watts and Mrs Watts, whose sympathy encouraged me to put on record in verse these deeds of heroism'. Furthermore, Watts wrote the preface to the book and a reproduction of his 1884 painting *The Happy Warrior*, depicting an armoured heroic medieval knight over whom a female spirit hovers as the patriotic young man breathes his last, featured as the frontispiece. In the preface, Watts summarized the overarching definition of everyday heroism employed by him and his associates, writing 'these poems were inspired by deep and reverential admiration for affecting and splendid self-sacrifice, even unto death, and for brave endeavours to save the lives of others often unknown.'[76] Two of the cases featured were well known within those circles, these being, once again, Alice Ayres and also an incident at an East Ham sewage works in which four workmen died. Watts and Rawnsley were close friends and associates, as this quotation from Eleanor Rawnsley's biography of her husband shows,

> Hardwicke greatly valued the friendship of G. F Watts and his wife, for they were in sympathy with him in many of his aims and ideals. The work of the Keswick School of Industrial Arts, the National Trust and the crusade against the massacre of birds for plumage, were subjects of burning interest which they shared, and Hardwicke never lost an opportunity of being in the inspiring presence of the painter-seer, whose vision seemed to penetrate beyond the material to the spiritual world.[77]

Rawnsley was also firmly a part of the extended intellectual and artistic network in which Watts circulated. The Rawnsley family were closely acquainted with the Tennysons; Hardwicke's father Drummond was a lifelong friend of Alfred and performed the poet's wedding ceremony in 1850. After spending his formative years at Uppingham public school, Hardwicke went up to Balliol College, Oxford, where, among others, he was tutored by the then Slade Professor of Art, John Ruskin. According to Rawnsley, Ruskin had the ability to get at the hearts of Oxford undergraduates and Hardwicke was one of several notable students who participated in voluntary work rebuilding local village roads.[78] In 1875, having decided to follow his father into the church, Hardwicke undertook voluntary work as a lay-chaplain at the Newport Market Refuge in Soho. On the recommendation of Ruskin, Hardwicke introduced himself to Octavia Hill, with whom he went on to enjoy a long and profitable friendship. Later the same year, Hardwicke was ordained a Deacon and took up a post in a poor working-class area of Bristol where he was responsible for establishing a charitable mission. In addition to this, Rawnsley also worked on a scheme to provide liquor-free clubs for working men where they could enjoy organized games and debating clubs. This endeavour was undertaken with Frank Barnett, the brother of Canon Barnett, yet another associate of G. F. Watts.

In addition to placing Rawnsley physically within these circles, it is also possible to position him intellectually within the wider radical network that was concerned with everyday heroism. As already mentioned above, Rawnsley shared many interests and opinions with G. F. Watts. Rawnsley and Octavia Hill shared, among other things, a love for and appreciation of the benefits of nature and open spaces which would ultimately lead them, along with solicitor Robert Hunter, to form the National Trust. Rawnsley was a member of the Kyrle society and, more importantly, an advocate of the arts and crafts movement, which situates him closely with the work and ideas of Walter Crane. In 1884, Rawnsley established the Keswick School of Industrial Arts (KSIA) which through evening classes taught practical craft skills, such as wood carving and metalwork, to local people. One of the founding objectives of the KSIA was 'to counteract the pernicious effect of turning men into machines without possibility of love of their work', which suggests that Rawnsley also, to some extent, shared Crane's socialist beliefs regarding the nobility of labour.[79] Crane visited, what he described as, the 'well equipped and housed Arts and Crafts School at Keswick, which owes much to the zeal of Canon and Mrs Rawnsley' in 1897.[80] It is clear then that in composing his ballads, Rawnsley must have drawn ideas and inspiration from the same radical network that conceived the Red Cross Hall murals and other commemorations of everyday heroism.

For Rawnsley, though, it would appear that an additional factor to his 'Ballads of Brave Deeds' were, unsurprisingly, his religious beliefs. In a sermon at his church, St Kentigern's, Crosthwaite, on 24 April 1898, he spoke of the religious meanings that such acts communicated. The previous day had been St George's day and Rawnsley instilled the virtues of chivalry into his congregation by informing them that it was a true Christian virtue. Furthermore, he went on to make the connection between chivalry and self-sacrifice, stating that 'the crown of true knightliness is clearly self-sacrifice.'[81] Citing John 15:13, 'greater love hath no man than this, that he lay down his life for his friends', Rawnsley then proclaimed that 'the test of God as to the Christlikeness of men's souls is not whether they accept certain statements about Christ's life and death, but whether, as he loved the brethren even unto death, so they too are willing to lay down their lives for the brethren also'. Such virtues, the Canon claimed, were more 'quick and alive among us' than might be realized, and he cited the case of a recent act of self-sacrifice in a Leicestershire pit as an example. Acts such as these demonstrated man's willingness to give up his own life for another and this, Rawnsley proposed, allowed them to 'realise something of the joy of the Lord – Self-sacrifice unto death'.

For Hardwicke Rawnsley, everyday heroes were chivalric and chivalry encapsulated the Christian virtues of self-sacrifice and the giving of life for one's brethren. In this way, Rawnsley differed from those in the Home Office who set the standards for State-sanctioned recognition of civilian heroism. They did not, on the whole, subscribe to chivalric ideals and would, it can be argued, have placed service to the nation above service to God in terms of self-sacrifice. Moreover, Rawnsley's focus on the self-sacrificial nature of heroic acts contrasted significantly with the State, which resisted the posthumous awarding of the Albert Medal and saw greater value in the publicity potential of living figures rather than exemplary martyrs. This was not, however, such a factor for those promoting everyday heroism as a radical alternative to the establishment viewpoint and perhaps one example that demonstrates this more than any other is G. F. Watts memorial dedicated to heroic self-sacrifice.

The Watts memorial to heroic self-sacrifice

On 5 September 1887, *The Times* published a letter from G. F. Watts, in which he proposed a scheme to commemorate Queen Victoria's Golden Jubilee. In his letter, the artist suggested: 'The character of a nation as a people of great deeds is one, it appears to me, that should not be lost sight of. It must surely be a matter of regret when names worthy to be remembered and stories stimulating and instructive are allowed to be forgotten.' In order to help prevent this, Watts put forward a plan 'to collect a complete record of the stories of heroism in every-day life [and] to erect a monument . . . to record the names of these likely to be forgotten heroes', arguing that 'the material prosperity of a nation is not an abiding possession; the deeds of its people are.'[82] The idea for a commemorative jubilee monument to everyday heroism was not taken up in 1887, despite an offer of funding from the newspaper proprietor John Passmore Edwards. According to Watts, 'little or no notice was taken of my suggestion' and he sardonically remarked to one acquaintance, 'if I had proposed a race course round Hyde Park, there would have been plenty of sympathisers.'[83] Undeterred, the essence of the project remained an enduring passion in the life and thought of the artist. Watts and his second wife Mary were, in fact, so passionate about constructing a monument that they had their wills redrafted so as to leave the greatest part of their estate to the purpose and considered selling their London property, Little Holland House, to fund it. Mary took solace in the fact that, should she survive her husband, she would finally be in a position to erect the 'beautiful colonnade' as a memorial to him, but Watts himself was determined to see it carried out in his lifetime, a desire he was finally able to realize some years later.[84]

It has been suggested that Watts was friendly with Henry Gamble, the vicar at St Botolph's without Aldersgate on the edge of the City of London and that during a stroll in Postman's Park, a small public garden adjacent to the church and so-called because of its proximity to the Post Office headquarters on the eastern side of nearby St Martin's le Grand, it suddenly struck the artist that the park would provide an ideal site for his memorial to everyday heroism.[85] Unfortunately, there is no evidence to support this charming tale and far more likely is the explanation given by Gamble at a vestry meeting of 24 February 1899. According to this report, in 1898 St Botolph's was trying to raise funds to purchase a patch of nearby land so as to incorporate it into Postman's Park and this newly enlarged site would provide a suitable opportunity for Watts to carry out his plan. When the idea was subsequently put to the artist, he had agreed and once the land was purchased work on the memorial began in around 1899.[86]

The Watts Memorial to Heroic Self-Sacrifice, as it has become known, is a large wooden cloister structure, approximately 50 feet (15 metres) long and 9 feet (2.5 metres) high, with a red tiled roof, fixed at the rear to a supporting wall and supported at the front by seven sturdy timber uprights (see Figure 1). The design was by Ernest George, the architect who designed Limnerslease, Watts's residence in Compton, Surrey, and it was constructed by the building firm J. Simpson and Son for a cost of £402.[87] Watts personally financed the design and construction of the cloister and the total outlay was substantial: around £600–700.[88] The purpose of the cloister was to shelter and protect the wall beneath, upon which would be displayed the records of heroism that Watts had for so long wished to commemorate. These records took the form of tablets or panels, made up of a number of smaller, glazed ceramic tiles, upon which were recorded the details of the incident (see Figure 2). Ceramic tiles might, at first, appear to be an unusual choice for the purpose, but for Watts they were cheaper and more straightforward to procure than engraved stone, as the artist was acquainted with one of the foremost producers of decorative ceramics at that time, namely William De Morgan. De Morgan was, unsurprisingly, another familiar figure within the extended network discussed in this chapter, being also associated with Edward Burne-Jones, Walter Crane, Frederick Leighton and William Morris.

Initially, in July 1900, when the memorial was unveiled there were only four tablets in place. These four were, however, quickly followed by a further nine and over the course of the next thirty-one years, a total of fifty-three tablets were erected within the cloister. Eleven were placed there in 1905 and, combined with the thirteen already in place, this formed a complete row of twenty-four tablets across the breadth of the monument and one of five rows that Watts had outlined for completion. In 1908, a complete row of twenty-four tablets, manufactured by Doulton of Lambeth rather than by De Morgan who had abandoned ceramics for a career as a novelist, was erected on the wall, making a total of twenty-four. Apart from a single tablet, dedicated to a Metropolitan Police Office, erected in 1919, no further progress was made until May 1929 when a public subscription was launched to raise funds for continuing the memorial. Just over £250 was raised and this funded four tablets, three new cases and one replacement for an original tablet which had been removed, which were unveiled in October 1930. In 1931, the space left by the removed tablet was filled with a new one, and in 2009 a single tablet was installed commemorating an individual who died in 2007.[89]

There are many layers of meaning hidden beneath the timber and ceramic of the Watts memorial, but on the surface it is fundamentally a narrative of remembrance, a record of those who might otherwise have been forgotten. Watts's 1887 letter to *The Times* made reference to 'likely to be forgotten heroes', and in another interview that year, he lamented that such individuals often received no more recognition than a paragraph in the newspaper; something more, he argued, was required. Watts summarized his idea in an interview with the *London Argus* in January 1899, saying: 'My intention was, and is, to institute some permanent memorial to the deeds of those heroic men the sacrifice of whose lives is being constantly made and as quickly forgotten.'[90] Given his artistic credentials and his association with Barrington and the Kyrle Society, it might be expected that, in a similar fashion to Brown, Crane, Scott and Sharples, Watts would have sought to promote his interest in everyday heroism through the medium of his art.

Watts, however, stated on numerous occasions that, with regard to the commemoration of everyday heroism, he did not consider art to be a suitable vehicle for the message he wished to communicate. On one occasion, he quipped that 'I would not ask for a monument that could be looked upon or carped at as an artistic scheme promoted by an artist' and on another that 'I would have absolutely no attempt at art, at anything ornate.'[91] Furthermore, with regard to the decorative scheme at the Red Cross Hall, Watts actually had similar reservations to Leighton regarding the use of fine art as a vehicle for communicating ideas to the general public. When asked by an acquaintance if he objected to this venture, Watts replied: 'It is not quite my project, but there is nothing in it I can disapprove of.'[92] The artist feared that anything overtly artistic would distract viewers from the facts of the case and that the truly important message of the records, the heroic self-sacrificial act of the individual, would be lost. Communicating this message in a straightforward manner was crucial to Watts for, as with those within the network undertaking projects to recognize everyday heroism, he too intended his monument to serve a deeper and more radical purpose than straightforward commemoration.

One of the major characteristics of the latter half of the nineteenth and early twentieth centuries was a conscious awareness of the physical and moral degradation of the poor in society, and, generally speaking, late Victorians and Edwardians were more inclined than their predecessors to address this matter and to seek solutions.[93] First-hand social explorations, such as those undertaken by the journalist Henry Mayhew and the architect George Godwin in the 1850s, were continued through the 1880s and 1890s by writers like Andrew Mearns and William Booth, the founder of the Salvation Army. Meanwhile, businessmen such as Charles Booth and Seebohm Rowntree were attempting to address the issue through systematic empirical surveys.[94] Initially prompted by concerns over living standards, these investigations uncovered crippling poverty, appalling working conditions and poor levels of education while stimulating perceptions of an alarmingly criminal and morally corrupt underclass.

Watts himself had a keen sense of the problems in society and was not afraid of tackling sociopolitical issues, as his paintings *Found Drowned, Under a Dry Arch, The Irish Famine* (all three c.1848–50) and *The Seamstress/The Song of the Shirt* (c.1849–50) demonstrate. Furthermore, he was forthright with his opinions as to the causes of the problems, as in one 1898 interview when he lamented that 'drunkenness is sapping our character and gambling threatens to destroy it', both of which were vices he had previously condemned in paintings such as *Jonah* (1894–95) and *Can These Bones Live* (1897–98). With particular reference to the monument, Watts believed that 'it is our duty to encourage what is good and vigorous and noble [and] I hope that the memorial of humble heroes will not be without its value in that direction.'[95] How, though, did this liberal-radical, social reformer envisage his monument contributing to the rehabilitation of society?

Heroic acts, Watts argued, should be commemorated because they were 'stimulating and instructive', and, in doing so, he was reflecting a key social initiative of the time. This was that moral guidance and instruction, taught through the exemplary actions or narratives of the great and the good, could help to address the problems in society. This thinking fuelled projects designed to 'educate' the poor by offering them practical moral examples that they would seek to emulate. As previously mentioned one such project was implemented by the clergyman Samuel Barnett in 1884 and involved a number of clerics and middle-class reformers taking up residence in a poor East London neighbourhood in the hope that they would inspire the local residents.[96] Watts formed a close friendship with Barnett and was instrumental in establishing art exhibitions at Barnett's church, St Jude's in Whitechapel. Another exponent of this idea was the British historian J. A. Froude, who, in one of his *Short Studies on Great Subjects* entitled 'Representative Men', championed the idea of improvement through example. Froude called for great biographies that could be presented with the injunction: 'Read that; there is a man – such a man as you ought to be; read it, meditate on it; see who he was and how he made himself what he was, and try to be yourself like him.'[97]

In essence, reformers such as Froude and Barnett were advocating the promotion of 'exemplary lives' as guidance for right and proper behaviour, and Watts, too, had this in mind when creating his monument. It might be argued that, with its focus on a single fatal act, the memorial would have failed to impress upon its viewers the requisite sense of an exemplary life, offering instead merely exemplary death. However, as historians have shown, heroism and exemplarity do work together, because essential messages about an individual's life can be encapsulated and communicated via one particular dramatic incident or moment. Furthermore, the tendency to undertake a single heroic act is often seen as a component of a virtuous or courageous life, as Geoffrey Cubitt has suggested, 'Heroes do what they have to do, in the nature of their being; they become what they have to become, in the nature of their destiny'[98] Take, for example, Grace Darling, the daughter of a lighthouse keeper who in 1838 rowed through a tremendous storm to save nine lives from the wreck of the *Forfarshire*. Darling was subsequently hailed as the very model of a young woman of high virtue and from a single act an entire exemplary life was constructed in the imagination of those who read about her.[99]

With regard to the Watts memorial, one feature in particular allowed it to communicate its message of exemplarity, and it is the one that has captivated observers ever since. In addition to the name of the individual and the date of the tragic event, one or two lines of narrative were also added to describe the act in which the hero or heroine had perished. These narratives dramatized the events concerned, describing individuals running into burning buildings, leaping from Thames steamboats, descending gas-filled wells and venturing into deadly quicksand. In one highly evocative case, the eleven-year-old hero is even allowed to speak from beyond the grave, delivering his dying words of 'mother I saved him but I could not save myself'.[100] Furthermore, the narratives were not only designed to explain, but also intended to instruct, and the message in the action was one of exemplary behaviour on the part of the individual. When standing before the tablets, viewers were encouraged to conceive the act of heroism as a product of an ideal life rather than just a single brave moment. In this way, the intended didactic message was not one of how to behave in the rare instance of being faced with disaster, but a blueprint for how to live as a respectable, honourable and purposeful member of society. Essentially, Watts hoped that highlighting and commemorating the exemplary qualities of everyday heroes would encourage the poor, the destitute and the morally corrupt to climb out of their own personal circumstances and, thus, his Memorial to Heroic Self-Sacrifice was intended to achieve something far beyond simple commemoration and instead it was to be an instructional and didactic tool.

Furthermore, Watts clearly recognized the same important principle as Barrington, Crane and Hill, namely that everyday heroes were important as exemplars for a working-class audience, because they represented 'the heroism displayed by people of their own way of living'. Watts made this clear in an 1888 letter, writing that a memorial to everyday heroism would 'apply more to the lower class than any other' because 'nothing can be more desirable than to excite in that class, in every good direction, the good feeling that would always be awakened by warm appreciation of its qualities'. He then went on to assert that 'the higher classes do not or ought not to require reminders or inducements'.[101] The 'higher classes', according to the artist, already possessed the necessary character and qualities required to perform acts of heroism and therefore had little need of examples to teach them how they should behave. Large swathes of the working classes, on the other hand, with their loose morals, distasteful vices and abandonment of social responsibility, appeared deficient in character, and therefore, the monument was more applicable to them because they required the education and instruction that it would provide. The great biographies of great men doing great things were all very inspirational but they did not always serve the aspirational purpose that was required. Consequently, because Watts intended the monument to have a practical influence on the working classes, it was, he believed, working-class individuals who should predominantly feature.

Conclusions

George Frederic Watts was a man with a powerful sense of social conscience, who paternalistically believed in the didactic and improving influence of exemplary individuals and who viewed everyday heroes as ideal examples of good and decent behaviour. As a result, in 1887 he originated the idea to erect a monument to commemorate them, a goal he eventually achieved in 1900 with the unveiling of his Memorial to Heroic Self-Sacrifice. He was, though, most certainly not alone in his thinking and, as this chapter has demonstrated, Watts must be situated within a growing liberal-radical network of influential people, all of whom were working to promote and disseminate examples of everyday heroism. There was a high degree of interconnection between projects, most notably in terms of personnel, but also in relation to the core values and belief that underpinned them. For one, they all sought to offer education and instruction for the purposes of stimulating or fostering social and cultural improvement of the lower classes. In addition to this, they all specifically employed acts of everyday heroism because they believed them to be more relevant and better understood by their intended working-class audience and consequently would have a greater didactic potential. However, while the projects shared these key characteristics, some of the people behind them did differ in their underlying objectives.

Mrs Barrington, unlike Watts who actively spoke against such a use, employed the commemoration of everyday heroism as a vehicle by which to uplift and educate through the beautification of surroundings. The Red Cross Hall scheme, for Barrington, was a way to apply her Kyrle Society orientated belief that cultural and aspirational education was as valuable to the working classes as alleviating social and financial hardships. Everyday heroes were ideal because they provided relevant and approachable subject matter through which to engage a working-class interest in and develop a greater understanding of fine art. For Crane, on the other hand, it was art that was the vehicle through which to communicate certain ideas about the working classes and the nobility and class consciousness of labour. The idealization he employed in his depiction of everyday heroes created or emphasized an explicit working-class contribution to the heroism of the event. Through this, Crane was attempting to communicate and promote a sense of unity or class consciousness which in turn was designed to endorse and encourage working-class support of socialism. In this respect, he too differed from Watts who did not believe that everyday heroism was particularly restricted to the working classes but simply to acts of heroism undertaken by civilians in the course of their everyday life. The examples of Barrington and Crane demonstrate that, even within this united circle of people, everyday heroism was still a flexible idea and one that could be adapted or constructed to suit different agendas and purposes.

This chapter has also shown that this circle of influential people was very much at the forefront of establishing and promoting a radical idea of everyday heroism that challenged the more establishment construction. This clearly has an important bearing on how we are to understand and study heroism in general as a concept. Clearly, Watts, Hill, Crane, Rawnsley and others considered everyday heroism to be an important and relevant idea. Moreover, it can be inferred that these people must also have viewed or believed everyday heroism to be relevant and highly regarded by the working classes or else they would not have considered it such a valuable vehicle for communication. As previously mentioned, those behind projects which promoted everyday heroism to a working-class audience did so because they believed it had more relevance or importance to that audience. It is likely that this belief stemmed from a perception in which the working classes were effectively homogenized into a single entity, in which all shared the same views and opinions primarily because of their social class. From this, then, we might adopt a similar theory about heroism and exemplarity more generally, which is that it is predominantly dependent on a sense of affinity with the heroic individual. However, assuming for a moment that the working classes did especially associate with acts of everyday heroism and view them as relevant to their own lives, there is another possibility to consider and this is the nature of the heroic act itself.

Acts of everyday heroism involved, by and large, reasonably familiar activities and generally took place within recognizable and familiar environments, examples being industrial accidents, house fires, inland water incidents and problems with out-of-control horses or livestock. Conversely, the imperial and military examples tended to take place overseas, in relatively exotic landscapes, and featured incidents which were alien to many ordinary working-class people. Characters such as General Gordon or Henry Havelock were undoubtedly recognized and celebrated by people across the social spectrum, but, to many, these great men were unreachable and, more pertinently, their actions were largely irrelevant to the 'ordinary' lives that the majority were personally leading. Everyday heroes, on the other hand, had encountered challenges and dangers that were all too real and recognizable to the majority of the working classes, who could associate and understand the nature of the heroic acts much more clearly. So, if those from the working classes did relate to or regard everyday heroism in particular, it may not necessarily have been because they viewed themselves as akin to those *people*, but more because they appreciated and could relate to the *incident* in which they had risked, and sometime given, their own life while attempting to save another. From this perspective, understanding the radical nature of everyday heroism will inform and broaden our overall understanding of the relationship between heroism and exemplarity beyond studies of individuals and allow a more nuanced evaluation that also considered the influence of the location and circumstances of the incident.

Obtaining this nuanced understanding of heroism also involves, as outlined in the introduction, an engagement with the reception of heroism by the masses and an understanding of popular, public participation in the processes of recognition and commemoration. The Albert Medal was essentially administered by an elite body of government officials, based in London, working under the guidance of the Crown and concerned with how the recognition of heroism could stimulate loyalty to the nation-state. Although the recipients of the awards were civilians, the public had little involvement with the process of recognizing them. Likewise, the various projects undertaken by Watts and those within his extended network originated from within that liberal, philanthropic middle-class cohort and were predominantly autonomous and self-funded with little public involvement beyond being the unwitting subjects of attention and exemplification. If we are to fully understand heroism, and particularly everyday heroism, in the period under discussion, it is vital to locate and examine it beyond these limited metropolitan circumstances and, more importantly, try to understand and appreciate the level of public engagement with the idea. Watts certainly understood the power and influence that public memorials to everyday heroes could have upon their audience but, again, he was certainly not alone in this and his was not the only monument dedicated to commemorating them.

'Erected by Public Subscription':
Monuments to Everyday Heroism

Newark-on-Trent is a small market town in Nottinghamshire. Around twenty miles from the city of Nottingham, it is particularly noted for its ruined castle, destroyed by parliamentary troops following surrender orders issued by Charles I in May 1646. Perhaps less well known is that the local branch of the Women's Institute is known as Newark Fountain and on Sherwood Avenue, a short distance from Fountain Gardens, there is a medical practice called the Fountain Medical Centre. This is far from simple coincidence and all three take their name from a water fountain situated alongside the bustling junction of the B6326 London Road and Balderton Gate (see Figure 9). Time and the elements have taken their toll on the soft Mansfield stone and the once clear and crisp letters of the inscriptions are now heavily eroded and barely legible. Fortunately, tactful and sympathetic restoration has been undertaken with the result being reproductions of the original engravings on small tablets at the foot of the fountain. One of these reads, 'To the memory of Ethel Harrison of this town who was drowned near Chester while gallantly saving the life of a child under her care, December 7 1906', the other, 'This memorial was erected by public subscription by her fellow townspeople to commemorate the heroic act.'

While not unique, this memorial is one of only a handful of public monuments erected prior to 1914 to commemorate a civilian individual, or individuals, who died undertaking an act of heroism. From a survey of sixty-five English, fourteen Scottish and eleven Welsh County archives and record offices, twelve such monuments have been identified for the period 1850 to 1914.[1] This is not to suggest that others do not, or did not, exist, for it is highly likely that they did or still do. However, as extensive attempts to identify and locate further examples have been unsuccessful, it is possible that previously existing monuments have since been removed or, in the case of surviving examples, they are located in obscure places or on private ground. Also excluded from this study are monuments that were erected some considerable time after the event, or which have since been wholly replaced with modern examples. The memorials examined in this study were located through various means. Those for Mark Addy, Alice Ayres, Alice Denman, William Hunter and Mary Rogers were identified while researching the Albert Medal, the Carnegie Hero Fund and the Watts Memorial. The memorials for Ethel Harrison, Albert Lee, Timothy Trow and William Walton have been catalogued in the database of the *Public Monuments and Sculpture Association*, while

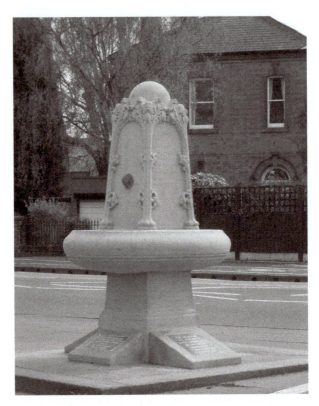

Figure 9 Drinking fountain commemorating Ethel Harrison, Newark-on-Trent, 2008 (*John Price*).

those for Percy Gordon and Edgar Wilson were discovered through internet searches using terms such as 'heroism memorial'.

The Watts Memorial for Heroic Self-Sacrifice in Postman's Park, London has already been discussed and will not be examined in any great detail in this chapter. The remaining eleven monuments, however, provide a rich and detailed seam of evidence which allows a great deal to be learnt, not only about the monuments themselves, but also about attitudes towards civilian heroism and public commemoration.[2] The eleven monuments are situated at various locations around Britain and one particularly striking thing about the geographical location of these monuments is that they are, more often than not, to be found in areas that were largely working-class centres of industry or manufacturing. If we look briefly at the individuals being commemorated, they consist of seven men and four women and their ages ranged from fifteen to fifty-two, although the majority of them were below thirty. Two out of the seven men were married while for the women it was a 50/50 split.

With regard to the form of the memorials, there are six stone obelisks, three drinking fountains, a bronze memorial plaque and finally what can be best described as an ornamental headstone. With regard to the design element of the memorials, this chapter will not go into any great detail, largely because it can be suggested they are reasonably straightforward constructions. The common use of obelisks is unsurprising for two reasons. First, they were a form that was classically associated with commemorating triumph or glory in death and second, they would have been relatively cheap and easy to construct, requiring only the services of a mason, rather than a sculptor. The use of drinking fountains is interesting for the fact that they appear to have been the preferred choice for commemorating women. Again, it is not the purpose of this chapter to discuss the history of the drinking fountain, but it might be concluded that they were chosen in this context to communicate ideas of purity, nurturing and life-giving or life-saving through clean water, which tied in with the image of these women as mother-figures or saviours.[3]

Before going any further, it is useful to consider the rationale for studying memorials and monuments and, more importantly, what they can provide in terms of historical evidence. Most obviously, monuments provide a snapshot of the period in which they were created and they symbolize the attitudes and opinions of the society which conceived them. They were not, however, uncontested objects and therefore they allow us to see not only the dominant attitudes and opinions, but also gauge and understand alternative views and more popular movements. In this respect, monuments provide a static time-locked capsule of evidence. However, although locked in a specific time, these monuments remain in the ever-changing public domain and therefore they also allow us to study changes in attitudes and ideas by examining how people continued to engage with them. Some memorials, such as World War I monuments, remain frequently revisited sites of memory and the focus for public ceremony and organized collective remembrance. Others, however, become neglected and overlooked, left to the ravages of time and vandalism. Monuments are, therefore, reflections of our own attitudes and relationship to the ideas of the past as well as being embodiments of the consciousness into which they were born.

This chapter is, however, less concerned with what these monuments tell us about commemoration and memorialization in general, and more with what they communicate about heroism and, in particular, 'everyday' heroism. This is a much understudied area, with historians more often examining monuments to military or imperial heroism or the 'great actions of great men'. War memorials in general and World War I memorials in particular enjoy an extensive range of examinations, with Alan Borg's 1991 study *War Memorials from Antiquity to the Present* and *Memorials to the Great War in Britain* by Alex King, published in 1998, being notable examples.[4] Individuals such as Admiral Nelson, The Duke of Wellington and Henry Havelock have also attracted much attention from historians such as Alison Yarrington and Graham Dawson.[5] There have been some attempts to engage with arguably less notable or more contested figures, such as several works on monuments to the nurse Edith Cavell and a volume of essays by Paul Pickering and Alex Tyrell looking at the commemoration of key individuals in the politics of reform, but generally speaking there has been little or no engagement with the heroism of otherwise ordinary individuals.[6]

So that, fundamentally, is the overriding purpose of this chapter: to examine these monuments, the processes by which they were conceived and realized and the people who were involved, in order to gain a better understanding of how 'everyday' heroism was viewed and understood, particularly by the general public, at a local and regional level. Along the way, the research will reveal a certain amount about the processes of commemoration and the methods by which monuments, and the individuals they commemorated, could be appropriated or manipulated to convey particular messages or promote certain ideas. These messages were not, as will be demonstrated, always concerned with the actual heroism of the individual, and more often were about promoting a set of ideals or characteristics which were believed to be represented by those who undertook heroic acts. As throughout this book, what this case study reveals is that heroism, during this period, was not – as is often concluded by historians – a single uncontested concept, but a multifaceted one which could be constructed in different ways to suit different purposes.

Throughout this chapter, the case of the Newark-on-Trent nursemaid Ethel Harrison will effectively act as a spine, running from beginning to end, with each stage in the commemorative process being examined in detail and then examples regarding the other monuments being employed to flesh out the argument. Areas under examination will include the purposes and objectives of those administering the commemorative process and the evidence for the levels of actual public engagement. The discussion will start, however, at the beginning of the process, by looking at how and why these monuments originated and who was involved in the processes to erect them.

'Erected by public subscription by her fellow townspeople': Conceiving and realizing a memorial

Jimmy Adamson was teasing one of the family dogs by throwing stones into the Shropshire Union Canal in the hope of encouraging the animal to follow. The canal was familiar to the five-year-old Jimmy and his two siblings as it was a regular walking spot, not far from their home at Croughton cottage, Stanney. The children were accompanied on this cold day in early December by their two nursemaids: twenty-four-year-old Ethel Harrison and her young under-nurse, Louisa Thompson. Ethel, the daughter of Thomas Harrison Captain of the Newark Fire Brigade, had been under the employ of Mr and Mrs Adamson for around five years and was said to live happily alongside the family. On this particular day, the dog was in no mood for swimming and as Jimmy's efforts to provoke it became more animated the lad lost his balance and toppled into the icy waters of the canal.

Without a moment's hesitation, Ethel rushed to the spot and plunged in after the stricken child whom she proceeded to drag to the bankside where Louisa was able to pull him from the water. Ethel, however, was not so lucky and with the intense shock of the cold combined with the weight of her clothing, she was unable to prevent herself being pulled down into the icy waters. As Ethel cried for help, Louisa made frantic attempts to attract attention but the only help available was a nearby ploughman who sadly could not swim. The under-nurse's screams eventually attracted assistance in the shape of a local constable but it was too late for Ethel, who exhausted from her exertions to stay afloat, sank from sight. The body was recovered within the hour, and although artificial respiration was attempted, it was clearly far too late. Ethel Harrison had perished, drowned while heroically attempting to save a child in her care.[7]

Ethel's body was returned to Newark, and despite inclement weather, her funeral attracted large crowds of mourners and saw blinds drawn across the district. Six members of the Newark Fire Brigade carried her polished oak coffin through Newark cemetery where it was laid to rest amidst a sea of floral tributes, among them, wreaths from the Adamson family, other staff at Croughton cottage, 'Workmen from the Corporation' and the Newark Fire Brigade.[8] Thomas Harrison and his wife received hundreds of letters of condolence and sympathy including one from Mrs Adamson in which she expressed her sorrow, 'it is a great grief to me as I thought so much of her [Ethel], I do not know what we shall do without her.'[9] The only element of the tragic circumstances that appeared to dull the grief was the manner in which Ethel had lost her life. One letter received by the Harrisons sympathized, 'there is something surprisingly beautiful in the love and self sacrifice your dear child made . . . and her unselfish aim was rewarded in the saving of the little child's life.'[10] The *Newark Herald* suggested that 'while deep pathos surrounds the episode, it is illuminated by a great act of self sacrifice and devotion, and no nobler deed can be imagined than that in which she gave up her life.'[11] Furthermore, the *Herald* believed that, Harrison's 'noble effort, ending so tragically . . . [had] caused a sensation mingled with regret and admiration', and this stirred it into action.[12]

In its 26 January edition, the *Herald*'s editor asked, 'ought not so courageous an act of devotion to receive some public recognition from our townsmen? Miss Harrison's intrepid example is a rare one and surely deserves to be perpetuated and honoured by some further memorial.'[13] It called upon its readers to submit their ideas and suggestions while offering, 'to receive contributions . . . towards carrying out any idea commending itself generally'.[14] The following week, it printed a letter signed A Townsman which stated 'I quite agree with you that the townspeople of Newark ought to do something to show their recognition and appreciation of such an heroic act of self-sacrifice. I see no reason why a subscription list should not be opened at once and a memorial erected in a prominent position in the town.'[15] To this end, a committee was formed and it held its first meeting, presided over by the Mayor, in the Council Chamber of the Town Hall on 6 May 1907.

The committee consisted largely of influential or well-connected individuals from the Newark area, Alderman W. F. Atter, Councillor J. Stennett, Councillor Peet, Mr and Mrs Blagg, Mr and Mrs T. A. Smith, Mr P. J. C. Staniland, Mr J. Burgess, Mr G. A. Rouston, Mr J. T. Mills and Mr J. Saunders. Although chaired by the Mayor and meeting in the Town Hall, the committee was not working under the official auspices of the town council and was, in effect, a private committee with the backing and support of the Mayor. This is substantiated by the fact that none of the committee proceedings appear in any official council documents. Furthermore, although largely composed of dignitaries the outlook of the committee was very much that the monument should be representative of the whole community. Councillor Stennett proposed that the amount required for a monument should be raised in small sums, with amounts as small as 6d being accepted 'so that the memorial should be as general as possible'.[16] This motion was passed and the *Newark Herald* summed up the committee's position thus, 'it was thought that the masses as well as the classes would be anxious to subscribe to such a worthy object, and it was therefore proposed to raise the sum required in small rather than large donations, so that the memorial, when erected, will be really a general appreciation of the brave young woman.'[17]

This type of committee composition, with councillors, alderman and influential local figures such as merchants and industrialists taking the lead in establishing and directing the organization, is repeated in the case of many of the other monuments considered here. Often, the committee also included representatives of local churches, although as with the councillors, they appear to have been involved more as an individual than as an official representative of their church. However, in the cases of two monuments, a religious organization did take the central role in the process. The Young Men's Christian Association (YMCA) was formed in 1844 by George Williams, a twenty-two-year-old draper based in London. Initially conceived as a prayer group to provide London drapers with a sense of their obligation and responsibility as Christians in diffusing religious knowledge to those around them, it rapidly grew into a national, and subsequently international, organization. Although a non-denominational evangelical Christian movement, the YMCA focused mostly on educational work and providing opportunities for social and physical activities for its members.[18]

One such member was seventeen-year-old William Hunter who, returning from a Sunday morning service at Townhill Church near Dunfermline on 25 July 1886, heard cries that a swimmer was in need of help at the town loch. A fifteen-year-old local lad, Andrew Robson, had attempted to swim the loch but had become entangled in a bed of pondweed from which he was unable to free himself. William, who had run to the spot, waded in and proceeded to swim out to Robson but was apparently struck with cramp and with a cry of 'Chaps, I canna go further' he suddenly disappeared into the deep water. Robson was eventually saved through the use of a long ladder and, a short time afterwards, William's lifeless body was recovered from the loch (see Figure 10).[19] William Hunter was, at the time of his death, a member of the Townhill YMCA and consequently when the *Dunfermline Journal* appealed for a committee to organize and promote a memorial subscription, it seems to have been logical for the organization to take the lead. There was also the practical aspect of collecting subscriptions to which the YMCA, as a locally based membership group, would have been ideally suited.

Edgar Wilson, on the other hand, was not a YMCA member, but as his father, Rev George Wilson, was the Minister at the Commercial Road Baptist chapel, it was no surprise when the Oxford branch of the non-denominational movement established the movement to erect a memorial. Edgar had, in fact, been visiting his father for lunch on the afternoon of 15 June 1889 and was returning to his job as a chemists' assistant in Oxford via the Isis towpath between Osney and St Aldgate's when he saw two young boys in the water. According to two men who were in a nearby boat, Wilson, perceiving that the boys were in danger, immediately jumped in and succeeded in getting them out onto a breakwater. The two men rowed over to Wilson and attempted to assist him by throwing their oars to him, but it would seem he was exhausted and before catching hold of one, he was pulled under by the current (see Figure 11).[20] It later transpired that the twenty-one-year-old Edgar was, at best, a poor swimmer and that he may also have become entangled in some discarded fishing line. Whatever the case, Wilson's actions, which the coroner suggested would otherwise have earned him a medal, ultimately cost him his life.[21] Interestingly, the Wilson Memorial Committee

Figure 10 Monument to William Hunter in Townhill Cemetery, Dunfermline, Scotland, 2008 (*John Price*).

also included the Rev Bowring of Holy Trinity Church and at the unveiling ceremony on 7 November 1899, he stated that 'although Wilson did not belong to the Church of England, he could frankly be present that day as a sympathiser with the family, and as an admirer of his noble act', not though, it would appear, as an official representative of his Church.[22]

In many cases, the initial call for the formation of a committee came through the editorial columns of the local press, but was then taken up by a relevant party, be it local men of influence, local organizations or, as in the case of William Walton, the individual's employer. William was an Overman at the Dean and Chapter Colliery in Ferryhill, and on 8 August 1906 he was returning home when he spotted two apparently unconscious boys hanging from a metal cable supporting a pole carrying electricity wires. The colliery generated is own electricity which ran overground to supply the colliery manager's house and a nearby pug mill. It would appear that a section of insulation was worn away on the electricity wire and that this had come into contact with the metal support cable which, according to local rumour, children were prone to swinging on. William rushed to assist the children but in doing so, brushed

Figure 11 Monument to Edgar George Wilson, Thames towpath, Osney Lock, Oxford, 2008 (*John Price*).

against the still-live cable and was himself fatally electrocuted. The current was quickly switched off and whereas the two boys were able to be resuscitated, sustained efforts to revive William were unsuccessful.[23] William's funeral was described as 'one of the most impressive scenes ever witnessed in the district' and, as with Ethel Harrison, the graveside was surrounded by floral tributes, among them wreaths from William's co-workers, 'the collier officials', 'deputies at no.3 pit' and 'the colliery joiners'.[24]

These men were also to make up the committee that oversaw and coordinated the memorial to William that was erected in front of Ferryhill Town Hall and unveiled on 18 April 1908 (see Figure 12). Mr Dixon, the committee's secretary, was among a number of overmen on the committee, and the Colliery manager and under-manager were both members. The committee was composed primarily of colliery management rather than the more general working men of the pit and in this respect it was similar in composition to that of the Ethel Harrison Memorial Committee in which local dignitaries or men of influence predominated. However, as with Harrison, the Walton Memorial Committee also recognized the central importance of including all sections of the community in the process of funding and realizing the memorial.

Figure 12 Monument to William Walton, Town Hall Gardens, Ferryhill, Durham, 2008 (*John Price*).

At the unveiling ceremony, Mr Bell, the colliery Check-weightman, moved a vote of thanks to 'all the colliery workmen [and] the public generally for their sympathy and contributions towards the erection of the monument'.[25] The organization behind the monument to William Walton may have been composed of colliery management, but it is clear that the monument itself was supported and funded by a far wider selection of the community.

This insistence that any commemoration of the hero had to be supported by and representative of the entire community is a present and visible aspect in every case under consideration. Individual subscriptions to the Edgar Wilson fund were limited to a maximum of 3d, which according to the committee was implemented because 'This system was a means of making the matter representative.'[26] This was also the prerogative of the committee formed to administer a memorial to Mark Addy, the Salford Hero (see Figure 13). Addy spent most of his life living and working beside the River Irwell in Salford and during his lifetime was reputed to have saved over fifty people from a watery grave, feats that earned him a clutch of bravery medals.[27] During the Whit Monday parade through Salford in 1889, Addy, heeding a cry of 'child in the water' rushed to

Figure 13 Monument to Mark Addy, Weaste Cemetery, Salford, 2008 (*John Price*).

the nearby Factory lane and to the 'admiration of the frightened crowd', plunged into the foul and polluted waters of the Irwell to save the young boy.[28] Although seemingly just another rescue for Addy, this was to be his last and after a prolonged period of ill health he died on 9 June 1890, aged fifty-three, apparently from tuberculosis hastened by his frequent exposure to the cold and filthy water of the Irwell.

On 2 July 1890, a deputation met with the Mayor of Salford and after stating 'that they represented the whole of the community', they presented a memorandum signed by over one hundred local ratepayers, which declared, 'we are of the opinion that such distinction merits that some lasting memorial should be erected by his fellow-townsmen as a record of his [Addy's] humane deeds of daring and as an example to posterity, and we should be glad if you would call a public meeting for the purpose of promoting this object'.[29] This public meeting was convened by the Mayor on 8 July 1890 at Salford Town Hall. During the proceedings, several of the committee members expressed opinions about the nature of the commemorative process. Councillor Rudman declared, 'the crowd of people who witnessed Addy's funeral were proof of the appreciation of his heroism by the residents in that district, and he took it that they would only be too glad to subscribe their mite to the memorial fund'; Alderman Mottram, 'asked the working men of Salford to put their shoulders to the wheel and to open subscription lists amongst their fellow workmen (hear hear)';

The Rev G. W Petherick 'hoped that a worthy monument would be erected to his memory and let them all feel they had a brick or stone in that monument'; and The Mayor concluded that 'he should like to see the workingmen of Salford raise a memorial to Addy'.[30] It is clear, then, that the committees formed to undertake the commemorations wanted the full involvement of the local community, but to what extent did this actually occur?

At a meeting of the Harrison Memorial Committee on 6 May 1907, the procedure by which the subscriptions should be raised was discussed. One proposal was to distribute collection books among the members of the committee so as to allow them to actively collect contributions on behalf of the fund. The Mayor expressed his concerns over this, saying he 'did not like the idea of collecting for such an object. It would be far better for the money to be sent spontaneously and left entirely to their own inclination'.[31] It was suggested that it might be better for Councillor Stennett to open and publicize a subscription list in the *Newark Herald* for contributors to send subscriptions to the newspaper, to which he replied that 'he was quite willing to do that, but he considered there were many who would subscribe to collectors who would not send to the office'.[32] The underlying implication here is that relying solely on the submission of subscriptions to the newspaper office might exclude people on grounds of literacy or because they felt unfamiliar or intimidated by such formalized systems, whereas if they could simply put money directly into the hand of someone they knew and trusted, they would be more likely to donate. This second process, coupled with the knowledge that people could give as little as 6d, would limit the chances of the fund being overwhelmed by large donations from influential patrons. The committee finally agreed that a subscription list would be opened in the *Herald* but also that 'there was no objection to members of the committee having a book as well'.[33]

The first list of subscribers appeared in the *Newark Herald* on 1 June 1907, and subsequently on 22 June, 6 July, 20 July and 27 July, with the complete list being published on 5 October. On that occasion, it was stated that the fund currently stood at £30 11s 0d which was sufficient for the proposed design to be carved in white Mansfield stone. However, the paper reported that there was a feeling that red or grey granite would be more imposing, but that as it would cost around £40 to produce, the subscription would remain open until 14 October in the hope of raising the difference.[34] In the end, the closing amount of the fund was reported as £33 so it would appear that the extra money was not forthcoming. Furthermore, this demonstrates that the committee members stuck to their remit of the fund being realized through small donations, as it is clear that for them to have made up the outstanding balance themselves would not have been financially difficult. It would, however, have rendered the monument less representative of the community at large and consequently it was produced and erected, using Mansfield stone, for a cost of £32 7s 6d.

The final subscription list, published in the *Newark Herald*, makes for interesting reading and suggests that the funds were raised, after all, more through collection books rather than by direct submission to the newspaper. The printed list of subscriber names was divided up into sections according to the committee member through whom the money was received, which would seem an odd approach to take unless the subscriptions were being collected through subscription books. At the end of the main list, there was a 'summary' in which the total amount raised by each member was given, in descending order of sum raised. From this, it can be seen that Mrs Stennett, the wife of Councillor Stennett, topped the list with a total of £18 2s 6d raised, while Mr J Saunders, the architect who designed the memorial, only managed to submit 4s. This way of demarcating the total amount subscribed, whether wittingly or otherwise, placed the emphasis on the committee member rather than the individual subscriber, although each individual donor was named individually in the list. The total number of subscriptions was 224 and this was attributed to the collecting efforts of ten committee members. The largest subscriptions were those of the Mayor of Newark; Alderman Earp; Ethel's employer, Mr Adamson; and a Mr R Hodgkinson, each of whom gave a guinea. The lowest subscription was that of a Mr S Bulley, jnr., presumably a child, who gave a single penny. The most common amount subscribed was 2s 6d with seventy subscriptions and closely behind that was 1s with fifty-six. It does not appear that the minimum subscription of 6d was that closely observed as the vast majority of subscriptions (196 out of 224) were for more than sixpence.

Despite the publication of the list, ascertaining exactly who was subscribing to the fund is difficult.[35] For example, thirty-seven of the subscribers are identified only by initials or simply as 'A Friend', while even those who are listed by name often only give a surname or surname and initial. Furthermore, as the fund was collected in 1907, the 1901 census listings are of limited use in obtaining information regarding the contributors. What can be said is that the fund was distinctly local in its composition. In a few instances, the name of the subscriber is followed by a location, such as Liverpool, London, Chester and Lincoln, which suggests that these were exceptions to the others whom it might be presumed were therefore local people. Furthermore, in one case, a Mr E. H. Bailey submitted ten subscriptions of a shilling each on behalf of 'Newarkers residing in Scunthorpe', who although living elsewhere still apparently considered themselves connected to the town and therefore to the memorial fund. The majority of subscribers were men, but forty-two women were listed as subscribing on their own terms and of those, eighteen were listed as single women. It is possible that these single women were other nursemaids or servant girls as generally they gave less than the 2s 6d most often donated. There are no donations attributed to large-scale places of work such as mills or factories, although collections could have been made in such places by committee members and the individual subscribers listed rather than the total for that location.

Aside from the subscription fund, there is further evidence for a more widespread public involvement outside of those on the committee or their immediate circle. The memorial fountain to Ethel Harrison was unveiled on the evening of 6 August 1908 by the then Mayoress of Newark, Mrs Quibell, and the *Newark Herald* reported that the ceremony took place 'in the presence of over five hundred townspeople'.[36] Even allowing for the fact that around 200 local people had contributed to the fund, this still represented a significant crowd. Furthermore, what the crowd witnessed was the unveiling of a statue which, as testified by its inscription, 'was erected by public subscription by her fellow townspeople to commemorate her heroic act'.[37] The memorial does not contain the names of any of the committee members, nor the architect or stone-mason. Following the unveiling, a postcard was produced which carried a picture of the memorial fountain with an inset portrait of Ethel Harrison. It is not known how many of these postcards were sold, but the fact that it was produced at all suggests that there was, at the very least, a perceived level of public engagement with the monument.[38]

Evidence of general public engagement with the funding and erection of monuments to civilian heroes can be clearly seen in all of the memorials under discussion. Without exception, they were funded through a public subscription and more importantly, every monument has an inscription that states this. Apart from the Harrison memorial fund, exact details of the subscribers to two other funds were published, those for Percy Henry Gordon and Mary Rogers. Gordon was a twenty-eight-year-old from Bermondsey who, along with his friend, Charles May, travelled down to Rochester in Kent for an Easter excursion in April 1912. On Good Friday, 5 April, he was walking on Rochester Esplanade when, drawing near the pier, he heard cries for help and assistance. Apparently, a young girl had fallen from the pier and was struggling in the rough waters of the river Medway. Gordon ran to the pier and, jumping in to the river, began making his way towards the girl. However, before he could reach her, he himself got into difficulties and was pulled under and swept away by the current. The girl was eventually saved through the use of a lifebelt but Percy Gordon lost his life through his unsuccessful attempt (see Figure 14).[39] As with Ethel Harrison, a letter was written to a local newspaper asking it to instigate a subscription fund in order to erect a memorial to Gordon and the paper agreed to do so. A 'meeting of citizens' was also convened at which a committee of local worthies presided. It was agreed that the subscription should be raised via donations directly to the newspaper and also via subscription lists which would be 'printed and circulated', especially to local elementary and Sunday schools.[40]

The fund for the Gordon memorial differs from that for Ethel Harrison in that it contains entries for both individual subscriptions and collections on behalf of particular

Figure 14 Bronze memorial plaque commemorating Percy Henry Gordon, Rochester Esplanade, Kent, 2010 (*John Price*).

groups. There are ninety-nine subscriptions listed in the fund and of these, twenty-eight, which raised £16 9s 4d of the total £24 9s 2d, can be identified as collections on behalf of an organization or particular group of people. These include 'Employees of Rochester, Chatham and District Laundry Ltd', 'Rochester Printing Company, Compositors', 'Rochester Baptist Sunday School', 'Rochester City Police', 'Kings Head Hotel, Rochester', 'Messrs Avering and Porter's Works', 'Rochester Post Office Staff', 'Proprietors and Employees of the Star Hand Laundry Company', 'Employees of the Oil Mills, Strood', 'Bull Hotel, Rochester', 'A Jewish Tribute', 'Luton Rovers Cycle Club', and 'Seven Shipwright Admirers of a Brave Young Fellow'. The most popular sum for an individual subscription was 1s, although the 2s 6d donation that was so popular in the case of Ethel Harrison was a close second. It is very difficult to gauge the average individual subscription from the collections made within workplaces or other organizations in which the totals ranged from nearly £2 in one case to just 7s in another. What can be said is that these collections demonstrate that there was a breadth of public engagement and involvement with subscribing to the memorial funds.

Even in cases where the memorial fund was not published in full, there is still evidence of general public involvement with regard to fundraising. Queen's Park, which is situated on the outskirts of Heywood in Lancashire, was opened in 1879, and among the usual Victorian attributes such as a bowling green and an ornamental fountain, there is also a memorial obelisk to Albert Lee, a fifteen-year-old lad who died in the nearby River Roch while attempting to save the life of his friend (see Figure 15). It was 15 June 1907 when Lee's companion, David Ashworth, fell into the swollen river while trying to catch some floating wood. Lee jumped in to save him but the strong current of the flooded river carried them quickly downstream and before help could reach them, both boys were drowned. At the inquest, the jury expressed the opinion that Lee had drowned while 'making a gallant attempt to save his companion from drowning' and several jury members became instrumental in arranging for a subscription fund to be set up.[41] However, as they later explained, 'it was not entirely the jury who were doing that, but the bulk of the town. They had not really pushed it forward themselves. The public thought that something ought to be done, and as they sat on the jury they seemed to wish them to take it up.'[42]

The *Heywood News* reported, following a meeting of the committee on 25 June 1907, that 'there are to be elaborate arrangements for the carrying on of the fund, and for the insuring of a considerable amount being subscribed. Lists are to be opened in various shops and envelopes with the deceased lad's photo are being sent out for the convenience of those who wish to drop their contributions into the boxes.'[43] The shops in question included 'the Co-operative store, Rochdale Road East', 'Hooley Bridge Post Office' and 'Mr Ashworth, tobacconist', all of which, it might be expected, would have been frequented by most of the town at some point or another. In addition to this, the use of Lee's picture on the collecting envelopes would not only have made a poignant statement, but would also have left people in no doubt as to what they were contributing to, whether they were literate or not. Other places of collection were Hornby Street school and Bethel Street school, both of which Lee had connections with and also the Mutual Cotton Mills where Lee had been employed. In fact, when asked about the collection that had been undertaken at the Mills, its representative

Figure 15 Memorial to Albert Lee, Queens Park, Heywood, Rochdale, 2008 (*John Price*).

Arthur Dawson replied, 'as far as interest was concerned there was no dissention at their mill. The feeling of the town seemed to be that some recognition ought to be made to the noble act the lad did.'[44] When the collecting boxes were opened and the various collections combined, the subscription raised £57 5d. Although no list of the subscribers was published, it was reported that 700 postcards, presumably produced to support the fund, had been sold and that a further 500 had been ordered which as one of the committee stated, 'that gives you some idea of the interest in the case.'[45]

The previously outlined case of minister's son Edgar Wilson also provides evidence of the breadth of public involvement. At the unveiling ceremony, Mr Souttar of the Oxford YMCA stated that the society 'had inaugurated a three-penny subscription list and the monument represented the subscriptions of something like 2000 Oxford residents (applause).'[46] Unfortunately, the calculations do not exactly add up – the fund reportedly raised £17 which at 3d per person would represent something closer to 1400 contributions – which suggests that Mr Souttar was, to some extent, playing to the crowd. However, even at 1400 contributions, or even 1000 for that matter, the fund would still appear to represent the backing of a wide and general audience. Furthermore, in the case of the memorial fund for William Walton in Ferryhill, it was stated that, 'the committee had no difficulty in raising the money and might have got as much more as they had got,' and in another case, that of Timothy Trow, the local press reported that 'the heart of the public was so deeply moved by the pathetic incident, that when the idea of a public memorial was mooted, subscriptions flowed in'.[47]

Timothy Trow was a tramcar conductor in the employ of the North Staffs Tramways Company, and on the afternoon of 13 April 1894, he was travelling along the London Road, part of the Stoke to West End line. As the modern steam-driven tram neared the West End Hotel, Trow would have had a clear view of the Trentham and Mersey Canal which ran alongside the road but he could have had no idea of what was to happen. The driver of the tram, John Hulme, reported hearing a splash and, looking over to the canal, saw a small child, four-year-old Jane Ridgway, in the water. At once, Trow jumped down from the platform of the tram, pushed his way through the brambles that lined the canalside and jumped into the water. Although able to swim, Trow suddenly became helpless and cried out 'oh Jack, I have got the cramp' at which point he began to struggle in the water. Two onlookers, Henry Lloyd and John Forrester, jumped in to give assistance and while Forrester managed to get Jane out to safety, Lloyd was unable to rescue the frantic Trow for fear of being drowned himself. Lloyd later claimed that he could have saved Trow's life, had the latter not struggled so much, but sadly this was not the case and Timothy Trow lost his life (see Figure 16).[48]

As with other cases, a memorial committee was formed and a public subscription announced on the basis that 'Public spirit was very greatly stirred in the matter; the heart of the public was very deeply moved'.[49] Unfortunately, no details of how the subscription should be administered or indeed the final total collected were announced. However, at the unveiling ceremony, the Rev J. E. Walker, Priest-in-charge at nearby All Saints, Boothen, announced, with regard to donations, that 'most of them were collected in the tramcar in its journey between Stoke and Boothen' and that 'much was given by poor working men and women, who showed they knew how to recognize and to admire an act of this kind'. He went on to add that the fund had attracted 'something like 300 subscribers' to which a hearty 'hear hear' is reported to have emanated from the assembled crowd.[50] The committee was able to erect not only the monument on the London Road opposite the West End Hotel, but also a cross on Trow's grave in Hanley borough cemetery, which suggests that the subscription fund raised something in the region of £40–50. If this was achieved through around 300 subscribers, it would place the average contribution at about 3s, which, although slightly higher than other monuments, still demonstrates that many people gave a little, rather than a few people giving a lot.

This is interesting with regard to our understanding of heroism because it demonstrates that people from different levels of the public at large, including the lower and working classes, did actually engage with the concept. Frequently, in studies of heroism during this period, historians offer the objectives and purposes of those projecting and promoting an idea of heroism, as evidence for how heroism was accepted and understood without considering the importance of how such ideas were actually received. As discussed in the introduction, Michael Lieven's examination of Anglo-Zulu war heroes, Stephen Heathorn's work on martial heroes in school text books and much of John MacKenzie's engagement with imperial heroes are prime examples of

Figure 16   Monument to Timothy Trow, London Road, Stoke on Trent, 2008 (*John Price*).

this tendency.[51] However, similar to the approach taken by Max Jones in his work on Captain Scott, the evidence presented in this chapter, and throughout the book, reveals the prevalence and importance of grass roots agitation, as opposed to governmental or ruling class orchestration, in the staging of commemorative events and the erecting of monuments to commemorate everyday heroism.[52]

'A drinking fountain in the castle gardens': The importance of location

Having proposed, in its edition of 26 January 1907, that a subscription fund should be established to erect a commemoration to Ethel Harrison, the *Newark Herald* outlined two possible suggestions as to the form that this should take. The first 'that an inscription on brass be placed in some suitable position in the town hall' and second that 'an additional inscription should be made to the cross at the cemetery'.[53] The *Herald* welcomed the suggestions of its readers and the following week it published two letters. The first was signed 'A Townsman' who suggested that 'a drinking fountain in the castle grounds with a suitable inscription thereon, I think would be as suitable as anything.' The second letter was from a Percy Deed, of Lincoln, who thought that, 'some sort of memorial should be erected in the centre of the market-place.'[54]

Similar views to these, on both form and location, were expressed by the members of the committee at a meeting held in the Council Chamber at Newark Town Hall on 15 May 1907. Councillor Stennett announced that two proposals had been suggested to him, 'to erect a drinking fountain in some public place in the town or the endowment of a cot at the hospital'.[55] The cot, he added, had been investigated and was thought to be too expensive, and therefore he had approached Messrs. Saunders (architects) and asked them to draw up some plans for a drinking fountain, which he then submitted to the committee. The committee agreed that a drinking fountain was 'a very good idea' and that 'the design was an excellent one'.[56] The only concern with the design was expressed by the Mayor who felt that, 'it appeared to him to be a bit heavy, and he wondered whether it could be made a little lighter and more ornamental'.[57] The original design had been submitted on the basis of an estimated cost of £27 but when the fund raised £33, the architect offered to redraft the plans to include the improvements. It would appear, by comparing the originally proposed design published in the *Herald* with the finished article, that some additional decorative carving of climbing foliage was added to the edges of the portion of the tapered shaft above the bowl of the fountain. It is debatable as to whether or not this made the monument appear 'lighter' but it did certainly make it appear more ornamental and less utilitarian.

The focus of the meeting then turned to establishing a suitable site for the purpose. Two positions in the marketplace were suggested: one 'in the place where the old iron pump now stood', and a second, 'a corner in the market-place near Messrs Saunders' offices'.[58] However, both of these were dismissed as unsuitable, and by far the most popular location emerged as Castle Gardens. The formal gardens in the grounds of the ruined Newark castle were created by the eminent landscape gardener Henry E. Milner to commemorate Queen Victoria's golden jubilee and were officially opened on her 70th birthday, 24 May 1889. The committee were unanimous in their desire to see the fountain placed there, but as the Mayor explained, there was a problem in that the Chairman of the Castle Gardens Committee had privately expressed his opinion that the Gardens should be reserved only for national monuments. The matter would, however, be placed before the Castle Gardens committee and so there was still a possibility. One final suggestion put forward was that if the use of Castle Gardens was not permitted, then 'the junction of the London Road and Balderton Gate would be a fine position'.[59]

There was also consensus between the public and the committee with regard to the reasoning behind the correct location. 'A Townsman' favoured the Castle Gardens because 'many people visit there, and amongst them are nurses who take their charges, and it would remind them of their duty and be a splendid example'.[60] Furthermore, in a second letter to the *Herald*, Percy Deed wrote that he was decidedly in favour of a really public memorial and argued his case in an eloquent fashion,

> Where one would see it if it took the form of a cot in the hospital, five hundred or a thousand would see it in the Castle grounds, which were much frequented by nursemaids. Shut up in a hospital, the memorial would be deprived of very much

power of inspiration. My hope, is that it will not be shut up within brick walls; but open to the breath of heaven, and to the sight of passers-by. Especially it should be prominently placed where those who, like the subject of the memorial, having the charge of children, congregate mostly.[61]

Castle Gardens was popular with the committee for the same reasons, with the Mayor stating that 'the reason the castle gardens was thought so highly of as a site was, that so many nurses with children visited the place daily, that the memorial would keep the heroic deed of a fellow nurse constantly in their minds (hear hear)'.[62]

Unfortunately, the Castle Gardens Committee did not permit the use of the site on the basis that it, 'hardly liked to start putting up memorials there, other than national memorials'.[63] Undeterred, the committee instead opted for the patch of ground at the junction of London Road and Balderton Gate, previously occupied by the Post Office. The Mayor was of the opinion that this was an ideal site because 'many children and nurses take their walks up that road' and 'more people went up the London Road than anywhere else on a Sunday afternoon', and the committee agreed.[64] When the fountain was unveiled, the Mayor likened its role to the portraits of great men which hung in the council chamber and inspired those who sat there, but in this case, the inspiration was in a public position where all could see it and presumably be inspired by it.[65] Mr and Mrs Harrison wrote a letter for publication in the *Herald* in which they thanked all the subscribers and the committee for their efforts in realizing the memorial: 'the drinking fountain we regard as both tasteful and appropriate and we shall always look upon it with feelings of gratitude to those who have shown so much interest in commemorating my daughter's life-sacrifice'.[66]

The Harrison Memorial Committee gave little indication as to why it regarded a drinking fountain as the most appropriate form of public commemoration and this lack of explanation was repeated in the case of the other memorials. In most cases, the initial suggestion was accepted by the committee with little published debate, as in the case of the Rochester hero Percy Gordon whereby the suggestion of having a memorial tablet fixed to the Esplanade wall was simply proposed and accepted. When Gordon's father was contacted for his opinion, he wrote no more than to say that he 'acquiesced in the committee's proposal to erect a tablet' and his only request was 'that they would not make it too showy'.[67] There was a little discussion as to whether the tablet should be in metal or granite and, depending on the choice, which design should be selected, but nothing in particular regarding the choice of a tablet. In the case of Timothy Trow, there *was* some debate among committee members between either an obelisk or a tablet on the canal bridge, but why the obelisk won out and was ultimately selected was not reported.[68]

Clearly, cost would have been an important and influential factor in determining the exact form of any commemoration. With the Gordon memorial tablet, although the metal design was selected, it was decided that 'If funds permit . . . the tablet is to have a framing of granite', and sufficient money must have been raised as the tablet was produced to that design.[69] In most cases, it was thought sensible to delay the decision on the precise nature of the monument until the subscription fund was closed and the final sum was known. In the early stages of planning for the memorial to Albert Lee, there was some suggestion of a clock tower being erected. However, once the subscription had been collected no further mention was ever made of this and it is likely that, despite having raised a highly creditable £57 5d, such a project was simply too costly to implement.[70] When a committee knew the amount of money that was available to them, they would then have had a better idea of what they could do.

Once a monument had been decided upon, and a design selected, there was still the all important factor of where the monument should be located. There were a number of possible options: at the place of burial, at the site of the heroic act where the individual died, in their town of birth or in some other significant public place. Yet, even this was not always as straightforward as it might seem; take, for example, the case of Mary Rogers. Mary Rogers was a stewardess on the Channel steamer, the SS *Stella*, which had sunk on Good Friday, 30 March 1899, after striking the Casquets rocks off Alderney in thick fog. Reports emanating from survivors of the wreck painted a vivid picture of how Rogers had given up her lifebelt to a passenger and refused to get into an overcrowded lifeboat, before voluntarily going down with the ship (see Figure 17).[71]

When it came to erecting a monument to Rogers, the choices for location were many, but problematic. The stewardess had been born in Frome, Somerset, providing

Figure 17 Monument commemorating Mary Rogers, Western Esplanade, Southampton, 2008 (*John Price*).

that town with a good claim, but at the time of her death Rogers was officially a resident of Southampton. Furthermore, it transpired that Rogers actually spent most of her time living in Jersey and not Southampton, which prompted the *Jersey Weekly Press* to suggest that 'the town of St Helier would be the proper place for the memorial and the neighbourhood of the piers a suitable site.' Many of these monuments to everyday heroes were erected either at the location of the incident or over the grave of the individual. However, with Rogers losing her life at sea and her body never being recovered for burial, even these options were denied to the organizing committee. The initial letter to *The Times* that began the movement to commemorate Rogers suggested 'a simple monument . . . at Southampton, or elsewhere', and this idea appears to have stuck in the minds of those who undertook the task.[72] There was no explicit reason given as to why Southampton was chosen, and one possibility is that, as it was erected on the newly built Western Esplanade, it was perceived as forming an element of an overall civic development scheme. Incidentally, no official memorials to the *Stella* were erected in the Channel Islands until 1997 when a metal plaque was installed on the harbour wall at St Peter Port, Guernsey.[73]

Three of the eleven monuments, those to Mark Addy, Alice Ayres and William Hunter, are located over or adjacent to their place of burial in municipal cemeteries. In the case of Mark Addy, it is possible to see something of the necessity of this, as the publican did not die while actually undertaking a single act of heroism and his commemoration was in respect to many acts over a number of years. The most logical place to commemorate him was his grave, but a very good case could, no doubt, have been made for placing a monument outside the Old Boathouse Inn where Addy had performed so much of his heroism, or at another prominent position in the town which claimed him as their hero. After all, it was the people of Salford who had raised the funds. Perhaps the plan to erect the cemetery memorial was finalized before a proposal to place a bust in Peel Park was shelved, but this is not clear. Alice Ayres performed her act of heroism at the house in Southwark where she lived and worked, but her body was returned and laid to rest in Isleworth, where she had been born and where her family still lived (see Figure 18). The subscription fund collected money from numerous locations and the people of Southwark were said to speak of her as 'our Alice', yet there was no suggestion of placing the memorial outside the house or anywhere else in Southwark. Perhaps that location, where two young children and their parents had died, was considered too tainted with tragedy or simply, as with Addy, the grave was seen as the most apt position; whichever the case, there is no evidence either way.

The decision is even less clear in the case of Hunter, and it is hard to see why a memorial was not erected adjacent to Townhill Loch where Hunter drowned. In fact, in all the other cases where the individual drowned while saving the life of another, aside from Ethel Harrison, the memorial was placed at the scene of the incident. Percy Gordon, Albert Lee, Timothy Trow and Edgar Wilson all perished under these circumstances and, in the case of the memorials to Lee and Trow, reference is made in the memorial inscription to the fact that the act occurred close to the spot of the monument. It might appear that these references are now, to some extent, redundant as, in the case of Trow, the canal no longer exists and the river at the spot where Lee drowned is now little more

Figure 18 Monument commemorating Alice Ayres, erected over her grave in Isleworth Cemetery, 2004 (*John Price*).

than a stream. However, that was the very point of the reference in the inscription. It was designed to conjure up the dramatic and heroic scene in the minds-eye of the casual observer so that in the years to come, the monument would still evoke the emotion of the moment. Even where there was no explicit reference in the inscription to being at the location of the incident, the proximity of the site still resonates. And this was exactly the purpose of placing the monument close to the spot itself. Any monument, at any location, might evoke sympathy, but the fact that the visitor was drawn to the very site of the tragedy instilled a deep sense of empathy with what had been undertaken and the sacrifice that had been made. These monuments were designed to touch people and, what is more, to touch people for very particular reasons.

'Miss Harrison's intrepid example': Commemorating and communicating the exemplary life

At the unveiling ceremony for the Harrison memorial, the Mayoress spoke of her hope that 'many would follow the example of Miss Harrison and be faithful even unto death if need be.'[74] This proposition, that the monument should convey a message of example, is also visible in the previously discussed debate over the location of the monument. Harrison's act, as clearly stated in the monument's inscription, was 'saving the life of a child under her care', so in addition to being heroic, it also communicated messages of faithfulness, commitment, responsibility and, most crucially, dedication to duty. These were all excellent qualities to promote to the general public at large, but they would have been particularly pertinent to one group. The Castle Gardens site was suggested because it was a popular spot for nursemaids to congregate and, likewise, the London Road because it was a popular route for them while out walking. It was intended that, by placing the memorial in such a location, nursemaids would look upon the memorial to Ethel Harrison and see an example of a dutiful and responsible servant who had undertaken a heroic act to protect the children in her care, an example they would respect and consequently seek to emulate. This was certainly the desire of the Mayoress, who believed that 'the calling of a nurse was a very high one, only second to that of a mother's, and she could not help thinking that if mothers and nurses did their work faithfully they would be serving their country far better than in talking about their rights to vote (laughter and applause).'[75] Ethel Harrison had been viewed as one such nursemaid, and the monument that commemorated the act that proved it, was designed to inspire and encourage such behaviour in others.

As might be expected, these goals of inspiration and prescription were not restricted to the Harrison memorial alone and were present in the motives behind others. At the unveiling ceremony in Queen's Park, assembled dignitaries came to the platform one after another and spoke of the public role they saw for the monument to Albert Lee. Councillor Smith hoped that it 'would be a source of inspiration to many young men to be prepared to make sacrifices for the good of others', the Mayor believed that 'the loss of Lee's life was one of the grandest and greatest teachings that they could have had for their boys and girls' and that Lee 'recognised instantly that he had a duty to perform [which] was a noble lesson and one they could all profit by'.[76] It was said that those who had conceived of the monument saw it as 'an inducement to others not to shrink from taking their part, from doing their duty in elevating and sustaining those who were in a more unfortunate position than themselves'.[77] Finally, in officially handing responsibility for the monument to the Park's Committee, the Mayor expressed his confidence that 'the committee would see that it was kept in sound condition and handed down to future generations as an illustration of the highest nature which can be shown in this life'.[78] The memorial to the Durham miner William Walton was intended to 'inspire the people of Ferryhill to good and noble deeds', as was that for the publican Mark Addy, which would 'inspire to like heroic deeds generations yet unborn'.[79] Children, townspeople and future generations would all, apparently, learn and take instruction from the monuments to these individuals.

In some cases, the prescription was not aimed at the general audience alone but, as with nursemaids in the case of Ethel Harrison, at a more specific target. Percy Gordon's mother was reported to have 'made very kind enquiries about the little girl whom her son rescued, and had expressed a hope that she would grow up to be a good and useful woman', while the two men who had attempted to save Timothy Trow were told, 'In the years to come they might have to trust to the noble efforts . . . of some passers-by in order that their own life, or the lives of someone near and dear to them might be preserved . . . and the spirit of Trow would always be found in such a case.'[80]

Strikingly, the two lads, Green and Hazel, whom Edgar Wilson had attempted to save, were actually present on the platform at the unveiling of the monument and it was said of them that 'already the noble act was appreciated by the boys themselves, and would doubtless have a moral effect on their lives when they were in a position to fully appreciate it (hear hear)'.[81] Furthermore, the instructive nature of the monument itself was impressed upon the boys by the Mayor who advised them, 'when they required consolation and help . . . to come there sometimes and look at that monument for that purpose and for the inspiration which it would give them (applause)'.[82] So even for those who had been personally and profoundly touched by the event itself, the monuments were seen as offering a continual reminder of the type of person they should strive to be.

For that is, to some extent, what these monuments were commemorating. It is highly unlikely that any of the individuals commemorated would have attracted such attention had they simply lived out their lives without incident. In that respect, it was, in effect, more the example that the individual had set through their behaviour and the moral values that underpinned such actions, than the actual individual themselves that was being celebrated and promoted. Of course, one was intrinsically linked to the other and not simply because without the individual you could not have the act, but because the character of the individual and the act of heroism were effectively coupled in a reciprocal relationship. The intended message was that acts of heroism were undertaken by people of good character, and it was the presence of good character that inspired and enabled people to undertake acts of heroism. This can be seen in a number of cases: publican Mark Addy 'had many excellent, noble and heroic qualities which they revered and admired and were proud of'; Rochester hero Percy Gordon 'was a fine, good-living fellow [who people] spoke in the highest terms of him'; Dunfermline people 'all knew William Hunter as a much respected, quiet, inoffensive, well behaved lad' and Durham miner William Walton was understood to be 'a man of excellent character, a good husband, a tender father and an industrious workman'.[83] This supposition is, of course, harder to test in the case of deceased heroes than it is with living ones, as it can be argued that people do not like to speak ill of the dead. Notwithstanding this, the way in which those commemorated were described would seem to suggest that character was a major contributory factor in the ability and willingness to perform an act of heroism, and ultimately, to die for it.

Another element in the way in which heroic individuals were commemorated was concerned with what can best be described as ownership or appropriation. This varied in its motives with issues such as local and national identity as well as labour and gender politics being key. The manner in which both subscribers and committee regarded Ethel Harrison as a local heroine and the movement to erect a memorial to her as the responsibility of Newark people has already been shown. Furthermore, the Heywood youngster Albert Lee was described as 'not exactly the son of his mother, but a son of the town', while it was reported that the Stoke tram conductor Timothy Trow 'would rank amongst the heroes produced by the Potteries'.[84] Mark Addy was, of course, referred to as the 'Salford Hero', and it is clear from discussions surrounding his commemoration that he was very much seen in that light, as Alderman Mottram announced to the committee at their July meeting, 'they could justly claim him as a Salfordian and certainly a Salford hero (cheers)'. At the same meeting, it was also said that 'Salford would do honour to herself by erecting a memorial' and that 'a memorial would show what manner of man Salford men delighted to honour (cheers)'. As might have been expected, the Rev Petherick claimed that 'not only was he [Addy] a Salford hero, but a Salford Martyr as well (cheers)', and he also claimed him not only for the town, but for the county as well, 'they had reason to be proud he was a Lancashire man; he was a good sample too (hear hear)'.[85]

It was not just local identity that was recognized, national identity was important as well. The heroism displayed by Timothy Trow was not just individual heroism, it was the heroism of a nation, as summed up by the committee chairman, 'though they all deplored the disaster they could not help feeling gratified that in their midst the courage which was proverbial of Englishmen was certainly not wanting'. The memorial was needed, it was said, 'so that those who saw it in the days yet to come could see that self-sacrifice still lived amongst the English people' and because it would demonstrate that 'the prevailing spirit of Englishmen' was always be found in such cases.[86] It was also, apparently, to be found in the case of the cross-channel stewardess Mary Rogers. The lengthy inscription on the memorial fountain commemorating her act gives a brief account of the incident in which she lost her life, before going on to assert that her actions 'constitute the glorious heritage of our English race'. Furthermore, in her letter to *The Times*, the novelist Lucy Walford wrote, 'may we not claim that the noble heroine of the *Stella* belongs to the nation' and she described Mary as 'England's latest heroine'.[87]

While considering commemoration, it is interesting to note that the condition of the nation was also a prominent and consistent theme in the reasoning behind G. F. Watts' memorial to everyday heroism. In 1887, Watts declared that his monument would demonstrate 'the character of a nation as a people of great deeds' and that it would make the nation richer by offering an 'infinitely honourable' record.[88] In the artist's eyes, heroic acts constituted 'a grand and honourable feature of the national character' and were the glory of that nation's people.[89] Furthermore, Watts saw the existence and prevalence of heroic individuals as an indicator of the condition of the nation as a whole, as he told the *Pall Mall Gazette*: 'The frequency of such noble acts leads me to look hopefully to the future of a nation that can produce such heroes.'[90] The individuals offered by the monument were to be understood and emulated not just as models of exemplary individual character but as representatives and examples of a glorious and honourable nation. It was the artist's hope that his monument in Postman's Park, originally conceived as featuring only London-based acts, would be replicated across the country. Every town and city would erect its own memorial to its own heroes, and in this way heroism would be shown to be a national rather than simply a local concept.[91] In this respect, the artist's vision, essentially one of pride and focused on celebrating and promoting the nation's strengths, can be interpreted as patriotic. Watts, however, was not only concerned with how Britain viewed itself but also with how it was viewed from outside and he walked a fine and often blurred line between patriotism and jingoism.[92]

In 1888, the artist had written to Lord Wemyss to express his fears regarding the position of the country: 'Every nation stands by with unfriendly feeling . . . we are neither loved, which is a pity, nor trusted which is a disgrace, nor feared which is a disaster!'[93] Watts declared that in his championing of heroes he was 'an Englishman, proud of what an Englishman can do', and when asked if the memorials to heroes would be wholly national or international, he replied: 'British, decidedly British; they would be the honour of our nation.' However, he was also concerned with the ways in which Britain was viewed and, more importantly, how it matched up to other nations, going on to add: 'Foreigners come over here and are not slow to note our many vices . . . but they look in vain for any record of noble deeds amongst our people [who] are moved by many noble impulses [and] compare favourably with any people on the face of the earth.'[94] This confident affirmation has, it can be argued, vague hallmarks of jingoism about it with Watts as the 'blustering and blatant' patriot advocating the greatness of the British Nation. When the second Boer War broke out in October 1899, Watts asserted that the Boers were uncivilized and deficient in character and suggested that the British were an 'active and progressive' race, well suited to replace them.[95] Once again, there are hints of a bellicose nationalism that suggest vaguely jingoistic beliefs in the thinking of Watts.

Notwithstanding this assertion, the Boer war inspired Watts to paint *Love Steering the Boat of Humanity* (1899–1901), which, according to Mary Watts, was conceived to show 'Man's . . . recognition of his own importance to control, yet with the sustaining faith that the hand of love directs his course.'[96] Perhaps, then, there was less of the jingo in Watts and more of the well-intentioned paternalist, who believed wholeheartedly in the superiority of British national character and the capacity to educate and civilize through the exportation of it.[97] In the logic of its creator, the Watts monument would explicitly demonstrate exemplary individual character and, with its focus on British subjects, implicitly suggest a superior national character. This in turn would help to bolster and substantiate Britain's position as a social and political world leader. Essentially, Watts, and many of the others who were involved with instating or erecting monuments, hoped that highlighting and commemorating the exemplary qualities of everyday heroes would not only assist and encourage the poor, the destitute and the morally corrupt to climb out of their own personal circumstances, but also that their new-found sense of duty and responsibility would help improve the reputation and position of the nation.

In addition to being claimed for the nation, these heroic individuals and the monuments erected to them were also appropriated or called upon to assert or promote other ideas as well. The monument to the miner William Walton was unveiled outside Ferryhill Town Hall on 18 April 1908 by Mr John Johnson. Mr Johnson was not a member of staff from the colliery, nor was he a representative of Ferryhill or Durham. He was, in fact, MP for Gateshead but, more than that, he was a lib/lab MP, attached to the Durham Miners Union and an ardent campaigner for improving conditions for miners. Although he alluded to Walton's good character and offered his condolences to the family, the majority of his speech addressed the fact that bravery was simply a daily occurrence in the life of a miner and while 'poets sang of the brave deeds done on the battlefield [and] monuments erected to the memory of brave men in many walks of life', the heroism of miners seldom came to light.[98] He praised the King for introducing the Edward Medal, but claimed that many more would be needed than thought of, such was the lot of the miner. William Walton was a working miner and had certainly lost his life undertaking a heroic act, but that act had not been undertaken in a mine or in relation to a mining accident, which makes Johnson's speech appear slightly wide of the mark, given the occasion. Essentially, he was attempting to harness the emotional power communicated by the memorial and use it to direct attention not only onto the individual bravery of William Walton, but also onto the collective everyday bravery of all miners. While being an admirable and understandable objective for someone in Johnson's position, his use of Walton's monument shows how easily everyday heroism could be appropriated and constructed to suit various purposes.

There seems to have been a similar political agenda at work in relation to the commemoration of Mark Addy, although not quite so explicitly. In calling for a subscription fund to be established, there was much reference to the working men of Salford. Alderman Bailey had no doubt that 'the working men of Salford would contribute their sixpences and shillings.' Similarly, Alderman Richard Mottram 'asked the working men of Salford to open subscription lists amongst their fellow workmen' and also 'to put their shoulders to the wheel' in providing both a cemetery memorial and a monument in Peel Park. Even the Mayor, Benjamin Robinson, professed that 'he should like to see the workingmen of Salford raise a monument to Addy.'[99] Quite why the committee were so adamant that there should be working-class involvement is not clear and it would appear that they did not want the subscription to be exclusively funded by the working classes, as Mottram made clear, 'the memorial should not only have the support of the rich with their gold, but the middle classes with their silver and the poor with their copper.'[100] It is possible that the committee viewed Addy as being a relatively poor working man and consequently believed that appealing to other working men who would better associate and relate to him would both increase subscriptions and encourage working-class engagement with a didactically intended monument. This suggestion is substantiated by a published comment made by Alderman Bailey, in that the committee 'had not met to do honour to a man who had become distinguished on the field of battle; but to do honour to a poor man, a working man, who had risked his life in saving human beings.'[101]

However, it is highly unlikely that the committee members would have considered or believed Addy to be a poor man. Addy had been a prominent and highly successful professional sculler earning hundreds of pounds from competing in head-to-head races for cash prizes and in 1878, he had been awarded a £210 testimonial.[102] Considering that around the same time an average annual salary for a working-class man would have been around £70, this was a substantial sum and one that Addy would have been unlikely to have expended in the intervening years. Quite the opposite, in fact, as Addy's wealth at his death in 1890 was £819 14s 3d.[103] Rather than believing Addy to be a poor working man, what is more likely is that an idea or image of Addy as such was constructed and promoted so as to encourage and foster a sense of the working-class hero figure among the 'lower' classes. Consequently, when the working classes viewed the monument, they would, it was hoped, feel more inspired or impelled by the example because they could relate to Addy on their own terms rather than him being simply an icon handed down to them from above.

It would appear that these monuments to everyday heroes were, in conceptual terms, highly malleable objects which provided a versatile platform from which it was possible to project and promote different points of view. This was possible because heroism, rather than being a single, static and rigidly understood idea, was actually a flexible and adaptable concept which could be assembled or constructed in different ways to serve different purposes. The design of any monument to a heroic act, its location, its inscription and the way in which it was unveiled and presented to the public could all be tailored so as to communicate specific messages. But more often than not these messages, and their possible public appeal, were limited because they were locked in a military or imperial context. Everyday heroes, on the other hand, could provide qualities and characteristics which were far more universal to the general public, and consequently, they provided ideal vehicles in which elements could be included or discarded as appropriate to different constructions.

Conclusions

This chapter has demonstrated that the planning and erecting of a monument to a heroic civilian individual was a collective effort and one which involved widespread and general engagement across all social classes. It is true to say that, in most cases, the formal procedures and practical mechanisms for administering the memorial were undertaken by committees formed from those at the upper end of the social spectrum. Furthermore, there is no doubt that the commemoration of 'Miss Harrison's intrepid example' and other acts of everyday heroism were capitalized upon by influential men and women in the local area, and sometimes nationally, in order to promote a didactic message of exemplary behaviour or call for greater recognition of particular groups in society. In this way, they do share things in common with both the Albert Medal and the various liberal-radical projects discussed in Chapter 2. Notwithstanding this, the evidence shows that there was actual and demonstrable engagement with every stage of the commemorative process from the general public, including those at the lower as well as the upper ends of society.

The memorial committees were adamant that the commemorative process for these 'everyday' heroes had to be public, not private, and that involvement in it had to be open to all, irrespective of their social or financial position. This finding has an important bearing on our understanding of how everyday heroism was viewed and understood during this period, especially when examined in relation to the process for erecting other sorts of commemorative monuments. The *Public Monuments and Sculpture Association* (PMSA) was formed in 1991 with the aim of increasing the public awareness and enjoyment of public art, and as part of its work it publishes a series of volumes which catalogue and examine the public sculpture of Britain.[104] Through a study of monuments which were erected to commemorate the death of an individual which feature in these volumes, it is possible to discern a rough pattern within the general process of commemoration from around 1830 up to around 1914.

It would appear that public subscription rather than private patronage was chosen as a method of realizing a monument when it was believed that the public at large, including the working and lower classes, would want to contribute their time and money to the project. Furthermore, it appears that this judgement was based upon assumptions about which types of individual these sections of society would have appreciated and therefore wished to commemorate. As Terry Cavanagh has concluded in his introduction to the PMSA volume for Liverpool, 'when it was felt that the person to be commemorated was held by them [the working classes] in particular affection, special arrangements might be made to organise collections door to door or within workplaces'.[105] Choosing to open the planning and funding of these monuments to public consultation and subscription suggests that those on the committee viewed everyday heroes and heroism as something which society at large understood, took an interest in and, most importantly, appreciated sufficiently to wish to commemorate.

The precise reasons or motivations behind the engagement of the public at large remain unclear, but as it has been shown that everyday heroism could be variably constructed and understood, it is not unreasonable to suggest that those who gave their money may have had their own construction, rather than that handed down to them by the committee. In this regard, although the committee painted a picture of Nurse Harrison – a dutiful and dedicated nursemaid who conscientiously sacrificed her own life for that of her master's children – the people of Newark might have viewed her as something else. Perhaps they viewed her simply as Ethel Harrison – a brave and selfless young woman who compassionately attempted to save the life of a small child and who tragically but heroically lost her life in the process – and this was why they put their hands in their pockets to ensure that she and her act were fittingly commemorated.

This chapter also suggests that historians need to revaluate their attitudes and approaches to the study of heroism. There is, as previously outlined, a distinct tendency in work which engages with heroism to employ it as nothing more than a fixed lens through which to study other subjects and concepts. Studies of military or imperial heroism tend to be concerned with what the research reveals about the military or the empire, rather than examining the heroism aspect as a subject in and of its own right.[106] The danger with approaches such as this is that they give the impression that militarism and imperialism were the major influences and the dominant components in the Victorian conception of the idea of heroism. With regard to the study of heroism, these monuments and the processes behind them demonstrate that this really was not the case. From the early 1860s right through until the World War I, the idea of everyday heroism became well established and widely promoted alongside the more general discourse on the subject. The Crown instituted medals to recognize it, private organizations were founded to reward it, G. F. Watts put his own money into a grand plan to commemorate it and, as shown here, local communities came together to erect monuments to those who died while undertaking it. Heroism was not a static and rigid concept, as historians have generally speaking concluded, but a flexible and adaptable one in which everyday heroes from all walks of life played an important and central role. What is more, it was this flexibility that allowed heroism, and especially everyday heroism, to be successfully appropriated by both establishment and radical groups in order to promote particular ideas, suggest alternative positions or to try and persuade people around to an alternative point of view. As the popular profile of everyday heroism and the public's willingness to acknowledge and engage with a non-establishment concept of the idea increased through the latter half of the nineteenth century and into the twentieth, it became an even more potent vehicle through which to publicize alternative or challenging points of view, something that was not lost on one of the richest men in the world at that time.

'Heroes for Hire': The Carnegie Hero Fund Trust

From its establishment in 1866 until the introduction of the Edward Medal in 1907, the Albert Medal was the only award for civilian heroism explicitly awarded by the Crown. However, it was far from being the only award for civilian heroism given during this period, with others being awarded by several subscription-based organizations. The foremost of these were the Liverpool Shipwreck and Humane Society (1839), The Order of St John of Jerusalem (1874), The Royal Humane Society (1776), the Royal National Lifeboat Institution (1824) and the Society for the Protection of Life from Fire (1836).[1] The majority of these organizations were primarily concerned with the saving of life or the prevention of circumstances in which life was put at risk and, while they all gave awards for it, their recognition of civilian heroism was, to some extent, a by-product rather than a central focus of their work. They all shared a common goal, which was to endorse and encourage a particular set of ideas or practices, directly linked to the ethos and objectives of the organization, and they all utilized incidents of everyday heroism to promote and further their work. In doing so, they also increased the public profile of everyday heroism and demonstrated that it could be a powerful and potent mechanism for attracting press attention, bringing publicity to a particular cause and affecting real change in terms of behaviour or best practice.

By the beginning of the twentieth century, the Royal Humane Society (RHS) had stimulated and facilitated a fervent and effective life-saving culture, the Royal National Lifeboat Institution (RNLI) had significantly reduced loss of life at sea and the Society for the Protection of Life from Fire (SPLF) had played a key role in the foundation and work of the Metropolitan Fire Brigade. Undoubtedly, heroism in all walks of life attracted publicity and such publicity could certainly influence public opinion and, potentially, put pressure on government policy. Into this atmosphere and context, an organization was launched, which was explicitly created and designed to recognize 'heroism' as distinct from life-saving or the protection of life. This organization was the Carnegie Hero Fund Trust (1908), the brainchild of the retired steel magnate and philanthropist Andrew Carnegie. This organization set out from the start to acknowledge and assist 'heroes' as opposed to those who had simply saved or attempted to save life, and consequently it has much to reveal about the construction of everyday heroism.

The Carnegie Hero Fund Trust was announced in September 1908, when a letter from its founder was read before the Board of Trustees of the Carnegie Dunfermline Trust.[2] Carnegie opened his letter with a bold statement, 'Gentlemen . . . we live in an heroic age. Not seldom are we thrilled by acts of heroism where men or women are injured or lose their lives in attempting to preserve or rescue their fellows; such are the heroes of civilisation'.[3] He went on to explain that he had long felt that 'such true heroes and those dependent upon them should be freed from pecuniary cares resulting from their heroism' and consequently he intended to provide $1.25 million in bonds, yielding an annual income of £12,500, as a means of addressing the issue.[4] Such an amount, Carnegie believed, would be sufficient to 'meet the cost of maintaining injured heroes and their families during the disability of the heroes [and] the widows and children of heroes who may lose their lives'.[5] Essentially, the purpose of the Hero Fund was to provide pensions or one-off payments to individuals who had been injured or financially disadvantaged as a result of undertaking an act of heroism or in the case of those who lost their lives through such an act, to provide for the family or other dependants.

The Hero Fund Trust was the first extension of a US Hero Fund Commission, founded by Carnegie in 1904 and based in Pittsburgh, Pennsylvania.[6] The noted palaeontologist and first president of the Commission, William J. Holland, recalled a conversation with Carnegie a couple of years prior to the founding of the commission. Following reports of a dramatic rescue from a burning building, Carnegie commented, 'I intend some day to do something for such heroes. Heroes in civic life should be recognized.'[7] Following the establishment of the US commission in 1904 and the UK Hero Fund Trust in 1908, a further nine Hero Funds were established across Europe between 1909 and 1911, and in total Carnegie endowed $10.5 million to the foundation of funds recognizing everyday heroism.[8] It is, however, the foundation and work of the UK Hero Fund Trust that this chapter will examine in detail.

First and foremost, the stated purpose of the Hero Fund was to ensure that an individual who undertook a heroic act, or those dependent upon them, did not suffer financially as a result of the action. This is the first point that Carnegie made in his 12 September 1908 letter to the Trustees in which he outlined that individuals should be provided for until able to work again, widows until remarriage and children until they reached a self-supporting age. He also allowed for other dependants to be supported at the discretion of the trustees.[9] The Chairman of the Trust, Dr John Ross, echoed this in an address he gave to the Trustees on 1 October 1908 in which he stated the purpose of the Trust as, 'saving heroes from pecuniary loss, and . . . lessening the pain which may ensue from a heroic action to the hero himself, his wife, or children, or dependants'.[10] The explicitly stated primary concern of the Trustees was to be providing recognition through practical relief to those in need rather than simply giving out cash prizes for bravery.

The press, both national and local, were very much in favour of the general principle of the Fund, that being recognition and assistance for those who undertook heroic acts. Indeed, *The Scotsman* declared that 'such objects present no opening for adverse criticism', while the *Dundee Advertiser* contended that 'it is difficult to imagine the state of mind of one who would say that it is not a thing worth doing.'[11] Some editorials simply voiced their own opinions, such as the *Daily News* which considered the Trust to be 'as wise as it is generous', and the *Daily Express* which thought it to be 'an entirely excellent scheme'.[12] Other editorials sought to speak for the wider public; 'There was no reason to expect anything but warm public sympathy' stated *The Scotsman*, and 'none of the previous donations of the Pittsburgh millionaire have been received with such a universal chorus of applause' reported the *Glasgow Evening Citizen*.[13] The *Sheffield Daily Telegraph* wrote that it believed, 'the community at large will not be slow in showing its appreciation of it [the Hero Fund]', while the *Manchester Courier* ambitiously suggested that 'the world will sympathise with and approve the motives that have prompted the scheme'.[14] Whether stating their own opinions or appearing to reflect those of the public, the general consensus of the press was that the Hero Fund was an excellent idea and it was highly praised.

This chapter will focus primarily upon the work of the Hero Fund although the work of other organizations will be considered, albeit in less detail, as they certainly helped to create the background context and set the stage. As preceding chapters have shown, by 1908 the public recognition and commemoration of everyday heroism was relatively commonplace and it had become a reasonably well-known and well-understood idea. The Hero Fund was, then, something of a latecomer and this proved to be both beneficial and problematic to Carnegie and those responsible for administering his project. On the positive side, everyday heroism had developed into a prominent and important idea that captured the public's imagination and it could be usefully employed when attempting to influence popular opinion. Everyday heroism had also been shown to be an idea that could challenge conventions and provide a radical discourse alongside more establishment constructions. This made it an ideal vehicle through which to garner or galvanize public support for less conventional or accepted ideas, provided that a reasonably widespread acceptance and approval for a project could be achieved.

This, however, was not necessarily straightforward and because everyday heroism was generally well regarded, there were strong feelings about the correct methods of recognizing it. Acts of heroism were viewed as stemming from pure motive or the best aspects of human nature and any method of recognition perceived to be interfering with those motivations or stimulating others could be viewed with suspicion and concern. Carnegie's plan was to facilitate and encourage civilian heroism by providing financial support or reward to those who undertook such acts and this aspect made his project particularly contentious. Thus, as this chapter reveals, the Hero Fund Trustees had to tread a careful path to achieve the right balance. To maximize publicity, an egalitarian and all-encompassing attitude towards candidates was required and, in contrast to the Albert Medal, Carnegie believed that the more often awards were made, the better. However, many of the core nineteenth-century views and definitions of heroism still underpinned the idea in the minds of many and negotiating these while still trying to achieve the aims of its founder created a conundrum for the Trustees of the Hero Fund. As revealed in this chapter, this eventually led them into a position of rewarding acts of everyday heroism with cash payments, something which Carnegie had originally denied was his intention, but which became necessary if his goals were to be achieved.

The *Gospel of Wealth: The Hero Fund as a vehicle for philanthropy*

The Hero Fund was one of Carnegie's charitable trusts and therefore his views on philanthropy are an important consideration when seeking to understand the reasoning behind it. Fortunately, Carnegie was not backward in coming forward with regard to what he saw as the correct way of administering wealth and the most notable example of this is his 1889 article *The Gospel of Wealth*.[15] Carnegie proposed that 'the man who dies rich dies disgraced' and there might at first appear to be parallels here with religious ideas of atonement and the unlikelihood of rich men passing through the gates of the Kingdom of God which were prevalent in the nineteenth century.[16] However, Carnegie generally had little time for organized religion and was from a non-conformist background, his father having been a Swedenborgian. Instead, and as professed in his *Gospel of Wealth*, Carnegie believed that wealth accumulated in the hands of the few partly as a result of the efforts of the community or society that surrounded that individual. He cited a fictional example of how two similar farmers with similar values of land or capital might work equally hard throughout their lives but one becomes wealthier than the other simply because the land around his farm becomes a prosperous city rather than remaining a rural backwater. Consequently, Carnegie viewed wealthy individuals as an inevitable and essential product of a satisfactory development of society.

However, Carnegie was also influenced by an underdeveloped understanding of Herbert Spencer's ideas of Social Darwinism which led the former to believe that the wealthy were in a position to administer the accumulated wealth of the poorer classes better then they themselves could.[17] To quote Carnegie,

> the surplus wealth of the few will become, in the best sense, the property of the many because administered for the common good; and this wealth, passing through the hands of the few, can be made a much more potent force for the elevation of our race than if distributed in small sums to the people themselves.[18]

Carnegie did not believe in indiscriminate charity or in assisting those who were the architects of their own poverty through vices such as laziness, drunkenness or gambling. Such individuals, according to Carnegie, should be given refuge by the state, but only as long as it isolated them from the ranks of the 'well doing and industrious poor' whom they would demoralize with their vices. With regard to dominant ideas about philanthropy and charity, Carnegie was not particularly out of step, for, as Frank Prochaska has observed, 'it was tacitly agreed that charity was to assist deserving cases, those who could be helped by preventative or remedial actions; the poor law would cope with undeserving paupers.'[19] Hero Fund payments were intended to support those who *could not* work, not those who *would not* and dependants who had lost their breadwinner through no fault or action of their own. Carnegie, then, was in the business of helping only those who were willing, but unable, to help themselves, essentially those whom he considered the deserving poor. Why, though, civilian heroes in particular rather than any other deserving individual who could not work because of accidental incapacity?

By 1908, everyday heroism was relatively well understood and, as outlined in this book, there had been numerous public activities which had shaped and forwarded various constructions of the idea. Something, though, which consistently ran through all of these activities was the perception that heroism was the preserve of morally decent people, and the performance of a heroic act was indicative of a respectable and upstanding character. Therefore, recognizing acts of everyday heroism provided Carnegie with a practical 'quality control' mechanism through which to sieve the wheat from the chaff and provide a steady stream of people who, by this reckoning, must have the requisite qualities to be fitting and worthy of his financial benevolence. An indication of this belief is provided by the inclusion of a clause in the original deeds for the Hero Fund which stipulated, 'No grant is to be continued unless it is being soberly and properly used, and the recipients remain respectable, well-behaved members of the community . . . no exceptions will be made to this rule'.[20] This is very similar, in essence, to clause six in the Albert Medal warrant, which allowed for awards to be revoked in the event of 'disgraceful conduct' by the recipient. Interestingly, this is not the only similarity between the Hero Fund and the Albert Medal in terms of how to judge qualification for an award.

In the Hero Fund Annual Report for 1908, details of six awarded cases were given but reference was also made to 'many reported cases which the Trustees, after careful investigation, felt compelled to set aside as not falling within the scope of the Fund'.[21] These cases, it was reported, were 'judged to fall short of what is required for recognition as heroes, or of what is required to qualify for benefit from the hero fund'.[22] Given that the Fund was concerned with the practical issue of providing pecuniary relief to injured heroes or their dependants, it might be expected that such shortfalls would concern the level of disablement, the personal or financial circumstances of those under consideration or the volume of any other means of support being forthcoming. However, this was not necessarily the case and, instead, the 'General Principles' upon which the decision should be based were, as with the Albert Medal, much more concerned with the heroism of the act and the character of the individual undertaking it.

The first qualification was that 'an action which has as its object the saving of human life cannot be regarded as one of heroism, unless the rescuer incurs serious personal risk in doing it'.[23] The basis given for this judgement was that it was within 'the ordinary claims of humanity that a man shall make every reasonable effort . . . to save the life of another, and the discharge of this duty does not necessarily make a man a hero'.[24] Cases of a man with a boat rescuing someone who was drowning, or a strong swimmer doing likewise without incurring any serious risk to themselves, were given as examples of such acts. This is the same criteria as with the Albert Medal where significant personal risk to the life of the rescuer was a key factor. This judgement also makes it possible to define the perceived difference between life-saving and heroism. It was possible to save or attempt to save life without it being heroism, but a constituent part of a heroic act was the risking of life to save life; you could save life without being a hero but you could not be a hero without risking your life.

Another key factor listed in the 1908 Annual Report was that 'the action must be voluntary and not one that is performed under the compulsion or pressure of duty.' This, it was stated, referred to the 'numerous callings in which the discharge of one's duty involves an element of risk' and cited the medical profession and the railway service as examples.[25] This certainly mirrors the decisions taken by those administering the Albert Medal, who also excluded anyone with any sort of perceived duty or responsibility to save life, whether in a professional or personal capacity. There was, though, more ambiguity with the Hero Fund than there was with the Albert Medal as to how stringently to apply this qualification. In his 1908 letter to the Trustees, Carnegie explicitly cited doctors, nurses and railroad employees as suitable candidates for awards.[26] However, in the 1908 Annual Report, The Chairman of the Hero Fund, Dr John Ross, stated that 'There are professions, such as the medical profession, and occupations such as that of the railway and shipping services, which have to do with the safety of human life, and in connection with which the ordinary discharge of duty involves risk.'[27] According to Ross, the fact that such action was not voluntarily performed but undertaken as a result of professional duty, excluded such individuals from awards, apart from in exceptional circumstances, 'where the ordinary requirements of duty have been exceeded in effort to save life.'[28] This is, perhaps, more in keeping with the ethos of G. F. Watts, who applied a similar rationale when questioned about lifeboat men, than with the secretaries in the Home Office. What is clear from this is that Carnegie and his trustees were acutely aware of the antecedents of the Hero Fund and were very keen to ensure that they were in tune with existing frameworks for recognition and support, rather than conflicting with them.

For example, when challenged that some cities already provided pensions for policeman, fireman and others, Carnegie stated that 'Nothing could be further from my intention than to deaden or interfere with these most creditable provisions, doubly precious as showing public and municipal appreciation of faithful and heroic service.'[29] Another suggestion made by the Press was that 'The fund will save the community from the reproach which sometimes can be bought against it,' suggesting that local communities would be relieved of the financial responsibility for maintaining injured heroes.[30] Carnegie, though, disagreed, stating that the Trustees should not act in making awards 'until employers and communities have done their parts, for their contributions benefit both givers and recipients.'[31] This is more than merely an example of Carnegie wishing to avoid stepping on local toes, but is entirely consistent with his ethos on communities and charity which, as already discussed, were based in the realms of self-help. Furthermore, it indicates that Carnegie was, to some extent, aware that recognition existed at the local or community level and wanted to ensure that, rather than interfere, his fund would work in synthesis with it.

These community or publicly orientated schemes of support, described in one newspaper as 'the normal current of public beneficence' and the 'ordinary fountain of charity', were clearly seen as important and as much for the benefit they provided to the benefactors as the beneficiaries.[32] 'We do not want the springs of compassion that usually flow readily enough to be closed by the liberal outpouring of one man's generosity. Townspeople might with more profit to themselves make provision for the hero . . . rather than allow the practical sympathy to come from outside' was the opinion of the *Yorkshire Post*, which also cited that in places where Carnegie libraries were not universally accepted the objection was that people appreciated things more if they paid for them themselves.[33] This sense of 'social responsibility' was also present in *The Scotsman* editorial which praised Carnegie for providing against 'the danger of relieving public bodies from the duty they have hitherto performed', and another which considered the only danger of the Trust to be that, 'those who can well afford not to let the brave among them suffer because of their bravery, should willingly allow their responsibility to be passed to the trust'.[34] The *Dundee Courier* agreed and suggested that the responsibility for supporting civilian heroes should lie with the state but that 'Mr Carnegie has helped us . . . by stepping in to remove a reproach in regard to which the State has had to confess its helplessness'.[35] Others suggested that it was 'society' that should step in and support heroes; 'Society ought itself to provide handsomely and gratefully for these heroes of peace' wrote the *Daily News*, although it was not clear about exactly what 'society' meant.[36] Perhaps, it too was referring to the actions of the local community including, as highlighted in Chapter3, the public involvement in the planning and funding of memorials.

Ross was certainly in agreement with Carnegie that 'it is most desirable that our verdict should coincide with the verdict of the neighbourhood in which the hero resides,' and in order to ensure this it would be necessary for the Trustees to gain some knowledge of 'the social and economic condition amidst which each scene is situated'.[37] It was suggested that this should be achieved by employing an officer who would travel to the area and conduct the necessary enquiries, but that 'he must largely be dependent on local knowledge, because numerous circumstances which he might overlook or fail to ascertain must be considered before we can arrive at a safe and appropriate decision'.[38] Ross was more than clear about the consequences of not adopting such a policy: 'if we act alone without regard to the opinions of others, and especially of the opinions of the neighbours of the heroes, our actions cannot possibly earn the same respect as if they were endorsed by neighbourly opinion'.[39] As the Chairman of the Carnegie Dunfermline Trust, Ross was no stranger to administering a large financial endowment, but unlike the Dunfermline Trust, the Hero Fund was a nation-wide project and this appears to have given him some cause for concern. In his 1908 address, he drew the Trustees' attention to the fact that,

> It may puzzle the public to know why we have been given so much power and . . . are supposed to possess so much knowledge of human nature as to be able to assign suitable awards to proper cases.[40]

Ross declared that, as Trustees, they must 'remove all idea of our presuming to ride upon our commission, or act arbitrarily or pompously as if we felt ourselves self-sufficient'.[41]

One particularly interesting way in which the Hero Fund trustees sought to ensure validity and authority for their awards was to allow other bodies to make the decisions for them. With regard to Crown awards, notably the Albert and Edward Medals, Ross considered them to be not only a 'source from which we will derive authentic information for our guidance' but also as recommendation and justification, as 'no one will be honoured by the King who does not well deserve it'.[42] He also saw similar benefits in cases forwarded from local authorities as they would, 'afford us information' and 'give moral sanction to our decisions'.[43] This apparent desire for someone else to take responsibility for deciding whether or not an act was heroic could be seen as an attempt to avoid having to make difficult judgements upon acts of heroism themselves. However, Ross also made it clear that 'I do not mean to advise you to shrink from your responsibilities or to abdicate your duties' and, as demonstrated earlier, the Trustees had no difficulty setting forth a definition of heroism from which to work with.[44] Rather than evasion, the desire for authentication stemmed, to some degree, from anxiety and a wish to 'act in harmony with public opinion'. Far from not wanting to be charged with making the decisions, the Trustees were actually more concerned that they may not carry sufficient authority to do so, a far cry from the undersecretaries in the Home Office.

The Hero Fund, then, was launched at a time when there were already well-developed ideas about the nature and construction of everyday heroism and various bodies had set their own benchmarks for defining it and judging those who performed it. It is clear that the Trustees were aware of this and recognized that, if the fund intended to utilize everyday heroism as an indicator of exemplary character, they would need to stay broadly within these established nineteenth-century definitions. Consequently, key qualifications from the Crown approach, such as risk to life and professional duty, were adopted and the decisions made by the Home Office and other local government officials were taken as trustworthy indicators of correct judgements. Basically, the initial belief of Carnegie and his trustees was that the Hero Fund could and would draw upon the records and decisions of other bodies, utilize their judgements and decisions to provide validity and authority, allow local communities the time and space to do their bit, and then make their own pecuniary award, safe in the knowledge that the money was going to a decent and morally sound individual whose action had broad public approval. This would, perhaps, have been an ideal approach and would have greatly assisted the trustees in undertaking their task of awarding money in line with Carnegie's philanthropic perspective. However, they quickly encountered a key problem with utilizing these existing foundations. Relying simply upon cases which presented themselves would not necessarily generate a plentiful amount of opportunities for making awards and, furthermore, adopting the exceptionally high standards set by the Home Office would restrict that field even further. Meanwhile, the trustees were under increasing pressure from their patron to not only spend his money but spend it wisely, generously and often. It was this pressure which essentially motivated the actions of the trustees and, more crucially, shaped the nature and methods of the work they undertook and the construction of heroism they adopted.

The administrative approach of the Hero Fund

Andrew Carnegie was acutely aware that, as a practical and philanthropic undertaking designed to distribute relatively large quantities of money to worthy individuals, his fund would be of little or no use if it did not reach and assist a significant quantity of suitable people. The prevalence and urgency of this concern for Carnegie is illustrated by his criticism of the Fund's Chairman for failing to capitalize on an opportunity to attract publicity,

A live sec'y would know to use the unsurpassed act of heroism reported in the Scotsman (libellous to use the word providential, but that is our theology). Properly recorded and copy to send to each newspaper would give you a start as nothing else would and stir the hearts of the people. So much depends on first impressions and here the fates favoured you. Utilize this incident and your start is assured, nothing could give you such a start.

This was, perhaps, a fair criticism, but Carnegie was, to some extent, overlooking the point that the ability to make awards ultimately relied upon a plentiful and reliable supply of information regarding potential heroes and details of acts of heroism. Utilizing the records of State awards, including the Albert Medal, initially appeared to provide the Trustees with a solution, but there were two predominant problems. One of these was the relatively low number of State awards and the second, related in part to the first, concerned the restrictions applied by State officials as to who should and should not qualify.

As discussed in Chapter 1, the award of an Albert Medal was a relatively rare and unusual occurrence. Between 1850 and 1914, the decoration was awarded just forty-two times, considerably less, on average, than once a year. There was much concern among the Home Office undersecretaries about the possibility of 'cheapening' the decoration by awarding it too often and, consequently, the Albert Medal was administered in such a way as to keep it sought after and highly prized. This generally meant not making awards very often, and in particular, not awarding to acts which were particularly common, such as stopping runaway horses. As an award of the State, it was important to those administering it that the Albert Medal was regarded by the public as representing the pinnacle of achievement and something that was out of reach to all but a select few. Only the details of awarded cases, rather than all those nominated, were published in the *London Gazette*, so if the Hero Fund Trustees had relied solely upon those, they would have had very little to work with.

The low number of awards made by the Home Office was partially related to the relatively low number of cases it had to work with. Between 1850 and 1914, the Home Office received and considered just 398 nominations for the Albert Medal, an average of six cases a year. Although the desire was to increase public knowledge and opinion of the State recognition of civilian heroism, there was no attempt to solicit or proactively identify cases for recognition. Instead, the Home Offices secretaries believed that the kudos associated with its Crown-sanctioned honours and the prestige of State recognition would provide ample publicity to generate sufficient nominations. This was not, however, the case and the fact that the Albert Medal was awarded so infrequently and was promoted as being the ultimate recognition of civilian heroism made it appear virtually unattainable and lessened the publicity around it. Furthermore, there was very little information or publicity about how to submit nominations for the Albert Medal, so even if people had been aware and engaged with the decoration, they might well have struggled to make their admiration known. Essentially, the Home Office officials were happy to sit back and wait for Albert Medal cases to be presented to them, and low numbers of nominations were less of an issue because there was no pressure to make high numbers of awards.

This was not going to be an option for the Hero Fund Trustees, who had their benefactor pushing them to make awards and attract publicity in order to achieve his philanthropic endeavour to free himself of his wealth in a satisfactory manner. For the Trustees, the position was more or less opposite to those in the Home Office. The more acts the Hero Fund recognized, the more publicity it would attract; the more publicity it attracted, the more public recognition it would achieve; the more public recognition, the more nominations; and the more nominations, the more potential heroes to recognize and so on. This is another reason why the Trustees were particularly concerned with securing public support and approval, because if they acted out of concordance with popular ideas they risked damaging their supply of nominations. It was also why they were proactive in seeking-out details of cases of heroism, as opposed to simply hoping that they would find their way to the office. By the time of the 1908 report, 9,000 copies of a pamphlet containing the text from Carnegie's 1908 letter, Ross' 1908 address and a letter from the Trustees inviting cooperation, had been distributed around the country to local authorities and other local bodies such as Police forces and Coroner's courts. The stated purpose of this was to ensure that 'no case of genuine heroism, in however remote a part of the country, will be overlooked' but it was also an astute mechanism for prompting organizations into action and for actively identifying cases and soliciting information about them.[45]

This initiative and others, including establishing direct channels of communication with Police forces and other life-saving organizations, were immensely successful and the figures speak for themselves. In just four years, between 1908 and 1912, the CHFT considered 1276 cases, an average of 319 per year and between September 1908 and September 1914, it made 1355 awards, an average of around 225 a year.[46] In comparison with the award of the Albert Medal, the Carnegie Hero Fund recognized more than five times the number of civilian heroic acts between 1908 and 1914. There was simply no way that the Trustees could have achieved this by relying solely upon State recognition to provide information and authentication. Furthermore, extensively widening their mechanism for acquiring potential cases and utilizing channels outside of the State system provided the Trustees with a far broader range of people and incidents to consider and recognize. This was important for them, as it helped to stimulate public engagement and approval for their project. It also did a great deal to alter and widen the recognition of everyday heroism beyond the narrow channels established by the State.

Before moving on to examine the work of the Hero Fund in more detail, it is important to acknowledge that it was not the only organization at the time to award to considerably higher numbers of people or adopt a broader and more varied model of heroism than that constructed by the State.

Between 1908 and 1914, the Royal Humane Society (RHS) made over 6000 awards including 960 bronze medals, 4044 testimonials on either parchment or vellum and 1023 pecuniary awards.[47] It is fair to say that the RHS did differ from both the State and the Hero Fund in that its awards, and in particular its pecuniary awards, were not solely restricted to what would have been considered acts of heroism. The Society was founded in 1774 by two physicians, Dr William Hawes and Dr Thomas Cogan, and started life as 'The Institution for affording immediate relief to persons apparently dead from drowning'. It became The Humane Society in 1776 and the Royal Humane Society when it received the patronage of King George III in 1787. The Society's interest in preventing death from drowning derived from its wider purpose of investigating, establishing and promoting means of resuscitation. Consequently, awards could be given to those who had recovered an individual from water and attempted to resuscitate them, as long as they had used RHS approved methods, regardless of whether or not their own life had been at risk.

However, the RHS medals, and to a lesser extent the testimonials, were most often given for exceptional attempts to save life and as these rescues usually included personal risk to the rescuer, they would have been perceived as representing acts of heroism rather than simply life-saving. This is further substantiated by the fact that one of the approved inscriptions for the bronze medal was 'The Royal Humane Society presented this gift to [name] his life having been exposed to danger.'[48] Although it was, to some extent, a secondary element to its work, the RHS recognized a substantial number of civilian heroism cases between 1908 and 1914, an average of 145 medals per year plus testimonials, which although slightly less than the Hero Fund is still substantially more than that recognized by the State. Its work was, though, almost exclusively restricted to cases involving drowning or asphyxiation and, therefore, although it made a great many awards to a wide range of people, its contribution to the public perception and understanding of the construction of everyday heroism was, to some extent, limited to a particular type of incident.

Another organization that although less prolific than the RHS and the Hero Fund still recognized considerably more individuals than the State was the Society for the Protection of Life from Fire (SPLF). The Society was formed in 1836, received Royal patronage in 1837 but lost it again in 1901 when King Edward declined to renew it after the death of Queen Victoria. In its 1837 annual report, the Society stated its purpose as 'the preservation of Life from Fire, by organising a body of men who shall be provided with . . . public fire escapes . . . and also by exciting Fireman, Policemen and others to a prompt attention to the scene of danger – by holding out rewards, as the merit of the case may deserve.'[49] Its main work at this time was the provision and maintenance of fire escapes at around eighty central London locations and although individual actions were important, it was certainly life-saving from fire rather than heroism that was paramount to the Society.

However, in 1865, the Metropolitan Fire Brigade Act placed the responsibility of providing an efficient fire brigade onto the Metropolitan Board of Works and the equipment and staff of the SPLF was absorbed into the new organization. Consequently, by 1908 the remit of the Society had changed, and was now stated as, 'promoting the Protection of Life from Fire, by the grant of rewards for saving life from fire, to persons who shall have distinguished themselves or received injury while engaged in the rescue of life from fire.'[50] This specific definition of its work, with an emphasis on the risk to life or exertions of the rescuer rather than just the attempt to save life, places the rewards given by the society into the realm of heroism, rather than simply life-saving.

In the period 1908 to 1914, the SPLF recognized 547 individuals with awards including eighty-one bronze and forty-six silver medals, eighteen silver watches and 293 certificates.[51] With an average of seventy-eight awards a year, the SPLF was considerably more prolific in its recognition of civilian heroism than the State and even if only the medals it awarded are considered, it still presented an average of eighteen a year compared to the average of six Albert Medals a year presented during the same period. As with the RHS, it can be argued that the contribution of the SPLF to the development of the idea of everyday heroism, while nevertheless very important, was limited to one type of incident.

The Hero Fund was certainly working alongside these organizations and there would, undoubtedly, have been communication between them regarding suitable cases. It was also not unknown for individuals to be recognized by more than one organization, if the circumstances allowed. There were, though, several major differences between the Hero Fund and these other organizations. First, the RHS and the SPLF both relied upon public subscriptions and this, inevitably, meant that they were, to some extent, reliant upon their subscribers for their funding and also answerable to them for their actions and the decisions they took. The Hero Fund Trustees, on the other hand, although answerable to Carnegie, had a high level of autonomy and, although Carnegie was an exacting task-master, there was no shortage of money and his objective was, in many ways, a straightforward one.

A second difference was that the Hero Fund was not restricted in terms of the incidents it recognized, and therefore, awards could be made to heroic acts of every conceivable nature. One implication of this was that it established far wider boundaries for what was considered to be everyday heroism. For example, preventing someone from being killed by tackling a runaway horse was highly unlikely to merit an Albert Medal and would have been outside of the remit of the RHS and SPLF. Yet it was something that the Hero Fund could recognize and, as a result, such acts became regarded as heroic when they might not have otherwise. A second implication was that it removed a specific element of qualification and this meant that different elements of the acts could be differently weighted when making decisions. For example, the SPLF was solely concerned with acts relating to fires and, as that was their principle qualification, it carried a certain amount of weight in the decision-making process. The Hero Fund Trustees, however, were not bounded by such qualifications and were at liberty to base their judgements on a wider range of factors.

A third difference was that the Hero Fund was making pecuniary awards rather than presenting medals and certificates. This is not to suggest that these other organizations did not provide financial support or reward because it is clear from their records that they did. But, unlike the Hero Fund, it was an exception rather than a rule, and their methods of recognition were, generally speaking, much more in keeping with those more usually related to the recognition of heroism. As discussed below, the pecuniary element of the work of the Hero Fund was contentious and did cause problems for the Trustees, which was something the other organizations did not have to contend with. In terms of the development of the idea of everyday heroism, the implication was that the bestowal of money in relation to an act of heroism became a contested point and stimulated thought and discussion about exactly how heroism should be recognized and understood. While the Hero Fund was certainly not acting in isolation and the extent and scope of its work was not unique, it did stand somewhat apart from other organizations undertaking similar work. Most notably, it effectively extended the boundaries of what could be considered heroic and, as a result, it set out a new landscape of the types of acts, and individuals, who could and should be considered heroic.

The volume and reach of Hero Fund awards

The Albert Medal was almost exclusively awarded to men with women representing just 2.5 per cent of the awards (see Table 5). A further breakdown of the figures demonstrates that it was not just men that predominated, but adult men, with only one award out of 238 going to a boy. It could be argued that this was simply reflective of the cases being put forward and that women and children could not be recognized simply because they were not being nominated. However, this is not the case, as an examination of all nominations demonstrates that, while they were still very much in the minority, women and children *were* being nominated but more often than not their applications were refused.[52] Evidence suggests that, with the Albert Medal, this stemmed from a belief that, due to their perceived weaknesses, acts undertaken by women inherently represented a lower standard than those undertaken by men and honouring such acts would devalue the award (this issue is discussed in more detail in Chapter 5). It can be reasoned that this was probably also the influencing factor with regard to acts undertaken by children and that awarding Albert Medals to them was also viewed as lowering the overall prestige of the award. The Albert Medal was to be reserved only for recognizing the very pinnacle of civilian heroism and in the eyes of those making the awards, acts of that nature were the preserve of men.

However, this was not an opinion shared by the Hero Fund Trustees. Although the vast majority of awards still went to men, there was significantly more recognition for the acts of women and children (see Table 5). Out of the 96.5 per cent of awards made to men, 8.4 per cent of these were boys under the age of 16. From the remaining 3.5 per cent of total awards, adult women account for 2.7 per cent while girls under the age of sixteen make up the remainder. Unfortunately, the records for refused or rejected cases for the Hero Fund are not as detailed as for the Albert Medal and it is therefore not possible to determine if the increased recognition of women and children stemmed from higher levels of nominations or a greater willingness on the part of the Trustees to recognize such acts. However, it has been shown that the Hero Fund proactively sought out cases rather than solely relying on nominations and therefore the increased numbers of women and children suggests that, either way, the Trustees regarded such individuals as more than suitable candidates for recognition, unlike the undersecretaries at the Home Office.

An examination of occupations also reveals that the Trustees of the Hero Fund were less restrictive and more open-minded than the Home Office undersecretaries about the status of those that they recognized. The relatively low number of Albert Medal awards made to men (232) means that the occupation of each individual can be shown (see Table 6). However, with the Hero Fund, the large numbers of subtly different occupations recorded, including job titles such as Professional Football Player, Tube Sweeper and even a Donkey Proprietor's Assistant, means that it would be

Table 5 Number and percentage of men, women and minors who received the Albert Medal (AM) or awards from the Carnegie Hero Fund Trust (CHFT) or the Society for the Protection of Life from Fire (SPLF)

Award	Period	Total awards	Male adult	%	Female adult	%	Male minor	%	Female minor	%
AM	1866–1914	238	231	97.1	6	2.5	1	0.4	0	0.0
CHFT	1908–1914	1355	1194	88.1	37	2.7	114	8.4	10	0.7
SPLF	1908–1914	547	439	80.2	84	15.4	14	2.6	10	1.8

Sources: Home Office (HO) and Board of Trade (BT) documents, The National Archives; CHFT Annual Reports, British Library; SPLF Annual Reports, London Metropolitan Archives.

Table 6 Occupations of men who received the Albert Medal (AM) or awards from the Carnegie Hero Fund Trust (CHFT) and the Society for the Protection of Life from Fire (SPLF)

Occupation	AM	%	Occupation	CHFT	%	Occupation	SPLF	%
Mine worker	36	15.6	Other	172	18.8	Police officer	180	42.1
Seaman	35	15.2	Mine worker	119	13.0	Other	62	14.5
Soldier	34	14.7	Police officer	94	10.3	Labourer	38	8.9
Naval seaman	25	10.8	Labourer	80	8.7	Fireman	27	6.3
Manager	16	6.9	Fisherman	74	8.1	Mine worker	11	2.6
Not given	15	6.5	Seaman	69	7.5	Soldier	10	2.3
Coastguard	8	3.5	Workman	40	4.4	Engineer	8	1.9
Railway worker	8	3.5	Railway worker	35	3.8	Clerk	7	1.6
Civil servant	7	3.0	Coastguard	26	2.8	Manager	5	1.2
Labourer	7	3.0	Boatman	17	1.9	Milkman	5	1.2
Workman	7	3.0	Clerk	16	1.7	Gardener	4	0.9
Engineer	5	2.2	Manager	16	1.7	Plumber	4	0.9
Police officer	4	1.7	Farm worker	13	1.4	Porter	4	0.9
Boatman	2	0.9	Foreman	12	1.3	Railway worker	4	0.9
Doctor	2	0.9	Engineer	11	1.2	Scaffolder	4	0.9
Farmer	2	0.9	Blacksmith	10	1.1	Seaman	4	0.9
Accountant	1	0.4	Carter	10	1.1	Bus conductor	3	0.7

(continued)

Table 6 (continued)

Occupation	AM	%	Occupation	CHFT	%	Occupation	SPLF	%
Artisan	1	0.4	Postman	10	1.1	Fisherman	3	0.7
Asylum attendant	1	0.4	Carpenter	9	1.0	Furrier	3	0.7
Blacksmith	1	0.4	Joiner	7	0.8	Vegetable dealer	3	0.7
Cinema proprietor	1	0.4	Coachman	6	0.7	Workman	3	0.7
Clergyman	1	0.4	School teacher	6	0.7	Baker	2	0.5
Diver	1	0.4	Soldier	6	0.7	Carpenter	2	0.5
Lock keeper	1	0.4	Crane worker	5	0.5	Commercial traveller	2	0.5
Merchant	1	0.4	Butcher	3	0.3	Cooper	2	0.5
Mines inspector	1	0.4	Doctor	3	0.3	Dairyman	2	0.5
Newspaper lad	1	0.4	Moulder	3	0.3	Decorator	2	0.5
Painter	1	0.4	Painter	3	0.3	Greengrocer	2	0.5
Plumber	1	0.4	Porter	3	0.3	Horse keeper	2	0.5
Postman	1	0.4	Rescue worker	3	0.3	House painter	2	0.5
Sailmaker	1	0.4	Shop worker	3	0.3	Joiner	2	0.5
Salesman	1	0.4	Stevedore	3	0.3	Motor driver	2	0.5
School teacher	1	0.4	Baker	2	0.2	Painter	2	0.5

Occupation	No.	%
Waiter	1	0.4
Total	**231**	
Minor	1	
Total	**232**	

Occupation	No.	%
Bath attendant	2	0.2
Boilermaker	2	0.2
Bricklayer	2	0.2
Commercial traveller	2	0.2
Electrician	2	0.2
Iron dresser	2	0.2
Mill worker	2	0.2
Plasterer	2	0.2
Plumber	2	0.2
Roadman	2	0.2
Slater	2	0.2
Tinsmith	2	0.2
Wheelwright	2	0.2
Woodsawer	2	0.2
Total	**917**	
Minor	114	
Not given	277	
Total	**1308**	

Occupation	No.	%
Paperhanger	2	0.5
Shop worker	2	0.5
Victualler	2	0.5
Clergyman	1	0.2
Coastguard	1	0.2
Doctor	1	0.2
Domestic servant	1	0.2
Postman	1	0.2
School teacher	1	0.2
Total	**428**	
Minor	14	
Not given	11	
Total	**453**	

Sources: Home Office (HO) and Board of Trade (BT) documents, The National Archives; CHFT Annual Reports, British Library; SPLF Annual Reports, London Metropolitan Archives.

impractical and unwieldy to list them all. Therefore, only occupations that are attributed to two or more individuals have been tabled; the rest being classified as 'other'. Notwithstanding this approach, what is immediately apparent from the figures is that Hero Fund awarded to a far greater and more diverse range of occupations than the Home Office.

A more detailed breakdown shows that, of those awarded the Albert Medal, 25 per cent were servicemen and a further 10 per cent were made up by managers and civil servants while labourers, workmen and engineers only make up 8 per cent collectively. Conversely, labourers, workmen and engineers account for 14 per cent of Hero Fund awards while civil servants are absent and managers represent less than 2 per cent. Although mine workers top the Albert Medal list with thirty-six medals awarded, this is somewhat misleading as this represents recognition on just nine occasions, with thirty-one of the awards being derived from just four large-scale mining disasters.[53] In comparison, the 119 awards to mine workers by the Hero Fund are derived from recognition on sixty-nine different occasions and forty-nine of these were separate incidents, albeit not all actually in mines. The lack of police officers and fireman in the Albert Medal list is not surprising as the Crown had introduced The King's Police and Fire Brigades Medal in 1909 to recognize bravery by those individuals. For the Hero Fund, it might be expected to find a range of emergency service personnel in the list, but this is not the case. Police officers do account for 10 per cent, but others including coastguards and rescue workers and firemen are almost entirely absent. With regard to police officers, it was not necessarily that they were more likely to be heroic or more often in a position to undertake acts considered to be heroic. The official and hierarchical structure within which they worked meant that cases were more likely to be recorded and recognized, and the Hero Fund had been proactive in establishing direct lines of communication with Police forces across the country so cases were less likely to be overlooked.

With regard to women, the exceptionally small sample group for the Albert Medal limits the comparative usefulness of female occupation data (see Table 7). Nonetheless, out of the six Albert Medal cases, five noted the occupation although two of these were listed as housewife and therefore not formally a paid occupation. Of the remaining three, two were nurses and one a school teacher. Both of these occupations were, arguably, professional careers more than simply paid work but the small sample size precludes the formulation of any other useful analysis. What is striking is that domestic servants do not feature at all with regard to the Albert Medal whereas they top the list for Hero Fund awards to women. Given that domestic service was the largest employer of women during this period, it seems reasonable that it would feature highly yet not one Albert Medal was presented to such an individual.[54] This was not solely related to the decision of the undersecretaries as only one of the nineteen nominations for women was on behalf of a domestic servant. It would appear that, where the Albert Medal was concerned, neither the nominating public nor the Home Office undersecretaries considered female domestic servants as suitable candidates for recognition. Yet it is clear that, relatively often, they undertook acts perceived by many to be heroic and were duly recognized as such.

It is interesting to briefly note, by way of comparison, that the SPLF recognized more cases of female heroism than the Hero Fund and this was probably related to the nature of their work. Although it did actually give many awards simply in recognition of heroic action, the Hero Fund was officially established to provide pecuniary support to those in need and primarily individuals (or their dependants) who could not work due to incapacity. This inevitably shifted its focus onto paid workers or breadwinners who were, in the majority of cases, men. However, the SPLF was, by its very nature, only concerned with acts undertaken at fires and judging from the causes given for the incidents which led to awards, the majority of these were domestic rather than industrial fires (see Table 8). Many were the result of lamps and stoves being upset, carelessness with candles or children playing with fire, all incidents which more often than not occurred in the home. There were also a large number of cases where flammable materials, particularly those used in ladies' dresses, were ignited by either candles or lamps. Grouped together (those marked (D) on Table 8), this variety of causes can be described as domestic incidents and collectively they account for 90 per cent of the awards made to women by the SPLF. The disparity in female recognition stems more from the circumstances of the incidents recognized than it does from the motives of the organizations. By and large, men were more likely to encounter mining or industrial accidents or be around harbours or railways, while women spent more time in the domestic sphere of the home where, it would appear, accidents involving fires were particularly common. It is also interesting to note that the Albert Medal covered all of these types of incidents, yet it was still overwhelmingly awarded to men, something discussed in more detail in Chapter 5.

It was not just women who were overlooked by the State, but also minors. Defined for the purposes of this study as those under sixteen years of age, only one boy received the Albert Medal between 1866 and 1914, despite eight boys and one girl being nominated. This is in stark contrast to the Hero Fund, which, between 1908 and 1914, made awards to 114 boys and 10 girls (see Table 5). Table 9 shows the breakdown of the type of awards given to minors in relation to the reason stated and while, unfortunately, 'no reason given' dominates the statistics, there are also some other items of note. Minors were far more likely to be given just an honorary award than an adult (58% minors, 20% adults), which suggests that the Trustees were not comfortable with making monetary awards to minors for undertaking acts of heroism. In the case of an award made directly to the individual, with minors they were more likely to award a pension rather than a one-off payment than they were with an adult (13% minors, 3% adults). When the Trustees did make these pension payments, they were almost always for the purposes of providing educational support, either through schooling or practical instruction such as an apprenticeship. In general, it would appear that the Hero Fund was much more reluctant to reward minors with money than it was with adults and when it did reward with money it was far more conscious of ensuring that it was targeted at education rather than simply presented as a one-off payment.

Again, it is interesting to compare the Hero Fund with the SPLF, which in 79 per cent of its awards to minors chose only to present an honorary token, in almost all cases a silver watch or a certificate, rather than a pecuniary payment (see Table 10). Another notable aspect of the recognition of minors by the SPLF is that in every case bar one, the minor was responsible for rescuing another minor, rather than rescuing an adult. Of course, it seems reasonable to assume that many incidents involving fire

Table 7 Occupations of women who received the Albert Medal (AM) or awards from the Carnegie Hero Fund Trust (CHFT) and the Society for the Protection of Life from Fire (SPLF)

Occupation	AM	%	Occupation	CHFT	%	Occupation	SPLF	%
Housewife	2	40.0	Domestic Servant	3	25.0	Domestic servant	7	18.4
Nurse	2	40.0	School teacher	3	25.0	Nurse	6	15.8
School teacher	1	20.0	Nurse	2	16.7	Charwoman	4	10.5
Total	**5**		Factory worker	1	8.3	School teacher	4	10.5
			Lady missionary	1	8.3	Lady's help	3	7.9
Not given	1		Newsagent	1	8.3	Dressmaker	2	5.3
Total	**6**		Weaver	1	8.3	Housekeeper	2	5.3
			Total	**12**		Laundress	2	5.3
						Spinster	2	5.3
			Minor	10		Clerk	1	2.6
			Not Given	25		Companion	1	2.6
			Total	**47**		Newsagent	1	2.6
						Private means	1	2.6

Scholar	1	2.6
Shop assistant	1	2.6
Total	**38**	
Minor	10	
Not given	46	
Total	**94**	

Sources: Home Office (HO) and Board of Trade (BT) documents, The National Archives; CHFT Annual Reports, British Library; SPLF Annual Reports, London Metropolitan Archives.

Table 8 Number and percentage of awards given by the Society for the Protection of Life from Fire (SPLF) between 1908 and 1914 and the nature of the incident

Cause of fire	All cases	%	Cause of fire	Female cases	%
Clothing caught alight (D)	80	23.1	Clothing caught alight (D)	30	39.0
Lamp or stove incident (D)	72	20.8	Children playing with fire (D)	19	24.7
Children playing with fire (D)	63	18.2	Lamp or stove incident (D)	15	19.5
Candle incident (D)	44	12.7	Airing clothes (D)	3	3.9
Gas or petrol explosion	16	4.6	Other	3	3.9
Other	14	4.0	Candle incident (D)	2	2.6
Airing clothes (D)	9	2.6	Spark from fire	2	2.6
Spark from fire	9	2.6	Defective equipment	1	1.3
Match incident	8	2.3	Gas or petrol explosion	1	1.3
Defective equipment	7	2.0	Match incident	1	1.3
Tar boiling over	7	2.0	Arson	0	0.0
Arson	6	1.7	Boiler explosion	0	0.0
Electrical	5	1.4	Cigarette	0	0.0
Cigarette	4	1.2	Electrical	0	0.0
Boiler explosion	2	0.6	Tar boiling over	0	0.0
Total	**346**		**Total**	**77**	
No cause given	19		No cause given	3	
Cause given as unknown	182		Cause given as unknown	14	
Total	**547**		**Total**	**94**	

Source: SPLF Annual Reports, London Metropolitan Archives.

Table 9 Number of awards made to minors by the Carnegie Hero Fund Trust (CHFT) between 1908 and 1914 and the reason given for making the award

Reason for award	One-off payment to individual	Pension to individual	Pension to dependants	One-off payment to dependants	Honorary award only	No award recorded	Total
Convalescence	1	0	0	0	0	0	1
Educational support	0	14	0	0	0	0	14
Family support	0	0	1	2	0	0	3
Funeral expenses	0	0	1	2	0	0	3
Life-saving record	0	0	0	0	0	0	0
Loss of earnings	0	0	0	0	0	0	0
Losses sustained	0	0	0	0	0	0	0
No reason given	26	2	0	0	59	0	87
Recognition of action	2	0	0	0	13	0	15
Special circumstances	0	0	0	1	0	0	1
Total	**29**	**16**	**2**	**5**	**72**	**0**	**124**

Sources: CHFT Annual Reports, British Library.

Table 10 Nature of awards made to minors by the Carnegie Hero Fund Trust (CHFT) and the Society for the Protection of Life from Fire (SPLF) in comparison with awards of the Albert Medal (AM)

Type of award to children	AM	%	CHFT	%	SPLF	%
Honorary award only	1	100	72	58.1	19	79.2
One-off pecuniary payment	0	0	34	27.4	5	20.8
Pecuniary pension	0	0	18	14.5	0	0.0
Total	**1**		**124**		**24**	

Source: CHFT Annual Reports, British Library; SPLF Annual Reports, London Metropolitan Archives.

may have occurred when minors were either left alone or left to supervise one another and this could explain these statistics. However, it could equally suggest that the fact that a minor saved another minor rather than saving an adult had some bearing on the recognition of heroism. With the Albert Medal, it has been suggested that the heroism of minors was not perceived to be of the required standard and was not recognized due to concerns that it would lower the overall prestige of the decoration. Similar ideas may have been at work in the SPLF which was prepared to recognize the heroism of minors but only as long as it related to the rescue of other minors which was perceived to be an acceptable domain for them to occupy.

It is clear, then, that maximizing the number of potential awards was of key importance to the Hero Fund Trustees. In order to do so, they moved away from the limited State model of judging and assessing everyday heroism and, instead, adopted a more egalitarian approach that would broaden the field and encompass a wider, and more representative, social spectrum of society. One of the reasons why they were able to do this was because, unlike other organizations at the time, they were more or less unrestricted in terms of the types of acts and individuals that they could make awards to. They were also, unlike the Home Office, relatively unconcerned with limiting the number of awards they made and were proactive in identifying cases and encouraging nominations through publicity. It was not, though, just a case of them being more able than the Home Office to award to a greater and more varied range of individuals. It was also that they were more willing to do so and better positioned, both as individuals and as a group, to assess and evaluate cases in a more open and less judgemental manner.

'Empanelled as a jury': The Hero Fund Board of Trustees

The Carnegie Hero Fund Board of Trustees was made up of sixteen life Trustees, originally appointed by Carnegie; six members appointed by the Corporation of Dunfermline; and a further three appointed by the School Board of Dunfermline. The original Hero Fund life Trustees were all members of the 1903 Carnegie Dunfermline Trust's Board of Trustees and Carnegie had been adamant, when establishing the Dunfermline Trust, that 'there had to be representatives of the working class on the commission along with the more wealthy professional men and town and county officials.[55] Consequently, the sixteen men that took responsibility for the Hero Fund in 1908 were an eclectic mix of individuals and, as desired by Carnegie, covered the full spectrum of social standing.

At the top of the social ladder was the youthful aristocrat, Sir Edward James Bruce, 10th Earl of Elgin, 14th Earl of Kincardine and distant relative to King Robert II.[56] In the middling ranks, the public-serving Hay Shennan, a dedicated advocate who spent much of his career in Sheriff-Substitute positions and the Rev Robert Stevenson, 1st charge at Dunfermline Abbey.[57] Next, a clutch of middle-class professionals, Lawyers James Macbeth, one of Scotland's foremost practitioners of the Workmen's Compensation Act and solicitor to the miner's union and David Blair, who at his death aged ninety-two, was the oldest practising lawyer in Dunfermline.[58] The chairman of the Trust, Dr John Ross, described by Andrew Carnegie as 'emphatically the right man in the right place', had also had a career in law but was better known for his thirty-five-year association with the local school board and twenty years as Sheriff-Substitute. Ross was granted the freedom of Dunfermline in 1905 and awarded a Knighthood in 1921.[59] The Architect, Andrew Scobie had been responsible for designing Carnegie's first public swimming baths and was also noted for his designs for social housing, while Alan Smith Tuke, was a noted surgeon and local physician who pioneered the physical training and inspection of schoolchildren and set up the Dunfermline College of Hygiene and Physical Education.[60]

The other middle-class contingent of the committee was made up of local businessmen, most of who were connected with the damask linen industry. James Brown, aside from his wool dying business, was also one of the founders of the Fifeshire Property Investment and Building Society and an enthusiastic freemason, who went on to hold all principal offices in his lodge.[61] George Mathewson and Robert Walker helped to found the Dunfermline and West Fife hospital, while William Robertson served for four years on the town council and was president of the Dunfermline Rotary Club.[62] Although both involved in linen manufacture, Andrew Shearer was better known for his military career in which he rose to lieutenant colonel in the Royal Highlanders and Henry Beveridge for his purchase of Pitreavie Castle in 1884.[63] Albeit wealthy manufacturers by the time of their association with the Hero Fund, many of these men had worked their way up through the ranks of the business, such as Mathewson, who entered his father's firm as a joiner, then worked as a mechanic before progressing into warehousing where he learnt the financial aspects of the business.

Although in the minority, the Carnegie Hero Fund Board of Trustees did include two working-class individuals. John Hynd was a working miner and had worked at Rosebank Colliery for most of his life.[64] It is not clear exactly what the arrangements were for Hynd to attend Trustee meetings but it must be presumed that he was compensated in some way for his loss of earnings. Hynd was also a keen horticulturalist and Secretary of the Dunfermline Horticultural Society. The other Board member with a keen insight into working-class life was John Weir. Although no longer a working miner, Weir had worked below ground from the age of eleven until 1878 when, aged twenty-four, he was appointed interim president of the Fife and Kinross Miners Union. He went on to become president of the Union in 1880 and was described as 'a shrewd, cautious leader of men. Eminently practical and sane in his judgements, he rarely erred on questions affecting the welfare of those under his care'.[65] Elected as a Scottish trade union representative to the federation of labour convention in 1900, Weir was a strenuous advocate of the minimum wage and a consistent supporter of the conciliation board. In addition to his union work, Weir was also a manager of the Dunfermline and West Fife Hospital and served on the town council for eighteen years.

In comparison with the undersecretaries at the Home Office, most of whom were university-educated sons of wealthy industrialists or government officials, the Hero Fund Board of Trustees was certainly more balanced in its composition and, at least in part, closer in social standing to the people it was considering. Furthermore, speaking of the Trustees in their capacity as board members for the Dunfermline Trust, which carried out a wide and varied range of projects, Ross described how each of them 'undesignedly fell into groups according to our predilections for one department of work rather than another, and in each one of these it is not difficult to see that one Trustee is more expert than his fellows'.[66] However, with regard to the Hero Fund, Ross believed that 'we must feel that we are much more on a footing of equality. We must always remain empanelled as a jury, each with a vote of equal value, and not easily led by the foreman.' This is different to the situation in the Home Office where, although each undersecretary could give his opinion as to whether or not the medal should be awarded, the final overriding decision rested, in theory, with the monarch but in practice with the Secretary of State who could overrule as he chose. The danger of one man's will setting the agenda for the way the award was administered was, therefore, more prevalent at the Home Office than it was for the Hero Fund Board of Trustees.

The Hero Fund Trustees were also more willing to seek advice and guidance from different sections of society than the Home Office undersecretaries, who mostly liaised with police force Chief Constables or magistrates when seeking opinions on nominees or corroboration of eyewitness accounts. Although the Hero Fund Trustees claimed to 'know nothing of politics and shall commit ourselves to no opinions in respect to labour questions', they sent their introductory pamphlet to Trade Unions and those MPs that they understood as representing labour.[67] This, it was stated, was because these people would know the localities and occupations of the men they represented and would be 'conversant with the feelings of the working classes', from among which the Trust expected the largest number of heroes.[68] This expectation, one would imagine, stemmed more from the dangerous nature of working occupations at this time rather than from any notion that the working classes were inherently more heroic than any other class. It does, however, demonstrate that the Hero Fund Trustees were trying to reach balanced decisions informed by a wide range of different opinions and ones pertinent to the status of those being rewarded.

The Hero Fund Trustees were, as individuals, reasonably representative of a broader social spectrum and, as a group, more likely to be in touch with the attitudes of the general public (or more willing to identify and consider such attitudes before making their decisions) than those at the Home Office. As a result, the evidence suggests that they were more egalitarian and open minded about the individuals they were considering for recognition and more inclined to judge each case on its facts and merits rather than seek out faults or shortcomings. This was not, however, the attitude taken by everyone and the manner in which the fund operated, as well as its overall ethos, its objectives and the types of people it might potentially reward, attracted a significant level of criticism.

'Beset with plenty of difficulties': Problems and challenges faced by the Hero Fund

The founding of the Hero Fund in 1908 stimulated a great deal of press interest and not only were the details of the Fund reported as a news story, but many of the papers took time and space in their editorial columns to debate the pros and cons of Carnegie's latest philanthropic endeavour: 'The path of him who endeavours to show the practical side of his hero worship is beset with plenty of difficulties both of his own making and the making of others' was the view of one editor.[69] Examining the views expressed in these editorials about certain problems and challenges that the Hero Fund was perceived to generate provides an insight into what may have been some of the dominant public ideas about heroism at this time. Two key concerns appear most often: first, that the Hero Fund would unduly encourage or stimulate people to undertake acts of heroism and, second, that the provision of monetary awards rather than honorary ones, such as medals and certificates, would devalue and vulgarize the purity of the heroic act being recognized to the detriment of both the particular individual and heroism in general.

The *London Standard* raised what it termed, 'certain unpleasant consequences of self-advertisement and pretence' and cited the 'nauseating spectacle' of 'undoubtedly brave men tempted by money to display themselves on the music-hall stage' as one potential consequence of the fund that must be stringently guarded against.[70] The *Yorkshire Post* also highlighted that there were some 'who were never content unless they are in the limelight, and the acclamation which follows a gallant action in saving life is music to their ears', but assured its readers that 'happily [the Trust] is as little likely to deter as promote heroism'.[71] The general opinion proffered by the editorials was that the Trust would not, and largely because it was not possible to, encourage heroism; 'Heroism will never be "encouraged" into being and the "encouragement" of heroes, we take it, is no part of Mr Carnegie's design', being the opinion of the *Dundee Advertiser*, or as the *London Standard* put it, 'we do not so far insult Mr Carnegie's understanding as to suppose that he expects to make a single hero the more by his great gift'.[72]

The second concern that aroused the press was that the Trust appeared to be offering money in return for acts of heroism and this located it in the realm of reward, rather than recognition, which was a position that some were uncomfortable with. The *Aberdeen Free Press* editorial was particularly critical, asking, 'will Mr Carnegie's well intentioned endowment of heroism be for good or evil?' Heroism, it argued, was its own greatest reward and while it accepted that such heroism should be acknowledged it accused Carnegie of creating an 'intimation in advance that heroism will be paid for'. This, by associating heroism with monetary reward in the public mind, would effectively 'take the bloom off heroism'.[73] Others, while raising concerns about the reward aspect of the awards, were confident that the true nature of heroism, as they saw it, would out. *The Scotsman*, for example, was resolute that the purpose of the fund was 'not to give pecuniary rewards for heroic action' as 'honourable and public recognition is the only fitting reward for heroic conduct'; anything else, it believed, would amount to the 'vulgarisation of heroism' and a 'degradation of the heroic'.[74]

Carnegie's defence was that his fund provided pensions or support only to those who required it, rather than rewarding all who performed acts of heroism. As Carnegie himself noted in the early period of the Hero Fund,

> It is said that heroism cannot be purchased. This is quite true and the founder knew this perfectly – and had no such purpose in view. It is simply for rewarding Heroism after it is performed and where the hero or those dependant upon him suffer injury or require assistance. In that case, the Carnegie Fund steps forward and provides that he and they suffer no loss.[75]

Carnegie was arguing that, rather than trading in the vulgar or degrading business of rewarding heroism, his Hero Fund undertook benevolent and justified recognition of heroism by supporting heroes or their families in the event of the individual being injured or killed while undertaking a heroic act. This approach attracted no criticism from the Press which reveals that it was not necessarily pecuniary awards that it disagreed with but the reasons why they were awarded. Furthermore, this is clearly demonstrated in the attitudes towards other non-State organizations.

Both the RHS and the SPLF gave pecuniary awards in relation to acts of civilian heroism yet neither appears to have attracted criticism of their policy. One element to this was that both organizations were primarily concerned with the saving of life, and therefore, the pecuniary awards were perceived to be rewarding life-saving rather than explicitly heroism, something which, it would appear, was considered acceptable. The RHS, in particular, placed no qualification on the rescuer's risk to life when making pecuniary awards and reserved their bronze and silver medals for cases they considered heroic for that reason, thus avoiding any accusations of rewarding heroism with money. The SPLF, on the other hand, openly stated that 'income [was] devoted to rewarding meritorious services', and that, in 1908, the remit of the organization was 'the grant of rewards for saving life from fire, to persons who shall have distinguished themselves or received injury while engaged in the rescue of life from fire, either by the gift of medals, testimonials, or sums of money'.[76] This description, with its focus on the behaviour or risk to life of the rescuer rather than just the act of life-saving places the work of the organization firmly into the realm of recognizing and rewarding heroism, yet it attracted no criticism for its actions. The best explanation that can be forwarded for this is that the SPLF was a relatively small organization, and one that had originated in 1865 with far different objectives to those it pursued in 1908. Consequently, its actions of rewarding civilian heroism with money were either just overlooked or the organization was still perceived as one that dealt more with fire prevention and safety than with heroism.

Part of the reason why the Carnegie Hero Fund attracted criticism was because its pecuniary awards were specifically targeted at 'heroes' as opposed to those who saved life and the Press appear to have had clear ideas about what motivated heroism. 'Men and women do not perform deeds of heroism for the sake of monetary reward; they do it because it is their nature to,' stated the *Sheffield Daily Telegraph* and the *Yorkshire*

Post was confident that 'all the rewards that can be promised to heroes will not promote heroism . . . a man will not speculate before taking the plunge . . . he will be brave, if he is built that way, because he can not help it . . . human nature will not be influenced by rewards of decorations and money'.[77] The *Dunfermline Press* was more concise in its evaluation that 'those who would calculate on such an award are not of the stuff of which heroes and heroines are made of' and the *Daily Express* colourfully explained that the fund would not result in the manufacture of 'pseudo-heroes' because, 'no chicken-hearted loafer will dive into the Regent's Canal to save a drowning child in order to share in the Carnegie Fund'. It also added that it might be a benefit if the Trust was to have this effect as 'the loafer would, without question, be a better man after his dive'.[78]

The criticisms of the Hero Fund reveal the Press' disdain for the encouragement and pecuniary reward of civilian heroism. The reasoning behind this is revealed in one editorial which stated that 'the great virtue of heroism is that it is purely spontaneous, the outcome of noble self-denying impulse. It is the element of overmastering altruism which promotes heroism.'[79] This reflects the attitudes and opinions of those administering the Albert Medal, who viewed sound moral character and pure motive to be the defining characteristics of those who undertook truly heroic acts. This explains why the Press viewed the actions of the Hero Fund to be so potentially damaging to the concept of heroism. Offering pecuniary rewards introduced an alternative and selfish motive for undertaking an act of heroism and one which would appeal to those of deficient moral character who might be looking only to their own benefit. Pecuniary awards presented in relation to injuries sustained or even death were acceptable because such individuals had displayed the ultimate altruism in their wiliness to suffer for others, but those who escaped unscathed were perceived as less than true heroes. Of course, it was suggested that such individuals as the 'chicken-hearted loafer' would not undertake heroic acts in the first place because of their deficient moral character, but there was still the fear that widespread pecuniary rewards would eventually dilute or contaminate the pure motives that stimulated true heroism.

Ironically, it would appear that the Press was correct in suggesting that the Hero Fund would ultimately be rewarding heroism rather than solely recognizing it through the practical support of pensions and compensatory payments. The Trust essentially gave three types of award, a pecuniary award directly to the individual, a pecuniary award to the dependants of the individual and an honorary or 'token' award which was given (either on its own or in addition to a pecuniary award) both directly to the individual or to the dependants. Pecuniary awards consisted of either a one-off payment or a type of pension whereby payments were made on a regular basis for a specific period of time. The honorary awards were objects such as watches or certificates as well as the Trust's medallion (see Table 11). Table 12 shows the breakdown of the total awards in relation to the type of award given. The majority of payments made (67%) were one-off cash payments made directly to the hero or heroine, with honorary awards accounting for nearly 20 per cent and pensions (either to the individual or to dependants) and one-off payments to dependants accounting for just under 13 per cent. With over 80 per cent of the cases involving a monetary award of some kind, it is clear that although it did on occasions give honorary awards, the core of the Trust's work was, just as it had set out to be, pecuniary in nature.

Table 11 Number and type of honorary awards given by the Carnegie Hero Fund Trust (CHFT) between 1908 and 1914

Type of honorary award	Honorary award only awarded	In addition to pecuniary award	Total
Honorary certificate	38	274	312
Inscribed watch	179	83	262
Watch	23	22	45
Medallion	17	22	39
Memorial medallion	8	23	31
Memorial certificate	0	19	19
Other	1	0	1
Total	**266**	**443**	**709**

Source: CHFT Annual Reports, British Library.

Table 12 Number and percentage of the type of awards given by the Carnegie Hero Fund Trust (CHFT) between 1908 and 1914

Type of award	Awards given	%
One-off payment to individual	911	67.2
Pension to an individual	41	3.0
One-off payment to dependants	27	1.9
Pension to dependants	107	7.9
Honorary award only	266	19.6
No award recorded	3	0.2
Total	**1355**	

Source: CHFT Annual Reports, British Library.

However, when giving details of the cases in the Annual Report, it was not uncommon for the reason for the award to be explicitly stated, such as 'awarded £5 in recognition of his action' or 'awarded £10 to compensate him for losses sustained in the act'. These explicitly stated reasons provide an interesting insight into the motives of the Trustees when making certain types of awards, as shown in Table 13. This table provides a breakdown of each type of award in relation to the reason given for making it. Only where a reason was explicitly given has it been recorded and unfortunately, as can be seen, there were 833 cases in which no reason was explicitly given. This problem, and an attempt to reconcile the data, will be discussed below. Also, in three cases the details of the award were not recorded and it has not been possible to ascertain the type of award made through recourse to other sources such as the press reports.

Table 13 Number of awards made by the Carnegie Hero Fund Trust (CHFT) between 1908 and 1914 and the reason given for making the award

Reason for award	One-off payment to individual	Pension to individual	Pension to dependants	One-off payment to dependants	Honorary award	No award recorded	Total
Convalescence	9	4	1	1	0	0	15
Educational support	1	15	0	0	0	0	16
Family support	0	0	102	19	0	0	121
Funeral expenses	0	0	1	3	0	0	4
Life-saving record	1	0	0	0	0	0	1
Loss of earnings	23	15	2	1	0	0	41
Losses sustained	59	0	0	1	0	0	60
No reason given	632	4	0	0	194	3	833
Recognition of action	179	2	1	1	72	0	255
Special circumstances	7	1	0	1	0	0	9
Total	**911**	**41**	**107**	**27**	**266**	**3**	**1355**

Source: CHFT Annual Reports, British Library.

Although the omission of explicit reasons in such a large number of cases is a distinct disadvantage, a fair idea of the approach of the Trustees can still be obtained.

With regard to both pensions and one-off payments made to the dependants of heroes and heroines, there are few surprises in the results. In the overwhelming majority of cases where a pension was given to dependants, it was done in order to support the family due to the loss of the main breadwinner and this is also reflected in relation to one-off payments to dependants. One-off payments instead of pensions were almost always given to dependants who were awaiting a financial settlement, for example under the regulations of the Workman's Compensation Act or from an employer, and needed short-term relief rather than long-term assistance. The reasons given for the pensions made directly to the individual who undertook the act are also those which might be expected with 'loss of earnings' and 'convalescence' accounting for around 46 per cent of the awards. This was, essentially, what the Trust was set up to do, namely support those who could no longer support themselves on account of undertaking an act of heroism. The Trust also gave pensions for 'educational support' and these awards were predominantly made to individuals under the age of sixteen and were intended to support either an academic or practical education. What, though, about the one-off cash payments, made directly to heroic individuals, that was attracting so much negative attention.

The one-off cash payment made directly to the individual is particularly interesting as not only did it, surprisingly, account for the majority of the awards made (67%) but also because it was frequently given for (in terms of the Fund) a controversial reason. Table 14 isolates the figures for one-off payments to individuals and the reasons why

Table 14 Number of one-off payments awarded to individuals by the Carnegie Hero Fund Trust (CHFT) between 1908 and 1914 and the reason given for making the award

Reason for award	One-off payment to individual	%
No reason given	632	69.4
Recognition of action	179	19.6
Losses sustained	59	6.5
Loss of earnings	23	2.5
Convalescence	9	1.0
Special circumstances	7	0.8
Educational support	1	0.1
Life-saving record	1	0.1
Family support	0	0.0
Funeral expenses	0	0.0
Total	**911**	

Source: CHFT Annual Reports, British Library.

they were awarded and, as can be seen, the table is dominated by the 632 awards (69%) where no explicit reason was given. Aside from these, the next most often cited reason for giving a one-off payment was 'in recognition of action' which accounted for 20 per cent of the awards. With 'loss of earnings', 'losses sustained' and 'convalescence' accounting in total for just 10 per cent of the awards it starts to look as though one-off payments were primarily given to reward what someone had done, rather than to relieve them of any particular loss. However, the high number of awards for which no explicit reason was recorded has a significant bearing on the validity of such a conclusion. Completely discounting these cases and recalculating the percentages from the new total is one approach to the problem, but it would be a blunt and less than satisfactory solution. What is required, then, is evidence as to whether or not any of the 'no reason' cases could have been given in recognition of action and, if so, how many.

Well, in 309 of the 632 awards in which a one-off payment was made but no reason was given, the Trustees also chose to make an honorary award in addition to the pecuniary one. It could be argued that these cases, with the additional mark of admiration in the shape of a separate honorary gift, demonstrate that the payment was intended as reward rather than assistance. If these 309 awards are reclassified as being 'in recognition of action' rather than 'no reason', the number of one-off payments to individuals given in recognition of action rises to 83 per cent (see Table 15).

Of course this still leaves 323 awards for which no reason can be satisfactorily determined and if, for arguments sake, all of these *were* given to compensate for losses sustained or earnings lost, then the picture would be a very different one (recognition of action would still just predominate but only with 54% rather than 83% of the total). However, examining the sums involved in one-off payments suggests that they were

Table 15 Number of one-off payments awarded to individuals by the Carnegie Hero Fund Trust (CHFT) between 1908 and 1914 and the reason given for making the award (with figures for cases adjusted to include honorary awards as recognition of action and percentages recalculated)

Reason for award	One-off payment to individual	%
Recognition of action	488	83.0
Losses sustained	59	10.0
Loss of earnings	23	3.9
Convalescence	9	1.5
Special circumstances	7	1.2
Educational support	1	0.2
Life-saving record	1	0.2
Family support	0	0.0
Funeral expenses	0	0.0
Total	**588**	

Source: CHFT Annual Reports, British Library.

unlikely to have been made for those reasons (see Table 16). In over 80 per cent of the cases, the one-off payment was either £5 or £10, both very exact figures, and would appear to represent a 'token' payment rather than an exact compensatory figure based upon an actual loss. It could be that the Trustees simply decided to 'round-up' the sum required to replace a suit of clothes and a pair of boots or a period of time without wages, but these sums appear to be not only round but also generous for such purposes. What is more likely is that these payments were being given to recognize that the person was considered to have displayed behaviour that deserved it; in essence, a 'well done' for doing what they did and as such, it should be seen as a reward, rather than practical support.

Table 16 Sum of money awarded by the Carnegie Hero Fund Trust (CHFT) in the case of a one-off payment to an individual and the number of times that sum was awarded between 1908 and 1914

Payment	Awards	%
£5	435	47.7
£10	319	35.0
£3	53	5.8
£15	38	4.1
£20	26	2.8
£2	10	1.1
£25	6	0.6
£7	5	0.5
£30	2	0.2
£1	1	0.1
£4	1	0.1
£11	1	0.1
£12	1	0.1
£21	1	0.1
£40	1	0.1
£50	1	0.1
Other	10	1.1
Total	**911**	

Source: CHFT Annual Reports, British Library.

This position is also substantiated by an editorial piece in the *Dunfermline Press*, 25 November 1911. The work of the Trust was well underway by this point and somewhere in the region of 700 awards had been made, the majority of which the *Press* had reported on. However, the editorial was critical of the manner in which the Trust was carrying out its duties,

> As for the question of money awards, these should be discountenanced as much as possible. Mr Carnegie did not found the Trust for the purpose of giving a pound note to a man who might stop a runaway horse. The main purpose of the fund is to secure that those who have been injured, and the dependants of those who have lost their lives in attempting to preserve or rescue their fellows; "should be freed from pecuniary cares resulting from such heroism". . . we think it would be a wise rule to limit the money payments to cases where a personal injury or loss has been caused.[80]

This editorial demonstrates that the one-off pecuniary payments being made in relation to people who had not been injured or killed were, in keeping with the stance taken by the Press in 1908, still viewed as being a wholly unsuitable way to recognize civilian heroism; yet this seems to have been the mainstay of the Hero Fund's work.

It is curious that while the Hero Fund, according to Carnegie himself, was conceived and established with the explicit remit of providing pecuniary support where needed, it moved so quickly into giving reward where merited. It could be argued that this was simply down to economics as it quickly became clear to the Trustees that Carnegie's endowment of £12,500 a year was far in excess of what was required. Coupled with the fact that the Trustees had distributed around 9000 copies of the leaflet promoting its work and soliciting cases of possible heroism, there were, as illustrated above, no shortage of acts to recognize or money to reward them. Moreover, Carnegie himself had stipulated to Ross, in no uncertain terms, that the Trust had to seek publicity for its work by getting the details of awards into the press and presumably when there was nobody in need of assistance, other awards were made to fill the gap. The human element must also not be overlooked and it is likely that the Trustees were considering somewhere in the region of twenty-five cases a month. While a small percentage of these would probably have been cases where the risk was so low or the act so mundane that it did not merit reward, the majority would have been acts where an individual had put themselves at considerable risk to save others. Such stories must have moved the Trustees, who were not bureaucrats or government officials, and limiting themselves to only recognizing those who had been injured or killed, while disregarding the remarkable bravery or heroism of those who had not was, perhaps, just something they felt unable to do.

The 'false heroes of barbarism': The Hero Fund and the quest for world peace

Before concluding this examination of the Hero Fund, there is one important aspect of Andrew Carnegie's life and work that needs to be considered in more detail as it is one that was highly influential in his decision to establish his heroism projects. Carnegie placed little restriction on who could receive awards, although by stating that 'whenever heroism is displayed by man or woman in saving human life in peaceful pursuits the fund applies,' he ensured that servicemen were excluded.[81] This decision was related to Carnegie's other great enthusiasm, alongside philanthropy, during his retirement years, namely his quest for world peace. Between 1904 and 1914, Carnegie gifted over $25 million to the cause of achieving world peace.[82] This money was spent on, among other things; establishing a Church Peace Union that called upon all religions to work together for peace; constructing three 'Peace Palaces', including the International Court of Justice at The Hague, dedicated to encouraging dialogue and justice between nations; and finally in 1910, founding the Carnegie Endowment for International Peace with its professed aim 'to hasten the abolition of international war'.[83]

As with philanthropy, Carnegie wrote extensively about his attitudes and opinions of war and peace in publications such as *Armaments and their Results* (1909), *The Path to Peace upon the Seas* (1909) and *War as the Mother of Valor and Civilization* (1910).[84] Carnegie believed that man killing man to settle disputes between countries was uncivilized and that arbitration was the key to settling conflicts and achieving world peace, as he wrote in 1910, 'The greatest force is no longer that of brutal war, which sows the seeds of future wars, but the supreme force of gentleness and generosity'.[85] Some biographers of Carnegie, such as Geoffrey Tweedale, have suggested that the once ruthless and Machiavellian businessman saw peace as just another industry that could be carefully and successfully managed.[86] Others, such as Joseph Wall, have instead proposed that Carnegie, having conquered the business world, was seeking a new mission in life and that the peace movement provided him with just such an opportunity.[87] The majority of biographers, however, share one view in common and that is that they all interpreted the Hero Funds as being a part of Carnegie's quest for world peace; and there is much evidence to suggest that they were correct to do so.

In his 1920 memoir *Personal Recollections of Andrew Carnegie*, Frederick Lynch, the Educational Secretary of the Church Peace Union, suggested that Carnegie's Hero Funds, 'grew out of his [Carnegie's] intense conviction that it took just as much heroism to save life as it did to take it, whereas the man who took it got most of the recognition'.[88] Carnegie, Lynch went on to recall, was often frustrated that 'the more men you kill the greater hero you are' and that 'most of the monuments in the world are to somebody who has killed a lot of his fellowmen'.[89] This frustration is further evident in Carnegie's 1908 letter instituting the fund in which he branded those who were rewarded for maiming or killing others as 'the false heroes of barbarism'.[90] One might conclude from this that Carnegie had a relatively negative view of heroism. However, he actually had a very strong belief in it and in particular that 'there is an instinct in man that seeks to wrestle with some foe. The heroic impulse demands expression'.[91] For Carnegie, heroism was not something that could be ignored or overlooked; it was something that would find expression through one means or another. He believed that it was civilian heroism that produced 'the heroes of civilisation' and that when heroism no longer meant to kill but only to assist or save fellow men, then wars would cease. As Carnegie explained the idea to Lynch, 'We have got to show young men that there are just as great battles to be fought in peace-time as in war-time and just as much heroism demanded, just as much opportunity for the hero'.[92] The goal, then, was to direct the heroic impulse into, in Carnegie's opinion, a more desirable area and this was the purpose of the Hero Funds.

The press reaction to Carnegie's attack on military heroism was mixed. The *Dundee Advertiser* suggested that 'A single sentence in Mr Carnegie's letter we can imagine arousing to the point of retort, temperaments differing from his own.' It went on to argue that painting military heroes as 'the false heroes of barbarism who maimed and killed' was 'to pass censure on humanity in all ages', as military heroes had always received honour and although military courage had 'on countless occasions been devoted to bad and oppressive ends', it still represented 'the greatest of public assets'.[93] It did, however, concede that due to these historical antecedents, the honouring of military heroism needed no conscious effort and consequently it overshadowed the heroism of civil life, denying it the recognition it deserved. This, it asserted, was what needed addressing, and it was not alone in expressing that view. The *Dundee Courier* editorial, misquoting from a sonnet by John Milton, stated that 'the recognition that peace hath not only her victories but her heroes as well as war is one of the most trustworthy signs of the real progress of civilisation' and the *Daily Chronicle*, agreed by praising the fund for its, 'recognition that peace hath her heroes no less than war'.[94] The *Aberdeen Free Press*, having drawn attention to the fact that heroism in war had previously been 'inordinately magnified' and had consequently 'falsified values and put other manifestations of heroism, equally impressive, on an unduly moral plane', was pleased to note that 'the tendency in question has been in the course of correction'.[95] So in 1908, Carnegie's Hero Fund, with its focus on civilian rather than military heroism, was launched into a reasonably receptive environment.

Moreover, it was, from Carnegie's perspective, an entirely applicable and necessary time to be accelerating his campaigns for peace. A destabilization of many nineteenth-century military and political alliances was generating a resurgence of imperialism in Europe and the formation of new agreements and powerbases, coupled with an accelerating arms race, was visibly building towards conflict in the region. Carnegie believed that endorsing and recognizing civilian rather than military heroism would promote a message that peace, not war, was the true path for civilized nations and demonstrate that peace provided just as many opportunities as war for the expression of the heroic impulse. Carnegie's intention was to remove one of the arguments for the necessity for young men to go to war, that being that it provided the best opportunity for the performance of heroism. This objective can be seen in the work of the Hero Fund and, although awards were made to women and children, it was overwhelmingly men that were recognized. Furthermore, although the age of the recipients was not systematically recorded, an average age of 22 and a median age of 16 can be obtained from the data, suggesting an inclination towards men of a suitable age for military service.[96] Carnegie considered military heroism to be hampering peace between nations, because young men were not sufficiently aware of avenues other than war and military service through which to exercise the heroic impulse that burned within them. The Hero Funds were designed to highlight alternative options and show young men that heroism in peaceful pursuits could be every bit as rewarding and well regarded as the military variety.

Conclusions

This chapter has revealed that by 1908, when the Hero Fund was founded, everyday heroism was sufficiently embedded in the public consciousness that, while Carnegie attracted some criticism, the general ethos of the Fund, recognition and assistance for civilian heroes, was more or less accepted and endorsed without comment. Moreover, by this time the recognition of everyday heroism was not only present but was a reasonably prominent element in the more general discourse on heroism in the period between 1850 and 1914. State recognition and endorsement was provided by the Albert Medal, which had been awarded 238 times since its introduction in 1866, and the newly introduced Edward Medal, which reinforced the Crown's commitment to acknowledging the bravery of its civilian citizens. Furthermore, there were at least six large organizations publicly and enthusiastically recognizing, promoting and endorsing acts of civilian heroism. Between 1908 and 1914, two of those organizations, the Royal Humane Society (RHS) and the Society for the Protection of Life from Fire (SPLF), collectively recognized the heroism of over 6000 civilian individuals who had risked their lives in saving or attempting to save the lives of others. The Hero Fund was, then, something of a latecomer in the development of the idea of everyday heroism and, as such, it had to locate itself within the existing landscape.

The Hero Fund Trustees undoubtedly recognized the expediency of drawing upon and utilizing cases of State-sanctioned recognition, which they believed would provide a ready supply of authenticated and reliable cases. The problem with this approach was that the Home Office, concerned with maintaining the prestige of its decorations and restricting them to only, as they viewed it, the very pinnacle of heroic achievement, sought to limit the number of medals it awarded and applied extremely high and exacting standards. Conversely, organizations such as the RHS and the SPLF were, largely for the purposes of promoting and disseminating their beliefs, awarding to a higher number and wider demographic of individuals, which was more in keeping with the aims of the Hero Fund. However, these bodies were relatively limited by the focused nature of their work, the need to satisfy their subscribers and the somewhat precarious nature of their funding. Furthermore, although needing to accommodate itself within this existing framework, the Hero Fund did, to some extent, present a challenge to it by emphasizing the idea that acts of heroism could and should be recognized through pecuniary support. It was this difficult position that the Trustees were charged with negotiating.

That said, all those administering awards for civilian heroism were, to some extent, placed in the same sensitive predicament of trying to decide who was worthy and who was not. Those in the Home Office faced the problem as was expected of bureaucrats and so they consulted precedent, applied a stringent set of self-determined rules and regulations and, when all else failed, they fell back on their own personal judgements of what was and was not heroic. Conversely, the Hero Fund Trustees, being upper-, middle- and working-class individuals, were a body of men very different in their composition from that at the Home Office. Furthermore, they could provide a range of perspectives, formed through different life experiences, and, when drawn together to make the decisions, each man's voice apparently carried equal weight. This would, inevitably, have widened their perspective and insight into the lives of the mainly working-class men upon whom they were being asked to pass judgement, a benefit not shared by those at the Home Office. In addition to this, unlike those administering other organizations, the Hero Fund Trustees were not answerable to subscribers nor concerned about funding and, thus, if they were moved or minded to make awards, there was little, beyond perhaps public opinion, to prevent them from doing so.

Public opinion was openly expressed, most notably through the press, on numerous occasions and there were prominent points of view. Recognizing civilian heroism was not particularly new or novel and so attracted little overall criticism or, for that matter praise, beyond those who saw it as ultimately worthwhile if not without its pitfalls. Appearing to offer money as a reward for heroism was, though, a contentious issue that stimulated debate and, as such, it provides an opportunity to gain insight into how heroism was viewed and considered at the time. It would appear that public opinion was, to some extent, in line with what Carnegie and others believed and that there was a common view that heroism, and particularly civilian heroism, was stimulated and facilitated by pure motive and moral decency on the part of those who undertook it. Generally speaking, people believed, or certainly wanted to believe, that individuals who acted heroically were essentially 'good' people and that heroic acts reflected all that was right and decent about society and the nation. There was much concern about heroism being corrupted by money but, equally, much confidence that it was a deeply held conviction in people that could not be inspired or encouraged by financial incentive.

Recognition and financial compensation were acceptable, but blatant monetary reward was not considered appropriate and the Trustees had to defend their actions on several occasions against accusations that they were partaking in prize-giving rather than assistance. The evidence would seem to suggest that these accusations were, in fact, correct and that the Trustees did, more often than not, present one-off payments to individuals in recognition of their heroic action rather than to directly compensate for financial losses. It would seem unlikely that the Hero Fund inspired people to actively seek out and perform acts of heroism in the hope of financial reward but, even if it did, stimulating such actions was certainly not the intention of Carnegie or his Trustees. Their main concern was to redistribute Carnegie's wealth to the decent and deserving people that he believed had, in a roundabout way, assisted him in accumulating it and everyday heroes appeared to provide a useful yardstick for identifying just such people.

Examining the work of the Hero Fund reveals that it awarded prolifically, partly on the basis of fulfilling its founder's desire to philanthropically redistribute his wealth, but also to increase the public profile of the organization so as to generate further nominations. Consequently, the Hero Fund Trustees were highly proactive in soliciting cases and facilitating lines of communication rather than simply waiting for people to come forward. Ensuring a high number of awards also required a wider and less stringent set of qualifications than those employed by the state and other organizations. This is not to say that the Hero Fund Trustees were unconcerned with the character, morality and motives of the individuals, because it is clear that these were important attributes that Carnegie wanted to endorse and recognize. However, the Hero Fund was not adverse to recognizing individuals who had already been refused the Albert Medal or other awards, suggesting that, although character judgements may well have been an issue, the qualifications applied in relation to them must have been significantly lower. The broader remit of the Hero Fund can also be seen through the range of occupations, and therefore social status, that its awards encompassed, as well as its more frequent recognition of women and children. This was partly because the Trustees were relatively unconcerned with preserving rarity, but also because they were not so heavily influenced by the idea that such acts would lower the perceived quality of their awards. Consequently, the approach of the Hero Fund was relatively flexible and diverse, which allowed it to court a wide and varied public opinion, something which Carnegie was keen to achieve as a means for disseminating his somewhat alternative views on war and militarism.

Endorsing the actions of brave individuals, through recognition of their heroic life-saving acts, could be used to publicize and promote a particular cause and facilitate the dissemination of particular ideas and beliefs. Carnegie would have been acutely aware of this process and that demonstrating, through the recognition of heroism, that resuscitation worked, that first-aid stabilized accident victims or that fire escapes saved lives had done much to further the work and ideas of particular organizations. Likewise, the Albert Medal could be seen to represent the State's attempt to reinforce a belief in the supremacy of British character and the importance of paternalistic imperialism, so as to encourage active and patriotic citizenship and inculcate an allegiance to defend the Crown that could then be called upon if and when required. In this respect, all those recognizing civilian heroism were trying to achieve a similar objective, the endorsement of particular actions or behaviour that promoted their particular cause, and for Carnegie, the cause was peace. It could be argued that while both the State and Carnegie wanted to utilize civilian heroism to capture the hearts and minds of British citizens, the two positions were somewhat at odds, with the State attempting to link it to allegiance to the nation while Carnegie wanted it to reflect a deeper philosophy of allegiance to humanity. In this sense, although it undoubtedly shared elements of both, the Hero Fund can be seen as being more in tune with the liberal-radical philanthropy outlined in Chapter 2 than it was with approach taken by the State.

The various Carnegie Hero Funds, then, appear to stem from a more complex assembly of motivations and intentions than it might first appear. In many ways, they were entirely typical of Carnegie's philanthropy and represented a mechanism for identifying suitably moral and upstanding citizens upon which to bestow the substantial fruits of his enterprises. The focus upon those who had been physically and/or financially disadvantaged, those who *could not* rather than *would not* work, was both apt and appropriate. But Carnegie also wanted to generate maximum publicity for his project so as to promote and endorse civilian heroism as an alternative to military heroism. In doing so, he was seeking to disseminate his alternative ideas on war and military service to the general public through the vehicle of everyday heroism which, as demonstrated in earlier chapters, was already regarded as being differently constructed to the establishment view. In order to deliver this level of publicity, the Trustees of the Hero Fund needed to maintain a high number of awards and recognize a broad social range of people so as to stimulate wide public support and approval. It was also important, though, that they remained in tune with public opinion and this relationship between the shifting perspectives and beliefs of a body of people and those that they are willing to endorse and accept as heroic is fundamental to any wider academic study of heroism.

The Hero Fund also provides a particularly useful case study for the study of everyday heroism because it is one of the last major initiatives relating to the idea before 1914. It is an opportunity to take stock and to examine how the idea had grown and developed in relation to the context around it, in the fifty or so years since it emerged and began to be more widely recognized and acknowledged. The Hero Fund certainly slotted-in to an existing discourse on civilian heroism and adopted a position alongside others who considered the idea a vehicle for challenging preconceived establishment ideas and promoting radical-liberal social change. It also, though, modified the discourse and introduced a range of new elements that altered how people understood the idea. The Hero Fund effectively endorsed and defined as 'heroic' a range of actions and individuals who would not, until then, have been considered eligible or suitable for recognition by other bodies or organizations. Actions involving dangerous or out of control animals, incidents with road or railway vehicles, particular types of medical treatment, or common industrial accidents all became seen as heroic in a manner that would not necessarily have been the case without the Hero Fund. It also, to some extent, subtly altered the parameters for acceptable methods of rewarding civilian heroism and suggested that, under certain circumstances and with effective judgement, financial reward could be seen as appropriate recognition. Of particular note, though, is that the Hero Fund was reflective of the societal changes that had occurred in the preceding years and those that were prescient at the time. Social, cultural and political reforms had gradually widened participation and the positions of working-class men and all women and children had, and were continuing, to alter significantly, something which was mirrored by their increasing inclusion in mechanisms recognizing heroism, as the final chapter will now discuss in more depth.

'Courage for a man is heroism for a girl': The Gendered Nature of Heroism

In the early hours of 28 October 1884, the steamship *William Hope* was en route between Fraserburgh and Burghead on the north-east coast of Scotland when it was caught up in a ferocious storm. As its engines failed, the seventy-seven-tonne vessel became unmanageable in the rough seas and the fifteen-man crew were left helpless as the ship was driven into Aberdour bay, close to the small village of Pennan. On the shores of Aberdour Bay stood the Waulkmill, a small woollen mill that was part of the nearby Bankhead Farm and at that time tenanted by John Whyte, the farm foreman, his wife Jane and their nine children. John had already left for work and Jane was alone in the mill with the children when she saw the ship being washed into the bay. Despite high winds and the driving rain and hail, Jane rushed down to the shoreline where she was able to retrieve the end of a rope that had been thrown from the ship. Wading out into the rough surf and wrapping the rope around her body, Jane pulled hard upon it and tightened it sufficiently to assist the men to disembark the ship. Once all the men were safely ashore, they were taken to the mill where Jane supplied them with dry clothes, hot tea and a warm meal.[1]

In the days that followed, the bravery of Jane Whyte was recounted in both local and national newspapers and she soon became known as the 'Aberdour Heroine'. Initial plaudits were quickly followed by a number of generous and, in some cases, high-profile acts of recognition. Locally, a collection was undertaken that resulted in the presentation of a purse of money (of an unspecified amount); an award of £10 was given by the executors of a legacy left by an Aberdeen woman for 'humane purposes' and another unspecified gift from a 'gentleman who withheld his name'.[2] The owners of the *William Hope* also presented Jane with a sum of money in gratitude for her assistance. On 6 December 1884, at a meeting held in the Fordyce Street Hall in nearby Rosehearty, Mrs Whyte was presented with £5 and a letter of thanks from the committee of the Shipwrecked Mariners Benevolent Society, 'in recognition of her brave services on the occasion of the wreck of the *William Hope*'.[3] In January 1885, two further accolades were announced; the silver medal of the RNLI and a Board of Trade bronze gallantry medal. The first of these was presented, along with a testimonial on vellum and £10 in money, during a ceremony at the Town Hall in Fraserburgh on 20 January 1885, while the Board of Trade medal was formally presented by the Lord Provost during a meeting of the Local Marine Board in Aberdeen on 3 February 1885.[4]

Jane Whyte, it would appear, was generously and publically acknowledged and accepted by her contemporaries as nothing less than a shining and noteworthy example of heroism.

Historians, however, have been slow to note or examine the existence, representation or construction of female heroism and with regard to civilian females have almost entirely overlooked them. There are, of course, a few exceptions to this: women whose stoicism and commitment were interpreted as heroic, such as Florence Nightingale and Edith Cavell; women who undertook public or political roles, such as Elizabeth Fry and Josephine Butler; and occasionally women who undertook a single act of bravery, the most notable being Grace Darling.[5] However, studies of such women, as would be expected, tend to focus on the life and character of the individual and, by and large, the 'heroic' element is either uncritically subsumed into the biography or briefly explored as an adjunct to the examination of the individual's reputation. Another example of a study of women which can loosely be interpreted as heroic but which is largely concerned with exemplarity and reputation is Krista Cowman's examination of the construction of the 'good woman socialist'.[6] There has, however, been one particularly useful short study in which Judith Rowbotham has examined the martyrdom of late-Victorian missionary women.[7]

Through an engagement with life-risking acts of bravery undertaken by women and an examination of the implications of an acceptance and promotion of female heroism for wider and predominant ideas of gender stereotyping in late-Victorian society, Rowbotham has, to some extent, provided a starting point from which to work. The article does, however, operate within a limited remit and while it has much to conclude about the treatment of female missionaries and does raise some interesting questions about how narratives of female martyrdom were actively and purposefully constructed so as to help preserve and reinforce male dominance and control of the missionary movement, it is less conclusive about the more general construction of female heroism during the Victorian period. This is far from being a shortcoming as the article does not set out to reach such conclusions, but it does leave the field open for an examination of the wider picture, as this chapter will demonstrate.

The choice to focus a chapter of this book on female heroism in particular, rather than looking at everyday heroism in relation to the wider field of gender, stems partly from constraints of space but more crucially from the nature of the discourse of everyday heroism. Accommodating civilian and largely working-class men alongside the existing discourse on heroism was, as this study has demonstrated, far from straightforward. However, because that discourse had, up until around the 1860s, been largely concerned with military and imperial exploits and consequently almost exclusively male, the gap to span was relatively narrow. In contrast, the inclusion of women, and to some extent children, into discourses on heroism was a far larger step to begin with and consequently required greater and deeper adaptations of the idea. A discourse of heroism that included civilian men was one step, but the inclusion of women was a further and far greater step. Furthermore, because female heroism was, to some extent, one of the defining features of everyday heroism that significantly marked it apart from the more general discourses on heroism, it makes it of central importance for this study.[8]

This is not to say that the construction of the male everyday hero was unproblematic and much could be gained by examining everyday heroism in relation to nineteenth-century constructions of masculinity. In particular, situating everyday heroes against the backdrop of what some historians have termed the 'flight from domesticity' could contribute much to the understanding of Victorian idea of 'manliness'.[9] It has been argued that the period 1870–1914 saw an increase in men eschewing marriage and family life in favour of manly pursuits and overseas adventure, an argument partly substantiated by the rise in imperial and militaristic adventure narratives aimed at men as well as boys.[10] As with the idea of 'separate spheres', discussed below, the rigidity of such a paradigm has been challenged and, instead, the view that 'men were continually seeking to reconcile and integrate the contradictory impulses of domestic responsibility and escapism' is now more generally accepted.[11] That said, it would still be interesting to consider the position and idea of everyday heroes in relation to a period, 1870–1914, which, as a reaction to the perceived threat of male domestication and the rise of the more independent woman, saw an increase in the celebration and promotion of the hyper-masculine military or imperial hero. For example, were traits such as compassion, sympathy and modesty, which were inherent in acts of everyday heroism, and the everyday (or certainly not exotic) locations of the acts themselves, negotiated or reconstructed so as not to stimulate an uneasy and potentially problematic feminization of civilian male heroes, and if so, how was this achieved? This study is not the place to examine these issues but they certainly provide avenues for future scholarship.

This chapter will closely engage with narratives and accounts of acts of heroism undertaken by women in order to examine the construction of female everyday heroism and ascertain how it differed from other constructions and the purposes for which it was appropriated and employed by various groups or individuals in society. The chapter will reveal that female heroism could be specifically constructed for political reasons, for example in attempts to further the cause of women's rights or conversely to reinforce the notion that a woman's place was within the domestic sphere. Furthermore, although considered to be important and worthwhile, there was also a strong belief that female heroism naturally represented a lesser standard than that undertaken by men, and consequently, promoting or recognizing it as equally worthwhile could undermine perceptions of the overall idea. Set within the wider context of the Victorian understanding of heroism as examined and outlined throughout this book, it can be argued that the creation of a distinctly female construction was as much concerned with protecting and defending the integrity of the idea itself, as it was about restricting women to their own limited sphere of influence. This, it will be argued, helps to explain why a specifically gendered construction of heroism was deemed necessary for women.

What will also become apparent from the evidence provided in this chapter is that the construction of female heroism grew and developed in parallel with the changes and developments in the status and position of women in Victorian and Edwardian society. What is more, in the same way that these political and societal changes took place gradually and some elements of change existed alongside one another for periods of time while society negotiated or adjusted to the shifts, so too did elements within the construction of female heroism. Consequently, although heroines at the turn of the nineteenth century were differently constructed to those of the mid-Victorian period, such differences were often subtle in nature or elements of existing constructions were carried over briefly as part of adjusting to the change. Not only does this illustrate the complexities of the construction of female heroism in particular but it also serves to once again underline the malleable and adaptable nature of the overall idea.

'Heroines of Daily Life': Locating and revealing female heroism

Given that this is a period for which historians, by tending to focus on the military or the empire (areas where women were either absent or had a limited role), have given the impression or generally concluded that performing acts of heroism was the exclusive domain of men, it is necessary to begin by showing that this was purely and simply not the case.[12] Table 5 provides a basic gendered analysis of the number of Albert Medals awarded between 1863 and 1914 and the number of awards made by the Carnegie Hero Fund Trust (CHFT) and the Society for the Protection of Life from Fire (SPLF) between 1908 and 1914. Clearly, cases involving women represent something of a minority, 17 per cent at the most and just 2.5 per cent at the least. However, these figures demonstrate that not only were civilian women undertaking acts of heroism, but also that prominent elements in Society were willing to recognize women for doing so. In this respect, although the actual numbers are low, the implications for the study of civilian heroism during the period are significant. Women were most certainly performing acts of heroism, and consequently, an examination of this is long overdue.

Furthermore, in addition to quantitative data, which paints a general but impersonal portrait, a substantial amount of qualitative material was also produced which can be employed to flesh out the statistical bones of these heroines. Evidence is primarily drawn from two sources, these being newspaper reports and volumes of biographical literature. Much biographical literature was didactic in nature, with individuals being offered as exemplars for emulation, and studies of heroic individuals certainly featured heavily in the genre. However, the term heroic could be employed to represent actions or behaviour other than single acts of life-risking bravery which are the central focus of this study of everyday heroism. Consequently, volumes such as Edwin Hodder's *Heroes of Britain in Peace and War* (1878), which included chapters entitled 'Heroes of the Slave Trade Abolition', 'Early Arctic Heroes' and, in particular, 'Prison Heroines' which detailed the work of Elizabeth Fry and Anna Buxton, are less than entirely useful.[13]

Fortunately, there were also a significant number of volumes which detailed the exploits of civilian women who had undertaken brave and life-risking acts of heroism, notable examples being Frank Mundell's *Heroines of Daily Life* (1896) and Charles D. Michaels' *Heroines: True Tales of Brave Women* (1904).[14] These volumes are useful for a number of reasons. First, they offer numerous accounts of actual heroic acts which can then be examined further using newspaper reports. More importantly, however, they provide a deliberate selection of particular cases and in doing so, they can offer an insight into which types of women or types of heroic acts undertaken by women were viewed, by those editing or compiling these volumes, as particularly important or exemplary. In a number of instances, the same case was selected and retold in several different volumes, which further substantiates the idea that some incidents were considered to be of more value, or more entertaining, than others. Also, through examining the language used or the emphasis placed on certain characteristics within the accounts, it is possible to identify whether and to what extent the women who featured were being constructed in a specific way so as to communicate specific qualities. However, before moving on to undertake this analysis, it is necessary to gain a broad overview of the type of women who were being recognized or noted for their heroism.

Two of the most consistent pieces of information supplied for women awardees were their marital status and their occupation. Table 17 shows the numbers of married and unmarried women who either received an Albert Medal or were recognized by the CHFT or the SPLF. Any discussion of the data relating to the marital status of women has to be considered within the context of Victorian attitudes towards married and unmarried women. Around the 1860s, there was a growing awareness and concern regarding the disproportionate number of single women in England. One solution, famously offered by the journalist W. R. Greg in 1862, was that single women over the age of thirty should be shipped to Australia, Canada and the United States where there was a surplus of unmarried men or, if they remained in England, they should more actively and coquettishly encourage men into marriage.[15] While attitudes such as Greg's were at the extremes of opinion, underlying concerns about the damaging effects of women remaining unmarried and living independent lives remained pertinent within middle-class didactic commentary throughout the century. Notwithstanding this, marriage appears to have remained far more popular, desirable or necessary for women than the single life as by the 1890s only around 16 per cent women remained unmarried.[16]

By the law of averages alone, then, it might be expected to see these figures generally reflected in the differentiation between married and unmarried women being recognized for undertaking acts of heroism, with a higher percentage of married women being represented. Furthermore, much of the public recognition of heroic individuals was didactically concerned with influencing society for the better and as there was some concern as to the impact on society if women did not marry, it would not be altogether surprising to see higher levels of awards being made to married rather than single women. However, as Table 17 shows, there was no discernable pattern one way or the other with regard to marital status with a more or less 50/50 split. So, it would appear that when it came to celebrating or honouring a woman for undertaking an act of heroism, her marital status was not a significant factor; both married and unmarried women were, more or less, equally recognized.

Moving on to work, Table 18 shows a breakdown of the occupations, where recorded, for female recipients of recognition. Three categories have been excluded from the total used for the percentage calculation: minors, not because they did not

Table 17 Number and percentage of married and unmarried women who received the Albert Medal (AM) or awards from the Carnegie Hero Fund Trust (CHFT) or the Society for the Protection of Life from Fire (SPLF)

Award	Period	Married	%	Unmarried	%	Total	Not specified	Total
AM	1866–1914	2	33.3	4	66.7	**6**	0	**6**
CHFT	1908–1914	16	47.1	18	52.9	**34**	3	**37**
SPLF	1908–1914	45	54.9	37	45.1	**82**	2	**84**

Sources: Home Office (HO) and Board of Trade (BT) documents, The National Archives; CHFT Annual Reports, British Library; SPLF Annual Reports, London Metropolitan Archives.

work but simply because official occupations were seldom given for them; those for whom the term 'married woman' was used in relation to occupation, particularly in the reports of the SPLF; and individuals for who no official occupation was recorded. The only category where specific job titles have been consolidated is 'domestic service' which includes those listed as 'housekeeper', 'lady's help' and 'charwoman' as well as the straightforward 'domestic servant'. In all other cases, the job description is exactly as recorded in the original document.

As with marital status, female employment and suitable work for women is also something that needs to be put into context. Generally speaking, employment opportunities for women only existed in limited occupations and even then these were further demarcated by class.[17] For working-class women, domestic service was the most available type of work and was overall the largest employer of women. On average, between 1851 and 1901, 43 per cent of working women were employed in domestic service.[18] Domestic service was usually nothing more than a financially necessary hardship for working-class women and their families, but it was perceived by middle-class observers as the most fitting occupation for single working-class women because it provided an environment and opportunity for both social control and the inculcation of middle-class morals and standards.[19] Towards the latter half of the nineteenth century, increased educational provision led to greater opportunities for women from the more prosperous working classes to move into teaching or nursing, both of which were viewed as good, stable and, most importantly, respectable occupations for women. By and large, however, these roles were more the domain of the middle-class woman, as were occupations such as shop assistant, governess and clerk.

Moreover, the nature of women's work was significantly shaped by an adherence to strict notions of gender difference. On the most basic level, women's work was almost universally lower paid than men's; typically, a woman could expect to earn between one-third and one-half of that paid to a man for similar work and even at the highest levels of an occupation, a woman would be lucky to earn two-thirds of a male salary.[20] Furthermore, gender distinctions were not restricted to pay alone. For example, there was a belief, certainly among the middle classes, that women had a natural ability to teach and to nurse, thus their innate suitability and the public acceptability of such occupations. Although retailing was open to both men and women, roles within the industry were strictly gender specific. Grocering or the retailing of luxury items such as jewellery, fine food or wine, or quality books, was regarded as skilled work and consequently the domain of men, women being restricted to the realms of the lower-status bakery, stationers or tobacconists. It would appear, then, that working women were increasingly accepted, but only as long as they were undertaking 'women's work'.

When considered against this contextual backdrop, the occupations listed in Table 18 and the frequency with which certain ones occur is, to some extent, unremarkable. Top of the list, with nearly 35 per cent, is domestic service, with nurse and school teacher reasonably close behind with 18 per cent and 15 per cent,

Table 18 Occupations of women who received the Albert Medal (AM) or awards from the Carnegie Hero Fund Trust (CHFT) and the Society for the Protection of Life from Fire (SPLF)

Occupation	AM	CHFT	SPLF	Total	%
Domestic service	0	3	16	19	34.5
Nurse	2	2	6	10	18.2
School teacher	1	3	4	8	14.5
Dressmaker (D)	0	0	2	2	3.6
Housewife (D)	2	0	0	2	3.6
Laundress (D)	0	0	2	2	3.6
Newsagent	0	1	1	2	3.6
Spinster	0	0	2	2	3.6
Clerk	0	0	1	1	1.8
Companion	0	0	1	1	1.8
Factory worker	0	1	0	1	1.8
Lady missionary	0	1	0	1	1.8
Private means	0	0	1	1	1.8
Scholar	0	0	1	1	1.8
Shop assistant	0	0	1	1	1.8
Weaver	0	1	0	1	1.8
Sub-total	**5**	**12**	**38**	**55**	
Not given	1	25	46	**72**	
Minor	0	10	10	**20**	
Total	**6**	**47**	**94**	**147**	

Sources: Home Office (HO) and Board of Trade (BT) documents, The National Archives; CHFT Annual Reports, British Library; SPLF Annual Reports, London Metropolitan Archives.

respectively. Of the other occupations that appear more than once, three (marked with a D) can be considered as taking place within a distinctly domestic environment, which, as detailed above, would have reinforced the gendered distinction of the work. The remaining occupations were only recorded on single occasions and so provide less of a quantitative picture, but by and large, they represent jobs that were not out of the ordinary for a woman to undertake.

Given the unremarkable pattern of this data, it might at first appear difficult to discern whether occupation had any impact on the selection of women with a view to offering them as exemplars. The evidence does indeed show that, similarly to marital status, whether or not a woman undertook paid work outside of the home does not appear to have particularly influenced the decision. Furthermore, given that the occupations listed for female awardees represent some of the most prominent employment opportunities for women at the time, the likelihood is that they would feature highly. However, they were certainly not the only employment opportunities and it is striking not to see other occupations featuring. Where, for example, are the textile workers, the colliery workers, the chain makers, the machine operators and, to a lesser extent, the agricultural workers and those who worked in the small manufacturing industries? Although it is true to say that when such employment was undertaken by women there was a tendency for under-recording – because it was considered occasional or seasonal or undertaken from home – these are still occupations that women were documented as undertaking in great numbers in the period under consideration. For example, in 1881, 745,000 women were recorded as working in the textile industry; 667,000 in the clothing industry; 49,000 in metal manufacturing industries; 27,000 in brick and pottery manufacture; 8,000 in mining and quarrying and 116,000 in agriculture.[21] Despite this, women working in these areas were almost completely overlooked by the awarding organizations. To understand fully why this might have been the case, it is necessary to engage with one of the major elements in the study of nineteenth-century gender relations: the concept and theory of 'separate spheres'.

As Leonore Davidoff, one of the pioneers and developers of the theory, has concluded of the historiographical terrain, 'the debate over separate spheres has been complicated and the terms slippery'.[22] Nonetheless, a limited engagement with the theory is required in order to fully contextualize and understand social reactions to female heroism.[23] The term 'separate spheres' essentially refers to a proposition forwarded by, among others, Catherine Hall and Martha Vicinus, that by the middle of the nineteenth century a dominant 'ideology of domesticity' was effectively confining women to the 'private' sphere of the home and consequently limiting them to roles of wives and mothers.[24] This ideology most obviously manifested itself through a physical separation of the sexes, men in the public world of business, commerce and politics and women in the private domestic world of the house or nursery. But it also created and reinforced gender differences and stereotypes of a more biological, social or emotional nature. Women were not only perceived as being physically weaker than men but their biology also determined for them the innate and natural role of motherhood. Emotionally, women were considered timid and unassuming, unable to act decisively and dependent on men to lead and take charge. Women *were* regarded as the ethical compass in society and the custodians of religious and moral standards, thus equipping them for teaching, but these were still seen as values subordinate to those of men.

The theory of separate spheres in Victorian society has received much criticism and has been substantially and successfully challenged. Arguably, the most significant revision has been the acceptance that the 'cult of domesticity' and the strict separation of spheres along gendered lines was a prescriptive ideal rather than a descriptive reality.[25] For many women, especially those in working-class families, paid work was a reality and simply a financial necessity. For others, in the middle and upper classes, although it may have been a lifestyle choice it was often one motivated by a genuine desire to contribute to society or from a sense of redundancy within a large family, rather than any conscious effort to challenge gender stereotypes. In fact, it has also been suggested that rather than being a confident and proactive prescriptive ideology, separate spheres was actually a nervous and concerned reaction to rising levels of single working women and a perceived breakdown of family and moral values.[26] Whichever the case, it is clear that the idea of separate spheres, even though it was a prescriptive ideology, still represented a pervasive and influential discourse in Victorian Society. For many, it was how they lived, for many more, it was how they would have been happy to live had it been financially or practically viable and for the vast majority it was a set of ideas with which they would have been familiar, even if it had little or no direct influence on their particular life.

When viewed within the context of the idea of separate spheres, the data for the occupations of those women who received recognition for an act of heroism becomes more revealing. There is certainly an argument to be made that the working women who were recognized did not necessarily represent just the most prominent female occupations, but more importantly occupations that were viewed by the middle classes as representing acceptable and respectable work for women. This same social class perceived industrial, agricultural or manufacturing jobs as being unsuitable for women, not simply because the work was considered to be hard and physical – the tasks of a domestic servant were not exactly light – but more because they removed women from their socially acceptable sphere. Conversely, other occupations such as those undertaken within the domestic sphere, those for which women were considered to be naturally adept, or those which upheld or reinforced gendered separation, were regarded not only as suitable but also as ideal occupations, and consequently those which could be endorsed and promoted. The issue of marriage, raised earlier, was not such an influential factor because, although the separate spheres ideology prescribed marriage as the ideal course for a woman, there were socially acceptable occupations within the ideology that a single woman could follow, such as domestic service or teaching, which would be less likely to challenge gender stereotypes.

This is not to argue, for instance, that the Home Office secretaries or the Trustees of the CHFT consciously or systematically evaluated the occupation of every woman considered, with a mind to only recognizing those who represented idealized models of femininity. However, the consistent absence of certain types of occupation which were significant but less socially acceptable employers of women is intriguing and, it can be argued, suggests that a latent or unconscious adherence to the idea of separate spheres was having some influence. Examining similar occupational data for male awardees (see Table 6) reveals that manual or industrial workers featured considerably in the records and this, it might be argued, was because such jobs were relatively dangerous and accidents or incidents that might require the performance of life-saving heroism were more common. Yet, these very same occupations are almost entirely absent from the list of female awardees and arguably because the type of work was not seen as suitable or desirable for women to be undertaking.[27]

This is tantalizing evidence for a gendered construction of female heroism, but the quantitative analysis alone is not sufficient to fully substantiate such an argument; this requires an analysis of qualitative evidence as well. Every act of heroism, whether undertaken by a man or a woman, is more or less unique in its own right, but, as has already been shown in previous chapters, there can be common and consistent elements across a range of such acts, which serve to unite or categorize them together along specific lines. Looking more closely at some specific acts of heroism performed by women and identifying those unifying characteristics should help to demonstrate whether or not there is further evidence of gender consideration in the construction of the heroine.

'Decidedly not a day for a woman': Acts by women and comparisons to men

One striking and consistent element that manifests itself in both journalistic and more dramatized accounts of acts of heroism undertaken by women is the suggestion that the act itself, and in particular the level of bravery, is all the more remarkable because of the fact that it has been undertaken by a woman. This appears to stem from an assumption that heroism is the preserve of men and is usually expressed through some sort of comparison to the bravery of men. Take, for example, a comment made by the representative of the Shipwrecked Mariners Benevolent Society during the public presentation to Jane Whyte of her £5 award. Having expressed his pleasure at being able to recognize her acts, he went on to add that 'at the time the *William Hope* came ashore it was blowing a perfect tornado, and decidedly not a day for a woman to be outside, far less to proceed to the scene of a shipwreck and do such a heroic deed'.[28] In another case, documented by Frank Mundell in his *Heroines of Daily Life*, a Miss Evans dived from Southampton Pier to attempt a rescue of three people who had overturned their pleasure boat. In remarking upon this act, Mundell concluded that 'it was a feat of which the best male swimmer would have every right to feel proud, and executed as it was by a young lady, was almost, without precedent'.[29] While perceived as remarkable, it would appear that women could be considered brave and heroic, but only in relation or comparison to men.

An exception to this could occur if there was a wish to disparage the masculinity of particular men and in these cases, the woman was portrayed as being considerably more heroic. One such case is that of Catherine Vasseur, a seventeen-year-old servant girl, who rescued three men from a sewer in the French town of Noyen. According to the accounts narrated in several collections of true-life stories of heroic women,

Catherine alone volunteered to descend into the well when there was also present a crowd of French men who refused. In one account, it is reported that 'not a man in the crowd was brave enough to risk his life for his fellow-men' and that even 'the frantic entreaties of the poor wives failed to stir them to act like men.'[30] Even Catherine's willingness to undertake the act 'did not shame any of the strong fellows standing by into taking action' and this prompted one writer to conclude 'that a woman should dare to do what men are afraid to attempt is a fact of which every woman may feel proud and every man ought to feel shamed. Such cases, though rare, are not unknown.'[31] The men concerned were, of course, French men and as such it was less of an issue, for the British and American authors of the accounts, to find their bravery wanting in relation to that of a woman. In fact, portraying French men as cowards in relation to a French woman could well have been more an attempt to disparage and parody the cowardice of Frenchmen and less about celebrating the bravery of a French servant girl.

Generally speaking, though, women were portrayed as unusual candidates for heroism and this was partly linked, as might be expected under the influence of Victorian ideas of gender, to their perceived fragility and weakness. With regard to the Noyen incident, it was asserted that 'rescue came from an unexpected quarter' because Vasseur was 'a delicate looking servant girl' and 'it seemed impossible that this slightly built young girl could rescue the men.'[32] If women did display physical strength and fortitude, it was usually considered to be a one-off and stemming from a particularly female characteristic. This sentiment is suitably exemplified by a comment in *The Englishwoman's Domestic Magazine*, 'notwithstanding the physical weakness of her constitution, there is an internal energy of character and strength of endurance fed from the deep and solemn sources of affection, that render women capable of performing the most heroic and glorious acts.'[33] For example, in one incident, a Mrs Walker, who while searching for her two children during a snowstorm in the High Peaks area of Derbyshire, 'tore the cold snow-clods asunder with the miraculous strength that comes to mothers when their children are in peril' after discovering her son buried in a snowdrift.[34] Another case was that of a Norah Halinstrom who went to the rescue of her husband who had fallen down a cliff while servicing a frozen reservoir. The fact that she, 'by no means a muscular woman', had achieved the physical act of pulling him, 'a strongly built man cumbered with heavy clothing', back up using a rope was attributed to her love for her husband; 'it was love that gave her strength, love that made her indifferent to bodily pain and weakness – love, that inspires even the frail and feeble with courage and devotion and enables them to perform noble and heroic deeds.'[35]

It was not only the acts of women towards their loved ones that received such treatment; working women (in respectable occupations of course) were also accorded unnatural strength on account of other more natural abilities. On 14 October 1881, a dreadful storm raged across the north of England and in the small village of Sutton in Lancashire, a young school mistress, Hannah Rosbotham, endeavoured to calm the fears of her infant pupils as the wind howled around the building. High above the schoolhouse, the stone belfry was unable to withstand the relentless buffeting and without warning, a large portion broke away and collapsed down through the roof of the classroom, burying many of the children beneath the ruins. Without hesitation and still at risk from falling debris 'Hannah Rosbotham tore away the timber, stone and slate that were crushing the little sufferers, whose pale faces and pleading voices filled her heart with anguish, but gave strength to her arms'.[36] It was also reported that for those children who were not completely buried but 'too terror stricken to move from their seats, the sight of their teacher put new life into them and by her directions they made their way down the steps'.[37] It was, then, partly her natural ability for working with children, which in turn suggested an innate mothering instinct, that enabled Hannah to perform a heroic action seemingly beyond her physical womanly means.

The case of Hannah Rosbotham, among others, also contains an example of another highly prevalent element regarding the underlying physical and mental fragility of heroic women. Although women were portrayed as briefly attaining strength or capabilities beyond their gender *during* their act, as soon as it was completed they were strictly reassigned their womanly fragility. In the case of Rosbotham, it was reported that 'Now all the danger was over the brave schoolmistress broke down and cried hysterically' before calming herself and setting out to visit the homes of the children she had saved.[38] Other examples of this tendency include a Miss Wilkinson who, having performed 'strenuous exertions' in rescuing a six-year-old child who had fallen into a fast running stream in Twickenham, Middlesex, reportedly 'fainted on being assisted out of the water, and was afterwards confined to her bed with a severe attack of fever for three weeks'[39]; a Mrs Clinton, who helped to defeat a band of pirates who had murdered her husband and taken control of his ship, and of whom it was reported that 'it is a matter of no surprise that, when all was over, she completely broke down, and that for long months she was on the verge of insanity'.[40] Interestingly, the male seaman involved alongside her was apparently untroubled by the incident and had merely 'done his duty'; or finally the Scottish fisherman's daughter who ran for over four miles across moorland, along beaches and through the sea to raise the alarm when a ship was wrecked nearby and 'reaching the house where the coxswain of the lifeboat lived, she gasped out "the schooner – on the rocks – North!" and then fell fainting on the ground'.[41]

This is not to suggest that such exertions could not have placed pressures on the health of the individual or that the illnesses described were not genuine, for in many cases it is clear that those involved had endured a physically and mentally arduous task. However, it is relevant that, in the case of male heroes who undertook similarly strenuous actions, there was rarely any mention of fatigue or collapse and if there was, it usually stemmed from exposure to gas or some other factor that was beyond human means to withstand, such as smoke or poison. Moreover, this element of a man being 'insensible' through no direct fault of his own was often provided as an explanation in the rare cases where a young, fit, healthy man reportedly required rescue or assistance from a woman.[42] Furthermore, it is interesting that a woman was often reported to have fainted or become hysterical, rather than to have collapsed from exhaustion, suggesting more of a feminine weakness rather than a direct result of physical fatigue. It was crucial to the narrative that the heroine completed her heroic task, however arduous, before her collapse – as in the case of the fisherman's daughter – as this was a necessary component to her heroism. But it was also clearly important that her heroic actions were constructed and portrayed as being anomalous to her gender and that, as soon as possible, she was seen to reassume her fragile and vulnerable female role.

Another similar method employed within the discourse of heroism in order to accomplish this was to highlight the involvement or assistance of a man, either during the course of the act itself or immediately afterwards where he provided support for the incapacitated female. One of the most striking examples of this is in relation to a fire which took place above a tailor's shop in Dorking, Surrey in September 1888. In the early hours of the morning, a gas explosion ripped through the building, engulfing it in flames and smoke, and trapping Mr and Mrs Inglis, their three children and a fifteen-year-old maidservant called Minnie Murrell. Murrell, having raised the alarm turned her attention to the children in her care. The baby had already been accounted for, but the three- and five-year-olds were trapped on the first floor and Minnie ran to their assistance. Opening the window, she called to the crowd below 'catch the children' and then dropped each one safely from the window to the people below. At this point in the account, Mr Inglis reappeared, having forced his way through the flames to be of assistance to Minnie, and it would appear just as well that he did. For as the report continues,

> And now, having been hitherto as cool as a salamander and as gallant as a fireman, Minnie promptly regained the privileges of her sex, and was on the point of making a fool of herself by shrieking and jumping out of the window. She had at this crisis a sort of hysterical or fluttering fit, and would have leaped headforemost to probable death, had not her master caught hold of her in time and lowered her carefully to the enthusiastic arms below. [43]

This quotation clearly and succinctly illustrates the gendered stereotyping of heroines along the lines of separate sphere ideology. Minnie was a maidservant and as such was gainfully employed in what was considered to be fitting employment for a young woman. According to the construction in the narrative, her duty of care for the children provided her with the strength and courage required to undertake her heroic act, but when that was completed she 'regained the privileges of her sex' and consequently became hysterical. At this point, Mr Inglis, not only a man but her 'master', stepped in and rescued her from probable death, brought about by her irrational, yet distinctively female, behaviour, which needed to be checked or controlled by a man. In a nutshell, this, or slight variances upon it, were the most common types of narrative with regard to acts of female heroism and it situated the women firmly within the feminine role, as prescribed by the idea of separate spheres.

'The angel in the house': The acceptable theatre for female heroism

The principle of separate spheres was determined largely by the Victorian ideal of womanhood and the cult of domesticity. To those in the Victorian middle classes, the idea that 'a woman's place is in the home' was an ideal to be actively promoted and pursued. Take, for example, the English poet and critic Coventry Patmore. In a series of four poems, published between 1854 and 1862 and known under the collective title of 'the Angel in the House', Patmore expressed his reflections on the nature of ideal femininity.[44] The poem enjoyed a renaissance in the later nineteenth century through its suitability as didactic literature for use by advocates of domestic ideology and separate spheres. A central tenet of this domestic ideology was the locating of women firmly within the roles of mother and housewife but, as already outlined with regard to female occupations, the metaphorical boundaries of the 'domestic' sphere did not stop at the physical walls of the home. The idea of domesticity extended outside of this physical space into areas, such as nursing and teaching, which, although not strictly domestic in nature, were still considered suitable spheres for women. Heroism, however, was generally regarded as being the domain of men so when a woman undertook a heroic act, a mechanism or construction was required so as to acknowledge and celebrate that heroism without allowing it to challenge or devalue the dominant position of men. One way to achieve this was to ensure that the woman involved, or the act of heroism that she undertook, was intrinsically linked in some way with the domestic sphere. In this way, any potential challenge to the perceptions of men could be diffused via the safety valve of domestic ideology.

This retention of female heroism within the boundaries of the domestic sphere was achieved in different ways, some of which were more subtle than others. Within the narrative construction of female heroism, there was often a physical positioning of a woman within the home prior to her act of heroism and then a repositioning of her within it after her act. This was certainly the case with Jane Whyte, the 'Aberdour Heroine'. The most often recalled account states that while her husband had already gone to work on the farm, Jane was at home with the children when she saw the ship in difficulty. Her act of heroism required her to leave the home environment, but once it was completed it was clear where her true position lay, 'the brave woman welcomed those she has rescued to her cottage where, as far as her humble means would allow, she provided the refreshments they so sorely needed'.[45] This element of the account was given almost as much prominence as the act of heroism itself and served to situate Mrs Whyte squarely back into the domestic sphere. In another case, that of a Mrs Wallace and her daughter, who rowed out to rescue her husband, the Little Cumbrae lighthouse keeper, and their four other children whose boat had capsized in the Firth of Clyde, it was asserted that,

> It was while the wife and daughter were busy with their ordinary household duties that the call came to prove themselves heroines; and it was the same spirit of helpfulness which they brought to bear upon the uninteresting tasks of every day that enabled them to dare the fury of the storm in order to rescue those who appealed to them for aid.[46]

Not only did this situate the women within the domestic arena but it celebrated the skills they acquired from it and the inspiration that their role provided for them.

Acts of heroism involving domestic servants, such as Minnie Murrell or the Southwark heroine Alice Ayres, had the distinct advantage of usually taking place within a domestic space. However, even when incidents occurred far outside it, or the woman was temporarily unable to fulfil her normal duties, the discourse was still shaped so as to reinforce the domestic ideal in some way. In the case of Norah Halinstrom, who was badly injured during the rescue of her husband from a frozen reservoir, not only was she carried back into the house (the domestic space) by two men who came to her assistance, but once there, 'she rallied briskly, and busied herself in giving directions for hot coffee for the men'.[47] So even though she was not physically capable of providing domestic services, she fulfilled her role by directing them from her sickbed. Another incident which prompted a similar narrative construction was that of Grace Bussell, a sixteen-year-old English girl who, in December 1876, rescued a number of passengers from the wreck of the *Georgette* off the coast of Freemantle in Western Australia. Having made several trips on horseback out into the ocean to bring all the passengers ashore, she then, as so often was the case, collapsed from her efforts. However she then noticed the poor condition of those she had rescued and realized 'that unless food and warm clothing were given them quickly they would probably die'.[48] So, she rode the twelve miles to her family home where, after fainting once more, she finally recounted what had happened and the need for assistance. The next paragraph of the narrative perfectly encapsulates how the roles and spheres of women were acutely and strictly demarcated in these accounts:

> When at last she [Grace Bussell] told the story of the shipwreck her sister got together blankets and food and rode off to the sufferers, whom she carefully tended throughout the night. At daybreak Mr Bussell arrived with his wagon and conveyed the whole party to his home, where they remained tenderly nursed by mother and daughter for several days. Mrs Bussell, it is sad to say, died from brain fever brought on by her anxiety concerning the shipwrecked people whom she had taken into the house.[49]

This quotation barely requires further comment, such was the clarity with which the women were portrayed as the nursing and nurturing (although ultimately fragile) providers of care and tenderness, while always operating within a domestic sphere, which was clearly owned and controlled by Mr Bussell.

In other cases, the signs and indicators of domesticity were far more subtle, but nonetheless important. As already mentioned, it was highlighted that, having saved the infants from the collapsed roof of the Sutton National School, Hannah Rosbotham 'started out to visit at the homes of the little ones she had saved'.[50] In press reports of the Union Street fire in April 1885, during which Alice Ayres died while attempting to save the life of three children, it was reported that Henry Chandler, the man of the house, father of the children and proprietor of the shop below, was found dead at the bottom of the staircase with the money box from the shop clasped in his arms.[51] It is easy and tempting to regard the reporting of this information as a criticism of Mr Chandler, who appears to have prioritized saving his money over saving the lives of his family. However, from a gendered perspective, it could be argued that, in seeking to secure financial provision for his family in the event of them surviving the fire, Henry was actually being shown as performing his allocated role. As John Tosh has highlighted, 'masculine self-respect certainly demanded that a man provide for his family, and great shame was attached to one who "failed"'.[52] Meanwhile, the women of the house, the perceived custodians of the domestic and the nursery, performed their gender allocated role by attempting to save the children.

Another example of the influence of domestic ideology on the construction of heroism relates to an incident that occurred in January 1876. Following a shipwreck near to the village of Cresswell in Northumberland, three young women, Margaret Brown, Mary Brown and Isabella Armstrong, ran over five miles – along the coast, over rocks and through the sea – to a neighbouring village to raise the alarm.[53] The women were heralded as heroines and an award was made to each of them by the Hull District Coastguard. It was the nature of these awards, however, that particularly stands out in relation to the theme of this chapter. Margaret Brown received 'a very handsome solid silver teapot . . . enclosed in a pretty oak box' while Mary Brown and Isabella Armstrong both received 'an extremely handsome and massive silver broach, richly studded with rubies and large topazes . . . the broaches were of ample proportions and heart shaped.'[54] Not, then, for these young women the simple gold, silver or bronze medallions or even the cash awards presented to men who undertook similar actions. This is not to say that the awards to the three women were not valuable, or that they were not carefully chosen with a view to what would best be received or indeed that they were not well received and appreciated by the women themselves. However, representing, as they undoubtedly did, overtly domestic and feminine symbols, it reveals much about the perceptions and attitudes of the men who ultimately made the selection.

One final way in which heroic women were narratively and prescriptively located within the domestic sphere was by overtly highlighting their innate and natural mothering instinct. As Shani D'Cruze has written, 'although not all women were mothers, motherhood was clearly the manifest destiny of women.'[55] Even if the children involved were not theirs and in some cases when children were not even involved in the incident, the abilities of the woman with regard to motherhood were clearly emphasized in narratives of female heroism. For example, at the presentation of her Board of Trade bronze medal, it was highlighted that in addition to her act of heroism, Jane Whyte was also a mother of eight children.[56] Frank Mundell chose 'Brave Mothers' as the subject for the first chapter of his *Heroines of Daily Life*, asserting that, 'in times of unusual peril, mothers have faced dangers from which brave men have shrunk faint-hearted at the seeming hopelessness of the task.'[57] One of the stories he recounted in that chapter was that of a fire in the East End of London when two children became trapped, their mother having briefly stepped out of the house to buy groceries. A woman tried to enter the building but was forced back by the flames, then a man attempted the same but he too was beaten back. A third man who tried 'reached the door of the room, but was unable to affect an entrance, and only saved himself from suffocation by rolling down the stairs'. However, when the mother returned 'she threw off those who would have detained her, and made her way through the smoke and flame into the room', rescuing the children before the building was completely engulfed.[58] Such was the influence of motherhood, that it was stronger and more determined than the heroism of two men.[59]

Of course, it was only to be expected that a mother would risk everything and demonstrate enormous strength and determination to save her own children, but many women were attributed motherly qualities in other circumstances, regardless of the children involved. Mrs Mary Rogers, more of whom later, was a stewardess who perished during the sinking of the SS *Stella* in 1899. Mary's husband Richard, also a seaman employed by the London and South West Railway Company on their cross-channel route, had drowned in October 1880 aboard the SS *Honfleur* and this had left Mary with a two-year-old girl and a small baby boy to raise on her own.[60] It was reported that 'to bring her children up carefully and have them properly educated became Mrs Rogers' chief object in life, and to enable her to do this she obtained her position as stewardess', but this was not strictly the case.[61] It was common practice for railway companies to offer positions to the widows of deceased employees so as to avoid having to pay them compensation or provide a pension.[62] It is highly likely that Mary took the job out of financial necessity, and although this was clearly related to providing for her family, it was not quite the proactive decision as related in the narrative.

Furthermore, many years later, shortly before her ill-fated journey upon the *Stella*, her children had grown up and with her daughter about to marry and her son engaged as an apprentice ship-builder, the impression given was that Mary had successfully fulfilled her motherly duties with regard to her children. The role of a stewardess was essentially three-quarters domestic servant and one-quarter nurse, as they were responsible for treating the seasickness or other ailments of the women on board as well as providing for their needs and comforts. As one contemporary examination of the role of a stewardess reported, 'by far the most appreciable services they render is in attending upon and administering to the wants of lady passengers during sea sickness and other illnesses on board'.[63] When she died, aged forty-four, aboard the SS *Stella*, it was concluded of Mary that, although her death had been a terrible tragedy, 'her well-spent life had been crowned with an act of heroism'.[64] It can be imagined that by 'well-spent' the commentator was referring as much to an idealized construction of motherhood in which Mary had raised two prosperous children, as he was to her lengthy service as a stewardess, although, of course, either one of those aspects painted a picture of idealized domesticity.

It would appear, then, that the ideology of separate spheres and the belief in natural or preferable roles and arenas for women were influencing the discourse that surrounded female heroism and ultimately shaped the manner in which narratives and biographies were constructed. If 'the Angel in the House' was the ultimate middle-class prescription for how a woman should try to live her life and heroic women represented an ideal opportunity for presenting exemplary behaviour, it stands to reason that, in didactic narratives of female heroism, the key elements of one would simply map onto the other. This approach resulted in a particular type of heroism, namely one constructed along gendered lines and in which the virtues of domestic ideology could be shown to represent or result in the exemplary heroic behaviour of the heroine.

Further to this, it can be, and indeed has been, suggested that the mechanism of creating a particularly gendered construction of heroism was stimulated by a desire to preserve and reinforce male ruling-class hegemony in the face of challenges from an emerging women's political movement.[65] Constructing female heroism through metaphorically or symbolically locating it in the feminine or domestic sphere, it has been argued, diffused much of the possible political challenge presented by the idea of an independent woman undertaking actions on a par with, or in some cases beyond, those of a man. However, although convincing in relation to specific case studies, the more general picture of the recognition of female heroism is far more complex than this model of masculine hegemony suggests. Precisely because heroism is a variably constructible idea rather than a rigid and unalterable doctrine, it can indeed be shaped and moulded to suit different purposes and, more importantly, by different interest groups in society. Simply because female heroism was constructed along gendered lines does not necessarily mean that it was solely men who were shaping it for their own means or that it was a conscious attempt to discourage the emancipation of women.

'My place is here': Mary Rogers, stewardess of the *Stella*

On 30 March 1899, Maundy Thursday, the SS *Stella* left Southampton bound for St Peter Port in Guernsey. The route between Southampton and the island was the regular route for the London and South Western steamer, but this particular voyage was a special Easter excursion and the first daylight crossing of the season. One hundred and ninety passengers and crew were on board and while the passengers relaxed in the cabin area, the crew went about their usual duties. Later that afternoon, a dense fog came down and the ship's Captain, William Reeks, called his first and second mates alongside him on the bridge to keep watch and to listen for the foghorn that warned ships they were nearing the notorious Casquets rocks. It was reported that when the warning was eventually heard, it was too late and as the rocks loomed out of the mist, Captain Reeks was powerless to prevent the *Stella* from ploughing into them. The granite reef ripped an enormous gash into the hull of the vessel, which lurched violently as it veered along the jagged rocks (see Figure 19).

As water poured in, the fate of the ship was sealed and the Captain gave the order for the lifeboats to be launched. According to survivors, an orderly evacuation began with the women and children first to be lowered into the boats, followed by the male

Figure 19 Illustration of the wreck of the SS *Stella* with an inset of Stewardess Mary Rogers (*Illustrated London News, 1900*).

passengers where space allowed. It took just eight minutes for the ship to sink, and although four of the five lifeboats were successfully launched, eighty-six passengers and nineteen crew lost their lives, including the ship's captain who remained on the bridge and was seen to go down with the ship. The official conclusion of a Board of Trade enquiry was that the *Stella* 'was not navigated with proper and seamanlike care', that full speed had been maintained despite the thick fog and that the foghorn had probably not been heard because the ship was intermittently sounding its own whistle as a warning to other ships.[66] As to the highly prevalent rumours that the *Stella* had dangerously maintained full speed because it was unofficially engaged in a race to St Peter Port against the Great Western Railway service out of Weymouth, the enquiry would only admit that there was a tendency among Captains to increase speeds, but only in order to shorten passage times. It did, however, recommend that in future the arrival times of Southampton and Weymouth services should be staggered so as 'to reassure the public that racing is not practiced'. In summing up, the court recorded 'the greatest admiration of the master, officers, crew, stewards and the two stewardesses (M. Rogers and J. Preston) for the excellent discipline kept, and for their courage and devotion in aiding the women, children and other passengers to escape the vessel'.[67] To many, the gallant behaviour of the crew was the only silver lining to the tragic circumstances of the loss of the *Stella*.

In the days following the tragedy, surviving passengers began to relay their personal stories to the press and details emerged of a remarkable act by Mary Anne Rogers, the senior of the two Stewardesses. The *Jersey Times* of 15 April, quoting an unnamed female passenger, reported that,

> Mrs Rogers, with great presence of mind and calmness, got all the ladies from her cabin to the side of the ship and after placing life belts on as many as were without them, she assisted them into the small boats. Then, turning around, she saw yet another young lady was without a belt, whereupon she insisted on placing her own belt upon her and led her to the fast-filling boat. The sailors called out, "jump in, Mrs Rogers, jump in", the water being then but a few inches from the top of the boat. "No, no!" she replied; "if I get in I will sink the boat. Good-bye, Good-bye" and then with uplifted hands she said, "Lord, save me" and immediately the ship sank beneath her feet.[68]

This was not the only reported instance of such behaviour on board the *Stella*. A male crew member, a stoker, enquired of a female passenger if she had secured a life belt and when 'she said she had not, he took his off and placed it around her neck'. Another report stated that 'in more than one instance a member of the ship's company – a stewardess included – was seen to divest himself or herself of a lifebelt to give it to a passenger'. Another passenger was said to have given up his lifebelt to the daughter of another male passenger and there were numerous accounts of husbands and fathers securing lifebelts for their wives and daughters rather than for themselves.[69]

Nor was there any lack of emphasis on the heroism of the crew in general. One editorial commented that 'many acts of self-denial, devotion, gallantry and heroism are related and altogether would fill a large volume', while a survivor, Miss Drake, summed it up clearly and succinctly, 'the whole crew behaved like heroes'.[70] Others were more specific, such as the witnesses who described how the Master's boy declined to leave his post although urged by the Captain to do so or those who praised the second-mate Reynolds for his heroic actions in attempting to save passengers.[71] There were some who initially questioned the prevailing tide of adulation, such as the Rev John Penfold who had lost his sister in the accident. In a letter to *The Times*, Penfold asserted that 'in spite of the buncombe which has filled the newspapers about "chivalry," "pride of race" and so forth, women and children were left on deck while at least one boat full of men pulled away from the sinking ship. This appears to be borne out by the great number of men saved, while several women and little children perished.'[72] In another case, a Mrs Little who spent hours in one of the lifeboats before being rescued reported that,

> I took a turn at the oars because some of the men would not touch them. There were men who worked like heroes but others! Ah! Well. I won't talk about them, only it did make my blood boil to see them have a quiet pipe and then go to sleep. I confess I broke down when the Lynx rescued us, but perhaps that was due to being knocked down three times. There was a cry of "the lady first" but the men lost their heads and I was pushed everywhere.[73]

Eschewing this minority of dissent, it was the incident featuring Mary Rogers that really and truly captured the public's imagination. Furthermore, and central to the concerns of this chapter, her heroic and self-sacrificial behaviour was heralded as symbolic of the exemplary behaviour displayed by all, despite the fact that she was a woman.

This attitude towards Mary Rogers becomes even more remarkable when set within the context of the more general discourse regarding women at sea and, in particular, the behaviour of women during shipping accidents. In an article on gendered modes of behaviour during shipwrecks, Lucy Delap has shown that in the latter quarter of the nineteenth century the general perception was that 'feminine characteristics of hysteria, physical weakness and weakness of character meant that women could not successfully occupy the "male sphere" of the ship at sea.'[74] According to Delap, during shipwrecks women were usually viewed as either 'hysterical obstacles to evacuation' or 'passive inanimate objects, reliant on men to save them' and examples of this can be seen with regard to the *Stella* disaster. One woman passenger reported that 'she and the child were pressed into a boat by her husband, who refused her entreaty to be allowed to stay with him', another eyewitness told of how a gentleman went down with the ship after giving up his seat in a crowded lifeboat to the daughter of another male passenger, and there were numerous accounts of husbands 'putting' their wives into lifeboats against their protestations.[75]

Furthermore, during the Board of Trade enquiry, Mr Richards, who was the QC representing the Rev Penfold who had been so publically critical of the fact that many women and children had perished, made a statement concerning his client's change of heart after hearing the evidence presented. His statement read,

> During the last day or two the circumstances have been explained as being in no way due to the action of the crew or the passengers in crowding into the boats before the women. Two or three witnesses had clearly established the fact that these

poor women appeared to be rooted to the deck and did not realise the imminent danger. Having no male companions to make them enter the boats they remained and went down with the ship. If there had been more officers to superintend the departure of the women the unfortunate loss of life amongst them would not have occurred.[76]

Delap's conclusion that the gendered ideology of separate spheres influenced both the circumstances and behaviour of women at sea and, more crucially, the interpretation of their behaviour would appear to apply to the events of the shipwreck of the *Stella*, except, of course, in relation to Mary Rogers.

Rogers provided a very different example of how a woman could behave at sea and how she should be treated. In reporting that none of the stewardesses were saved, the *Jersey Evening Post* stated that this was 'due to the circumstances that the sixth and final lifeboat launched, into which the stewardesses were no doubt placed, was capsized in the vortex of the sinking steamer'.[77] This statement suggests that it was expected for all the crew, including the female stewardess, to be among the last to leave the ship. Acknowledging Mary's professionalism and dedication to duty, a *Derby Mercury* editorial contended that 'she appeared, from all accounts, to regard herself as part and parcel of the ship, nor did she move from her post until all the passengers, the women especially, were supplied with lifebelts, while she persistently refused to accept one for herself saying that she must stick to the ship'. Another eyewitness report simply stated that in response to a passenger's plea for her to save herself, Mary simply replied, 'no, my place is here.' Furthermore, in the narrative of Mary's last minutes on board, no man attempted to force her into a boat, as was the case with the female passengers. In the accounts, the male passengers and crew already in the lifeboat reportedly implored the stewardess to get in, and yet when she refused because it was overcrowded, none of them offered up their seat for her as they would undoubtedly have been expected to do for a female passenger.[78] It would appear that those on board the *Stella* viewed Mary Rogers more as a member of the crew than they did as a woman and as such she transcended the gap between the masculine and feminine spheres. Furthermore, in choosing to undertake her professional duty and stay with the ship, rather than exercising her accepted priority for escape accorded on the basis of her gender, it would appear that Mary also, in this respect, viewed herself as a stewardess first and a woman second.

To some extent, these attitudes can be explained within the context of significant social and political changes during the last quarter of the nineteenth century which, in the words of one historian, 'challenged the rigid doctrine of separate spheres for men and women and showed that women could play a part in public and professional life'.[79] Improvements in educational provision for women were important in their own right, but coupled with the general expansion of white-collar work and technological advances such as the telephone and typewriter, they dramatically widened the occupational field for women. The increasing availability of safer methods of contraception and more progressive attitudes towards female sexuality allowed women greater control over family planning and prompted revaluations regarding the domesticity of motherhood. Meanwhile, the repeal in 1886 of the Contagious Diseases Acts of the 1860s, largely as a result of a campaign by a female organization led by Josephine Butler, not only demonstrated a demand by women for control of their own bodies but also highlighted the positive effect they could have through political campaigning.[80] Legally, married women gained greater equality with the introduction of the Matrimonial Clauses Act in 1878 and the Married Women's Property Act in 1882. Even what might appear minor changes, such as increasing participation in sport or the enthusiastic female embracing of the bicycle, which in turn paved the way for reforms in clothing and styles of dress, had a distinct impact on shaping an alternative image of women. As Barbara Caine has concluded, 'one can see the whole discussion of the "new woman" of the 1890s as the reformulation of the early and mid-Victorian "woman question" in accordance with the broad economic, social, political and intellectual changes in society at large'.[81]

Women also began to make inroads into the political sphere. In 1870, school boards were created and these allowed female candidates, followed in 1875 by the election of the first female poor-law guardian, Martha Merrington, and from 1894 women were permitted to stand for election to parish and district councils.[82] Although it was to be many years before women would secure universal suffrage, the subject became an important focus for female campaign groups, especially in the light of limited successes and greater emphasis on parliamentary reform for men. The nineteenth-century movement for female suffrage was, however, beset by political and ideological differences, and even the formation of a unified suffrage organization, The National Union of Women's Suffrage Societies in 1897, failed to guard against influences from, among others, young female socialist and communist campaigners who believed universal suffrage was the goal. Furthermore, many campaigners for female suffrage were less firebrand radicals and more, as Martin Pugh has summarized them, 'determined but cautious reformers struggling to win support in a society which was far from favourably disposed to feminism'.[83] Change was being negotiated and acceptance would take time and a period of transition during which both old and new ideas operated alongside one another and competed for supremacy. This dialectic was clearly at work aboard the *Stella*, where a limited acceptance of new ideas permitted the treatment of Mary Rogers as a professional and independent woman, while an older belief, ingrained over many years, in separate spheres ideology determined the patriarchal behaviour towards female passengers. Further evidence for such a dichotomy is provided by the movement which was established to fund and erect a monument to commemorate Mary and recognize her heroic action.

On 13 April 1899, a letter appeared in *The Times*, which suggested that 'a short paragraph is far from being sufficient tribute of honour to the woman whose calm devotion and self-sacrificing death were chronicled in your columns yesterday'.[84] The letter went on to argue that all honour was accorded to a captain who went down with his ship and that sufficient money should be collected to erect 'a simple monument to Mrs Rogers's memory, and for the perpetuation of the honour she deserves'. The author of the letter stated that that she could not undertake such a collection, but that she would gladly contribute £25, a considerable sum considering that a modest public monument could be erected for around £40, to any fund that was established. The letter was from Francis Power Cobbe, a significant and prominent writer and spokeswoman on a range of political and social platforms. Like many middle-class women, Cobbe had been an active philanthropist, involved in activities for, among others, the Workhouse Visiting Society and the Societies for Friendless Girls who visited workhouse girls who had subsequently moved into domestic service. Cobbe was also extremely active in the anti-vivisection movement, running the Victoria Street Society and editing its newspaper the *Zoopholist*.[85] However, it was her work as a campaigner on women's rights issues, and more importantly the beliefs and ideas that underpinned that work, which are of particular relevance here. For, although Cobbe undoubtedly contributed much to significant debates regarding key issues for women, such as education, marriage and suffrage, her views were also deeply and complexly rooted in the ideology of separate spheres.

For Cobbe, Mary Rogers represented an absolute embodiment of exactly the construction of womanhood that she had been espousing throughout her career. Furthermore, the campaigning journalist was now in her late seventies and living alone in a remote part of Wales following the death of life-partner Mary Lloyd. Having recently severed her lifelong association with the antivivisection movement, she was perhaps looking for a last philanthropic opportunity with a socially political edge. Basically, Cobbe believed strongly in the moral autonomy of women, that women did not exist purely as a counterpoint to men or simply to serve men's needs and that women had a right to determine what they did and where they did it. She argued that women should not be restricted to the home, nor should they be financially dependent on men. However, Cobbe was also a defender of sexual difference and in particular the idea of women as the 'mother sex', which essentially predetermined them to be innately and naturally suited to the nurturing environment of home and family. For Cobbe, women should not be *restricted* to the home or to domesticity, but it was, she contended, where the vast majority were best suited to being.

Mary Rogers was an autonomous and financially independent woman, working outside of the home, and, by all accounts in a position where she would have been well regarded and, to some extent, respected by the women she tended to. Channel Stewardesses reportedly received, in addition to their 15s a week wage, a 'good income' from gratuities during crossings, which suggests that passengers regarded them highly enough to reward their service.[86] Consequently, she fitted well with Cobbe's ideas of moral autonomy. However, the role of a stewardess was in essence that of a lady's maid or nursery nurse and many of the duties were essentially domestic in nature, such as attending to the needs of ladies in their bedrooms or the female lounge and washing and tending to the children. Furthermore, stewardesses were given sole responsibility for the female passengers and the areas occupied by them aboard ship, which not only reinforced ideas of gendered spaces but also restricted the influence of stewardesses to the feminine sphere.

Stewardesses were, as already mentioned, responsible for the physical health and emotional well-being of the female passengers, and a nursing certificate or work experience was highly desired by those employing women for the role.[87] Yet, when illnesses were considered to be particularly serious, treatment was carried out 'under the direction of the ship's doctor', who would almost certainly have been a man. Nursing the seasick was perceived to be within the capabilities of a female stewardess, but anything more, it would seem, required the skill and knowledge of a man. A stewardess, then, was part 'angel in the house', part selfless nursemaid, and part nurturing mother figure, who took the sick or alarmed female passengers and children under her wing during the voyage. It is easy to see not only how and why the figure of Mary Rogers so appealed to Cobbe as an exemplar of late nineteenth-century womanhood, but also why she would have been so keen to facilitate a memorial to commemorate her and all she could be seen to stand for.

Cobbe's plea for a memorial fund was taken up by Annie Bryans, the wife of Herbert Bryans (a noted stained-glass artist) and following an appeal in *The Times* donations began to flood in.[88] The substantial sum of £570 was raised and as this was far in excess of what was required for the planned memorial, it was decided that £250 should instead be given to Mary's two children: her daughter receiving £50 as a wedding gift and her son £200 as an income to support his shipwright apprenticeship.[89] Cobbe, along with G. F. Watts, advised and assisted Bryans with the design and implantation of the memorial which, after a considerable delay caused by bureaucratic difficulties in agreeing a site with Southampton Council, was eventually unveiled on the newly constructed Western Esplanade in Southampton on 27 July 1901. Herbert Bryans designed the monument, a canopied drinking fountain in Portland-stone, upon the central column of which was a brass plaque with a lengthy inscription written by Cobbe (see Figure 17). In this inscription, after a brief narrative of the key points of Mary's act, Cobbe highlighted two characteristics which she believed made Mary worthy of such commemoration, 'steadfast performance of duty' and 'ready self-sacrifice for the sake of others'. While generally being noble elements to emphasize, they were also qualities that located Mary firmly within Cobbe's framework: the competent and independent working woman doing her duty and the selfless mother figure laying down her life for those in her care. Mary Rogers was therefore successfully promoted as an example, and to some extent a champion, of the reforming ideas being forwarded by campaigners for increased rights and opportunities for women, while still remaining an icon of the domestic ideology which had been a key idea of the previous quarter of a century.

The case of Mary Rogers provides one indication that female heroism was not necessarily constructed to only serve the gendered aims of men. It could also be constructed to support, for example, arguments for the suffrage rights of women or, as in the case of another example, calls for improved female pay and working conditions. Sarah Smith was a pantomime artist who, during a performance of Charles Perrault's *Riquet with the Tuft* at the Princess's theatre on Oxford Street in January 1863, was fatally burnt while trying to extinguish the flaming dress of a fellow performer which had ignited on an unprotected footlight.[90] There were, as might be expected, calls for more stringent safety precautions concerning lighting or the keeping of damp blankets in the wings. However, the incident revealed that dancers were usually required to purchase much of their own costume, and in particular their elaborate petticoats, out of their own money and that their wages were so low they could not afford to buy material that had been treated to make it more fire-retardant. One newspaper editorial stated, 'nor can ballet dancers afford, out of the miserable salaries they receive, to expend a fraction thereof on even taking precautions for the safety of their own lives'. It also went on to quote a correspondent to *The Times* who had written, 'I consider that the British female has an indefensible right to burn herself to death if she chooses, but for the poor girls at the theatre, whose inflammable costume is not a matter of choice, I do consider they have, at least, the right not to be unnecessarily burnt by the manager,' before bluntly and colourfully adding, 'when a *prima donna* has been roasted perhaps some improvement may take place, but I fear not till then'.[91] The politics of class is clearly more at work in this example than the politics of gender.

Another case in which class rather than gender politics appear to have directly influenced the way in which a heroine was constructed is that of the Southwark heroine Alice Ayres. Alice, who it will be recalled lost her life during a fire, was employed as a nursemaid by her sister Mary and was attempting to save her three nieces from the blaze. This family relationship was widely reported in the press and yet in the exemplary biographical accounts of the incident, she was almost universally referred to as an employed nursemaid rather than a relative of the family. In Charles Moore's account, Alice was presented, 'hurrying to the room where her master and mistress slept' to warn them of the fire.[92] G. F. Watts referred to the case in his 1887 letter to *The Times* regarding the recognition of everyday heroism, and in that letter he described Alice as 'the maid of all work, who lost her life in saving those of her master's children'.[93] It is unlikely that Watts, who collated the cases from newspaper reports, would not have been aware of Alice's relationship to the children and yet he chose not to mention it. Canon Rawnsley in his volume of poetry described Alice as 'the nursemaid in the household' and again, did not mention the family relationship.[94]

This emphasis can be explained in the light of previous evidence suggesting that Watts and his associates believed working-class examples to have a greater didactic influence upon the intended working-class audience. By focusing upon Alice's working-class status rather than her familial relationship, it was presumably hoped that the reports of her heroism would have greater resonance and influence in the working-class communities where encouraging self-improvement was viewed to be of considerable importance. Consequently, emphasizing her apparent dedication to duty and service to her master were more important characteristics to promote than the natural and nurturing instincts of a family member or the domesticity of Alice's role as nursemaid. Alice's heroism was also more blatantly constructed along class, and even republican, lines in the editorial of a particularly radical newspaper, which complained that,

> the Queen has at her disposal a large sum of money, which is supposed to be bestowed as rewards to needy persons for meritorious services and conduct . . . but in really conspicuous instances of bravery, devotion to duty and self sacrifice, as that of Alice Ayres the servant girl who lost her own life in saving the lives of her employers children, nothing is forthcoming from the Royal bounty fund. And wherefore? The cause is explained in the fact disclosed by the newspapers at her internment that, "the parents of this girl belong to the working classes.[95]

As with Sarah Smith, the heroism of Alice Ayres could be constructed in such a way so as to herald her as an icon for the emancipation of the working classes rather than as an example of the benefits of separate spheres ideology, despite the fact that her occupation and behaviour also suitably equipped her for such use.

'Courage for a man is heroism for a girl': The gendered scales of heroism

The evidence presented in this chapter suggests that female heroism was constructed in certain ways so as to present it as distinctly different to male heroism and, through the emphasis on domestic ideology and separate spheres, make it appear more remarkable but less 'heroic' in comparison with acts undertaken by men. However, female heroism was certainly not derided or disparaged and in some ways it was more celebrated than men's because it was perceived to be unusual or anomalous. Nonetheless, it was, by and large, regarded and constructed as being of a lower standard than men's and it would be tempting to conclude that this was related to reinforcing notions of female inferiority. But if, as this chapter has shown, not all constructions of female heroism were motivated by projecting such ideas, another conclusion must be sought and that conclusion might well be discovered by considering the evidence in relation to ideas about heroism, rather than ideas about gender politics.

It is certainly true to say that heroism was judged on a scale, with some acts ranking higher than others; an assertion that was substantiated in earlier chapters. Even the briefest of examinations of the history of the Albert Medal reveals that within months of its introduction, the decoration was reclassified into first-class and second-class awards because some acts were adjudged to be more heroic than others. The complex reasoning behind this, stemming from ideas of character and national identity, was examined in Chapter 1, but the very fact that heroism was being rated at all is also interesting. If, hypothetically, the Home Office secretaries who administered the Albert Medal had rated heroism on a scale of one to ten, it seems likely that the qualification for a second-class medal would have been around the six and over mark and for a first class, perhaps eight or even nine on the scale. This was because the Albert Medal was designed to reward only what was considered by those in the Home Office to represent the very pinnacle of heroic behaviour. If the act fell below a six, it would still be considered heroic and perhaps even really quite heroic, but it was, in the often repeated phrase of those who administered it 'not up to the standard of the Albert Medal'. There was a constant fear in the Home Office that Albert Medal standards would slip; hence, awards of the medal were kept rare and the first class was always reserved for only the very highest of the high.

So, if male heroism was judged on a scale, it is likely that female heroism would have been approached in the same way, with some women being regarded as more heroic than others. Furthermore, on the hypothetical scale of one to ten for female heroism, women would have been ranked in exactly the same way as men, starting with one at the bottom and rising to ten for those considered to have displayed the highest level of heroism. Thus, in its own right, there was nothing disparaging or inferior about women's heroism; it was rated in a similar way to that of men. However, and this is absolutely crucial, when those, for example in the Home Office, came to theoretically place the two scales up against one another, that is where the difference was marked. Rather than aligning them equally, with number one matching number one and so on, the scales were offset against one another with the ten of the female scale matched against the six of the male and everything else aligned accordingly. Using this model, it is possible to begin to see and understand why it was that female heroism, while highly regarded as important and valuable in its own right, could not match up with that of men. Even the very highest attainment for a woman was only half-way up the scale for a man.

The Albert Medal is the clearest example of this mechanism of evaluation at work. In the period between 1866 and 1916, six women received the decoration and all of these were second-class awards. In fact, in the entire lifespan of the medal, all nineteen awards made to women were of the second class; not a single woman ever received the first-class decoration. It would be easy to conclude that this was gender prejudice on the part of the male Home Office secretaries, who automatically degraded the heroism of women, but the evidence suggests something different. Gender was certainly never specifically given as a reason for refusal and in the case of Kate Chapman, a nine-year-old girl, it was expressly stated by one undersecretary that 'it ought not in my opinion to be a question either of age or sex'.[96] Refusals in female cases appear to have been made for largely the same reasons as refusals in male cases, with 'insufficient risk to life' once again the most common reason. However, while being female does not appear to have prevented an award, in several cases it appears to have been an influencing factor in allowing it. In the case of Hannah Rosbotham, the reasoning behind giving the award was that 'if this was the case of a man perhaps it would be hardly enough but what is an act of courage for a man is heroism for a girl'.[97] So although less likely to receive the award, it was actually because women were being judged on a scale which, when compared to that for a man, placed their highest achievements level with an average performance by a man. Thus, a woman attaining a ten on the metaphorical scale for female heroism rated only a six on the male equivalent and as the distinction for the first-class medal started at eight, it was impossible for even those women judged to have demonstrated the upmost bravery to reach the accepted standard.

Considered in this context, it becomes clearer that constructing female heroism in such a way as to project it as lesser than male could actually be about protecting the sanctity of heroism. As with the gradual shift in attitudes regarding the status of women, fundamental ideas about the nature of heroism were also ingrained in society and newer ones were slow to develop. Generally speaking, heroism was still seen to be the natural and innate domain of men and, particularly with regard to the undertaking of life-risking acts, much of this stemmed from the fact that the predominant theatres in which the public understanding of such heroism had been fostered were male dominated – the military, the emergency services, and overseas service or exploration in the British Empire. The introduction of decorations such as the Victoria Cross and the Albert Medal in the mid-nineteenth century paved the way for a more democratic understanding of gallantry and heroism. Later on, the increasingly publicized work of organizations like the Royal Humane Society and the Society for the Protection of Life from Fire, coupled with the ideas of people like Watts and Carnegie, widened the understanding of how and where heroism could be performed. This did a great deal to bring everyday heroism into greater prominence and did, at the least, offer a platform upon which women were included, much the same as the limited widening of the public and political sphere for women during the same period. However, attitudes were slow to change and true heroism of the very highest calibre was still seen as a predominantly male achievement, not so as to dismiss that of women, but simply because that was how it had generally been understood and constructed in the past.

Consequently, whereas female heroism might now be considered to have been constructed in certain ways so as to reinforce the inferiority of women, the gendered construction could actually have been more related to defending heroism against changes, which it was feared, could degrade or devalue the firmly held ideas and existing male constructions which had predominated since at least the 1850s. By 1900, however, when Mary Rogers was discussed and accepted as a heroine on equal terms with the male heroes on board the *Stella* and accorded an equal level of honour to the captain by having a memorial erected to commemorate her heroism, the gendered nature of the concept of heroism was, to some extent, on the wane. Some, such as Lucy Delap, might argue that, as far as gendered codes of heroism at sea were concerned, these ideas metaphorically sank in 1912 along with the *Titanic* when in the aftermath of the disaster it was argued that 'women and children first' should become simply 'children first' because if women demanded equality in daily life they should also expect it at sea.[98] Others might point to the treatment of female munitions workers during World War I, who were constructed as heroines if they died while assembling explosives, as the point at which gender could be considered to have ceased to have a significant bearing on the construction of heroism.[99] Or the very fact that women have continued to be referred to in terms of being 'heroines' rather than a more universal and gender-neutral use of 'hero' is, some might suggest, proof enough that little has actually changed and heroism still retains its deep-seated nature of gender separation.[100]

Conclusions

Female heroism was, especially in the mid to latter half of the nineteenth century, by and large, viewed and demarcated along similar lines to that prescribed within domestic ideology or the idea of separate spheres; women belonged in the domestic sphere as wives and mothers and were promoted or constructed as such when being held up as exemplary heroic figures. Moreover, it is clear that as the nineteenth century 'fin de siècle' approached and the ideas and attitudes of society towards the status and treatment of women began to change, so too did attitudes towards female heroism. Of course, because such arrivals and departures are never entirely synchronized and fundamental changes in ideology take time to embed themselves into the public psyche, ideas tend to run in tandem with one another for a period of time and this can be seen in relation to the ways in which female heroes such as Mary Rogers were treated around the turn of the century and in the period up to World War I. Nonetheless, female heroism was an adaptable construction, capable of adjusting to the prevailing ideas of the society in which it existed.

It is certainly conceivable that in some cases there may have been an agenda on the part of some men to restrict or control the activities that women could undertake so as to ensure that they did not encroach too far into the male domain; for example, the men in control of the nineteenth-century missionary movement highlighted by Rowbotham in her article.[101] Furthermore, it can be conceded that, while certainly not degraded or devalued on its own terms, female heroism was almost universally perceived to be innately and naturally of a lower standard when compared to the heroism of men. However, concluding that a male hegemonic agenda was at work in all constructions of female heroism and that the mechanism was symptomatic of wider discriminatory behaviour towards all women simply does not stand up when challenged with the evidence put forward in this chapter. What has been shown is that female heroism was differently constructed, but that the process was undertaken by both men and women and for the purposes of promoting or defending women's rights as much as for constricting or oppressing them. Also, examining the findings of how and why female heroism was being constructed in particular ways, against the backdrop of attitudes and ideas about heroism rather than gender, reveals a possibility that it was actually 'heroism' that was being protected and not necessarily male ruling-class hegemony.

Accepting that an act of heroism undertaken by a woman, who was ideologically perceived as physically weak, emotionally unstable and indecisive to the point of requiring male guidance, was equal to an act undertaken by a man, who was seen as innately and naturally able to represent the pinnacle of heroic behaviour, had the potential to devalue the whole concept. Given that the heroism of a country's men was one of the ways in which a nation not only shaped its own sense of its internal strength but also promoted and projected that strength to other nations, it was important that male heroism was always seen in the very highest of terms. Women could be seen to be extremely heroic, and could well be promoted as exemplary figures, as long as it was on their own terms and that their heroism was always second to that of men, lest it reduce the quality or ability of the heroic model in general. This is one possible reason why their heroism was seldom regarded on a par with that of men. However, what is essentially important to recognize, and has been explored in some depth throughout this book, is that male heroism was also variably constructed to take account of prevailing ideas in society and that men were subject to the same processes of rating and assessment as women. Furthermore, some men were just as likely as women to be regarded as lesser examples because their heroism was perceived or judged to have fallen short of what was required of a male hero; consider, for example, those whose nominations for the Albert Medal, or the various awards offered by non-State organizations, were refused. There was just as much 'construction' at work in the projected and promoted image of the Victorian male hero as there was for the heroine, and this is just one area in which this study provides a platform for further examination, as discussed in the conclusion.

Conclusion

> We have undertaken to discourse here for a little on Great Men, their manner
> of appearance in our world's business, how they have shaped themselves in the
> world's history, what ideas men formed of them, what work they did; on Heroes,
> namely, and on their reception and performance.[1]
>
> *Thomas Carlyle* (1841)

In 1841, when Thomas Carlyle decided to discuss the 'reception and performance'
of heroes and heroism, he chose to discourse on Great Men, but this book has selected
a different body of individuals upon whom to direct attention, namely, everyday
heroes and heroines. Carlyle focused on prophets, poets, priests and kings, whereas
it is workmen, seamen, women and the working classes who have populated this
study. Carlyle perceived heroes to be an inspirational intellectual elite, who drove
society and history forward with their creative initiative. This account, however, has
discovered that otherwise ordinary people, when undertaking extraordinary acts of
life-risking bravery, were also considered to be heroic and, more importantly, that
their reception had an impact upon the shape and structure of social relationships.
Heroes, in the Carlylean sense, were not products of their time, but rather men for
all time, enduringly constant in an ever-changing world. Yet, the heroic characters
in this examination have been shown to be, more often than not, social and cultural
constructions of the group or society that created them, mediations of the attitudes
and beliefs of the time, very much products of their age, albeit, in some cases, ones
that have subsequently endured. This study has identified and examined a far wider
nineteenth-century discourse of heroism than Carlyle outlined and in doing so has not
only encompassed the commonplace and the working classes, but has also determined
a new angle from which to understand the idea as a subject to be studied and analysed
in its own right. What conclusions, then, can be reached from this study?

Heroism, it has been shown, is not a free-floating idea or something uniform and
unchanging that exists independently of the time or society in which it is located. It is
a constructed idea and one which is assembled according to many variables, including
who is doing the constructing, when and where they are doing it, their intended
audience and their own objectives or purposes. This is not to say that there are not
constant characteristics which endure across every construction of heroism and the
risking of life to save life is one particularly consistent example. But many other factors,
some of which relate to the person undertaking the act and others which concern the
act itself, can be included or privileged, or equally be excluded or downplayed, so as to
create a specific type of heroism. This process is not always or necessarily a deliberate

or conscious action and is influenced as much by the social and cultural landscape of the time as by any explicit or premeditated objectives. Consequently, identifying and examining the various and differing constructions of 'everyday' heroism has revealed much about how the discourse was conceived, shaped and understood by various people and groups in society and how it altered and developed during particular periods of time. From this, it can be concluded that everyday heroism was a malleable and flexible idea, one that reflected and helped to shape a wide range of contemporary social and cultural ideas, and which was appropriated and constructed for the didactic purpose of promoting and promulgating certain types of individuals as models of correct and exemplary behaviour. Furthermore, it was precisely the flexibility of the discourse of everyday heroism, and the ease with which it could be appropriated and moulded, that made it so influential during this period and which contributed significantly to both the speed and nature of its development.

Throughout the first half of the nineteenth century, the acknowledgement and recognition of heroes and heroism tended to be undertaken through establishment channels and was largely limited to military and imperial heroism. In 1866, the State introduced the Albert Medal in the belief that raising the public profile of acts of everyday heroism would endorse a certain way of behaving. The aim was to associate civilian heroism with allegiance to the Crown and to foster active and constructive citizenship by inspiring or inducing the populace, and in particular the working classes, to adopt more moral and responsible attitudes and values. However, as a result of this approach, the secretaries and clerks at the Home Office based their judgements more on the personal character and moral integrity of the individual, rather than assessing the act itself. In turn, this led them to create and apply a particular model of everyday heroism that was constructed on the basis of certain criteria, this model being that individuals had to have freely, knowingly and willingly entered into circumstances where their own lives were at considerable risk, in order to save the life of another, without any professional or personal duty to do so and without any outside assistance. The application of these restricting criteria, coupled with a policy of maintaining unfeasibly high standards so as to preserve the prestige of the honour, meant that relatively few Albert Medals were awarded and it came to be regarded as establishment recognition of only the very pinnacle of civilian heroism.

However, this construction of everyday heroism was considered by many to be too limited, restrictive or inappropriate, and consequently, alternative models emerged and established themselves. One was the subscription-supported subject-specific model employed by organizations including the Royal Humane Society and the Society for Protection of Life from Fire. For these organizations, the regular and prolific recognition of heroism undertaken in particular circumstances was an important aspect of increasing publicity and support for their work. They generally had less fixed views about the types of people they recognized, but were each restricted to quite specific types of heroism and answerable to their subscribers. Another model, also reasonably restrictive, was that created by G. F. Watts and his liberally-minded associates, which tended towards the public commemoration of self-sacrificial heroism undertaken by working-class individuals or within working-class communities. As with other organizations, an egalitarian approach was adopted as it was important to include the full range of the working classes (men, women and children) so as to maximize the potential for didactic influence upon that class. A third model was conceived, far later than the others, by Andrew Carnegie who had to negotiate the prominent channels of recognition and commemoration that these existing initiatives had been establishing since the mid-nineteenth century. Carnegie undoubtedly benefited from the admiration and respect with which everyday heroism had come to be regarded, but this also meant that his alternative methodology of rewarding heroism with money raised anxieties and attracted criticism. The Hero Fund model was also different in that it significantly broadened the boundaries of what was considered to be a heroic act beyond the more commonly acknowledged parameters.

Despite their differences, all of these non-State organizations were, to some extent, united under an overarching radicalism that set them apart from and challenged the established point of view. Most notable in this was, perhaps, Andrew Carnegie who, alongside his desire to philanthropically dispense of his wealth, was also seeking a mechanism to encourage and stimulate pacifist ideas and ideals. Everyday heroism was, for Carnegie, the perfect alternative for young men to exercise their allegedly innate desire to be heroic, thus circumventing the need for war and conflict and presenting a potential challenge to the growing militarism of the early twentieth century. The involvement of figures such as Walter Crane and Octavia Hill in a prominent project utilizing the topic goes some way to demonstrating the radical credentials of everyday heroism but it is also something which ran though the wider circle of which they were a part. Watts and others were motivated by a progressive liberal agenda, concerned with highlighting and improving, albeit in a slightly narrow-minded and dogmatic way, the life and circumstances of the working classes. For them, the establishment's recognition of everyday heroism did not sufficiently provide what they believed to be the key to engaging the working-class audience, namely examples of life-risking bravery, indicative of sound moral character, undertaken in the everyday surroundings of working-class civilian life, and so they set out to do it themselves. Evidence that everyday heroism was perceived as presenting a challenge to establishment ideas is also provided by the fact that radical newspapers such as the *Morning Chronicle* and *Reynolds News* frequently ran reports championing or celebrating acts of everyday heroism and editorials deploring what it considered to be the shabby treatment of heroic individuals by the establishment, as outlined earlier in the cases of nursemaid Alice Ayres and actress Sarah Smith. What can be concluded from this is that radical, liberal and pacifist motivations all contributed significantly to shaping, consolidating and encouraging an alternative discourse on everyday heroism that existed alongside that presented by the State.

This is, however, only half of the process and, as this study has shown, it is crucial to also examine and understand the manner in which the idea of everyday heroism was received and understood by the general public at large. This is far from straightforward and most of the explicit evidence originates from sources which were, to borrow a term from Peter Karsten, a 'product of the articulate'.[2] Nevertheless, it is possible, by trying to uncover how middle-class or elite constructions were more widely received, to gain some insights and reach conclusions about the opinions and attitudes of the predominantly working-class audience at which they were aimed.

For example, the commemorative projects examined in Chapter 2 were motivated by a belief that everyday heroism was an especially potent didactic tool for presenting models of exemplary behaviour and character to a working-class audience, because it was undertaken by people of that class who consequently represented relevant and empathetic examples. However, this perception presupposed a homogenization of the working classes and a high level of class consciousness, both of which have been shown to be considerably overestimated by those at the top end of the social scale.[3] Nonetheless, the commemorative projects do appear to have been relatively well received by the working classes, and if this was not solely due to an affinity with the model characters that were put forward by the elites, why else might those constructions have been accepted by working classes?

'Everyday' heroism was characterized as such not only because it was undertaken by otherwise ordinary people, but also because it involved, by and large, reasonably familiar activities and generally took place within recognizable everyday environments, examples being industrial accidents, house fires, inland water incidents and problems with out-of-control horses or livestock. Everyday heroes and heroines had encountered challenges and dangers that were all too real and recognizable to the majority of the working classes, who could associate themselves with and understand the nature of the heroic acts. Consequently, their engagement with them may not necessarily have been because they viewed themselves as akin to those *people*, but more because they appreciated and could relate to the *incident* in which they had risked, and sometimes given, their life. In turn, this evidence suggests that the middle-class or elitist constructions of everyday heroism were focused on projecting the qualities and characteristics of the individual, whereas the working-class version appreciated and valued the nature of the act as well as the person who had undertaken it.

It is likely that this distinction was also a factor in relation to the public monuments erected to commemorate heroic individuals. It is clear that the administration and procedures behind these commemorations were largely controlled and driven by groups comprising middle-class and/or elite individuals. Furthermore, these groups were motivated by the opportunity to harness or appropriate the heroism of the individual for the purposes of encouraging and promoting exemplary behaviour, especially to an appropriate working-class audience. For example, the committee in control of the memorial to the Newark nursemaid Ethel Harrison ensured that the commemorative process was sufficiently open and affordable to encourage working-class engagement, and they selected the site of the monument on the basis of where it was most likely to be viewed by other working-class nursemaids. However, it is also clear, for example through evidence such as subscription lists and attendance at unveiling ceremonies, that there was popular and widespread working-class engagement with the commemorative process and the public monument once it was completed. Exactly why this occurred is very difficult to ascertain because those concerned rarely articulated the reasons behind their support or involvement. Nevertheless, as it has been shown that everyday heroism could be constructed and understood in a range of ways, it is not unreasonable to conclude that those from the working classes, who gave their money or voiced their support at public meetings, may well have had their own conceptions, rather than the one being constructed for them by the committee.

It can be concluded, then, that the working classes appear to not only have understood and constructed everyday heroism on their own terms, but also that their construction differed from that handed down to them from above. The latter generally employed a construction that judged the qualities and moral character of the individual person, rather than assessing the act of heroism; basically, it was more concerned with what people were rather that what they had done. This can be seen with regard to the Albert Medal, the projects of G. F. Watts and his associates, the ideas of memorial committees and those who sought to promote the actions of heroines. These constructions were not universally accepted by the working classes, but when they were, there is evidence to suggest that it was because public opinion had been sought and the working-class construction of the idea, which related to the everyday nature of the act as much as to the type of person who undertook it, had been taken into consideration.

The influence of this reciprocal relationship between the ideas and values of a particular group or society at a given time and the manner in which models of heroism are constructed can also be seen in relation to female heroism. Social and cultural ideas, such as domestic ideology, biological determinants, physical and emotional capabilities and prescribed roles or spheres, all implicitly contributed to a specific construction of female heroism which differed greatly to that for men. However, female heroism could also be explicitly constructed, as it was, for example, by Francis Power Cobbe, by G. F. Watts, by memorial committees and by the radical press, with particular intentions in mind, be they social, cultural or political in nature. This demonstrates how heroism is intrinsically related to the ideas and mindset of a given society at a given time. As social and political attitudes towards the position of women shifted and developed towards greater equality, so too did the construction of female heroism and contradictions within the processes of emaciation were mirrored in the development of the idea.

A further conclusion reached by this study is that, although certainly not degraded or devalued on its own terms, female heroism was almost universally perceived and constructed as being innately and naturally of a lower standard when compared to the heroism of men. It is tempting to see this as a mechanism for protecting or furthering male hegemony or restricting the development of female emancipation and this may well have had some influence. However, the close examination undertaken in Chapter 5 strongly suggests that the lower grading of female heroism in relation to the heroism of men was actually intended to protect and preserve the perceived integrity and superiority of the male model of heroism. The heroism of a country's men was one of the ways in which a nation shaped not only its own sense of its internal strength but also promoted and projected that strength to other nations, so it was important that male heroism was always seen in the very highest of terms. Women could be regarded as extremely heroic and could well be promoted as exemplary figures, as long as it was in relation to terms determined by their gender. Furthermore, their heroism was generally constructed as second to that of men, in order to guard against the possibility that it could reduce the quality or standing of the heroic model in general.

This study has sought to contribute to scholarship on the subject of heroism, and in particular everyday heroism, as well as the social, cultural and political history of the nineteenth and early twentieth centuries. It has demonstrated the flexible and variable nature of the idea of heroism and shown that, rather than being fixed and uncontested, it was actually something which was constructed and debated. This has an impact on the way in which heroism as a subject can be approached and understood, as it shows that it can be examined as a complex and multifaceted idea in its own right, rather than just an abstract lens through which to examine other topics. Furthermore, the idea of heroism was not only a construct, but it was one that differed from person to person, group to group and, indeed, from class to class, with those at the higher end of society viewing everyday heroism as a reflection of personal character and those lower down regarding it more as a significant and respectable life-risking action. This is an important conclusion for social and cultural historians, as well as historians who are interested in the nature of class identities and relationships, as it reveals the presence of distinctly different attitudes and beliefs between groups and classes. Identifying that differences existed in the construction of heroism, and outlining how and why they were shaped in certain ways, will assist and encourage historians to locate and explore other differences, thus leading to a greater understanding of class consciousness and identity. Furthermore, this investigation provides a springboard or stepping stone for further study in a range of different ways.

In a 2007 article, Max Jones posed the question 'What should historians do with heroes?' and in the light of this study, it might prove valuable to ask 'What should historians do with everyday heroes?'[4] By identifying and outlining the previously overlooked strand of everyday heroism, this book shifts the possibilities for investigation away from military and imperial subjects and consequently opens up previously overlooked areas for research. Everyday heroism is primarily defined by being non-military and while the focus here has been on otherwise ordinary people who undertook life-risking acts, there is no reason why studies of the idea should not approach it by examining more well-known or famous civilians or those who were considered to be heroic for reasons other than risking and saving life.

There have already been some examinations of subjects including re-evaluations of the warrior-queen Boudicca, the heroism and masculinity of Edwardian motor-racing drivers, twentieth-century icons such as Marilyn Monroe and Rock Hudson, and heroism as constructed in visual culture mediums such as comic books and feature films.[5] Studies such as these usefully explore connections between heroism and themes such as gender, celebrity, iconography, identity, communication, mediation and importantly, reception and influence. Another notable area that engages with non-military heroism is sport and leisure, and much interesting work has been done on local and regional sporting heroes as well as heroism in relation to specific pursuits such as mountaineering.[6] This study of everyday heroism can contribute to these areas by reinforcing the fact that heroes and heroines are mediations of a given time, place and set of ideas and this is where their ultimate value lies. As asserted throughout this book, if you want to understand a particular group or society at a particular time, examine the people, or more importantly the types of people it held up as heroic.

Chronologically, this study has focused upon the period 1850–1914 and, given the debates discussed in the introduction about the impact of World War I on ideas and concepts of heroism, a study which sought to trace everyday heroism through the interwar period of 1918–39 would undoubtedly represent a valuable and worthwhile exercise. Military heroism may well have been tarnished by the mud of the trenches, but it has yet to be proven whether everyday heroism suffered a similar fate. Likewise, studies situated in 1950s and 1960s Britain might, for example, provide interesting insights into the development of popular culture heroes and heroines as well the developing relationship between heroism and celebrity. Studies of non-military heroism in the 1970s and 1980s could conceivably illuminate the rise and fall of British industrial relations by examining the construction of working-class heroism within the context of challenges to trade unionism, communism and the rise of individualism and capitalism.[7]

Even the history of the last twenty years arguably has much to contribute. Questions about the extent to which terrorism or participation in unpopular conflicts might blur the lines between heroes, villains, victims and martyrs is one area into which studies of civilian heroism might fruitfully extend. Organizations including the Carnegie Hero Fund and the Royal Humane Society continue to recognize bravery and heroism displayed by individuals during specific incidents, as they have done throughout their long history, which might suggest that our ideas and definitions of heroism have changed little in that time. There is, however, also an increasing tendency to consider particular groups or bodies of people as collectively and universally heroic or to widen the scope of heroism to include attributes such as duty or stoicism.[8] Thus, heroism continues to be the product of multiple and variable constructions and as there is no single universally accepted definition it remains a valuable opportunity to examine and assess the identity of a society at a given time. Furthermore, everyday heroism, with its onus on the many rather than the few and the otherwise ordinary rather than the extraordinary or exotic, appears ideally positioned to assist with such studies.

Heroism is, of course, not restricted to the British Isles and everyday heroism is no different in this respect. The UK Carnegie Hero Fund Trust was a development of a US Carnegie Hero Fund Commission founded in 1904, a further nine European hero funds were founded between 1908 and 1911 and the Royal Humane Society established commonwealth branches in Australia in 1874, Canada in 1894 and New Zealand in 1898. In-depth research on these organizations, most of which continue to exist and function, and the nature of the individuals and acts that they recognized, would provide evidence of American, European and commonwealth perceptions and constructions of everyday heroism. In turn, comparative studies could then help to show what was particularly distinctive about British ideas on heroism. Although sidelined in this study, constructions of non-military heroism in imperial Africa and India, especially identifying the reception of a constructed British model upon native communities and the existence or endurance of pre-imperial constructions, could prove useful for both historians of heroism and of the British Empire.

Finally, in addition to offering possible avenues for further study, this book also provides one model of how everyday heroism can be researched, contextualized and analysed. It shows the value and benefit of an open-minded approach to locating and examining source materials and also an openness and willingness to engage with evidence on an interdisciplinary basis. Social and cultural sources have proved to be as useful and rewarding as institutional and political ones, and brief engagements with the discipline of Art History have illuminated visual culture sources. Within the historical discipline, this research demonstrates the importance of local and regional field study, the relevance of identity and memory studies, the centrality of contextualization and the validity of focusing on the lives and experiences of the working classes. The historian Christopher Hill once wrote, 'we may find that the obscure men and women who figure in this book, together with some not so obscure, may speak more directly to us than Charles I or Pym or General Monck, who appear as history-makers in the textbooks.'[9] Hopefully, the everyday heroes and heroines who have figured in this book will have served a similar purpose, and while the idea of everyday heroism may not have turned nineteenth-century Britain upside down, it did occupy a prominent and significant position in the thoughts and ideas of those who inhabited it, as this study has sought to demonstrate.

First Royal Warrant Instituting the Albert Medal, 7 March 1866

WARRANT Instituting a New Decoration to be Styled THE ALBERT MEDAL
VICTORIA, R.

VICTORIA, by the Grace of God, of the United Kingdom of Great Britain and Ireland, Queen, Defender of the Faith, &c., to all to whom these presents shall come, greeting:

Whereas, We, taking into Our Royal consideration that great loss of life is sustained by reason of shipwrecks and other perils of the sea, and taking also into consideration the many daring and heroic actions performed by mariners and others to prevent such loss, and to save the lives of those who are in danger of perishing by reason of wrecks and perils of the sea; and taking also into consideration the expediency of distinguishing such efforts by some mark of Our Royal favour:

Now, for the purpose of attaining an end so desirable as that of rewarding such actions as aforesaid, We have instituted and created, and by these presents, for Us, Our Heirs and Successors, institute and create a new Decoration, which We are desirous should be highly prized and eagerly sought after, and are graciously pleased to make, ordain, and establish the following Rules and Ordinances for the government of the same, which shall from henceforth be inviolably observed and kept:

First: It is ordained that the distinction shall be styled 'The Albert Medal', and shall consist of a gold oval-shaped badge or decoration, enamelled in dark blue, with a monogram composed of the letters V. and A. interlaced, with an anchor erect, in gold, surrounded with a garter, in bronze, inscribed in raised letters of gold 'For Gallantry in Saving Life at Sea', and surmounted by a representation of the crown of His Royal Highness the lamented Prince Consort, and suspended from a dark-blue riband of five-eighths of an inch in width, with two white longitudinal stripes.

Secondly: It is ordained that the Medal shall be suspended from the left breast.

Thirdly: It is ordained that the names of those upon whom We may be pleased to confer the decoration shall be published in the London Gazette, and a Registry thereof kept in the Office of the Board of Trade.

Fourthly: It is ordained that anyone who, after having received the medal again, performs an act which, if he had not received such medal, would have entitled him to it, such further acts shall be recorded by a bar attached to the riband by which the Medal is suspended, and for every such additional act an additional bar may be added.

Fifthly: It is ordained that the Medal shall only be awarded to those who, after the date of this Instrument, have, in saving, or endeavouring to save, the lives of others from shipwreck or other peril of the sea, endangered their own lives; and that such award shall be made only on a recommendation to Us by the President of the Board of Trade.

Sixthly: In order to make such additional provision as shall effectually preserve pure this most honourable distinction; it is ordained that if any person on whom such distinction is conferred be guilty of any crime or disgraceful conduct which, in our judgment, disqualifies him for the said Decoration, his name shall forthwith be erased from the registry of individuals upon whom the said Decoration shall have been conferred by an especial Warrant under Our Royal Sign-Manual, and his Medal shall be forfeited; and every person to whom the said Medal is given shall, before receiving the same, enter into an engagement to return the same if his name shall be so erased as aforesaid under this regulation. It is hereby further declared that We, Our heirs and successors shall be the sole judges of the circumstance demanding such expulsion. Moreover, We shall at all times have power to restore such persons as may at any time have been expelled, to the enjoyment of the Decoration.

Given at Our Court at *St James's*, this seventh day of *March*, one thousand eight hundred and sixty-six, in the twenty-ninth year of Our reign.

By Her Majesty's command,
G. GREY.

Catalogue of British Monuments to Everyday Heroism Erected Between 1850 and 1914

Name	Mark Addy
Location	Weaste Cemetery, Cemetery Road, Weaste, Salford, Greater Manchester
OS Reference	SJ 800 980
Unveiled	9 March 1891
Type of Monument	Obelisk
Material	Red Peterhead granite
Dimensions	Overall height: 15ft (4.5m); bottom base: 3ft 6in square (1.0m)
Inscriptions	**Front:** Sacred to the memory of/Mark Addy/the Salford hero/who died 9 June 1890/in the 52nd year of his age/he saved more than 50 persons from drowning in/the River Irwell for which he received/amongst other rewards/the Albert Medal (first class) from H. M the Queen/life's work well done/life's race well run/life's victory won/he rests in peace./erected by public subscription **Rear:** Memorial committee/Chairman/the Mayor of Salford Councillor B. Robinson, J. P./Vice Chairman/The Revd G. W Petherick, B. A [followed by names of committee]

Name	Alice Ayres
Location	Isleworth Cemetery, Park Road, Isleworth, Middlesex
OS Reference	TQ 165 764
Unveiled	March 1886
Type of Monument	Obelisk
Material	Red granite
Dimensions	Overall height: 16ft (5m)
Inscriptions	**Facing grave:** Sacred/to the memory of/Alice Ayres/aged 26 years/who met her death through/a fire which occurred in/Union Street, Borough/the 24th day of April 1885 A.D./Amidst the sudden terrors/of the conflagration/with true courage and clear judgement/she heroically rescued the children/committed to her charge./To save them she three times braved/the flames; at last leaping from the/burning house, she sustained injuries/from the effects of which she died/on 26 April 1885.//This memorial was erected by/public subscription/to commemorate a/noble act of unselfish courage./'be though faithful unto death, and I will/give thee a crown of life' **Right hand side:** Alice Ayres Memorial/Committee/[followed by names of committee members]

Name	Alice Maud Denman and Arthur Regelous ('Little Peter')
Location	Bethnal Green Museum Gardens, Cambridge Heath Road, London
OS Reference	TQ 350 827
Unveiled	1903
Type of Monument	Drinking fountain
Material	Granite

Dimensions	Total height: 8ft (2.5m); Width: 3ft 6in (1.0m); Bottom base: 6ft square (1.8m)
Inscriptions	Memorial to/Alice Maud Denman/and/Peter Regelous/who lost their lives in attempting/to save others/at a fire at 423, Hackney Road,/on the 20 April, 1902./Erected by public subscription/C. E. Fox, Mayor./R. Voss Junr Town Clerk.

Name	Percy Henry Gordon
Location	Castle Gardens, Rochester Esplanade, Strood, Rochester, Kent
OS Reference	TQ 740 685
Unveiled	3 November 1912
Type of Monument	Wall plaque
Material	Brass Plaque on granite tablet
Dimensions	
Inscriptions	To the glory of God. This tablet was erected by local public subscription to record the heroism of Percy Henry Gordon of Bermondsey, London, who while on visit to this city on Good Friday 1912, lost his life in bravely rescuing a little girl from drowning 'greater love hath no man than this'

Name	Ethel Harrison
Location	Junction of Baldertongate/London Road, Newark on Trent, Nottinghamshire
OS Reference	SK 803 533
Unveiled	6 August 1908
Type of Monument	Drinking fountain
Material	White Mansfield Stone

Dimensions	Height: 6ft 6in (2m); width: 1ft 6in (0.5m); depth: 1ft 6in (0.5m)
Inscriptions	**Balderton-facing side:** to the/memory of/Ethel Harrison/ of this town/who was/drowned near/Chester/while gallantly/saving the life/of a child/under her care/on 7 December/1906 **Newark-facing side:** This/memorial/was erected/by public/ subscription/by her fellow/townspeople/to commemorate/ the heroic act

Name	William Hunter
Location	Dunfermline Cemetery, Halbeath Road, Dunfermline
OS Reference	NT 102 880
Unveiled	November or December 1887
Type of Monument	Ornamental headstone
Material	Silver granite
Dimensions	Total height, 11ft 3in (3.5m)
Inscriptions	**Centre stone:** Erected/by the/inhabitants of Townhill and/ other friends/in loving memory of/William Hunter/son of David Hunter, Townhill/who on Sunday 23 July 1886/at the age of 17 years, perished/in the town loch, Townhill while/ attempting to save a Dunfermline/lad from drowning **Plinth:** The false heroes of barbarous man are those/who can only boast of the destruction of their fellows./The true heroes of civilisation are those alone who/save or greatly serve them. Young Hunter was one of those/and deserves and enduring monument – Carnegie

Name	Albert Lee
Location	Queen's Park, Queens Park Road, Heywood, Rochdale, Greater Manchester
OS Reference	SD 858 116

Unveiled	11 April 1908
Type of Monument	Obelisk
Material	White Halifax stone
Dimensions	Bottom base: 4ft 6in square (1.3m); centre stone carrying the inscription: 3ft 4in by 2ft 6in (1.0m × 0.7m); obelisk shaft: 2ft 6in by 14in (0,7m × 0.3m)
Inscriptions	THIS MEMORIAL/was erected by public/sub-scription to commemorate/the gallant and heroic/attempt of/ALBERT LEE/of 79 Starky Street Heywood/aged 15/who lost his life in/ attempting to rescue/his companion/DAVID ASHWORTH/ from drowning/in the river Roach at Crimble/opposite this spot on/Saturday afternoon the 15 June 1907

Name	Mary Anne Rogers
Location	Junction of Western Esplanade/Town Quay, Southampton
OS Reference	SU 417 111
Unveiled	27 July 1901
Type of Monument	Drinking fountain
Material	Brown Portland stone
Dimensions	Total height: 13ft 6in (4m); total width: 8ft 6in (2.5m); central column bearing inscription plate: 15in diam (0.3m)

Inscriptions	In memory of/the heroic death of/Mary Anne Rogers/ Stewardess of the 'Stella'/who/on the night of the 30th of March 1899/amid the confusion and terror of shipwreck/ aided all the women under her charge/to quit the vessel in safety/giving her own life-belt to one who was unprotected./ Urged by the sailors to make sure her escape/she refused/ lest she might endanger the heavily-laden boat./cheering the departing crew/with the friendly cry of 'good-bye, good-bye'/ she was seen a few moments later/as the 'Stella' went down/ lifting her arms upwards with the prayer/'lord have me'/then sank in the waters with the sinking ship./Actions such as these – revealing steadfast performance/of duty in the face of death, ready self-sacrifice for/the sake of others, reliance on God – constitute the/glorious heritage of our English race. They/deserve perpetual commemoration, because/among the trivial pleasures and sordid strife/of the world, they recall to us for ever the/nobility and love-worthiness of human nature

Name	Timothy Trow
Location	London Road, opposite James Street, Stoke on Trent, Staffordshire
OS Reference	SJ 872 441
Unveiled	22 October 1894
Type of Monument	Obelisk
Material	Grey granite
Dimensions	Total height: 10ft 6in (3m); obelisk height: 8ft 6in (2.5m)
Inscriptions	Erected/by public subscription/in grateful memory of/ Timothy Trow,/tram conductor, aged 21 years,/who lost his life by drowning /near this spot/in a heroic attempt to save/ that of a child. 13 April 1894

Name	William Walton
Location	Town Hall Gardens, Ferryhill, County Durham
OS Reference	NZ 287 327
Unveiled	18 April 1908
Type of Monument	Obelisk
Material	Hoyden Stone [Sandstone]
Dimensions	Total height: 12ft 6in (3.8m); bottom base: 3ft 6in square (1.0m)
Inscriptions	Erected/by the/officials and workmen/of Dean and Chapter colliery/to the memory/of the late/William Walton/ (Overman)/who sacrificed his life/in saving the lives/of two boys/at Dean Bank/8 August 1906

Name	Edgar George Wilson
Location	River Thames towpath, South-east of Osney Lock, towpath accessible from East Street, off Botley Road
OS Reference	SP 506 056
Unveiled	7 November 1889
Type of Monument	Obelisk
Material	Granite
Dimensions	Total height: c.10ft (3m)
Inscriptions	In memory of/Edgar George Wilson/who after rescuing two boys/from drowning lost his life/15 June 1889 aged 21 years// erected under the auspices of the/Oxford Young Men's Christian/Association by public subscription./Unveiled 7 November by the Mayor/of Oxford (Walter Gray Esq.)

Notes

Introduction

1 H. W. Mabie, *Heroes Every Child Should Know* (London, 1906), p. 4.
2 *The Independent*, 31 August 1989.
3 *The Guardian*, 20 October 2000.
4 P. Karsten, *Patriot Heroes in England and America* (London: University of Wisconsin Press, 1978).
5 For example, C. L. Balfour, *Moral Heroism; or, The Trials and Triumphs of the Great and Good* (London, 1846); L. Drake, *The Heroes of England. Stories of the Lives of the most Celebrated British Soldiers and Sailors* (London, 1843); J. M. Neale, *The Triumphs of the Cross. Tales and Sketches of Christian Heroism* (London, 1845).
6 T. Carlyle, *On Heroes and Hero-worship and the Heroic in History* (London, 1840), p. 1.
7 D. Birch, 'Ruskin and Carlyle: changing forms of biography in *Fors Clavigera*', in Cubitt, G. and Warren, A. (eds), *Heroic Reputations and Exemplary Lives* (Manchester: Manchester University Press, 2000), pp 178–91.
8 Ibid., p. 179.
9 A notable exception to this is C. P. Barclay, *Heroes of Peace: The Royal Humane Society and the Award of Medals in Britain, 1774–1914*, PhD thesis (University of York, 2009).
10 For example: G. Dawson, *Soldier Heroes: British Adventure, Empire and the Imagining of Masculinities* (London: Routledge, 1994); C. I. Hamilton, 'Naval Hagiography and the Victorian Hero', *The Historical Journal*, 23:2 (1980), 381–98; S. Heathorn, 'Representations of War and Martial Heroes in English Elementary School Reading and Rituals, 1885–1914', in J. Marten (ed.), *Children and War* (London: NYU Press, 2002b), pp. 103–25; M. Lieven, 'Heroism, Heroics, and the Making of Heroes: The Anglo-Zulu War of 1879'. *Albion*, 30 (1998), 419–38; J. M. Mackenzie, 'Heroic Myths of Empire', in J. M. Mackenzie (ed.), *Popular Imperialism and the Military 1850–1950* (Manchester: Manchester University Press, 1992), pp. 109–38; J. Richards, 'British Imperial Heroes', in J. Richards (ed.), *Films and British National Identity: From Dickens to Dad's Army* (Manchester: Manchester University Press, 1997), pp. 31–59.
11 For example, C. I. Hamilton, 'Naval Hagiography'; M. C. Smith, *Awarded for Valour: A History of the Victorian Cross and the Evolution of British Heroism* (Basingstoke: Palgrave Macmillan, 2008).
12 For example, S. Barczewski, *Antarctic Destinies: Scott, Shackleton and the Changing Face of Heroism* (London: Bloomsbury Academic, 2007); E. Berenson, *Heroes of Empire: Five Charismatic Men and the Conquest of Africa* (Berkeley: University of California Press, 2011); G. Dawson, *Soldier Heroes;* S. Heathorn, 'Representations of War and Martial Heroes'; M. Lieven, 'Heroism, Heroics, and the Making of Heroes'; J. M. Mackenzie, 'Heroic Myths of Empire'; J. Richards, 'British Imperial Heroes'.
13 C. I. Hamilton, 'Naval Hagiography', p. 381.

14 Ibid., p. 396.

15 Ibid., p. 382, emphasis in original.

16 This figure, and all those that follow in this paragraph, was obtained using the searchable online version of Hansard, http://hansard.millbanksystems.com/ (accessed 01/06/13).

17 T. Cavanagh, *Public Sculpture of Liverpool* (Liverpool: Liverpool University Press, 1997), p. xxi.

18 Studies which demonstrate this include, T. G. Grammer, *The Myth of Gentlemen Heroes in the Nineteenth Century: The Duke of Wellington and General Robert E. Lee* (Lampeter: Edwin Mellen Press, 2010); S. Heathorn, "'The Highest Type of Englishman": Gender, War, and the Alfred the Great Commemoration of 1901', *Canadian Journal of History*, 37:3 (2002), 459–84; i.d., 'A "Matter for Artists, and not for Soldiers"? the Cultural Politics of the Earl Haig National Memorial, 1928–1937', *Journal of British Studies*, 44:3 (2005), 536–61; A. Tyrell and J. Walvin, 'Whose History Is It? Memorialising Britain's Involvement in Slavery', in P. A. Pickering and A. Tyrell (eds), *Contested Sites: Commemoration, Memorials and Popular Politics in Nineteenth-Century Britain* (Aldershot: Ashgate, 2004), pp. 147–69.

19 O. Anderson, 'The Growth of Christian Militarism in Mid-Victorian Britain', *The English Historical Review*, 86 (1971), 46–72; R. H. MacDonald, 'A Poetics of War: Militarist Discourse in the British Empire, 1880–1918', *Mosaic*, 23:3 (1990), 17–36; J. A. Mangan, "Muscular, Militaristic and Manly': the British Middle-Class Hero as Moral Messenger', *International Journal of the History of Sport*, 13:1 (1996), 28–47; A. Summers, 'Militarism in Britain before the Great War', *History Workshop Journal*, 2 (1976), 104–23. For an insight into the revisionist debate see, A. Warren, 'Sir Robert Baden-Powell, the Scout Movement and Citizen Training in Great Britain, 1900–1920', *English Historical Review*, 101 (1986), 376–98; J. Springhall, 'Baden-Powell and the Scout Movement before 1920: Citizen Training or Soldiers of the Future', *English Historical Review*, 102 (1987), 934–42; A. Summers, 'Scouts, Guides and VADS: a note in reply to Allen Warren', *English Historical Review*, 102 (1987), 943–7.

20 G. Dawson, *Soldier Heroes*; P. Howarth, *Play Up and Play the Game: the Heroes of Popular Fiction* (London: Eyre Methuen, 1973); J. M. Mackenzie, 'Heroic Myths of Empire'; J. Richards, 'Popular Imperialism and the Image of the Army in Juvenile Literature', in J. M. MacKenzie (ed.), *Popular Imperialism and the Military: 1850–1950* (Manchester: Manchester University Press, 1992), pp. 80–108; S. Heathorn, 'Representations of War and Martial Heroes'.

21 J. Richards, 'Popular Imperialism', p. 81.

22 L. Lane, *Heroes of Everyday Life* (London, 1888); Christian Knowledge Society, *Everyday Heroes: Stories of Bravery During the Queen's Reign 1837–1888* (London, 1889); F. Cross, *Beneath the Banner* (London, 1894); H. D. Rawnsley, *Ballads of Brave Deeds* (London, 1896); C. D. Michael, *Deeds of Daring: Stories of Heroism in Every Day Life* (London: S. W. Partridge & Company, 1900).

23 W. Martin, *Heroism of Boyhood* (London, 1865), p. 2.

24 M. Trevelyan, *Brave little Women, Tales of the Heroism of Girls* (London, 1888); F. Mundell, *Heroines of Daily Life* (London, 1896); C. Moore, *Noble Deeds of the World's Heroines* (London: Religious Tract Society, 1903); C. D., Michael, *Heroines: True Tales of Brave Women* (London: S. W. Partridge & Company Limited, 1904).

25 G. Cubitt, 'Introduction', in G. Cubitt and A. Warren (eds), *Heroic Reputations and Exemplary Lives* (Manchester: Manchester University Press, 2000), p. 9.

26 Ibid., pp. 16–17.

27 T. Carlyle, *On Heroes and Hero-worship and the Heroic in History* (London: James Fraser, 1841), p. 1.

28 G. Cubitt and A. Warren (eds), *Heroic Reputations,* pp. 8–10.

29 S. Smiles, *Self-Help* (London, 1859), pp. 39–40.

30 S. Smiles, *Character* (London, 1871); i.d. *Duty* (London, 1880).

31 A. Briggs, 'Samuel Smiles: the Gospel of Self-Help', in G. Marsden (ed.), *Victorian Values: Personalities and Perspectives in Nineteenth Century Society* (London: Longman, 1990), p. 89.

32 T. Carlyle, *On Heroes and Hero-worship and the Heroic in History.*

33 For example see, J. F. Andrews, *William Shakespeare, his World, his Work, his Influence,* 3 vols. (New York: Scribner, 1985); S. Greenblatt, *Will in the World: How Shakespeare became Shakespeare* (London: Norton, 2005); J. S. Morrill, 'How Oliver Cromwell Thought', in J. Morrow and J. Scott (eds), *Liberty, Authority, Formality: Political Ideas and Culture, 1600–1900* (Exeter: Imprint Academic, 2008); D. L. Smith, *Oliver Cromwell: Politics and Religion in the English Revolution, 1640–1658* (Cambridge: Cambridge University Press, 1991).

34 A. Taylor, 'Shakespeare and Radicalism: the Uses and Abuses of Shakespeare in Nineteenth-Century Popular Politics', *Historical Journal,* 45:2 (2002), 357–79; R. E., Quinault, 'The Cult of the Centenary, c.1784–1914', *Historical Research,* 71 (1998), 303–23.

35 S. Heathorn, 'The Highest Type of Englishman'; J. Parker, *"England's Darling": The Victorian Cult of Alfred the Great* (Manchester: Manchester University Press, 2007); P. Readman, 'Commemorating the Past in Edwardian Hampshire: King Alfred, Pageantry and Empire', in M. Taylor (ed.), *Southampton: Gateway to the British Empire* (London: I.B. Tauris & Co Ltd, 2007), pp. 95–114.

36 F. Harrison, *The New Calendar of Great Men* (London, 1892).

37 M. Jones, 'What Should Historians Do With Heroes?', *History Compass,* 5/2 (2007), 439–54; other examples include: S. Barczewski, *Antarctic Destinies;* J. Seigel, 'Carlyle and Peel: the Prophet's Search for a Heroic Politician and an Unpublished Fragment', *Victorian Studies,* 26 (1983), 181–95; E. Bentley, *The Cult of the Superman: A Study of the Idea of Heroism in Carlyle and Nietzsche* (London: R. Hale, 1947).

38 J. M. MacKenzie, 'Heroic Myths of Empire', p. 111.

39 Examples of this include, J. M. MacKenzie, 'Heroic Myths of Empire'; M. Lieven, 'Heroism, Heroics, and the Making of Heroes'.

40 J. Campbell, *The Hero with a Thousand Faces* (New York: Pantheon Books, 1949).

41 J. M. MacKenzie, 'Heroic Myths of Empire', p. 113; other examples of this tendency include, G. Dawson, *Soldier Heroes;* M. Lieven, 'Heroism, Heroics, and the Making of Heroes'.

42 M. Lieven, 'Heroism, Heroics, and the Making of Heroes'.

43 J. Michelet, *History of the French Revolution,* Trans. C. Coeks (London, 1847).

44 For a broad overview of the development of the New History see, J. Black and D. M. Macraild, *Studying History,* 3rd edn (Basingstoke: Palgrave Macmillan, 2007).

45 A. Toynbee, *Lectures on the Industrial Revolution* (1884); S. & B. Webb, *History of Trade Unionism* (1894); J. L. & B. Hammond, *The Town Labourer 1760–1832: The New Civilisation* (1917).

46 For more on the New Cultural History see, L. Hunt (ed.), *The New Cultural History* (London: University of California Press, 1989).

47 P. Burke (ed.), *New Perspectives on Historical Writing* (Cambridge: Pennsylvania State University Press, 1991).

48 R. Samuel, 'People's History', in R. Samuel (ed.), *People's History and Socialist Theory* (London: Routledge and Kegan Paul, 1981), pp. xxx–xxxiii.

49 Ibid., p. xvi.

50 E. Hobsbawm, 'History From Below', in E. Hobsbawm (ed.), *On History* (London: Hachette, 1997), p. 216.

51 M. Jones, 'What Should Historians Do With Heroes?', p. 448.

52 M. Jones, *The Last Great Quest* (Oxford: Oxford University Press, 2003).

53 A similar approach to the reception of representations and commemorations was also adopted by Richard Price in his study of working-class attitudes and reactions to the Boer war: R. Price, *An Imperial War and the British Working Class; Working-Class Attitudes and Reactions to the Boer War 1899-1902* (London: Routledge & K. Paul, 1972).

54 M. Jones, 'What Should Historians Do With Heroes?', p. 441; P. Karsten, *Patriot Heroes*, pp. 1–12.

55 P. Karsten, *Patriot Heroes*, p. 2.

56 E. Hobsbawm, 'History From Below', p. 205.

57 Ibid.

58 For further reading on war correspondents in the Crimean war and the Victorian era see, A. D. Lambert and S. Badsey, *The Crimean War: The War Correspondents* (Stroud: Sutton Pub Limited, 1994); A. P. Ryan, 'The Journalist as Historian: William Howard Russell 1820–1907', *History Today*, 4 (1954), 813–22; R. T. Stearn, 'War Correspondents and Colonial War, c.1870–1900', in J. M. MacKenzie (ed.), *Popular Imperialism and the Military 1850-1950* (Manchester: Manchester University Press, 1992), pp. 139–61; R. Wilkinson-Latham, *From our Special Correspondent: Victorian War Correspondents and their Campaigns* (Sevenoaks: Hodder and Stoughton, 1979).

59 R. T. Stearn, 'Russell, Sir William Howard (1820–1907)', *Oxford Dictionary of National Biography* (Oxford, 2004); O. Anderson, *A Liberal State at War: English Politics and Economics during the Crimean War* (London: MacMillan, 1967).

60 HC Deb 15 December 1854 vol. 136 cc. 378–414.

61 HC Deb 19 December 1854 vol. 136 cc. 505–7.

62 The original wording of 'for the brave' was rejected by Queen Victoria on the grounds that it could give the impression that the only brave British men on the battlefield were those who won the Cross.

63 *London Gazette*, 5 February 1856, pp. 410–11.

64 In total, five of the fourteen lost their lives: John Hughes (50) and his son William (18) as well as father of seven, Edward Williams (35) and Robert Rogers, a boy of thirteen, were all drowned and William Morgan was killed by the collapse of rubble during a rescue attempt.

65 For example: Hartley Colliery, Durham, 16 January 1862, 204 men buried alive; The Oaks Colliery, Barnsley, 12 December 1866, 361 men killed in an explosion; Abercarn Colliery, 11 September 1878, 268 men killed in an explosion; Seaham Colliery, Sunderland, 8 September 1880, 164 men killed in an explosion.

66 *Merthyr Press*, 1 May 1877, quoted in K. Llewellyn, *Disaster at Tynewydd* (Cardiff: ap Dafydd Publications Ltd, 1975), p. 74.

67 *Western Mail*, 23 April 1877.

68 HC Deb 20 April 1877 vol. 233 c. 1544.

69 *The Leeds Mercury*, 25 April 1877.

70 Home Office case notes file, 'Tram Driver Wilton - refused' (1908), TNA: PRO HO45/10382/167115.

71 Home Office case notes file, 'HONOURS: Albert Medal: Jack Hewitt' (1911–28), TNA: PRO: HO 45/12941.

72 Home Office case notes file, 'ALBERT MEDAL: Award to Miss H Roabotham for saving lives from collapse of school roof' (1881–98), TNA: PRO: HO 144/88/A10053.

73 Letter from John Cooper, a fourth officer aboard the SS *Massalia*, who received a second-class medal in 1891, Home Office case notes file, 'Rewards. Award of the Albert Medal, 2nd Class to Fourth Officer A. J. Cooper' (1891), TNA: PRO: MT 9/402.

74 Letter from John McCandless, an Irish student on holiday in the United States, whose nomination was refused in 1906, Home Office case notes file, 'ALBERT MEDAL: Rescue by deaf mute students – refused' (1905–06), TNA: PRO HO 45/10322/129274.

75 G. F. Watts, letter to C. H. Rickards, 17 August 1866, National Portrait Gallery, Heinz Archive (hereafter NPG), v.2, ff. 25–8.

76 *The Times*, 5 September 1887.

77 For the full history of the memorial see, J. Price, *Postman's Park: G. F. Watts's Memorial to Heroic Self-sacrifice* (Compton: Watts Gallery, 2008).

78 *The Christian World*, 22 December 1898; *The London Argus*, 21 January 1889.

79 *The Christian World*, 22 December 1898.

80 *Irish Independent*, 10 August 1898.

81 *Daily Mail*, 7 July 1898.

82 *Daily Chronicle*, 20 July 1899; *Daily Mail*, 7 July 1898.

83 *The Christian World*, 22 December 1898.

84 Ibid.

85 Ibid.

86 *Daily Chronicle*, 20 July 1899; *City Press*, 1 August 1900.

87 Heroic Self-Sacrifice Memorial Committee (hereafter HSSMC) *Minutes Book*, P69/BOT1/B/036/MS18628, London Metropolitan Archives, meeting of 3 March 1904.

88 *The Times*, 5 May 1885.

89 *South London Chronicle*, 16 May 1885.

90 *The Graphic*, 16 May 1885; *South London Chronicle*, 16 May 1885.

91 L. Lane, *Heroes of Every-day Life*, pp. 55–6.

92 Ibid., p. 56.

93 Quoted in, R. Whelan (ed.), *Octavia Hill's Letters to Fellow Workers 1872–1911* (London: Kyrle, 2005), pp. 343–4.

94 C. D. Michael, *Deeds of Daring: Stories of Heroism in Every Day Life* (London: S. W. Partridge & Company, 1900).

95 Christian Knowledge Society, *Everyday Heroes: Stories of Bravery During the Queen's Reign 1837–1888* (London, 1889), p. 6.

96 E. Hodder, *Heroes of Britain in Peace and War* (London, 1878), p. 11.

97 C. D. Michael, *Deeds of Daring*, p. vi.

98 Anon, *Working-Men Heroes: A Roll of Heroic Actions in Humble Life* (London, 1879); cheap literature aimed at a working-class audience and approaches for the study of the reception of such literature are perceptively examined in J. Rose, *The Intellectual Life of the British Working Classes* (London: Yale University Press, 2001).

99 Examinations of the importance and influence of postcards include E. J. Evans and J. Richards, *A Social History of Britain in Postcards, 1870–1930* (London: Longman, 1980); S. Kearns, 'Picture Postcards as a Source for Social Historians', *Saothar: Journal of the Irish Labour History Society*, 22 (1997), 128–33; G. Teulié, 'Postcards,

Propaganda & National Identity: the Photographic Representations of the Anglo-Boer War (1899–1902)', in G. Hughes and K. Hildenbrand (eds), *Images of War and War of Images* (Newcastle upon Tyne, 2008), pp. 95–120.

100 F. McGlennon and G. Horncastle, *Heroes of Every Day Life* (London, 1892).

101 L. Senelick, 'Politics as Entertainment: Victorian Music-hall Songs', *Victorian Studies*, 19:2 (1975), 149–80; for further reading on politics and class in Victorian Music-hall see, P. Bailey, *Leisure and Class in Victorian England: Rational Recreation and the Contest for Control, 1830–1885* (London: Routledge & K. Paul, 1978); M. Huggins and K. Gregson, 'Northern Songs, Sporting Heroes and Regional Consciousness, c.1800-c.1880: "Wor Stars that Shine"', *Northern History*, 44:2 (2007), 141–58; D. Kift, *The Victorian Music-hall: Culture, Class and Conflict* (Cambridge: Cambridge University Press, 1996); P. Summerfield, 'Patriotism and Empire: Music-hall Entertainment, 1870–1914', in J. M. MacKenzie (ed.), *Imperialism and Popular Culture* (Manchester: Manchester University Press, 1986), pp. 17–48.

102 For a wealth of information on all these organizations and others, see C. P. Barclay, *Heroes of Peace*. For studies of specific organizations see, S. Jeffery, *The Liverpool Shipwreck and Humane Society 1839–1939* (Liverpool: Daily Post, 1939); W. K. R. Bedford, *The Order of the Hospital of St John of Jerusalem* (New York: Macmillan, 1978); D. Coke, *Saved from a Watery Grave: The Story of the Royal Humane Society's Receiving House in Hyde Park* (London: Royal Humane Society, 2000); A. Beilby, *Heroes All! The Story of the RNLI* (Somerset: Patrick Stephens Limited, 1992); B. Cox, *Lifeboat Gallantry* (London: Spink & Son, 1998).

103 B. Bergonzi, *Heroes' Twilight: A Study of the Literature of the Great War* (London: Coward-McCann, 1965), p. 17; Paul Fussell also forwards a similar argument in P. Fussell, *The Great War and Modern Memory* (Oxford: Oxford University Press, 1975).

104 M. C. Smith, *Awarded for Valour*, p. 111; see also pp. 131, 163, 165, 185.

105 G. Dawson, *Soldier Heroes*, p. 171.

106 Correspondence received by the author from the Royal Humane Society.

107 See, K. Llewellyn, *Disaster at Tynewydd*.

108 Correspondence received by the author from the relative in question.

109 *Who Do You Think You Are?*, issue 24 (August 2009), pp. 22–5.

110 Ibid.

111 Ibid.

112 *Bexley Times*, 20 September 2007.

113 *The Times*, 12 June 2009.

114 Ibid.

Chapter 1

1 For accounts of the incident see, *Leeds Mercury*, 28 March 1866; *Plymouth and Cornish Advertiser*, 28 March 1866.

2 *London Gazette*, 13 March 1866. For a complete transcript of the warrant see appendix one.

3 Board of Trade memorandum, 'REWARDS. Memorandum as to degree of bravery for award of Albert Medal and other life saving awards' (1866), TNA: PRO: MT9/29 (former dept reference W.3202/66). Board of Trade document files are often stored

in mixed boxes under a single TNA reference rather than being individually catalogued. In these cases, the former dept reference is provided to assist with identifying the specific file within the box.

4 *London Gazette,* 13 March 1866.

5 *The Times,* 16 June 1866.

6 Home Office memorandum, 'ALBERT MEDAL: Institution of the Albert Medal for gallantry in saving lives at sea' (1886–87), TNA: PRO: HO45/8846.

7 Home Office memorandum, 'ALBERT MEDAL: Amending Royal Warrant regulating awards' (1881), TNA: PRO: HO45/9552/63549H.

8 *London Gazette,* 20 September 1881.

9 Ibid., 27 May 1891.

10 Ibid., 25 March 1904; 9 June 1905.

11 Ibid., 31 August 1917.

12 E. C., Joslin, *Spink's Catalogue* (Exeter: Webb & Bower, 1983), pp. 75–6.

13 Board of Trade memorandum, 'REWARDS. Memorandum as to degree of bravery for award of Albert Medal and other life saving awards' (1866), TNA: PRO: MT9/29 (former dept reference W.3202/66).

14 Board of Trade memorandum, 'Original warrants and correspondence relating to institution of the Albert Medal' (1864–67), TNA: PRO: MT9/5969.

15 Literature on The Primrose League points to the importance of wearing honours to increase the prominence of the organization and also to occasions where such honours might be worn. For more details see, J. H. Robb, *The Primrose League 1883–1906* (New York: Columbia University Press, 1942), pp. 102–5. In 1867, the Royal Humane Society also reduced the size of its honorary medal so that it could be worn on the basis that it would make it 'prized by the wearer'. For more details see, C. P., Barclay, *Heroes of Peace: The Royal Humane Society and the Award of Medals in Britain, 1774–1914,* PhD thesis (University of York, 2009).

16 Home Office memorandum, 'ALBERT MEDAL: Extension of the Institution of the Albert Medal to cases of gallantry in saving life on land' (1877–81), TNA: PRO: HO45/9434/63549A.

17 Home Office case notes file, 'ALBERT MEDAL: Award to Miss H Roabotham for saving lives from collapse of school roof' (1881–98), TNA: PRO: HO144/88/A10053.

18 Board of Trade memorandum, 'REWARDS. Memorandum as to degree of bravery for award of Albert Medal and other life saving awards' (1866), TNA: PRO: MT9/29 (former dept reference W.3202/66).

19 Board of Trade memorandum, 'Rewards. Granting of awards; and interpretation of the terms "Distress at Sea" and "Peril of the Sea"' (1886), TNA: PRO: MT9/288 (former dept reference M.17381/86)

20 Ibid.

21 Board of Trade memorandum, 'Albert Medal. Presentation of Medals by H. M. the King' (1902), TNA: PRO: MT9/733 (former dept reference M.11051/02).

22 For more details on this see, F. Prochaska, *Royal Bounty: The Making of a Welfare Monarchy* (London: Yale University Press, 1995), Chs. 3 and 4.

23 For example see, M. C., Smith, *Awarded for Valour: A History of the Victorian Cross and the Evolution of British Heroism* (Basingstoke: Palgrave Macmillan, 2008).

24 Board of Trade memorandum, 'Original warrants and correspondence relating to institution of the Albert Medal' (1864–67), TNA: PRO: MT9/5969.

25 Home Office case notes file, 'ALBERT MEDAL: Dr Ryding for successful operation. Not granted' (1885), TNA: PRO: HO144/158/A41021; Home Office case notes file,

'Rewards. Award of the Albert Medal, Second Class, to Sub-Lieut. C. W. Robinson, R. N. R.' (1895), MT9/533 (former dept reference M.7498/95).

26 Home Office case notes file, 'ALBERT MEDAL: Mr. F. V. Nicholls – refused' (1908–09), TNA: PRO: HO45/10392/172692; Home Office case notes file, 'ALBERT MEDAL: Captain R. W. E. Knollys, Hasil of Chiral, Muhammad Ali of Dir' (1906–08), HO45/10348/144617.

27 Board of Trade memorandum, 'Rewards. Granting of awards; and interpretation of the terms "Distress at Sea" and "Peril of the Sea"' (1886), TNA: PRO: MT9/288 (former dept reference M.17381/86).

28 Ibid.

29 Ibid.

30 Ibid.

31 See clause six in the 1866 warrant in appendix one.

32 The three cases in question are: Thomas Davis in 1918, Home Office case notes file, 'ALBERT MEDAL: Lieutenant Commander T. K. Triggs – award Leading Seaman T. N. Davis – award Able Seaman Robert Stones – award Able Seaman William Becker – award Stoker Edward S. Beard. – award Albert C. Mattison – award' (1918–19), HO45/10890/354008; Arthur Hardiment in 1908, Home Office case notes file, 'ALBERT MEDAL: Misconduct of holder of Albert Medal – Arthur Hardiment' (1907–08), HO45/10368/157924; Thomas Lewis in 1909, Home Office case notes file, 'ALBERT MEDAL: Thomas Lewis - awarded' (1910–19), HO 45/10579/181121.

33 Home Office case notes file, 'ALBERT MEDAL: Thomas Lewis - awarded' (1910–19), HO 45/10579/181121.

34 Ibid.

35 Ibid.

36 Ibid.

37 Ibid.

38 Ibid.

39 London Gazette, 20 September 1881.

40 The bulk of these files are in the PRO: TNA: series' HO45, HO144 and MT9.

41 Figures for local individual, proposed recipient, relative of the proposed recipient, general individual and the individual rescued.

42 Ninety-one awards out of 128 nominations, 71 per cent success rate, based upon the top four nominating parties in table 2.

43 Thirty-seven awards out of seventy-six nominations, 49 per cent success rate, based upon top three local nominating parties in table 2

44 Home Office case notes file, 'ALBERT MEDAL: James Hodges - refused' (1906), TNA: PRO: HO/10347/143257.

45 Board of Trade memorandum, 'REWARDS. Memorandum as to degree of bravery for award of Albert Medal and other life saving awards' (1866), TNA: PRO: MT9/29 (former dept reference W.3202/66).

46 See, TNA: PRO: series MT/9 for details and examples of this.

47 The history of the Home Office and changes in the British Civil Service are well served by the following; E. W. Cohen, *The Growth of the British Civil Service 1780-1939* (London: Frank Cass, 1965); R. Moses, *The Civil Service of Great Britain* (London: Columbia University, 1914); R. A. Nelson, *The Home Office 1782-1801* (London: Duke University Press, 1969); F. Newsam, *The Home Office* (London: George Allen & Unwin, 1954); J. Pellew, *The Home Office 1848-1914: From Clerks to*

Bureaucrats (London: Heinemann Educational Books, 1982); E. Troup, *The Home Office* (London: Read Books, 1925).

48 J. Pellew, *The Home Office*, pp. 33–5.
49 Board of Trade memorandum, 'REWARDS. Memorandum as to degree of bravery for award of Albert Medal and other life saving awards' (1866), TNA: PRO: MT9/29 (former dept reference W.3202/66).
50 Ibid.
51 Home Office case notes file, 'ALBERT MEDAL: Edward James Battersby' (1906–07), PRO: TNA: HO45/10349/146953.
52 For examples of this see, Home Office case notes file, 'ALBERT MEDAL: Carmalt Jones – refused' (1911), HO45/10647/209658; Home Office case notes file, 'ALBERT MEDAL: Albert Medal – Capt. C.T.G.G.Plant – refused' (1905–06), HO45/10331/135695; Home Office case notes file, 'ALBERT MEDAL: Mrs. Connolly – refused' (1913), HO 45/10700/236176.
53 M. C., Smith, *Awarded for Valour: A History of the Victorian Cross and the Evolution of British Heroism* (Basingstoke: Palgrave Macmillan, 2008), p.47.
54 This is provided as a notional example and, in fact, the outcome of the rescue attempt was never actually a deciding factor in awarding the medal. The 1866 Royal warrant was specifically worded as 'saving or attempting to save' in order to accommodate this.
55 Home Office case notes file, 'ALBERT MEDAL: Charles Putman and Arthur Ruben – refused' (1911), TNA: PRO: HO45/10650/211533.
56 Board of Trade memorandum, 'REWARDS. Memorandum as to degree of bravery for award of Albert Medal and other life saving awards' (1866), TNA: PRO: MT9/29 (former dept reference W.3202/66).
57 Home Office case notes file, 'ALBERT MEDAL: Alfred Barlow and William D. McKay – awarded' (1912), TNA: PRO: HO45/10682/221805.
58 Home Office case notes file, 'ALBERT MEDAL: Mr.Urquhart – Vice-Consul at Baku' (1906), TNA: PRO: HO45/10332/136868; Home Office case notes file, 'ALBERT MEDAL: A. L. Bloom – refused' (1905–06), HO45/10329/134537.
59 Home Office case notes file, 'ALBERT MEDAL: Edward James Battersby' (1906–07), PRO: TNA: HO45/10349/146953.
60 Home Office case notes file, 'ALBERT MEDAL: Francis Ward' (1908), TNA: PRO: HO45/10378/162976.
61 Home Office case notes file, 'ALBERT MEDAL: James Hodges – refused' (1906), TNA: PRO: HO45/10347/143257.
62 Home Office case notes file, 'ALBERT MEDAL: P C Wotton – South Molton Workhouse fire. Refused' (1892), TNA: PRO: HO144/345/B13436.
63 For examples of this see Home Office case notes file, 'ALBERT MEDAL: Fireman A.Clark – refused' (1905), TNA: PRO: HO 45/10318/126728; Home Office case notes file, 'ALBERT MEDAL: Supt W Bailey, Hampton Volunteer Fire Brigade. Refused' (1900), HO144/462/B32468.
64 Home Office case notes file, 'ALBERT MEDAL: Guard Sullivan – refused' (1908), TNA: PRO: HO45/10382/167940.
65 Home Office case notes file, 'ALBERT MEDAL: Tram Driver Wilton – refused' (1908), TNA: PRO: HO45/10382/167115.
66 Home Office case notes file, 'ALBERT MEDAL: Award to Dr S C Thompson for dangerous operation' (1885), TNA: PRO: HO144/152/A39790.
67 Home Office case notes file, 'ALBERT MEDAL: Dr Saunders for successful operation. Not granted' (1885), TNA: PRO: HO144/158/A41020; Home Office case

notes file, 'ALBERT MEDAL: Dr Malcolmson for successful operation. Not granted' (1885), HO144/158/A41064; Home Office case notes file, 'ALBERT MEDAL: Dr Ryding for successful operation. Not granted' (1885), HO144/158/A41021.

68 Ibid., HO144/158/A41064.
69 *The Times*, 27 October 1884; 4 November 1884.
70 Home Office case notes file, 'ALBERT MEDAL: Dr Saunders for successful operation. Not granted' (1885), TNA: PRO: HO144/158/A41020.
71 Home Office case notes file, 'ALBERT MEDAL: Mrs. Connolly - refused' (1913), TNA: PRO: HO45/10700/236176.
72 Home Office case notes file, 'ALBERT MEDAL: John Gibson and John Wilson – refused' (1910), TNA: PRO: HO45/10594/186678.
73 Home Office case notes file, 'ALBERT MEDAL: Capt W D Andrews. Refused' (1888), TNA: PRO: HO144/298/B2644.
74 Home Office case notes file, 'ALBERT MEDAL: Henry William Curtis – refused' (1911), TNA: PRO: HO45/10650/211488.
75 S. Collini, *Public Moralists: Political and Intellectual Life in Britain 1850–1930* (Oxford: Clarendon Press, 1991), p. 94.
76 S. Smiles, *Character* (London, 1871: 1910 edition), p. vi.
77 Ibid.
78 S. Collini, *Public Moralists*, p. 100.
79 A. Bain, *On the Study of Character* (London, 1861); H. Maudsley, *Body and Mind* (London, 1870).
80 See, A. Secord, '"Be What You Would Seem to Be": Samuel Smiles, Thomas Edward and the Making of a Working-Class Scientific Hero', *Science in Context*, 16 (2003), 147–73; K. Fielden, 'Samuel Smiles and Self-Help', *Victorian Studies*, 12:2 (1968), 155–76; A. Jarvis, *Samuel Smiles and the Construction of Victorian Values* (Stroud: Sutton, 1997); T. Travers, *Samuel Smiles and the Victorian Work Ethic* (London: Garland Publishing, 1987).
81 S. Collini, *Public Moralists*, p. 62.
82 Ibid., pp. 75–9.
83 Ibid., p. 66.
84 Home Office case notes file, 'ALBERT MEDAL: John Barber, A. B. of H.M.S. "Lily". Awarded' (1889), PRO: TNA: HO144/315/B7501; Home Office case notes file, 'Rewards. Presentation of Albert Medal (2nd Class) to John Barber, Acting Boatswain' (1890), PRO: TNA: MT9/360 (former dept reference M.840/90).
85 M. Girouard, *The Return to Camelot: Chivalry and the English Gentleman* (London, 1981), p. 7.
86 Ibid., p. 62.
87 Some further insights into this area are provided in, L. Delap, '"Thus Does Man Prove to Be the Master of Things": Shipwrecks, Chivalry and Masculinities in Nineteenth- and Twentieth- Century Britain', *Cultural and Social History*, 3 (2006), 45–74.
88 M. Girouard, *The Return to Camelot*, p. 261.
89 Board of Trade memorandum, 'Rewards. As to grant of Albert medal to foreigner' (1875), PRO: TNA: MT9/110 (former dept reference M.5648/75).
90 Board of Trade memorandum, 'ALBERT MEDAL. Warrant instituting medal' (1866), PRO: TNA: MT9/28 (former dept reference M.754/66).
91 Home Office case notes file, 'ALBERT MEDAL: Kathleen Stewart. Refused' (1895), PRO: TNA: HO144/381/B19323.

92   Home Office case notes file, 'ALBERT MEDAL: Neighboni (Australian aboriginal) – awarded' (1911–13), PRO: TNA: HO45/10667/216857.

93   Home Office case notes file, 'Award of Albert Medal to African native for rescue of slave boy from sharks' (1881), PRO: TNA: MT9/192 (former dept reference M.6853/81).

94   Home Office case notes file, 'ALBERT MEDAL: Neighboni (Australian aboriginal) – awarded' (1911–13), PRO: TNA: HO45/10667/216857.

95   Home Office case notes file, 'ALBERT MEDAL: Lieut R H Macdonald, R. E. Awarded. Lance Naik Habib Khan, Awarded. Sapper Shekh Abdul Samand, Awarded. Sapper Kallan Khan, Awarded' (1898–99), PRO: TNA: HO144/433/B28046.

96   Home Office case notes file, 'ALBERT MEDAL: Captain R. W. E. Knollys, Hasil of Chiral, Muhammad Ali of Dir' (1906–08), PRO: TNA: HO45/10348/144617.

97   J. Richards, *Films and British National Identity: From Dickens to Dad's Army* (Manchester, 1997), p. 31.

98   J. M. MacKenzie, 'Imperialism and the School Textbook', in J. M. MacKenzie (ed.), *Propaganda and Empire* (Manchester: Manchester University Press, 1984), p. 181.

99   S. Heathorn, '"Let Us Remember That We, Too, Are English": Constructions of Citizenship and National Identity in English Elementary School Reading Books, 1880–1914', *Victorian Studies*, 38:3 (Spring 1995), 395–427; i.d., *For Home, Country and Race: Constructing Gender, Class and Englishness in the Elementary School, 1880–1914* (London: University of Toronto Press, 2000).

100 See, J. S. Bratton, *The Impact of Victorian Children's Fiction* (London: Croom Helm, 1981); J. Rose, *The Intellectual Life of the British Working Classes*, Ch. 5; J. Richards (ed.), *Imperialism and Juvenile Fiction* (Manchester: Manchester University Press, 1989); J. M. MacKenzie, 'Imperialism and Juvenile Literature', in J. M. MacKenzie (ed.), *Propaganda and Empire*.

101 J. S. Bratton, Children's Fiction, pp. 130–3.

102 M. C., Smith, *Awarded for Valour*, p. 43.

103 For a comprehensive summary of the debate around the concepts of 'Social control' and 'Socialisation' see, F. M. L. Thompson, 'Social Control in Victorian Britain', *The Economic History Review* (May 1981), pp. 189–208.

Chapter 2

1   H. Macmillan, *The Life Work of George Frederic Watts R.A* (London: J. M. Dent & co, 1903), p. 286.

2   B. Bryant, 'Watts, George Frederic (1817–1904)', *Oxford Dictionary of National Biography* (Oxford, 2004).

3   J. R. Gillis (ed.), *Commemorations: The Politics of National Identity* (Princeton: Princeton University Press, 1994), pp. 9–11.

4   R. Whelan (ed.), *Octavia Hill's Letters to Fellow Workers 1872–1911* (London: Kyrle, 2005), pp. 203–4; Bankside Open Spaces Trust, *Red Cross Gardens, Landscape Restoration Management Plan*.

5   All biographical information in this paragraph from, G. Darley, 'Hill, Octavia (1838–1912)', *Oxford Dictionary of National Biography* (Oxford, 2004).

6   O. Hill, 'The Kyrle Society', *Charity Organisation Review*, July–Dec 1905, p. 315.

7   R. Whelan (ed.), *Octavia Hill's Letters*, p. 704.

8   O. Hill, *Letter to my Fellow-Workers* (London, 1886).

9   *The Times*, 14 March 1887.

10 R. Whelan (ed.), *Octavia Hill's Letters*, pp. 221–9.

11 O. Hill, *Letter to My Fellow-Workers* (London, 1887).

12 Bankside Open Spaces Trust, *Red Cross Gardens, Landscape Restoration Management Plan*.

13 *The Times*, 2 June 1888; *The Graphic*, 30 June 1888.

14 E. Barrington, *G.F. Watts: Reminiscences* (London: Allen, 1905). Mary Watts' own personal copy of this book is heavily annotated with comments and corrections, including the addition of 'poisonous snake' beneath Barrington's name on the title page.

15 *The Times*, 5 September 1887.

16 *The Spectator*, 24 September 1887.

17 For more information on the People's Palace see, Anon, *The Queen's London* (London, 1896).

18 *The Spectator*, 24 September 1887.

19 All the quotes in this paragraph are taken from a letter from Leighton to Barrington reprinted in, A. Corkran, *Frederick Leighton* (London: BiblioBazaar, 1904), pp. 156–9.

20 E. Barrington, 'The Red Cross Hall', *English Illustrated Magazine*, x (June 1893), 610–18.

21 *The Times*, 30 March 1888.

22 C. A. P. Willsdon, *Mural Painting in Britain 1840–1940: Image and Meaning* (Oxford: Oxford University Press, 2000), p. 1; M. O'Neill, 'Art and Labour's Cause is One': *Walter Crane and Manchester, 1880–1915* (Manchester: University of Manchester, 2008), p. 45.

23 Willsdon, *Mural Painting*, p. 2.

24 W. Crane, 'Of the Decoration of Public Buildings', in *Art and Life and the Building and Decoration of Cities* (London, 1897), p. 138.

25 For further details see, M. O'Neill, *Art and Labour's Cause*, pp. 42–3.

26 W. Crane, 'Art and Character', in P. L. Parker, *Character and Life: A Symposium* (London: Williams & Norgate, 1912), p. 116.

27 Willsdon, *Mural Painting*, p. 3.

28 W. Crane, 'of Decorative Painting and Design', in W. Morris (ed.), *Arts and Crafts Essays* (London, 1893), p. 45.

29 W. Crane, 'Art and Character', p. 124.

30 Ibid., p. 113.

31 W. Crane, *Ideals in Art* (London, 1905), p. 98.

32 G. Smith, 'Developing a Public Language of Art', in G. Smith and S. Hyde (eds), *Walter Crane 1845–1915. Artist, Designer and Socialist* (Manchester, 1989), p. 13.

33 Ibid., p. 14.

34 For further details see P. Barlow, 'Local Disturbances: Ford Madox Brown and the Problems of the Manchester Murals', in E. Harding (ed.), *Re-Framing the Pre-Raphaelites: Historical and Theoretical Essays* (Aldershot: Scolar Press, 1996), pp. 81–97; J. Treuherz, 'Ford Madox Brown and the Manchester Murals', in J. Archer (ed.), *Art and Architecture in Victorian Manchester* (Manchester: Manchester University Press, 1985), pp. 81–97.

35 F. M. Brown, 'of mural painting', in W. Morris (ed.), *Arts and Crafts Essays* (London, 1893), p. 158.

36 I. Spencer, *Walter Crane* (London: Studio Vista, 1975), p. 133.

37 For further details see P. Usherwood, 'William Bell Scott's Iron and Coal: Northern Readings', in J. Vickers (ed.), *Pre-Raphaelite Painters and Patrons in the North East* (Newcastle: Tyne and Wear Museums Service, 1989), pp. 39–56.

38 W. Crane, 'Thoughts on House Decoration', *Ideals in Art* (London, 1905), p. 120.

39 M. O'Neill, 'Everyday Heroic Deeds: Walter Crane and Octavia Hill at the Red Cross Hall', *The Acorn*, 2003, p. 11.

40 W. Crane, 'of Decorative Painting and Design', p. 50.

41 *Pall Mall Gazette*, 8 October 1890.

42 E. Barrington, 'The Red Cross Hall', *English Illustrated Magazine*, x (June 1893), 610–18.

43 For detailed accounts of the incident see *Southwark Recorder and Bermondsey and Rotherhithe Advertiser*, 2 May 1885; *South London Press*, 2 May 1885; *South London Observer*, 29 April 1885.

44 *The Times*, 6 June 1888.

45 W. Crane, *An Artist's Reminiscences*, p. 359.

46 Reports of the incident appeared in, *Glasgow Herald*, 9 July 1874; *The Preston Guardian*, 11 July 1874.

47 T. Carlyle, *Past and Present* (London, 1843); for a detailed analysis of these two works and the depiction of labour in British Victorian art see, T. Barringer, *Men at Work: Art and Labour in Victorian Britain* (New Haven and London: Yale University Press, 2005).

48 Edwin Mead, in his 1912 pamphlet *Heroes of Peace* reported that the mural depicted George Eales, who in 1887 had descended a well near Basingstoke to rescue a five-year-old child who had fallen in.

49 O. Hill, *Letter to my Fellow-Workers* (London, 1888); Ibid., 1892.

50 W. Crane, *An Artist's Reminiscences*, p. 360.

51 O. Hill, *Letter to My Fellow-Workers* (London, 1911).

52 *The Times*, 30 March 1888.

53 Ibid.

54 W. Crane, 'Of the Decoration of Public Buildings', p. 163.

55 *The Spectator*, 24 September 1887.

56 *The Times*, 30 March 1888; *The Spectator*, 24 September 1887.

57 W. Crane, *An Artist's Reminiscences* (London: Macmillan, 1907), pp. 358–9.

58 L. Lane, *Heroes of Every-day Life* (London, 1888).

59 For example, L. Lane, 'A Character': *A Story for Girls* (London, 1879); i.d., *My Sister's Keeper: A Story for Girls* (London, 1879); i.d. *Ella's Mistake: A Tale* (London, 1882).

60 M. Bettison, 'Luffman, Lauretta Caroline Maria (1846–1929)', *Australian Dictionary of Biography*, 10 (1986), 167.

61 M. Bettison, 'Luffman, Lauretta Caroline Maria', p. 167.

62 L. Lane, *Heroes of Every-day Life*, p. v.

63 Ibid., pp. vi–vii.

64 Ibid., p. vii.

65 Ibid., pp. vii–viii.

66 Christian Knowledge Society, *Everyday Heroes*.

67 Both quotes taken from the preface to *Everyday Heroes*, pp. 5–6.

68 Ibid.

69 Christian Knowledge Society, *Everyday Heroes*.

70 F. Mundell, *Heroines of Daily Life* (London, 1896).

71 Ibid., *Heroines of History* (London, 1897); i.d. *Heroines of Travel* (London, 1897); i.d. *Heroines of Mercy* (London, 1896).

72 F. Mundell, *Heroines of Daily Life*, p. 12.

73 Ibid., p. 12.

74 Ibid., pp. 60–3.

75 H. D. Rawnsley, *Ballads of Brave Deeds* (London, 1896).

76 Ibid., p. vii.

77 E. F. Rawnsley, *Canon Rawnsley: An Account of his Life* (Glasgow: Maclehose, Jackson, 1923), p. 127.

78 This cohort were known as the 'Hinksey Road-Menders' on account of their work in the local Oxfordshire village and other notable participants were Arnold Toynbee and Oscar Wilde; G. Murphy, *Founders of the National Trust* (Bromley: National Trust Books, 1987), p. 77; E. F., Rawnsley, *Canon Rawnsley*, pp. 26–7.

79 E. F. Rawnsley, *Canon Rawnsley*, pp. 65–7.

80 W. Crane, *An Artist's Reminiscences*, p. 449.

81 All quotes in this paragraph taken from, H. D., Rawnsley, 'The Lamp of Chivalry', *Sermons* (Keswick, 1898), pp. 1–12.

82 *The Times*, 5 September 1887.

83 G. F. Watts, letter to Mrs Annie Bryans, 28 April 1899, NPG, v. 12, f. 56.

84 Mary Seton Watts Diaries (hereafter MSWD), 2 and 8 February 1891, 23 May 1891.

85 H. A. Roberts, 'The Heroes of Postman's Park', *The Lady*, 17 November 1959, p. 197.

86 Unreferenced news clipping, Watts Gallery Archive, Compton.

87 HSSMC, *Minutes book*, meeting of 14 November 1906.

88 The figure of £600–700 is quoted in E. Barrington, *Reminiscences*, p. 206.

89 For a full and detailed account of the development of the memorial see, J. Price, *Postman's Park: G. F. Watts's Memorial to Heroic Self-Sacrifice* (Compton: Watts Gallery, 2008).

90 *The Times*, 5 September 1887; *Pall Mall Gazette*, 1 November 1887; *London Argus*, 21 January 1899.

91 *Christian World*, 22 December 1898; *Pall Mall Gazette*, 1 November 1887.

92 G. F. Watts, letter to A. K. Hichens, 29 April 1888, NPG, v. 12, f. 189.

93 There are a number of excellent general studies of poverty during this period including, C. Chinn, *Poverty Amidst Prosperity: The Urban Poor in England, 1834–1914,* 2nd edn (Lancaster: Carnegie Publishing Ltd, 2006); G. S. Jones, *Outcast London* (Oxford, 1971); M. E. Rose, *The Relief of Poverty*, 2nd edn (Basingstoke, 1986); and J. Treble, *Urban Poverty in Britain 1830–1914*, 2nd edn (London, 1983).

94 H. Mayhew, *London Labour and the London Poor* (London, 1851), or for a more accessible selection see B. Taithe (ed.), *The Essential Mayhew* (London: Rivers Oram Press, 1996); G. Godwin, *London Shadows: A Glance at the 'Homes' of the Thousands* (London, 1854); A. Mearns, *The Bitter Cry of Outcast London* (London, 1883); W. Booth, *In Darkest England and the Way out* (London, 1890); C. Booth, *Life and Labour of the People in London* (London: Macmillan, 1902), or for a more accessible selection see A. Fried and R. Elman (eds), *Charles Booth's London* (Harmondsworth, 1969). The Charles Booth Archive is currently held by the London School of Economics; S. Rowntree, *Poverty: A Study Of Town Life* (London: The Policy Press, 1901).

95 *Daily Mail*, 7 July 1898.

96 The project was centred on Toynbee Hall in Commercial Street, Whitechapel, named after the historian and social reformer Arnold Toynbee; for further reading see

A. Briggs, *Toynbee Hall: The First Hundred Years* (London: Routledge, 1984), and S. Meacham, *Toynbee Hall and Social Reform 1880–1914: The Search for Community* (London: Yale University Press, 1987).

97 J. A. Froude, *Short Studies on Great Subjects* (London, 1888), pp. 583–4.
98 Theories concerning exemplarity and heroism are explored in G. Cubitt, 'Introduction', pp. 1–26.
99 H. Cunningham, *Grace Darling: Victorian Heroine* (London: Continuum, 2007).
100 This quote can be found on the tablet commemorating Solomon Galaman, who, in saving his four-year-old brother from being hit by a carriage, was himself knocked down and fatally injured while crossing Commercial Street on 6 September 1901. Transcriptions of all the tablet narratives are reproduced in, J. Price, *Postman's Park*, pp. 74–8.
101 G. F. Watts, letter to A. K. Hichens, 29 April 1888, NPG, v. 12, f. 189.

Chapter 3

1 A standard letter of enquiry was sent to the institutions listed below.
English Archives and Record Offices: Barnsley Archives and Local Studies Department; Bedfordshire and Luton Archives and Records Service; Berkshire Record Office; Bexley Local Studies and Archive Centre; Birmingham City Archives; Bromley Local Studies Library; Bury Archives Service; Cambridgeshire Archives and Local Studies; Centre for Buckinghamshire Studies; Cheshire and Chester Archives and Local Studies Service; Cornwall Record Office; County Record Office Huntingdon; Cumbria Record Office and Local Studies Library, Barrow; Cumbria Record Office and Local Studies Library, Whitehaven; Cumbria Record Office, Carlisle; Cumbria Record Office, Kendal; Derbyshire Record Office; Devon Record Office; Doncaster Archives; Dorset History Centre; Dudley Archives and Local History Service; Durham County Record Office; East Kent Archives Centre; East Riding of Yorkshire Archives and Local Studies; East Sussex Record Office; Gloucestershire Archives; Greater Manchester County Record Office; Hampshire Record Office; Herefordshire Record Office; Hertfordshire Archives & Local Studies; Isle of Wight Record Office; Lancashire Record Office; Lichfield Record Office; Lincolnshire Archives; Manchester Archives and Local Studies; Norfolk Record Office; Northumberland Collections Service; Nottinghamshire Archives and Southwell & Nottingham Diocesan Record Office; Oldham Local Studies and Archives; Oxfordshire Record Office; Oxfordshire Studies Centre; Plymouth and West Devon Record Office; Portsmouth City Museum and Records Office; Rotherham Archives and Local Studies Service; Sheffield Archives; Shropshire County Council; Somerset Record Office; Staffordshire Record Office; Stoke on Trent City Archives; Suffolk Record Office; Teesside Archives; Centre for Kentish Studies; Essex Record Office; Record Office for Leicestershire, Leicester & Rutland; Worcestershire Library & History Centre; Tyne & Wear Archives Service; Warwickshire County Record Office; West Sussex Record Office; West Yorkshire Archive Service, Bradford; West Yorkshire Archive Service, Calderdale; West Yorkshire Archive Service, Kirklees; West Yorkshire Archive Service, Leeds; West Yorkshire Archive Service, Wakefield Headquarters; Wigan Archive Service; Wiltshire and Swindon Archives; Wolverhampton Archives and Local Studies;

Worcestershire Record Office. **Scottish Archives and Record Offices**: Aberdeen City Archives; Angus Archives; Dundee City Archives; Ayrshire Archives; North Highland Archive; Dumfries Archive Centre; Glasgow Archives and Special Collections; East Lothian Local History Centre; Highland Council Archive Service; Perth Local Studies Department; Midlothian Local Studies Centre; Stirling Council Archive Service; Falkirk Library; West Lothian Local History Library. **Welsh Archives and Record Offices**: A. N. Palmer Centre for Local Studies and Archives; Anglesey County Record Office; Caernarfon Record Office; Carmarthenshire Archive Service; Ceredigion Archives; Conwy Archive Service; Denbighshire Record Office; Glamorgan Record Office; Holyhead Library; Llangefni Library; Powys County Archives Office.

2 See appendix two for full details of all eleven monuments.

3 The history of the nineteenth-century drinking fountain movement is covered in works such as Metropolitan Drinking Fountain and Cattle Trough Association, *A Century of Fountains: Centenary Report 1859–1959* (London, 1959); H. Malchow, 'Free Water: the Public Drinking Fountain Movement in Victorian London', *London Journal*, 4 (1978), 181–203; P. Davies, *Troughs and Drinking Fountains: Fountains of Life* (London: Chatto & Windus, 1989).

4 A. Borg, *War Memorials from Antiquity to the Present* (London: Leo Cooper, 1991); A. King, *Memorials of the Great War in Britain* (London: Berg Publishers, 1998).

5 G. Dawson, *Soldier Heroes*; A. Yarrington, *The Commemoration of the Hero*.

6 A. C. Hughes, 'War, Gender and National Mourning: the Significance of the Death and Commemoration of Edith Cavell in Britain', *European Review of History*, 12:3 (2005), 425–44; P. A. Pickering and A. Tyrrell (eds), *Contested Sites – Commemoration, Memorial and Popular Politics in Nineteenth Century Britain* (Aldershot: Ashgate, 2004).

7 Accounts of the incident were reported in, *The Newark Herald*, 8 December 1906; *Newark Advertiser*, 12 December 1906.

8 *Newark Advertiser*, 12 December 1906.

9 Ibid.

10 Ibid.

11 *Newark Herald*, 18 May 1907.

12 Ibid., 26 January 1907.

13 Ibid.

14 Ibid.

15 Ibid., 2 February 1907.

16 Ibid., 11 May 1907.

17 Ibid., 18 May 1907.

18 For further reading on the YMCA see, C. Binfield, *George Williams in Context:A Portrait of the Founder of the YMCA* (Sheffield: Sheffield Academic Press, 1994); N. Garnham, 'Both Praying and Playing: "Muscular Christianity" and the YMCA in Northeast County Durham', *Journal of Social History*, 35:2 (2001), 397–407; G. D. Spurr, 'The London YMCA: a Haven of Masculine Self-Improvement and Socialization for the Late Victorian and Edwardian Clerk', *Canadian Journal of History*, 37:2 (2002), 275–301.

19 An account of incident was published in the *Dunfermline Journal*, 31 July 1886.

20 An account of incident was published in the *Oxford Chronicle and Berks and Bucks Gazette*, 22 June 1899.

21 *Oxford Chronicle and Berks and Bucks Gazette*, 22 June 1899.

22 Ibid.

23 An account of incident was published in the *Durham Chronicle*, 17 August 1906.

24 *Durham County Advertiser*, 17 August 1906.

25 *Auckland Times*, 24 April 1908.

26 *Oxford Times*, 9 November 1889.

27 Price, J., 'Addy, Mark (1840–1890)', *Oxford Dictionary of National Biography* (Oxford: Oxford University Press, 2010b).

28 *Manchester Faces and Places*, vol. II (Manchester, 1890).

29 *Salford City Reporter*, 5 July 1890.

30 All quotes were taken from a report of the meeting in *Salford City Reporter*, 12 July 1890.

31 *Newark Herald*, 11 May 1907.

32 Ibid.

33 Ibid.

34 *Newark Herald*, 5 October 1907.

35 The details that follow have been collated from the series of subscription lists printed weekly in the *Newark Herald* between 1 June and 5 October 1908.

36 *Newark Herald*, 8 August 1908.

37 Ibid.

38 Postcard pictured in *Newark Herald*, 8 August 1908.

39 An account of the incident was given by witnesses at the inquest which was reported in the *Chatham, Rochester and Gillingham Observer*, 13 April 1912.

40 *Chatham, Rochester and Gillingham Observer*, 20 April 1912.

41 An account of the incident was given by witnesses at the inquest which was reported in the *Rochdale Observer*, 19 June 1907.

42 *Heywood News*, 28 June 1907.

43 Ibid.

44 Ibid.

45 Ibid.

46 *Oxford Times*, 9 November 1889.

47 *Auckland Times*, 24 April 1908; *Staffordshire Sentinel*, 27 October 1894.

48 Accounts of the incident were reported in the *Staffordshire Sentinel*, 14 April 1894; *Birmingham Daily Post*, 16 April 1894.

49 *Staffordshire Sentinel*, 27 October 1894.

50 Ibid.; *Birmingham Daily Post*, 23 October 1894.

51 M. Lieven, 'Heroism, Heroics, and the Making of Heroes'; S. Heathorn, 'Representations of War and Martial Heroes'; J. M. Mackenzie, 'Heroic Myths of Empire'.

52 M. Jones, *The Last Great Quest* (Oxford: Oxford University Press, 2003).

53 *Newark Herald*, 26 January 1907.

54 Ibid., 2 February 1907.

55 Ibid., 11 May 1907.

56 Ibid.

57 Ibid.

58 Ibid.

59 Ibid.

60 Ibid., 2 February 1907.

61 Ibid., 18 May 1907.

62 Ibid., 11 May 1907.

63 Ibid., 5 October 1907.

64 Ibid.

65 Ibid., 8 August 1908.

66 Ibid.

67 *Chatham, Rochester and Gillingham News*, 18 May 1912.

68 *Staffordshire Sentinel*, 25 April 1894.

69 *Chatham, Rochester and Gillingham News*, 18 May 1912.

70 *Rochdale Observer*, 3 August 1907; *Heywood News*, 28 June 1907.

71 An account of the accident and Mary Rogers' heroism was published in *The Times*, 10 April 1899.

72 *The Times*, 17 April 1899.

73 J. Ovenden and D. Shayer, *The Wreck of the Stella* (St Peter Port: Guernsey Museums & Galleries, 1999).

74 Ibid., 8 August 1908.

75 Ibid.

76 *Heywood Advertiser*, 17 April 1908; *The Bury Times*, 5 April 1908.

77 *Heywood Advertiser*, 17 April 1908.

78 Ibid., 17 April 1908.

79 *Auckland Chronicle*, 23 April 1908; *Salford City Reporter*, 16 May 1891.

80 *Chatham, Rochester and Gillingham News*, 18 May 1912; *Staffordshire Sentinel*, 27 October 1894.

81 *Oxford Times*, 9 November 1889.

82 Ibid.

83 *Salford Reporter*, 12 July 1890; *Chatham, Rochester and Gillingham Observer*, 18 May 1912; *Dunfermline Journal*, 31 July 1886; *Durham Chronicle*, 24 April 1908.

84 *Heywood News*, 28 June 1907; *Staffordshire Sentinel*, 27 October 1894.

85 All quotes were taken from a report of the meeting which appeared in the *Salford City Reporter*, 12 July 1890.

86 All quotes were taken from a report of a public meeting held at the West End hotel in Stoke on 24 April 1894 published in the *Staffordshire Sentinel*, 25 April 1894.

87 *The Times*, 5 May 1899.

88 *The Times*, 5 September 1887.

89 *Christian World*, 22 December 1898; *Daily Mail*, 7 July 1898.

90 *Pall Mall Gazette*, 1 November 1887.

91 *Daily News*, 22 September 1898; *Daily Chronicle*, 20 July 1899.

92 The Oxford English Dictionary (2001) defines 'jingoism' as the practices of 'one who brags of his country's preparedness for a fight, and generally advocates or favours a bellicose policy in dealing with foreign powers; a blustering or blatant "patriot"'.

93 G. F. Watts, letter to the Earl of Wemyss, 8 May 1888, quoted in Gould, *G. F. Watts*, p. 226.

94 *Daily Chronicle*, 20 July 1899; *Christian World*, 22 December 1898.

95 Quoted in W. Blunt, *England's Michelangelo*, p. 214.

96 Ibid.

97 S. Attridge, *Nationalism, Imperialism and Identity in Late Victorian Culture* (Basingstoke: Palgrave Macmillan, 2003); C. Bolt, *Victorian Attitudes to Race* (London: Routledge and K. Paul, 1971); D. A. Lorimer, *Colour, Class and the Victorians* (Leicester: Leicester University Press, 1978); P. Mandler, ' "Race" and "nation" in mid-Victorian thought', in S. Collini, R. Whatmore, and B. Young (eds), *History, Religion and Culture: British Intellectual History 1750–1950* (Cambridge: Cambridge University Press, 2000), pp. 224–44; K. Tidrick, *Empire and the English Character* (London: I. B. Tauris, 1990).

98 *Auckland Chronicle*, 23 April 1908.

99   Ibid.
100 Ibid.
101 *Salford City Reporter*, 12 July 1890.
102 *Manchester Faces and Places*, vol. II.
103 National Probate Calendar entry for Mark Addy.
104 Website, www.pmsa.org.uk(accessed 01/08/13).
105 T. Cavanagh, *Public Sculpture of Liverpool* (Liverpool: Liverpool University Press, 1997), p. xv.
106 C. I. Hamilton, 'Naval Hagiography', pp. 381–98; J. M. MacKenzie, 'Heroic Myths of Empire'; J. Richards (ed.), *Imperialism and Juvenile Fiction*.

Chapter 4

1   For a wealth of information on all these organizations and others, see C. P. Barclay, *Heroes of Peace: The Royal Humane Society and the Award of Medals in Britain, 1774–1914*, PhD thesis (University of York, 2009).
2   The Carnegie Dunfermline Trust was established by Andrew Carnegie in 1903 and was responsible for undertaking civic works for the benefit of the town of Dunfermline, Scotland, ranging from the construction of baths, gymnasium and playing fields through to the establishment of a children's home, a craft school and a college of hygiene. For further details of this organization see, *The Carnegie Dunfermline Trust 1903–1953* (West Fife, 1981).
3   Letter from Andrew Carnegie in Carnegie Hero Fund Trust (hereafter CHFT), *Report September 1908 to December 1908*, pp. 12–17.
4   Ibid.
5   Ibid.
6   For further reading on the US Hero Fund Commission, see D. R. Chambers, *A Century of Heroes* (Pittsburgh, 2004); T. S, Arbuthnot, *Heroes of Peace: A History of the Carnegie Hero Fund Commission* (Pittsburgh, 1935).
7   Quoted in, D. R. Chambers, *A Century of Heroes*, p. 29.
8   The European hero funds and the initial endowments were as follows: France (1909) $1 million; Germany (1910) $1.5 million; Norway (1911) $125,000; Switzerland (1911) $130,000; the Netherlands (1911) $200,000; Sweden (1911) $230,000; Denmark (1911) $125,000; Belgium (1911) £230,000; Italy (1911) $750,000. The US Hero Fund Commission (1904) received an initial endowment of $5 million.
9   CHFT, *Report September 1908 to December 1908*, pp. 12–17.
10 J. Ross, *Address* in CHFT, *Report September 1908 to December 1908*, pp. 36–44.
11 *The Scotsman*, 25 September 1908; *Dundee Advertiser*, 25 September 1908.
12 *Daily News*, 25 September 1908; *Daily Chronicle*, 25 September 1908; *Daily Express*, 25 September 1908.
13 *The Scotsman*, 25 September 1908; *Glasgow Evening Citizen*, 25 September 1908.
14 *Sheffield Daily Telegraph*, 25 September 1908; *Manchester Courier*, 25 September 1908.
15 A. Carnegie, *The Gospel of Wealth* (London, 1899).
16 See, B. Hilton, *The Age of Atonement* (Oxford: Clarendon Press, 1988).
17 For an overview of this subject, see G. Jones, *Social Darwinism and English Thought* (Sussex: Harvester Press, 1908).
18 A. Carnegie, *The Gospel of Wealth*, p. 12.
19 F. Prochaska, *The Voluntary Impulse* (London: Faber & Faber, 1988), p. 35.

20 Ibid.
21 CHFT, Report September 1908 to December 1908, pp. 12–17.
22 Ibid., p. 30.
23 Ibid.
24 Ibid.
25 Ibid.
26 Ibid.
27 CHFT, *Report September 1908 to December 1908*, pp. 44–6.
28 Ibid.
29 Ibid.
30 *Daily Mail*, 25 September 1908.
31 CHFT, *Report September 1908 to December 1908,* pp. 12–17.
32 *The Scotsman*, 25 September 1908.
33 *Yorkshire Post*, 25 September 1908.
34 *The Scotsman*, 25 September 1908.
35 *Dundee Courier*, 25 September 1908.
36 *Daily News*, 25 September 1908.
37 Ibid.
38 Ibid.
39 Ibid.
40 Address to the Trustees by John Ross, pp. 36–44.
41 Ibid.
42 Ibid.
43 Ibid.
44 Ibid.
45 Address to the Trustees by John Ross in CHFT, *Report September 1908 to December 1908*, pp. 36–44.
46 Figures were derived from, S. Goodenough, *The Greatest Good Fortune.*
47 Figures were derived from Royal Humane Society Minute Books 1908–14.
48 C. Barclay, *The Medals of the Royal Humane Society* (London: Royal Humane Society, 1998).
49 Society for the Protection of Life from Fire (hereafter SPLF), *First Annual Report of the Society* (London, 1837).
50 SPLF, *Annual Report of the Society* (London, 1908).
51 Figures were derived from SPLF, *Annual Reports*, 1908–14.
52 In the case of women, there were eighteen nominations of which twelve were refused and for children there were ten nominations of which nine were refused.
53 Abercarn Colliery, (1878), nine awards; Baddesley Colliery (1882), five awards; Clifton Hall Colliery, (1885), four awards; Tynewydd Colliery, (1877), thirteen awards.
54 On average, for the period 1851 to 1911, domestic service accounted for around 43 per cent of female workers. Figures were derived from B. R. Mitchell and P. Deane, *Abstract of British Historical Statistics* (Cambridge: Cambridge University Press, 1971), p. 60.
55 Wall, *Andrew Carnegie*, p. 851.
56 Burke's *Landed Gentry of Great Britain, The Kingdom in Scotland* (Wilmington: Burke's Landed Gentry, 2001).
57 Obituary for Shennan, *Dunfermline Press*, 30 January 1937; obituary for Stevenson, *Dunfermline Press*, 15 August 1931.
58 Obituary for Macbeth, *Dunfermline Press*, 12 April 1952; Obituary for Blair, *Dunfermline Press*, 18 February 1950.

59   Obituary for Ross, *Dunfermline Press*, 7 November 1931.
60   Obituary for Scobie, *Dunfermline Press*, 9 February 1924; Obituary for Tuke, *Dunfermline Press*, 29 May 1948.
61   Obituary for Brown, *Dunfermline Press*, 21 February 1920.
62   Obituary for Mathewson, *Dunfermline Press*, 27 August 1921; Obituary for Walker, *Dunfermline Press*, 27 September 1913; Obituary for Robertson, *Dunfermline Press*, 3 March 1923.
63   Obituary for Shearer, *Dunfermline Press*, 16 February 1935; Obituary for Beveridge, *Dunfermline Press*, 20 May 1922.
64   Obituary for Hynd *Dunfermline Press*, 21 December 1946.
65   Obituary for Weir, *Dunfermline Press*, 26 December 1908.
66   Address to the Trustees by John Ross, pp. 36–44.
67   Ibid.
68   Ibid.
69   *Dundee Courier*, 25 September 1908.
70   *London Standard*, 25 September 1908.
71   *Yorkshire Post*, 25 September 1908.
72   *Dundee Advertiser*, 25 September 1908; *London Standard*, 25 September 1908.
73   *Aberdeen Free Press*, 25 September 1908.
74   *The Scotsman*, 25 September 1908.
75   Quoted in T. S., Arbuthnot, *Heroes of Peace*, p. 34.
76   SPLF, *Annual Report of the Society* (London, 1908).
77   *Sheffield Daily Telegraph*, 25 September 1908; *Yorkshire Post*, 25 September 1908.
78   *Dunfermline Press*, 25 September 1908; *Daily Express*, 25 September 1908.
79   *Aberdeen Free Press*, 25 September 1908.
80   *Dunfermline Press*, 25 November 1911.
81   Ibid.
82   Figure derived from, S. Goodenough, *The Greatest Good Fortune: Andrew Carnegie's Gift for Today* (Edinburgh: Macdonald Publishers, 1985).
83   Ibid.
84   A. Carengie, *Armaments and their Results* (London: The Peace Society, 1909a); i.d., *The Path to Peace upon the Seas* (London: The Peace Society, 1909b); i.d., *War as the Mother of Valor and Civilisation* (London: The Peace Society, 1910).
85   A. Carnegie, *War as the Mother of Valor and Civilisation*, p. 12.
86   G. Tweedale, 'Carnegie, Andrew (1835–1919)', *Oxford Dictionary of National Biography* (Oxford, 2004).
87   F. J. Wall, *Andrew Carnegie* (London, 1970).
88   F. Lynch, *Personal Recollections of Andrew Carnegie* (London, 1920), p. 142.
89   Ibid.
90   CHFT, *Report September 1908 to December 1908*, pp. 12–17.
91   Quoted in, F. Lynch, *Personal Recollections*, p. 145.
92   Ibid.
93   *Dundee Advertiser*, 25 September 1908.
94   The sonnet in question being *Sonnet XVI: To the Lord General Cromwell* (1652) which contains the words, 'peace hath her victories/no less renowned than war'; *Dundee Courier*, 25 September 1908; *Daily Chronicle*, 25 September 1908.
95   *Aberdeen Free Press*, 25 September 1908.
96   Based upon 257 cases listed in the CHFT reports between 1908 and 1914 where an age was provided.

Chapter 5

1   The incident is recounted in several newspaper reports including *The Times*, 5 November 1884; *The Belfast News-letter*, 4 November 1884; *Reynolds's Newspaper*, 9 November 1884.

2   *Glasgow Herald*, 22 January 1885; *Aberdeen Weekly Journal*, 9 December 1884.

3   *Aberdeen Weekly Journal*, 9 December 1884.

4   *Glasgow Herald*, 22 January 1885; *Aberdeen Weekly Journal*, 4 February 1885.

5   M. Vicinus, 'What Makes a Heroine? Girls' Biographies of Florence Nightingale', in V. L. Bullough, B. Bullough and M. P. Stanton (eds), *Florence Nightingale and her Era: a Collection of New Scholarship* (New York: Garland Publishing, Inc., 1980), pp. 96–107; M. Bostridge, *Florence Nightingale: The Woman and her Legend* (London: Viking, 2008); K. Pickles, *Transnational Outrage: the Death and Commemoration of Edith Cavell* (Basingstoke: Palgrave Macmillan, 2007); S. M. Barney, 'The Mythic Matters of Edith Cavell: Propaganda, Legend, Myth and Memory', *Historical Reflections*, 31:2 (2005), 217–33; A. Summers, *Female Lives, Moral States: Women, Religion and Public Life in Britain, 1800–1930* (Newbury: Threshold Press, 2000); J. Jordan, *Josephine Butler* (London: John Murray, 2001); H. Cunningham, *Grace Darling*.

6   K. Cowman, ' "With a Lofty Moral Purpose": Caroline Martyn, Enid Stacy, Margaret McMillan, Katherine St John Conway and the Cult of the Good Woman Socialist', in G. Cubitt and A. Warren (eds), *Heroic Reputations and Exemplary Lives*, pp. 212–24.

7   J. Rowbotham, ' "Soldiers of Christ?": Images of Female Missionaries in Late Nineteenth-Century Britain: Issues of Heroism and Martyrdom', *Gender & History*, 12 (2000), 82–106.

8   Going forward, the universal and gender-neutral use of 'hero', in a similar manner to 'actor' or 'comedian', may well be widely adopted but, at this time, the more familiar terms 'female heroism' and 'heroine' have been retained in the interests of presenting a clear picture. The use of these terms is not intended to imply any critical differentiation between the heroism of men and women and is merely a shorthand for acts of heroism undertaken by women.

9   Seminal studies of nineteenth-century manliness include J. A. Mangan and J. Walvin (eds), *Manliness and Morality: Middle-class Masculinity in Britain and America, 1800–1914* (Manchester: Manchester University Press, 1987); N. Vance, *The Sinews of the Spirit: The Idea of Christian Manliness in Victorian Literature and Religious Thought* (Cambridge: Cambridge University Press, 1985).

10 J. Tosh, *A Man's Place: Masculinity and the Middle-Class Home in Victorian England* (London: Yale University Press, 1999), in particular chs. 7 and 8. Tosh cites authors such as and Rider Haggard, George Henty Robert Louis Stevenson as purveyors of this genre.

11 M. Francis, 'The Domestication of the Male? Recent Research on Nineteenth- and Twentieth-Century British Masculinity', *The Historical Journal*, 43/3 (2002), 637–52.

12 For example, M. Lieven, 'Heroism, Heroics, and the Making of Heroes'; S. Heathorn, 'Representations of War and Martial Heroes'; J. M. Mackenzie, 'Heroic Myths of Empire'.

13 E. Hodder, *Heroes of Britain in War and Peace* (London, 1878).

14 F. Mundell, *Heroines of Daily Life*; other examples include: F. J. Cross, *Beneath the Banner*; L. Lane, *Heroes of Everyday Life*; C. D. Michael, *Heroines: True Tales of Brave Women*; A. H. Miles, *A Book of Brave Girls at Home and Abroad: True Stories*

of Courage and Heroism (London, 1909); H. C. Moore, *Noble Deeds of the World's Heroines*; M. Trevelyan, *Brave Little Women.*

15 W. R. Greg, 'Why are Women Redundant?', National Review, 14 (1862), 434–60; discussed in M. Poovey, Uneven Developments: The Ideological Work of Gender in Mid-Victorian England (Chicago: University of Chicago Press, 1988).

16 Quoted in K. Gleadle, *British Women in the Nineteenth Century* (Basingstoke: Palgrave Macmillan, 2001), p. 183.

17 For an overview of this area see, S. Alexander, *Women's Work in Nineteenth-Century London* (London: Journeyman Press, 1976); A. Amsden, *The Economics of Women and Work* (Harmondsworth: Penguin, 1908); D. Blythell, 'Women in the Workforce', in P. O'Briedn and R. Quinault (eds), *The Industrial Revolution and British Society* (Cambridge: Cambridge University Press, 1993), pp. 31–53; S. Burman, *Fit Work for Women* (London: Croom Helm, 1979); K. Cowman and L. A. Jackson (eds), *Women and Work Culture: Britain c.1850–1950* (Aldershot: Ashgate, 2005); S. O. Rose, *Limited Livelihoods: Gender and Class in Nineteenth-Century England* (London: Routledge, 1992).

18 Figure derived from, B. R. Mitchell and P. Deane, *Abstract of British National Statistics*, p. 60.

19 K. Gleadle, *British Women*, pp. 104–6.

20 M. Vicinus, *Independent Women: Work and Community for Single Women, 1850–1920* (London: Virago Press, 1985), p. 25.

21 Figures derived from B. R. Mitchell and P. Deane, *Abstract of British National Statistics*, p. 60.

22 L. Davidoff, 'Gender and the 'Great Divide': Public and Private in British Gender History', *Journal of Women's History*, 15:1 (Spring 2003), 11.

23 A good introduction to the historiography is, A. Vickery, 'Golden Age to Separate Spheres? A Review of the Categories and Chronology of English Women's History', *The Historical Journal*, 36: 2 (June 1993), 383–414.

24 See, for example, C. Hall, 'The Early Formation of Victorian Domestic Ideology', in S. Burman (ed.), *Fit Work for Women* (London: Croom Helm, 1979), pp. 15–32; L. Davidoff and C. Hall, (eds), *Family Fortunes: Men and Women of the English Middle Class, 1780–1850* (London: Hutchinson, 1987); M. Vicinus (ed.), *Suffer and Be Still: Women in the Victorian Age* (Bloomington: Indiana University Press, 1972); C. Hall (ed.), *White, Male and Middle Class: Explorations in Feminism and History* (Oxford: John Wiley and Sons Ltd, 1992).

25 For example, F. B. Smith, 'Sexuality in Britain, 1800–1900: Some Suggested Revisions', in M. Vicinus (ed.), *A Widening Sphere: Changing Roles of Victorian Women* (Bloomington: Indiana University Press, 1977), pp. 188–93; M. J. Peterson, 'No Angels in the House: the Victorian Myth and the Paget Women', *American History Review*, 89:3 (1984), 693.

26 See, B. Caine, *Victorian Feminists* (Oxford: Oxford University Press, 1992), pp. 40–6.

27 Women certainly worked in manual or industrial occupations in large numbers, as noted earlier in this chapter.

28 *Aberdeen Weekly Journal*, 9 December 1884.

29 F. Mundell, *Heroines of Daily Life*, p. 46.

30 H. C. Moore, *Noble Deeds*, pp. 17–18.

31 C. D. Michael, *Heroines*, pp. 112–16.

32 H. C. Moore, *Noble Deeds*, p. 18.

33 'Female Heroism, Exemplified by Anecdotes', *The Englishwoman's Domestic Magazine* (London, date unknown), p. 11.

34 F. Mundell, *Heroines of Daily Life*, p. 30.

35 C. D. Michael, *Heroines*, pp. 76–80.

36 H. C. Moore, *Noble Deeds*, p. 33.

37 F. Mundell, *Heroines of Daily Life*, p. 40.

38 H. C. Moore, *Noble Deeds*, p. 34.

39 C. Young, 'The Courage of Women', *The Girl's Own Paper*, 7 February 1880.

40 F. Mundell, *Heroines of Daily Life*, p. 85.

41 Ibid., p. 137.

42 See, for example, the case of Mrs Wallace in C. D. Michael, *Heroines*, pp. 140–4.

43 *The Illustrated Police News*, 2 February 1889.

44 C. Patmore, *The Angel in the House* (London, 1863).

45 F. Mundell, *Heroines of Daily Life*, p. 47.

46 C. D. Michael, *Heroines*, p. 8.

47 Ibid., pp. 76–80.

48 H. C. Moore, *Noble Deeds*, p. 15.

49 Ibid., p. 16.

50 Ibid., p. 34.

51 For detailed accounts of the incident see *Southwark Recorder and Bermondsey and Rotherhithe Advertiser*, 2 May 1885; *South London Press*, 2 May 1885; *South London Observer*, 29 April 1885.

52 J. Tosh, *A Man's Place*, p. 14.

53 Accounts of this incident appeared in both, C. D. Michael, *Heroines*, pp. 172–5 and F. Mundell, *Heroines of Daily Life*, pp. 64–71.

54 *The Hull Packet and East Riding Times*, 21 April 1876.

55 S. D'Cruze, 'Women and the Family', in J. Purvis (ed.), *Women's History: Britain 1850–1945* (London: Chatto and Windus, 1995), p. 73.

56 *Aberdeen Weekly Journal*, 9 December 1884.

57 F. Mundell, *Heroines of Daily Life*, p. 15.

58 Ibid., pp. 16–17.

59 Studies of motherhood in the Victorian period include, A. Davin, 'Imperialism and Motherhood', *History Workshop Journal*, 5 (1978), 9–66; C. Nelson and A. S. Holmes, *Maternal Instincts: Visions of Motherhood and Sexuality in Britain, 1875–1925* (Basingstoke: Palgrave Macmillan, 1997); E. Ross, *Love and Toil: Motherhood in Outcast London, 1870–1918* (Oxford: Oxford University Press, 1993).

60 Genealogical information provided by the great, great niece of Mary Rogers.

61 H. C. Moore, *Noble Deeds*, p. 22.

62 J. Ovendon and D. Shayer, *The Wreck of the Stella*, p. 45.

63 'Employments for Women', *Myra's Journal*, 1 October 1889, p. 528.

64 H. C. Moore, *Noble Deeds*, p. 22.

65 J. Rowbotham, 'Soldiers of Christ?', pp. 86–7.

66 The full report of the Board of Trade enquiry into the loss of the SS *Stella* is held by The National Archives, ref: RAIL 411/411; national newspapers also extensively covered the enquiry and reported on the findings, for example, *Glasgow Herald*, 12 May 1899; *The Leeds Mercury*, 12 May 1899, *The Times*, 28 April, 12 May 1899.

67 *The Leeds Mercury*, 12 May 1899.

68 *Jersey Times*, 15 April 1899.

69 Quotes taken from reports in, *Daily News*, 1 April 1899, *Glasgow Herald*, 1 April 1899, *The Times*, 4 and 5 April 1889.

70   *Western Mail*, 3 April, 1899; *The Times*, 14 April 1899.
71   *Northern Echo*, 5 April 1899; *The Jersey Weekly Press and Independent*, 8 April 1899.
72   *The Times*, 7 April 1899.
73   *The Woman's Weekly*, 8 April 1899.
74   L. Delap, 'Thus Does Man Prove to Be the Master of Things', pp. 45–77.
75   *The Jersey Weekly Press and Independent*, 8 April 1899; *The Evening Post* (Jersey), 9 May 1899.
76   *The Times*, 6 May 1899.
77   *The Evening Post* (Jersey), 23 April 1899.
78   *Jersey Times*, 8 April 1899.
79   J. F. C. Harrison, *Late Victorian Britain 1875–1901* (London: Fontana, 1990) p. 173.
80   J. R. Walkowitz, 'Butler, Josephine Elizabeth (1828–1906)', *Oxford Dictionary of National Biography* (Oxford: Oxford University Press, 2004).
81   B. Caine, *Victorian Feminists* (Oxford: Oxford University Press, 1992), p. 250.
82   P. Hollis, *Ladies Elect: Women in English Local Government, 1865–1914* (Oxford: Clarendon Press, 1987).
83   M. Pugh, *Women and the Women's Movement in Britain 1914–1959* (Basingstoke: Palgrave Macmillan, 1992), p. 2; see also M. Pugh, *The March of Women* (Oxford: Oxford University Press, 2000); J. Purvis and S. S. Holton (eds), *Votes for Women* (London: Routledge, 2000).
84   *The Times*, 13 April 1899.
85   B. Caine, *Victorian Feminists*, pp. 103–30; S. Hamilton, *Frances Power Cobbe and Victorian Feminism* (Basingstoke: Palgrave Macmillan, 2006); L. Williamson, *Power and Protest: Frances Power Cobbe and Victorian Society* (London: Rivers Oram, 2005).
86   'Stewardesses in Steamships', *Myra's Journal*, 1 October 1889, p. 528.
87   'Stewardesses on Board Ship', *Hearth and Home,* 27 October 1892, p. 790.
88   *The Times*, 17 April 1899.
89   A. Bryans, *A Souvenir of the Unveiling of the Memorial Fountain in Southampton* (Southampton, 1901).
90   For accounts of the incident see, *Reynolds's News*, 25 January 1863; *Daily News*, 2 February 1863; *The Era*, 1 February 1863.
91   *Reynolds's Newspaper*, 1 February 1863.
92   C. H. Moore, *Noble Deeds*, p. 3.
93   *The Times*, 5 September 1887.
94   H. D. Rawnsley, *Ballads of Brave Deeds*, p. 151.
95   *Reynolds's Newspaper*, 10 May 1885.
96   Home Office case notes file, 'ALBERT MEDAL: Kate Chapman (aged 9). Refused' (1894), PRO: TNA: HO/144/368/B17244.
97   Home Office case notes file, 'ALBERT MEDAL: Award to Miss H Roabotham for saving lives from collapse of school roof' (1881–98), PRO: TNA: HO144/88/A10053.
98   L. Delap, 'Thus Does Man Prove'.
99   A. K. Smith, 'All Quiet on the Woolwich Front? Literary and Cultural Constructions of Women Munitions Workers in the First World War', in K. Cowman and L. A. Jackson (eds), *Women and Work Culture: Britain c.1850–1950* (Aldershot: Ashgate, 2005), pp. 197–212.
100 This is asserted in C. Pearson and K. Pope, *The Female Hero in American and British Literature* (New York: R.R. Bowker, 1981).
101 J. Rowbotham, *Soldiers of Christ*.

Conclusion

1 T. Carlyle, *On Heroes and Hero-worship and the Heroic in History* (London, 1841), p. 1.

2 P. Karsten, *Patriot Heroes*, p. 2.

3 Studies that demonstrate this include J. Benson, *The Working Class in Britain 1850–1939* (Harlow, 1989); J. Rose, *The Intellectual Life of the British Working Classes*; D. G. Wright, *Popular Radicalism: The Working-Class Experience 1780–1880* (Harlow: Longman, 1988).

4 M. Jones, 'What Should Historians Do With Heroes?'

5 Research papers on these subjects were, for example, presented at an AHRC-funded symposium 'My Hero: defining and constructing non-military heroism' held at King's College London in 2009. See also, M. Goodrum, '"Friend of the people of many lands": Johnny Everyman, critical internationalism and liberal postwar US heroism', *Social History*, 38.2 (2013); i.d. '"Hail to the King, baby": Bruce Campbell and the representation of US masculine heroism', *The BAAS Postgraduate Journal*, 16 (Spring 2010).

6 P. Gilchrist, 'The politics of totemic sporting heroes and the conquest of Everest', *Anthropological Notebooks*, 12:2 (2006), 35–52; i.d. '"Motherhood, ambition and risk"; mediating the sporting hero/ine in Conservative Britain', *Media, Culture and Society*, 29:3 (2007), 387–406; M. Huggins and K. Gregson, 'Northern songs, sporting heroes and regional consciousness, c.1800-c.1880: "Wor Stars that Shine"', *Northern History*, 44:2 (2007), 141–58; M. Huggins, 'Death, memorialisation and the Victorian sporting hero', *Local Historian*, 38:4 (2008), 257–65; P. B. Mukharji, 'the Culture and Politics of Local Sporting Heroes in Late Colonial Bengal and Princely Orissa: The Case of Santimoy Pati', *International Journal of the History of Sport*, 25:12 (2008), 1612–27; S. Wagg and D. Russell, *Sporting Heroes of the North: Sport, Religion and Culture* (Newcastle upon Tyne, 2010).

7 An in-depth analytical study of the *Daily Herald Order of Industrial Heroism* is also long overdue; see Fevyer, W. H., et al., *The Order of Industrial Heroism* (London, 2000) for further details.

8 For example, initiatives such as the 'Pride of Britain' awards and 'Help for Heroes'.

9 C. Hill, *The World Turned Upside Down: Radical Ideas During the English Revolution* (Harmondsworth, 1972), p. 18.

Bibliography

Primary sources

Manuscripts

The National Archives (TNA): Public Record Office (PRO): as follows:

HO/10347/143257, 'ALBERT MEDAL: James Hodges – refused' (1906)

HO/144/368/B17244, 'ALBERT MEDAL: Kate Chapman (aged 9). Refused' (1894)

HO144/152/A39790, 'ALBERT MEDAL: Award to Dr S C Thompson for dangerous operation' (1885)

HO144/158/A41020, 'ALBERT MEDAL: Dr Saunders for successful operation. Not granted' (1885)

HO144/158/A41021, 'ALBERT MEDAL: Dr Ryding for successful operation. Not granted' (1885)

HO144/158/A41064, 'ALBERT MEDAL: Dr Malcolmson for successful operation. Not granted' (1885)

HO144/298/B2644, 'ALBERT MEDAL: Capt W D Andrews. Refused' (1888)

HO144/315/B7501, 'ALBERT MEDAL: John Barber, A.B. of H.M.S. "Lily". Awarded' (1889)

HO144/345/B13436, 'ALBERT MEDAL: P C Wotton – South Molton Workhouse fire. Refused' (1892)

HO144/381/B19323, 'ALBERT MEDAL: Kathleen Stewart. Refused' (1895)

HO144/433/B28046, 'ALBERT MEDAL: Lieut R H Macdonald, R. E., Awarded. Lance Naik Habib Khan, Awarded. Sapper Shekh Abdul Samand, Awarded. Sapper Kallan Khan, Awarded'. (1898–99)

HO144/462/B32468, 'ALBERT MEDAL: Supt W Bailey, Hampton Volunteer Fire Brigade. Refused' (1900)

HO144/88/A10053, 'ALBERT MEDAL: Award to Miss H Roabotham for saving lives from collapse of school roof' (1881–98)

HO45/10318/126728, 'ALBERT MEDAL: Fireman A.Clark – refused' (1905)

HO45/10322/129274, 'ALBERT MEDAL: Rescue by deaf mute students – refused' (1905–06)

HO45/10329/134537, 'ALBERT MEDAL: A. L. Bloom – refused' (1905–06)

HO45/10331/135695, 'ALBERT MEDAL: Albert Medal – Capt. C. T. G. G. Plant – refused' (1905–06)

HO45/10332/136868, 'ALBERT MEDAL: Mr.Urquhart – Vice-Consul at Baku' (1906)

HO45/10347/143257, 'ALBERT MEDAL: James Hodges – refused' (1906)

HO45/10348/144617, 'ALBERT MEDAL: Captain R. W. E. Knollys, Hasil of Chiral, Muhammad Ali of Dir' (1906–08)

HO45/10349/146953, 'ALBERT MEDAL: Edward James Battersby' (1906–07)

HO45/10368/157924, 'ALBERT MEDAL: Misconduct of holder of Albert Medal – Arthur Hardiment' (1907–08)

HO45/10378/162976, 'ALBERT MEDAL: Francis Ward' (1908)

HO45/10382/167115, 'ALBERT MEDAL: Tram Driver Wilton – refused' (1908)

HO45/10382/167940, 'ALBERT MEDAL: Guard Sullivan – refused' (1908)

HO45/10392/172692, 'ALBERT MEDAL: Mr. F. V. Nicholls – refused' (1908–09)

HO45/10579/181121, 'ALBERT MEDAL: Thomas Lewis – awarded' (1910–19)

HO45/10594/186678, 'ALBERT MEDAL: John Gibson and John Wilson – refused' (1910)

HO 45/10622/197066, 'ALBERT MEDAL: Margaret Coutts – refused' (1910)

HO45/10647/209658, 'ALBERT MEDAL: Carmalt Jones – refused' (1911)

HO45/10650/211488, 'ALBERT MEDAL: Henry William Curtis – refused' (1911)

HO45/10650/211533, 'ALBERT MEDAL: Charles Putman and Arthur Ruben – refused' (1911)

HO45/10666/216363, 'ALBERT MEDAL: Harold Bould and Arthur Shakespear – refused' (1911–12)

HO45/10667/216857, 'ALBERT MEDAL: Neighboni (Australian aboriginal) – awarded' (1911–13)

HO45/10682/221805, 'ALBERT MEDAL: Alfred Barlow and William D. McKay – awarded' (1912)

HO45/10700/236176, 'ALBERT MEDAL: Mrs. Connolly – refused' (1913)

HO45/10890/354008, 'ALBERT MEDAL: Lieutenant Commander T. K. Triggs – award Leading Seaman T. N. Davis – award Able Seaman Robert Stones award Able Seaman William Becker – award Stoker Edward S. Beard. – award Albert C. Mattison – award' (1918–19)

HO45/12941, 'HONOURS: Albert Medal: Jack Hewitt' (1911–28)

HO45/8846, 'ALBERT MEDAL: Institution of the Albert Medal for gallantry in saving lives at sea' (1886–87)

HO45/9434/63549A, 'ALBERT MEDAL: Extension of the Institution of the Albert Medal to cases of gallantry in saving life on land' (1877–81)

HO45/9434/63549C, 'ALBERT MEDAL: Award to Mark Addey for saving several lives in River Irwell' (1878–79)

HO45/9552/63549H, 'ALBERT MEDAL: Amending Royal Warrant regulating awards' (1881)

MEPO 2/1925, 'Commendations, Awards and Commemorations' (1930)

MT9/110, (former dept reference M.5648/75), 'Rewards. As to grant of Albert medal to foreigner' (1875)

MT9/192, (former dept reference M.6853/81), 'Award of Albert Medal to African native for rescue of slave boy from sharks' (1881)

MT9/28, (former dept reference M.754/66), 'ALBERT MEDAL. Warrant instituting medal' (1866)

MT9/288, (former dept reference M.17381/86), 'Rewards. Granting of awards; and interpretation of the terms "Distress at Sea" and "Peril of the Sea"' (1886)

MT9/29, (former dept reference W.3202/66), 'REWARDS. Memorandum as to degree of bravery for award of Albert Medal and other life saving awards' (1866)

MT9/360, (former dept reference M.840/90), 'Rewards. Presentation of Albert Medal (2nd Class) to John Barber, Acting Boatswain' (1890)

MT9/402, 'Rewards. Award of the Albert Medal, 2nd Class to Fourth Officer A. J. Cooper' (1891)

MT9/533, (former dept reference M.7498/95), 'Rewards. Award of the Albert Medal, Second Class, to Sub-Lieut. C.W. Robinson, R. N. R.' (1895)

MT9/5969, 'Original warrants and correspondence relating to institution of the Albert Medal' (1864–67)

MT9/733, (former dept reference M.11051/02), 'Albert Medal. Presentation of Medals by H.M. the King' (1902)

Royal Humane Society, *Minutes Books; Case Books, Annual Reports,* LMA/4517, London Metropolitan Archives (1837–1914),

Carnegie Hero Fund Trust, *Annual Reports,* British Library (1908–14)

Carnegie Dunfermline Trust, *Annual Reports,* British Library (1903)

Heroic Self-Sacrifice Memorial Committee (HSSMC) *Minutes Book,* P69/BOT1/B/036/ MS18628, London Metropolitan Archives (1904)

George, Frederic Watts, *Correspondence,* MS 70-84 & 84a, Heinz Archive, National Portrait Gallery (1847–1904)

Society for the Protection of Life from Fire, *Minutes Books,* CLC/014, London Metropolitan Archives (1908–14)

Newspapers and periodicals

Aberdeen Free Press (1908)
Aberdeen Weekly Journal (1884–85)
Auckland Chronicle (1908)
Auckland Times (1908)
Belfast News-letter (1884)
Bexley Times (2007)
Birmingham Daily Post (1894)
The Bury Times (1908)
The Christian World (1898)
Charity Organisation Review (1905)
Chatham, Rochester and Gillingham News (1912)
Chatham, Rochester and Gillingham Observer (1912)
City Press (1900)
Daily Express (1908)
Daily Chronicle (1899–1908)
Daily Mail (1898–1908)
Daily News (1863–1908)
Dundee Advertiser (1908)
Dundee Courier (1908)
Dunfermline Journal (1886–1908)
Dunfermline Press (1908–52)
Durham Chronicle (1906–08)
Durham County Advertiser (1906)
English Illustrated Magazine (1893)
The Englishwoman's Domestic Magazine, (Date unknown)
The Era (1863–67)
The Evening Post, Jersey (1899)
The Girl's Own Paper (1880)
Glasgow Evening Citizen (1908)
Glasgow Herald (1874–89)

The Graphic (1885–88)
The Guardian (2000)
Hearth and Home (1892)
Heywood Advertiser (1908)
Heywood News (1907)
The Hull Packet and East Riding Times (1876)
The Illustrated Police News (1885–89)
Irish Independent (1898)
Independent (1989)
Jersey Times (1899)
The Jersey Weekly Press and Independent (1899)
The Lady (1959)
The Leeds Mercury (1866–99)
The London Argus (1889–99)
London Gazette (1866–81)
London Illustrated News (1885–90)
London Standard (1908)
Manchester Courier (1908)
Manchester Evening News (1990)
Manchester Faces and Places (1890)
Manchester Weekly Times (1877–90)
Merthyr Press (1877)
Myra's Journal (1889)
Newark Herald (1906–08)
Newark Advertiser (1906)
Newcastle Courant (1866–68)
Northern Echo (1899)
Oxford Chronicle and Berks and Bucks Gazette (1899)
Oxford Times (1889)
Pall Mall Gazette (1887–90)
Plymouth and Cornish Advertiser (1866)
Preston Guardian (1874)
Reynolds News (1863–85)
Rochdale Observer (1907)
Salford City Reporter (1890–1990)
Salford Weekly Chronicle (1887–90)
Salford Weekly News (1877)
The Scotsman (1908)
Sheffield Daily Telegraph (1908)
South London Chronicle (1885)
South London Observer (1885)
South London Press (1885)
Southwark Recorder and Bermondsey and Rotherhithe Advertiser (1885)
The Spectator (1887)
Staffordshire Sentinel (1894)
The Times (1866–2009)
Western Mail (1877–99)
Who Do You Think You Are? (2009)
The Woman's Weekly (1899)
Yorkshire Post (1908)

Published material

Alderson, B., *Andrew Carnegie: From Telegraph Boy to Millionaire* (London: Pearson, 1902).

Anon, *Working-Men Heroes: A Roll of Heroic Actions in Humble Life* (London, 1879).

—*The Queen's London* (London: Cassell and Co. Ltd, 1896).

Arnold, E., *My Book of Heroism* (London, 1896).

Arthur, W., *Heroes* (London, 1851).

Bailey, M. H., *A Terrible Experience: The Wreck of the Stella* (London, undated).

Bain, A., *On the Study of Character* (London: Parker, 1861).

Baker, H. J., *Lays and Ballads of Heroism* (London, 1884).

Balfour, C. L. *Moral Heroism; or, The Trials and Triumphs of the Great and Good* (London: Houlston And Stoneman, 1846).

Barrington, E., *G.F. Watts: Reminiscences* (London: Allen, 1905).

Besant, W., *All Sorts and Conditions of Men* (London: Chatto and Windus, 1882).

Booth, W., *In Darkest England and the Way Out* (London: International Headquarters of the Salvation Army, 1890).

Bryans, A., *A Souvenir of the Unveiling of the Memorial Fountain in Southampton* (Southampton, 1901).

Carlyle, T., *On Heroes and Hero-worship and the Heroic in History* (London, 1840).

—*Past and Present* (London, 1843).

Carnegie, A., *The Gospel of Wealth* (London, 1899).

—*Armaments and their Results* (London: The Peace Society, 1909a).

—*The Path to Peace upon the Seas* (London: The Peace Society, 1909b).

—*War as the Mother of Valor and Civilisation* (London: The Peace Society, 1910a).

—*Speech by Andrew Carnegie LL.D., at the Annual Meeting of the Peace Society, May 24th 1910* (London: The Peace Society, 1910b).

—*Autobiography of Andrew Carnegie* (London: Constable, 1920).

Carnegie United Kingdom Trust, *Andrew Carnegie, the British Trusts and their Works* (Edinburgh: Pillans & Wilson, 1935).

Christian Knowledge Society, *Everyday Heroes: Stories of Bravery During the Queen's Reign 1837–1888* (London, 1889).

Corkran, A., *Frederick Leighton* (London: BiblioBazaar, 1904).

Crane, W., *Art and Life and the Building and Decoration of Cities* (London, 1897).

—*Ideals in Art* (London, 1905).

—*An Artist's Reminiscences* (London: Macmillan, 1907).

Cross, F. J., *Beneath the Banner* (London, 1895).

Darby, E., *Lays of Love and Heroism, Legends, Lyrics and other Poems* (London, 1885).

Drake, L., *The Heroes of England. Stories of the lives of the most celebrated British Soldiers and Sailors* (London, 1843).

Engels, F., *The Condition of the Working Class in England* (London, 1844).

Faris, J. T., *The Book of Everyday Heroism* (London, 1924).

Foxwell, A. J., *Careless Charlie. A Temperance Story with Song* (London, 1889).

Froude, J. A., 'Representative men', in Froude, J. A., *Short Studies on Great Subjects* (London, 1888), pp. 465–85.

Gildea, J., *For Remembrance and in Honour of those Who Lost their Lives in the South African War 1899–1902* (London, 1911).

Godwin, J., *London Shadows: A Glance at the 'Homes' of the Thousands* (London, 1854).

Greenwood, J., *Outcast London: A Story of the Sufferings of the Poor* (London, 1884).

Greg. W. R., 'Why are women redundant', *National Review*, 14 (1862), 434–60.

Hammond, J. L. & B., *The Town Labourer 1760–1832: The New Civilisation* (London: Longmans, Green and co., 1917).

Hanson, R., *The Story of the Tablets* (Self Published, 1930).

Harrison, F., *The New Calendar of Great Men* (London, 1892).

Hill, O., *Letter to My Fellow-Workers* (London, annually).

Hodder, E., *Heroes of Britain in War and Peace* (London, 1878).

Hope, E., *Grace Darling: The Heroine of the Farne Islands* (London, 1875).

Lane, L. 'A Character': *A Story for Girls* (London, 1879a).

—*My Sister's Keeper: A Story for Girls* (London, 1879b).

—*Ella's Mistake: A Tale* (London, 1882).

—*Heroes of Everyday life* (London, 1888).

London, J., *The People of the Abyss* (London, 1902).

Lynch, F., *Personal Recollections of Andrew Carnegie* (London: Revell, 1920).

Mabie, H. W., *Heroes Every Child Should Know* (London, 1906).

Macaulay, J., *Thrilling Tales of Enterprise and Peril, Adventure and Heroism* (London, 1886).

Macmillan, H., *The Life Work of George Frederick Watts R.A.* (London: J. M. Dent & co, 1903).

Martin, W., *Heroism of Boyhood* (London, 1865).

Maudsley, H., *Body and Mind* (London, 1870).

Mayhew, H., *London Labour and the London Poor* (London, 1851).

McGlennon, F. and Horncastle, G., *Heroes of Every Day Life* (London, 1892).

Mead, E. D., *Heroes of Peace* (Boston, 1912).

Mearns, A., *The Bitter Cry of Outcast London* (London, 1883).

Michael, C. D., *Deeds of Daring: Stories of Heroism in Every Day Life* (London: S. W. Partridge & Company, 1900).

—*Heroines: True Tales of Brave Women – A Book for British Girls* (London: S. W. Partridge & Company Limited, 1904).

Michelet, J., *History of the French Revolution*, Trans. Coeks, C. (London, 1847).

Miles, A. H., *Fifty-Two Stories of Heroism in Life and Action for Boys* (London, 1899).

—*A Book of Brave Girls at Home and Abroad: True Stories of Courage and Heroism* (London, 1909).

Mill, J. S., *The Subjection of Women* (New York, 1869).

Moore, H. C., *Noble Deeds of the World's Heroines* (London: Religious Tract Society, 1903).

Morris, W. (ed.), *Arts and Crafts Essays* (London, 1893).

Moses, R., *The Civil Service of Great Britain* (London: Columbia University, 1914).

Mundell, F., *Heroines of Daily Life* (London, 1896a).

—*Heroines of Mercy* (London, 1896b).

—*Heroines of History* (London, 1897a).

—*Heroines of Travel* (London, 1897b).

Neale, J. M., *The Triumphs of the Cross: Tales of Christian Heroism* (London, 1846).

Parker, P. L., *Character and Life: A Symposium* (London: Williams & Norgate, 1912).

Patmore, C., *The Angel in the House* (London, 1863).

Rawnsley, E. F., *Canon Rawnsley: An Account of his Life* (Glasgow: Maclehose, Jackson, 1923).

Rawnsley, H. D., *Ballads of Brave Deeds* (London, 1896).

—'The Lamp of Chivalry', *Sermons* (Keswick, 1898).

Rowntree, S., *Poverty: A Study of Town Life* (London: The Policy Press, 1901).

Smiles, S., *Self Help* (London, 1859).
—*Character* (London, 1871: 1910 edition).
—*Duty* (London, 1880).
St Botolph's Aldersgate, *The Story of the Tablets* (London, 1908).
Toynbee, A., *Lectures on the Industrial Revolution* (London, 1884).
Trevelyan, M., *Brave Little Women: Tales of the Heroism of Girls Founded on Fact* (London, 1888).
Troup, E., *The Home Office* (London, 1925).
Various, *Tales of Heroism and Record of Strange and Wonderful Adventures* (London, 1847).
Watts, M. S., *The Annals of an Artist Life* (London, 1912).
Weaver, L., *Memorials and Monuments: Old and New: Two Hundred Subjects Chosen from Seven Centuries* (London, 1915).
Webb, S. & B., *History of Trade Unionism* (London, 1894).
Wilson, M. B., *A Carnegie Anthology* (New York, 1915).
Winkler, J. K., *Incredible Carnegie: The Life of Andrew Carnegie 1835–1919* (New York, 1931).
Yonge, C., *A Book of Golden Deeds of All Times and All Lands* (London, 1864).

Secondary sources

Published material

Alexander, S., *Women's Work in Nineteenth-Century London* (London: Journeyman Press, 1976).
Amsden, A., *The Economics of Women and Work* (Harmondsworth: Penguin, 1908).
Anderson, B., *Imagine Communities: Reflections on the Origin and Spread of Nationalism* (London, 1991).
Anderson, O., *A Liberal State at War: English Politics and Economics during the Crimean War* (London: MacMillan, 1967).
—'The Growth of Christian Militarism in Mid-Victorian Britain', *The English Historical Review*, 86 (1971), 46–72.
Andrews, J. F., *William Shakespeare, His World, His Work, His Influence*, 3 vols. (New York: Scribner, 1985).
Arbuthnot, T. S., *Heroes of Peace: A History of the Carnegie Hero Fund Commission* (Pittsburgh, 1935).
Armstrong, R., *Grace Darling: Maid and Myth* (London, 1965).
Ashplant, T. G., Dawson G., and Roper, M. (eds), *The Politics of War Memory and Commemoration* (London, 2000).
Bailey, P., *Leisure and Class in Victorian England: Rational Recreation and the Contest for Control, 1830–1885* (London: Routledge & K. Paul, 1978).
Bankside Open Spaces Trust, *Red Cross Gardens, Landscape Restoration Management Plan* (London, undated).
Barclay, C. P., *The Medals of the Royal Humane Society* (London: Royal Humane Society, 1998).
—*Heroes of Peace: The Royal Humane Society and the Award of Medals in Britain, 1774–1914*, PhD thesis (University of York, 2009).

Barczewski, S., '"Nations Make Their Own Gods and Heroes": Robin Hood, King Arthur and the development of racialism in nineteenth-century Britain', *Journal of Victorian Culture*, 2: 2 (1997), 179–207.

—*Antarctic Destinies: Scott, Shackleton and the Changing Face of Heroism* (London: Bloomsbury Academic, 2007).

—*Myth and National Identity in Nineteenth-Century Britain* (Oxford: Oxford University Press, 2000).

—*Titanic* (London, 2011).

Barlow, P., 'Local disturbances: Ford Madox Brown and the problems of the Manchester murals', in Harding, E. (ed.), *Re-Framing the Pre-Raphaelites: Historical and Theoretical Essays* (Aldershot: Scolar Press, 1996), pp. 81–97.

Barney, S. M., 'The mythic matters of Edith Cavell: propaganda, legend, myth and memory'. *Historical Reflections*, 31:2 (2005), 217–33.

Barringer, T., *Men at Work: Art and Labour in Victorian Britain* (New Haven and London: Yale University Press, 2005).

Bedford, W. K. R., *The Order of the Hospital of St John of Jerusalem* (New York: Macmillan, 1978).

Beilby, A., *Heroes All! The Story of the RNLI* (Somerset: Patrick Stephens Limited, 1992).

Ben-Amos, A., *Funerals, Politics, and Memory in Modern France, 1789–1996* (Oxford, 2000).

Bentley, E., *The Cult of the Superman: A Study of the Idea of Heroism in Carlyle and Nietzsche* (London: R. Hale, 1947).

Berenson, E., *Heroes of Empire: Five Charismatic Men and the Conquest of Africa* (Berkeley: University of California Press, 2011).

Bergonzi, B., *Heroes' Twilight: A Study of the Literature of the Great War* (London: Coward-McCann, 1965).

Best, G., *Mid-Victorian Britain 1851–75* (St Albans, 1973).

Bettison, M., 'Luffman, Lauretta Caroline Maria (1846–1929)', *Australian Dictionary of Biography*, 10 (1986), 167.

Binfield, C., *George Williams in Context: A Portrait of the Founder of the YMCA* (Sheffield: Sheffield Academic Press, 1994).

Bishop, P. J., *A Short History of the Royal Humane Society* (London, 1974).

Birch, D., 'Ruskin and Carlyle: changing forms of biography in *Fors Clavigera*', in Cubitt, G. and Warren, A. (eds), *Heroic Reputations and Exemplary Lives* (Manchester: Manchester University Press, 2000), pp 178–91.

Black, J. and Macraild, D. M., *Studying History*, 3rd edn (Basingstoke: Palgrave Macmillan, 2007).

Blythell, D., 'Women in the workforce', in O'Brien, P. and Quinault, R. (eds), *The Industrial Revolution and British Society* (Cambridge: Cambridge University Press, 1993), pp. 31–53.

Bolt, C., *Victorian Attitudes to Race* (London: Routledge and K. Paul, 1971).

Boorman, D., *At the Going Down of the Sun: British First World War Memorials* (York, 1988).

Borg, A., *War Memorials from Antiquity to the Present* (London: Leo Cooper, 1991).

Bostridge, M., *Florence Nightingale: The Woman and her Legend* (London, 2008).

Bouwers, E. G., 'Whose heroes?: The House of Commons, its commemorative sculptures and the illusion of British patriotism, 1795–1814', *European Review of History*, 15:6 (2008), 675–89.

Bratton, J. S., *The Impact of Victorian Children's Fiction* (London: Croom Helm, 1981).

Bryant, B. C., 'Watts, George Frederic (1817–1904)', *Oxford Dictionary of National Biography* (Oxford: Oxford University Press, 2004; online edn, May 2007).

Briggs, A., *Victorian People* (London, 1954).

—*Victorian Cities* (London, 1963).

—*Toynbee Hall: The First Hundred Years* (London: Routledge, 1984).

—*A Social History of England* (London, 1987).

—'Samuel Smiles: the gospel of Self-Help', in G. Marsden (ed.), *Victorian Values: Personalities and Perspectives in Nineteenth Century Society* (London: Longman, 1990).

Brooks, C. (ed.), *The Albert Memorial: The Price Consort National Memorial* (London, 2000).

Burke's *Landed Gentry of Great Britain, the Kingdom in Scotland* (Wilmington: Burke's Landed Gentry, 2001).

Burke, P (ed.), *New Perspectives on Historical Writing* (Cambridge: Pennsylvania State University Press, 1991).

Burman, S., *Fit Work for Women* (London: Croom Helm, 1979).

Burnett, J., *Useful Toil* (London, 1974).

—*A Social History of Housing 1815–1985* (London, 1978).

Burnett, J., Vincent, D. and Mayall, D., *The Autobiography of the Working Class: An Annotated Critical Bibliography*, three volumes (London, 1989).

Bushaway, B., 'Name upon name: the Great War and remembrance', in Porter, R. (ed.), *Myths of the English* (Cambridge, 1992), pp. 136–67.

Caine, B., *Victorian Feminists* (Oxford: Oxford University Press, 1992).

Campbell, J., *The Hero with a Thousand Faces* (New York: Pantheon Books, 1949).

Cannadine, D., *Admiral Lord Nelson: Context and Legacy* (Hampshire: Palgrave Macmillan, 2005).

Cavanagh, T., *Public Sculpture of Liverpool* (Liverpool: Liverpool University Press, 1997).

—*Public Sculpture of Leicestershire and Rutland* (Liverpool: Liverpool University Press, 2000).

Chambers, D. R., *A Century of Heroes* (Pittsburgh: Carnegie Hero Fund Commission, 2004).

Chinn, C., *Poverty amidst Prosperity: The Urban Poor in England, 1834–1914*, 2nd edn (Lancaster: Carnegie Publishing Ltd, 2006).

Cohen, E. W. *The Growth of the British Civil Service 1780–1939* (London: Frank Cass, 1965).

Coke, D., *Saved from a Watery Grave: the Story of the Royal Humane Society's Receiving House in Hyde Park* (London: Royal Humane Society, 2000).

Cole, G. D. H. and Postage, R., *The Common People 1746–1946* (London: Methuen, 1938).

Collini, S., *Public Moralists: Political and Intellectual Life in Britain 1850–1930* (Oxford: Clarendon Press, 1991).

—*English Pasts* (Oxford: Oxford University Press, 1999).

Collini, S., Whatmore, R. and Young, B. (eds), *History, Religion and Culture: British Intellectual History 1750–1950* (Cambridge: Cambridge University Press, 2000).

Conboy, M., *The Press and Popular Culture* (London: SAGE, 2002).

Connelly, M., *The Great War, Memory and Ritual: Commemoration in the City and East End London, 1916–1939* (London: Boydell & Brewer, 2002).

Cowman, K., 'With a lofty moral purpose': Caroline Martyn, Enid Stacy, Margaret McMillan, Katherine St John Conway and the cult of the good woman socialist', in Cubitt, G. and Warren, A. (eds), *Heroic Reputations and Exemplary Lives* (Manchester: Manchester University Press, 2000), pp. 212–24.

Cowman, K. and Jackson, L. A. (eds), *Women and Work Culture: Britain c.1850–1950* (Aldershot: Ashgate, 2005).

Cox, B., *Lifeboat Gallantry* (London: Spink & Son, 1998).

Cresswell, H., *The Story of Grace Darling* (London: Penguin Books, 1988).

Crook, M. J., *The Evolution of the Victoria Cross: A Study in Administrative History* (Tunbridge Wells: Midas Books, 1975).

Cubitt, G. and Warren, A. (eds), *Heroic Reputations and Exemplary Lives* (Manchester: Manchester University Press, 2000).

Cunningham, H., 'The Language of patriotism 1750–1914', *History Workshop Journal*, 12 (1981), 8–33.

—*Grace Darling: Victorian Heroine* (London: Continuum, 2007).

Curl, J. S., *The Victorian Celebration of Death* (Gloucestershire: Sutton Publishing, 2000).

Curtis, P. (ed.), *Patronage and Practice: Sculpture on Merseyside* (Liverpool: Tate Gallery Liverpool, National Museums & Galleries on Merseyside, 1989).

Dagnall, H., *Postman's Park and its Memorials* (self published, 1987).

Darke, J., *The Monument Guide to Britain and Wales* (London, 1991).

Darley, G., 'Hill, Octavia (1838–1912)', *Oxford Dictionary of National Biography* (Oxford: Oxford University Press, 2004).

Dawson, G., *Soldier Heroes: British Adventure, Empire and the Imagining of Masculinities* (London: Routledge, 1994).

Davidoff, L., 'Class and gender in Victorian England', in Newton, J. L., Ryan, M. P. and Walkowitz, J. R. (eds), *Sex and Class in Women's History* (London: Routledge, 1983), pp. 17–71.

—'Gender and the 'great divide': public and private in British gender history', *Journal of Women's History*, 15:1 (Spring 2003), 11–27.

Davidoff, L and Hall, C., *Family Fortunes: Men and Women of the English Middle Class, 1780–1850* (London: Hutchinson, 1987).

Davies, P., *Troughs and Drinking Fountains* (London: Chatto & Windus, 1989).

Davin, A., 'Imperialism and motherhood', *History Workshop Journal*, 5 (1978), 9–66.

D'Cruze, S., 'Women and the family', in Purvis, J. (eds), *Women's History: Britain 1850–1945* (London: Chatto and Windus, 1995), pp. 51–84.

De Groot, J., "Sex' and 'Race': The construction of language and image in the Nineteenth century', in Mendus, S. and Rendall, J. (eds), *Sexuality and Subordination. Interdisciplinary Studies of Gender in the Nineteenth Century* (London: Routledge, 1989), pp. 89–130.

Delap, L., ' "Thus does man prove to be the master of things": shipwrecks, chivalry and masculinities in nineteenth- and twentieth- century Britain', *Cultural and Social History*, 3 (2006), 45–77.

Downer, M., *Nelson's Purse* (London: Transworld, 2005).

Evans, E. J. and Richards, J., *A Social History of Britain in Postcards, 1870–1930* (London: Longman, 1980).

Evans M. and Lunn, K. (eds), *War and Memory in the Twentieth Century* (Oxford: Berg Publishers, 1997).

Fevyer, W. H., *Acts of Gallantry* (London, 1996).

Fevyer, W. H., Wilson J. W., Cribb J., *The Order of Industrial Heroism* (London: Orders & Medals Research Society, 2000).

Fielden, K., 'Samuel Smiles and Self-Help', *Victorian Studies*, 12:2 (1968), 155–76.

Francis, M., 'The domestication of the male? recent research on nineteenth- and twentieth-century British masculinity', *The Historical Journal*, 43/3 (2002), 637–52.

Franklin-Gould, V., *G.F. Watts: The Last Great Victorian* (London: Yale University Press for Paul Mellon Centre for Studies in British Art, 2004).

Fussell, P., *The Great War and Modern Memory* (Oxford: Oxford University Press, 1975).

Garnham, N., 'Both praying and playing: "Muscular Christianity" and the YMCA in northeast County Durham', *Journal of Social History*, 35:2 (2001), 397–407.

Gilchrist, P., 'The politics of totemic sporting heroes and the conquest of Everest', *Anthropological Notebooks*, 12:2 (2006), 35–52.

—'"Motherhood, ambition and risk"; mediating the sporting hero/ine in Conservative Britain', *Media, Culture and Society*, 29:3 (2007), 387–406.

Gillis, J. R., *Commemorations: The Politics of National Identity* (Princeton Princeton University Press, 1994).

Girouard, M., *The Return to Camelot: Chivalry and the English Gentleman* (London: Yale University Press, 1981).

Gleadle, K., *British Women in the Nineteenth Century* (Basingstoke: Palgrave Macmillan, 2001).

Goldie, S. (ed.), *'I have Done my Duty'. Florence Nightingale and the Crimean War 1854–56* (Manchester: Manchester University Press, 1987).

Goodenough, S., *The Greatest Good Fortune: Andrew Carnegie's Gift for Today* (Edinburgh: Macdonald Publishers, 1985).

Goodman, A., *The Street Memorials of St Albans Abbey Parish* (St Albans: St. Albans and Hertfordshire Architectural and Archaeological Society, 1987).

Goodrum, M., '"Hail to the King, baby": Bruce Campbell and the representation of US masculine heroism', *The BAAS Postgraduate Journal*, 16 (Spring 2010).

—'"Friend of the people of many lands": Johnny Everyman, 'critical internationalism' and liberal postwar US heroism', *Social History*, 38:2 (2013), 203–19.

Grammer, T. G., *The Myth of Gentlemen Heroes in the Nineteenth Century: The Duke of Wellington and General Robert E. Lee* (Lampeter: Edwin Mellen Press, 2010).

Greenblatt, S., *Will in the World: How Shakespeare Became Shakespeare* (London: Norton, 2005).

Grundlingh, A., 'The National Women's Monument', in Cuthbertson, G., Grundlingh, A. and Suttie, L. (eds), *Writing a Wider War: Rethinking Gender, Race and Identity in the South Africa War 1899–1902* (Ohio: Ohio University Press, 2002), pp. 18–36.

Hall, C. 'The early formation of Victorian domestic ideology', in Burman, S. (ed.), *Fit Work for Women* (London: Croom Helm, 1979), pp. 15–32.

—(ed.), *White, Male and Middle Class: Explorations in Feminism and History* (Oxford: John Wiley and Sons Ltd, 1992).

Halladay, E., *Rowing in England: A Social History* (Manchester: Manchester University Press, 1990).

Hamilton, C. I., 'Naval hagiography and the Victorian hero', *The Historical Journal*, 23:2 (1980), 381–98.

Hamilton, S., *Frances Power Cobbe and Victorian Feminism* (Basingstoke: Palgrave Macmillan, 2006).

Harlow, A. F., *Andrew Carnegie* (London, 1953).

Harris, J., *Private Lives, Public Spirit: Britain 1870–1914* (London: Oxford University Press, 1993).

Harrison, J. F. C., *Early Victorian Britain 1832–51* (London: Fontana Press, 1971).

—*Late Victorian Britain 1875–1901* (London: Fontana Press, 1990).

Hilton, B., *The Age of Atonement* (Oxford: Clarendon Press, 1988).

Himmelfarb, G., *Victorian Minds* (London, 1968).

Heathorn, S., ' "Let us remember that we, too, are English": constructions of citizenship and national identity in English elementary school reading books, 1880–1914', *Victorian Studies*, 38:3 (1995), 395–427.

—*For Home, Country and Race: Constructing Gender, Class, and Englishness in the Elementary School 1880–1914* (London: University of Toronto Press, 1999).

—' "The highest type of Englishman"? gender, war and the Alfred commemoration of 1901', *Canadian Journal of History*, 37 (2002a), 459–84.

—'Representations of war and martial heroes in English elementary school reading and rituals, 1885–1914', in Marten, J. (ed.), *Children and War: a Historical Anthology* (London: NYU Press, 2002b), pp. 103–15.

—'A "matter for artists, and not for soldiers"? The cultural politics of the Earl Haig National Memorial, 1928–1937', *Journal of British Studies*, 22:3 (2005), 536–61.

Henderson, D. V., *Heroic Endeavour: A Complete Register of the Albert, Edward and Empire Gallantry Medals and How They were Won* (London: J. B. Hayward, 1988).

Hobbs, C. A., *Florence Nightingale* (London, 1997).

Hobsbawm, E., 'History from below', in Hobsbawm, E.(ed.), *On History* (London: Hachette, 1997), pp. 201–16.

Hobsbawm, E. and Ranger, T., *The Invention of Tradition* (Cambridge, 1992).

Hollis, P., *Ladies Elect: Women in English Local Government, 1865–1914* (Oxford: Clarendon Press, 1987).

Hopkins, E., *A Social History of the English Working Classes 1815–1945* (London: Edward Arnold, 1979).

Houghton, W. E., *The Victorian Frame of Mind* (London: Yale University Press, 1957).

Howarth, P., *Play Up and Play the Game: the Heroes of Popular Fiction* (London: Eyre Methuen, 1973).

Huggins, M., 'Death, memorialisation and the Victorian sporting hero', *Local Historian*, 38:4 (2008), 257–65.

Huggins, M. and Gregson, K., 'Northern songs, sporting heroes and regional consciousness, c.1800-c.1880: "Wor Stars that Shine"', *Northern History*, 44:2 (2007), 141–58.

Hughes, A. C., 'War, gender and national mourning: the significance of the death and commemoration of Edith Cavell in Britain', *European Review of History*, 12:3 (2005), 425–44.

Hunt, L. (ed.), *The New Cultural History* (London: University of California Press, 1989).

Inglis, K. S., 'A sacred place: the making of the Australian war memorial', *War and Society*, 3 (1985), 99–126.

—*Sacred Places: War Memorials in the Australian Landscape* (Victoria: Melbourne University Press, 2001).

Ittmann, K., *Work, Gender and Family in Victorian England* (London: New York University Press, 1995).

Janson, H. W., *Nineteenth-century Sculpture* (London: Abrams, 1985).

Jarvis, A., *Samuel Smiles and the Construction of Victorian Values* (Stroud: Sutton, 1997).

Jeffery, S., *The Liverpool Shipwreck and Humane Society 1839–1939* (Liverpool: Daily Post, 1939).

Jones, G., *Social Darwinism and English Thought* (Sussex: Harvester Press, 1908).

Jones, G. S., *Outcast London* (Oxford: Clarendon Press, 1971).

Jones, M., *The Last Great Quest* (Oxford: Oxford University Press, 2003).

—'What should historians do with heroes?' *History Compass*, 5/2 (2007), 439–54.

Jordan, J., *Josephine Butler* (London: John Murray, 2001).

Jordonova, L., *History in Practice*, 2nd edn (London: Bloomsbury USA Academic, 2006).

Joslin, E. C., *Spink's Catalogue* (Exeter: Webb & Bower, 1983).

Karsten, P., *Patriot Heroes in England and America* (London: University of Wisconsin Press, 1978).

Kearns, S., 'Picture postcards as a source for social historians', *Saothar: Journal of the Irish Labour History Society*, 22 (1997), 128–33.

Kift, D., *The Victorian Music Hall: Culture, Class and Conflict* (Cambridge: Cambridge University Press, 1996).

King, A., *Memorials of the Great War in Britain* (Oxford: Berg Publishers, 1998).

Kitson-Clarke, G., *The Making of Victorian England* (London: Routledge, 1962).

Krass, P., *Carnegie* (New Jersey, 2002).

Lake, B., *British Newspapers, A History and Guide for Collectors* (London: Sheppard Press, 1984).

Lambert, A. D., *Admirals: The Naval Commanders who made Britain Great* (London: Faber and Faber Limited, 2008).

Lambert, A. D. and Badsey, S., *The Crimean War: The War Correspondents* (Stroud: Sutton Pub Limited, 1994).

Lamont-Brown, R., *Carnegie: 'The Richest Man in the World'* (Stroud: Sutton Pub Limited, 2005).

Lant, J. L., *Insubstantial Pageant: Ceremony & Confusion at Queen Victoria's Court* (London: Taplinger Publishing Company, 1979).

Levine, P., *Victorian Feminism 1850–1900* (London: Hutchinson Education, 1987).

Lieven, M, 'Heroism, heroics, and the making of heroes: The Anglo-Zulu war of 1879', *Albion*, 30 (1998), 419–38.

Llewellyn, K., *Disaster at Tynewydd* (Cardiff: ap Dafydd Publications Ltd, 1975).

Llewellyn, S., *Admiral Nelson: The Sailor who Dared All to Win* (London: Short Books, 2004).

Llinares, D., 'Idealized heroes of "retrotopia": history, identity and the postmodern in Apollo 13, *The Sociological Review*, 57 (2009), 164–77.

—*The Astronaut: Cultural Mythology and Idealised Masculinity* (Cambridge: Cambridge Scholars Publishing, 2011).

Lorimer, D. A., *Colour, Class and the Victorians* (Leicester: Leicester University Press, 1978).

MacDonald, R. H., 'A poetics of war: militarist discourse in the British empire, 1880–1918', *Mosaic*, 23:3 (1990), 17–36

Mackay, J., *Little Boss: The Life of Andrew Carnegie* (Edinburgh, 1997).

MacKenzie, J. M., 'Imperialism and the school textbook', in MacKenzie, J. M.(ed.), *Propaganda and Empire* (Manchester: Manchester University Press, 1984), pp. 174–97.

—*Imperialism and Popular Culture* (Manchester: Manchester University Press, 1986).

—'Heroic myths of empire', in MacKenzie, J. M.(ed.), *Popular Imperialism and the Military 1850–1950* (Manchester: Manchester University Press, 1992), pp. 109–38.

Malchow, H., 'Free water: the public drinking fountain movement in Victorian London', *London Journal*, 4 (1978), 181–203.

Mandler, P., ' "Race" and "Nation" in mid-Victorian thought', in S. Collini, R. Whatmore and Young B. (eds), *History, Religion and Culture: British Intellectual History 1750–1950* (Cambridge: Cambridge University Press, 2000), pp. 224–44.

—'The consciousness of modernity? liberalism and the English national character, 1870–1940, in Daunton, M and Rieger, B. (eds), *Meanings of Modernity: Britain from the Late-Victorian Era to World War II* (Oxford, 2001), pp. 119–44.

—*The English National Character* (London: Yale University Press, 2006).

Mangan, J. A., ' "Muscular, militaristic and manly": the British middle-class hero as moral messenger', *International Journal of the History of Sport*, 13:1 (1996), 28–47.

Mangan, J. A. and Walvin, J., *Manliness and Morality: Middle-Class Masculinity in Britain and America, 1800–1940* (Manchester: Manchester University Press, 1987).

McKenzie, R., *Public Sculpture of Glasgow* (Liverpool: Liverpool University Press, 2001).

McIntyre, C., *Monuments of War: How to Read a War Memorial* (London: Robert Hale, 1990).

McLean, J., 'Watts, historical thought and the schemes of painting in the 1840's', in Trodd, C. and Brown, S. (eds), *Representations of G.F. Watts. Art Making in Victorian Culture* (London: Ashgate, 2004), pp. 109–20.

Meacham, S., *A Life Apart: The English Working Class 1890–1914* (London: Harvard University Press, 1977).

—*Toynbee Hall and Social Reform 1880–1914: The Search for Community* (London: Yale University Press, 1987).

Metropolitan Drinking Fountain and Cattle Trough Association, *A Century of Fountains: Centenary Report 1859–1959* (London, 1959).

Michalski. S, *Public Monuments: Art in Political Bondage 1870–1997* (London: Reaktion Books Ltd, 1998).

Mitchell, S., *Francis Power Cobbe: Victorian Feminist, Journalist, Reformer* (London: University of Virginia Press, 2004).

Mitchell, B. R. and Deane, P., *Abstract of British Historical Statistics* (Cambridge: Cambridge University Press, 1971).

Moriarty, C., *Narrative and the Absent Body: The Mechanics of Meaning in First World War Memorials* (Sussex: University of Sussex, 1995).

—'Private grief, public remembrance', in Evans M. and Lunn, K. (eds), *War and Memory in the Twentieth Century* (Oxford: Berg Publishers, 1997), pp. 125–39.

Morrill, J. S., 'How Oliver Cromwell thought', in Morrow, J. and Scott, J. (eds), *Liberty, Authority, Formality: Political Ideas and Culture, 1600–1900* (Exeter: Imprint Academic, 2008), pp. 89–112.

Moses, R., *The Civil Service of Great Britain* (London: Columbia University, 1914).

Mosse, G., *The Nationalization of the Masses* (New York: H. Fertig, 1985).

Mukharji, P. B., 'the Culture and Politics of Local Sporting Heroes in Late Colonial Bengal and Princely Orissa: The Case of Santimoy Pati', *International Journal of the History of Sport*, 25:12 (2008), 1612–27.

Murphy, G., *Founders of the National Trust* (Bromley: National Trust Books, 1987).

Nelson, C. and Holmes, A. S., *Maternal Instincts: Visions of Motherhood and Sexuality in Britain, 1875–1925* (Basingstoke: Palgrave Macmillan, 1997).

Nelson, R. A., The *Home Office 1782–1801* (London: Duke University Press, 1969).

Newsam, F., *The Home Office* (London: George Allen & Unwin, 1954).

Newsome, D., *The Victorian World Picture* (London: John Murray, 1997).

Nora, P., *Les Lieux de Memoire* (Paris, 1984).

—'Between memory and history: les lieux de memoire', *Representations*, 26 (1989), 7–25.

Noszlopy, G. T., *Public Sculpture of Birmingham* (Liverpool: Liverpool University Press, 1998).

—*Public Sculpture of Warwickshire, Coventry and Solihull* (Liverpool: Liverpool University Press, 2002).

—*Public Sculpture of Staffordshire and the Black Country* (Liverpool: Liverpool University Press, 2005).

O'Moore, C. and Humphris, E. M., *The Victoria Cross, 1856–1920* (Polstead, 1985).

O'Neill, M., 'Art and Labour's Cause is One': *Walter Crane and Manchester, 1880–1915* (Manchester: University of Manchester, 2008).

Ovenden, J. and Shayer, D., *The Wreck of the Stella* (St Peter Port: Guernsey Museums & Galleries, 1999).

Owen, D., *English Philanthropy 1660–1960* (London: Belknap Press of Harvard University Press, 1964).

Parker, J., 'England's Darling': *the Victorian Cult of Alfred the Great* (Manchester: Manchester University Press, 2007).

Pears, I., 'The gentleman and the hero: Wellington and Napoleon in the nineteenth century', in Porter, R. (ed.), *Myths of the English* (Cambridge, 1992), pp. 216–36.

Pearson, C. and Pope, K., *The Female Hero in American and British Literature* (New York: R.R. Bowker, 1981).

Pellew, J., *The Home Office 1848–1914: From Clerks to Bureaucrats* (London: Heinemann Educational Books, 1982).

Penny, N., 'English sculpture and the First World War', *Oxford Art Journal*, 4:2 (1981), 36–42.

—' "Amor Publicus Posuit": monuments for the people and of the people', *Burlington Magazine*, 109:1017 (London, December 1987), 793–800.

Peterson, M. J., 'No angels in the house: the Victorian myth and the Paget women', *American History Review*, 89:3 (1984), 677–708.

Pickering, P. A. and Tyrrell, A., *Contested Sites: Commemoration, Memorial and Popular Politics in Nineteenth Century Britain* (Aldershot: Ashgate, 2004).

Pickles, K., *Transnational Outrage: the Death and Commemoration of Edith Cavell* (Basingstoke: Palgrave Macmillan, 2007).

Poovey, M., *Uneven Developments: The Ideological Work of Gender in Mid-Victorian England* (Chicago: University of Chicago Press, 1988).

Porter, R. (ed.), *Myths of the English* (Cambridge: Wiley, 1992).

Pound, R., *Scott of the Antarctic* (London: Coward-McCann, 1966).

Price, J., ' "Everyday Heroes": The memorial tiles of Postman's Park', *Journal of the Tiles and Architectural Ceramics Society*, 10 (2004), 18–23.

—' "Heroism in everyday life": the Watts Memorial for Heroic Self Sacrifice', *History Workshop Journal*, 63:1 (2007), 255–78.

—*Postman's Park: G. F. Watts's Memorial to Heroic Self-Sacrifice* (Compton: Watts Gallery, 2008).

—'Ayres, Alice (1859–1885)'. *Oxford Dictionary of National Biography* (Oxford: Oxford University Press, 2010a).

—'Addy, Mark (1840–1890)' *Oxford Dictionary of National Biography* (Oxford: Oxford University Press, 2010b).

Price, R., *An Imperial War and the British Working Class; Working-Class Attitudes and Reactions to the Boer War 1899–1902* (London: Routledge & K. Paul, 1972).

Prochaska, F., *Women and Philanthropy in Nineteenth-Century England* (Oxford: Oxford University Press, 1980).

—*The Voluntary Impulse: Philanthropy in Modern Britain* (London: Faber & Faber, 1988).

—*Royal Bounty: The Making of a Welfare Monarchy* (London: Yale University Press, 1995).

Pugh, M., *Women and the Women's Movement in Britain 1914–1959* (Basingstoke: Palgrave Macmillan, 1992).

—*The March of Women* (Oxford: Oxford University Press, 2000).

Purbrick, L., Aulich, J., and Dawson, G. (eds), *Contested Spaces: Sites, Representations and Histories of Conflict* (Basingstoke: Palgrave Macmillan, 2007).

Purvis, J. and Holton, S. S. (eds), *Votes for Women* (London: Routledge, 2000).

Putzell, S. M. and Leonard, D. C. (eds), *Perspectives on Nineteenth Century Heroism* (New York: J. P. Turanzas, 1982).

Quinault, R. E., 'The cult of the centenary, c.1784–1914', *Historical Research*, 71 (1998), 303–23.

Readman, P., 'The place of the past in English culture c.1890–1914', *Past and Present*, 186 (2005), 147–99.

—'Commemorating the past in Edwardian Hampshire: King Alfred, pageantry and empire', in Taylor, M. (ed.), *Southampton: Gateway to the British Empire* (London: I. B. Tauris & Co Ltd, 2007), pp. 95–114.

Richards, J. (ed.), *Imperialism and Juvenile Fiction* (Manchester: Manchester University Press, 1989).

Richards, J., 'Popular imperialism and the image of the army in juvenile literature', in MacKenzie, J. M.(ed.), *Popular Imperialism and the Military: 1850–1950* (Manchester: Manchester University Press, 1992), pp. 80–108.

—'British imperial heroes', in Richards, J.(ed.), *Films and British National Identity: from Dickens to Dad's Army* (Manchester: Manchester University Press, 1997), pp. 32–59.

Robb, J. H., *The Primrose League 1883–1906* (New York: Columbia University Press, 1942).

Robertson, W., *Welfare in Trust: A History of the Carnegie United Kingdom Trust 1913–1963* (Dunfermline: Carnegie United Kingdom Trust, 1964).

Rose, J., *The Intellectual Life of the British Working Classes* (London: Yale University Press, 2001).

Rose, M. E., *The Relief of Poverty*, 2nd edn (Basingstoke, 1986).

Rose, S. O., *Limited Livelihoods: Gender and Class in Nineteenth-Century England* (London: Routledge, 1992).

Ross, E., *Love and Toil: Motherhood in Outcast London, 1870–1918* (Oxford: Oxford University Press, 1993).

Rowbotham, J., "Soldiers of Christ? images of missionaries in late nineteenth-century Britain: issues of heroism and martyrdom', *Gender & History*, 12:1 (April 2000), 82–106.

Rowbotham, S., *Hidden from History* (London: Pluto Press, 1973).

Ryan, A. P., 'The journalist as historian: William Howard Russell 1820–1907', *History Today*, 4 (1954), 813–22.

Salveson, P., *The People's Monuments: A Guide to Sites and Memorials in North West England* (Manchester: Worker's Educational Association, 1987).

Samuel, R., 'People's history', in Samuel, R. (ed.), *People's History and Socialist Theory* (London: Routledge and Kegan Paul, 1981).

Samuel, R. (ed.), *Patriotism: the Making and Unmaking of British National Identity*, 3 vols. (London: Routledge, 1989).

—*Theatres of Memory, vol. two, Island Stories, Unravelling Britain* (London: Verso, 1998).

Saunders, N. J. (ed.), *Matters of Conflict: Material Culture, Memory and the First World War* (Oxfordshire: Routledge, 2004).

Schneer, J., *London 1900: The Imperial Metropolis* (Yale: Yale University Press, 1999).

Seaman, L. C. B., *Post Victorian Britain 1902–1951* (London: Methuen, 1966).

—*Victorian England* (New York: Methuen, 1973).

Secord, A., "'Be what you would seem to be": Samuel Smiles, Thomas Edward and the making of a working-class scientific hero', *Science in Context*, 16 (2003), 147–74.

Seigel, J., 'Carlyle and Peel: the prophet's search for a heroic politician and an unpublished fragment', *Victorian Studies*, 26 (1983), 181–95.

Segal, R. A., *Hero Myths: A Reader* (Oxford: Wiley, 2000).

Senelick, L., 'Politics as entertainment: Victorian music-hall songs', *Victorian Studies*, 19:2 (1975), 149–80.

Shipley, S., 'Tom Causer of Bermondsey: a boxer-hero of the 1890s', *History Workshop Journal*, 15:2 (1983), 28–59.

Sigsworth, E. M., *In Search of Victorian Values* (Manchester: Manchester University Press, 1988).

Smith, A. D., *National Identity* (London: Penguin Books, 1991).

—*The Nation Made Real: Art and National Identity in Western Europe, 1600–1850* (Oxford: Oxford University Press, 2013).

Smith, A. K., 'All quiet on the Woolwich front? literary and cultural constructions of women munitions workers in the First World War', in Cowman, K. and Jackson, L. A. (eds), *Women and Work Culture: Britain c.1850–1950* (Aldershot: Ashgate Publishing Ltd, 2005), pp. 197–202.

Smith, D. L., *Oliver Cromwell: Politics and Religion in the English Revolution, 1640–1658* (Cambridge: Cambridge University Press, 1991).

Smith, F. B., 'Sexuality in Britain, 1800–1900: some suggested revisions', in Vicinus, M. (ed.), *A Widening Sphere: Changing Roles of Victorian Women* (Bloomington: Indiana University Press, 1977), pp. 188–93.

Smith, G., 'Developing a public language of art', in Smith, G. and Hyde S. (eds), *Walter Crane 1845–1915. Artist, Designer and Socialist* (Manchester: Humphries, 1989), pp. 3–32.

Smith, G., and Hyde S. (eds), *Walter Crane 1845–1915. Artist, Designer and Socialist* (Manchester: Humphries, 1989).

Smith, M. C., *Awarded for Valour: A History of the Victorian Cross and the Evolution of British Heroism* (Basingstoke: Palgrave Macmillan, 2008).

Spencer, I., *Walter Crane* (London: Studio Vista, 1975).

Springhall, J., 'Baden-Powell and the scout movement before 1920: citizen training or soldiers of the future', *English Historical Review*, 102 (1987), 934–42.

Spurr, G. D., 'The London YMCA: a haven of masculine self-improvement and socialization for the late Victorian and Edwardian clerk', *Canadian Journal of History*, 37:2 (2002), 275–301.

Stapleton, J., 'Political thought and national identity in Britain 1850–1950', in Collini, S., Whatmore, R., Young, B. (eds), *History, Religion and Culture: British Intellectual History 1750–1950* (Cambridge: Cambridge University Press, 2000), pp. 245–69.

Stearn, R. T., 'War correspondents and colonial war, c.1870–1900', in MacKenzie, J. M. (ed.), *Popular Imperialism and the Military 1850–1950* (Manchester: Manchester University Press, 1992), pp. 139–61.

—'Russell, Sir William Howard (1820–1907)', *Oxford Dictionary of National Biography* (Oxford: Oxford University Press, 2004).

Strachey, L., *Eminent Victorians: The Definitive Edition* (London: Continuum International Publishing Group, 2002).

Summerfield, P., 'Patriotism and empire: music hall entertainment 1870–1914', in MacKenzie, J. M. (ed.), *Imperialism and Popular Culture* (Manchester: Manchester University Press, 1986), pp. 17–48.

Summers, A., 'Militarism in Britain before the Great War', *History Workshop Journal*, 2 (1976), 104–23.

—'Scouts, guides and VADS: a note in reply to Allen Warren', *English Historical Review*, 102 (1987), 943–7.

—*Female Lives, Moral States: Women, Religion and Public Life in Britain, 1800–1930* (Newbury: Threshold Press, 2000).

Taylor, A., 'Shakespeare and radicalism: the uses and abuses of Shakespeare in nineteenth-century popular politics', *Historical Journal*, 45:2 (2002), 357–79.

Teulié, G., 'Postcards, propaganda & national identity: the photographic representations of the Anglo-Boer war (1899–1902)', in Hugues, G. and Hildenbrand, K. (eds), *Images of War and War of Images* (Newcastle upon Tyne, 2008), pp. 95–120.

Thane, P., 'Late Victorian women', in Gourvish, T. R. and O'Day, A. (ed.), *Later Victorian Britain* (London, 1988), pp. 175–208.

Thompson, A., 'Publicity, philanthropy and commemoration: British society and the war', in Omissi D. E., and Thompson, A. S. (ed.), *The Impact of the South African War* (Basingstoke: Palgrave Macmillan, 2002), pp. 99–123.

Thompson, E. P., *The Making of the English Working Class* (London: Pantheon Books, 1963).

Thompson, F. M. L., 'Social control in Victorian Britain', *The Economic History Review*, 34:2 (May 1981), 189–208.

Tidrick, K., *Empire and the English Character* (London: I. B. Tauris, 1990).

Tosh, J., 'The making of masculinities: the middle class in late nineteenth-century Britain', in John, A. V. and Eustance, C. (eds), *The Men's Share: Masculinities, Male Support and Women's Suffrage in Britain 1890–1920* (London: Routledge, 1997), pp. 38–61.

—*A Man's Place: Masculinity and the Middle-Class Home in Victorian England* (London: Yale University Press, 1999).

—*Manliness and Masculinities in Nineteenth Century Britain* (Harlow, 2005).

Travers, T., *Samuel Smiles and the Victorian Work Ethic* (London: Garland Publishing, 1987).

Treble, J., *Urban Poverty in Britain 1830–1914*, 2nd edn (London: Methuen, 1983).

Treuherz, J., 'Ford Madox Brown and the Manchester murals', in Archer, J. (ed.), *Art and Architecture in Victorian Manchester* (Manchester: Manchester University Press, 1985).

Troup, E., *The Home Office* (London: Read Books, 1925).

Tucker, W., *The Language of Sculpture* (London: Thames and Hudson, 1974).

Tyrell, A. and Walvin, J., 'Whose history is it? memorialising Britain's involvement in slavery', in Pickering, P. A. and Tyrell, A. (ed.), *Contested Sites: Commemoration, Memorials and Popular Politics in Nineteenth-Century Britain* (Aldershot: Ashgate, 2004), pp. 147–69.

Usherwood, P., 'William Bell Scott's Iron and Coal: northern readings', in J. Vickers (ed.), *Pre-Raphaelite Patrons and Patrons in the North East* (Newcastle: Tyne and Wear Museums Service, 1989), pp. 39–56.

—*Public Sculpture of North-East England* (Liverpool: Liverpool University Press, 2000).

Vance, N., *The sinews of the spirit: the idea of Christian manliness in Victorian literature and religious thought* (Cambridge: Cambridge University Press, 1985).

Vicinus, M. (ed.), *Suffer and Be Still: Women in the Victorian Age* (Bloomington: Indiana University Press, 1972).

Vicinus, M., 'What makes a heroine?: girls' biographies of Florence Nightingale', in Bullough, V. L. Bullough, B, and Stanton, M. P. (eds), *Florence Nightingale and her Era: A Collection of New Scholarship* (New York, 1980), pp. 96–107.

—*Independent Women: Work and Community for Single Women, 1850–1920* (London: Virago Press, 1985).

Vickery, A. 'Golden age to separate spheres? A review of the categories and chronology of English women's history', *The Historical Journal*, 36: 2 (June 1993), pp. 383–414.

Wagg, S. and Russell, D. (eds), *Sporting Heroes of the North: Sport, Religion and Culture* (Newcastle upon Tyne, 2010).

Walkowitz, J. R., 'Butler, Josephine Elizabeth (1828–1906)', *Oxford Dictionary of National Biography* (Oxford: Oxford University Press, 2004).

Wall, F. J., *Andrew Carnegie* (London, 1970).

Waller, J. H., *Gordon of Khartoum: The Saga of a Victorian Hero* (New York: Atheneum, 1988).

Warren, A., 'Sir Robert Baden-Powell, the scout movement and citizen training in Great Britain, 1900–1920', *English Historical Review*, 101 (1986), 376–98.

—'Baden-Powell: two lives of a hero, or two heroic lives?', in Cubitt, G. and Warren, A. (eds), *Heroic Reputations and Exemplary Lives* (Manchester: Manchester University Press, 2000), pp. 123–41

West, S. (ed.), *The Victorians and Race* (Aldershot: Scolar Press, 1996).

Whelan, R. (ed.), *Octavia Hill's Letters to Fellow Workers 1872–1911* (London: Kyrle, 2005), pp. 203–4.

Whittick, A., *War Memorials* (Glasgow, 1946).

Wigglesworth, N., *A Social History of English Rowing* (London: Taylor & Francis Group, 1992).

Wilkinson-Latham, R., *From our Special Correspondent: Victorian War Correspondents and their Campaigns* (Sevenoaks: Hodder and Stoughton, 1979).

Williamson. L., *Power and Protest: Frances Power Cobbe and Victorian Society* (London: Rivers Oram, 2005).

Willsdon, C. A. P., *Mural Painting in Britain 1840–1940: Image and Meaning* (Oxford: Oxford University Press, 2000).

Winter, J., *Sites of Memory, Sites of Mourning* (Cambridge: Cambridge University Press, 1995).

Wood, A., *Nineteenth Century Britain, 1815–1914* (Harlow: Longmans, 1960).

Wolffe, J., *Great Deaths* (Oxford: Oxford University Press, 2000).

Wyke, T. J., *Public Sculpture of Greater Manchester* (Liverpool: Liverpool University Press, 2004).

—'Marginal figures? public statues and public parks in the Manchester region 1840–1914', in Eyres, P. and Russell, F. (eds), *Sculpture and the Garden* (Aldershot: Ashgate, 2006), pp. 85–98.

Yarrington, A., *The Commemoration of the Hero 1800–1864* (London: Garland, 1988).

Websites

Hansard 1803–2005, http://hansard.millbanksystems.com/

Public Monuments and Sculpture Association, http://www.pmsa.org.uk/

Index

Adamson, Jimmy   98
Addy, Mark   12, 95, 103–5, 115, 117–18,
      121, 207
Albert Medal   4, 1–18, 92, 125, 201
   administration   32, 60
   aim   198
   altruism   55–6
   awarded lists   44
   character and morality   53–5
   chivalry   56–7
   Crown sanctioned   36
   decision-making process   45–7
   exemplarity   53
   first and second-class distinctions   33
   gendered construction of   192–3
   land medal   33
   nationality   58–9
   nominations   42
   presentation ceremony   35–6
   qualifications   45
   refusals   47–8
      insufficient evidence   52–3
      not up to the standard   52
      professional duty   50–1
      use of safety equipment   53
   revoking   38–9
   Royal warrant   32–3, 205
   sea award   32–3
   women awardees
      marital status   172
      occupations   173
Anon
   Working-Men Heroes: a roll of heroic
      actions in humble life   26
Armstrong, Isabella   182
Arthurian legends   8
Ayres, Alice   22–4, 68, 72–7, 83–5, 95,
      115, 180–1, 191, 199, 208

Baden-Powell, Robert   1
Bailey, Alderman   121

Barber, John   55–6
Barrington, Emilie   20, 67
Battersby, Edward   49–50
Benson, Edward White   67
Bergonzi, Bernard   27
Beveridge, Henry   149
Birch, Dinah   2–3
Blair, David   149
Bloch, Marc   10
Board of Trade Medal for Saving Life
      at Sea   34–6, 45, 167
Borg, Alan
   War Memorials from Antiquity
      to the Present   97
Briggs, Asa   7
Brown, Ford Madox   70
   Work   78
Brown, James   149
Brown, Margaret   182
Brown, Mary   182
Bruce, Edward James   149
Bryans, Annie   190
Bryans, Herbert   190
Burke, Peter   10
Bussell, Grace   181
Butler, Josephine   168, 188

Caine, Barbara   188
Campbell, Colin   1
Campbell, Joseph
   The Hero with a Thousand Faces   9
Carlyle, Thomas   3, 6, 197
   On Heroes, Hero-Worship and the
      Heroic in History   2, 197
Carnegie, Andrew   199
   Armaments and their Results   160
   The Gospel of Wealth   128
   military heroism   161
   The Path to Peace upon the
      Seas   160
   Social Darwinism   128

War as the Mother of Valor and
    Civilization 160
Carnegie Dunfermline Trust 126
Carnegie Endowment for International
    Peace 160
Carnegie Hero Fund Commission 126
Carnegie Hero Fund Trust (CHFT) 4, 20,
    26–7, 126, 203
  administration 132–7
  and Albert Medal 129
  Annual Report 129–30
  awards 137–48
  Board of Trustees 131, 133–4, 136–7,
    148–51
  honorary awards 154
  one-off payments 156–7
  pecuniary awards 136, 152–3, 158–9
  pensions 156
  problems and challenges 151–2
  purpose 126
  reactions to 126–7, 151–2
  rewarding acts 127
  women awardees
    marital status 172
    occupations 173
  world peace 159–61
Castle Gardens Committee 112–13
Cavanagh, Terry 4, 122
Cavell, Edith 168
Chapman, Kate 192–3
Charles I 2
CHFT *see* Carnegie Hero Fund Trust (CHFT)
chivalry 8, 56–7
Church Peace Union 160
civic monuments *see* monuments
Cobbe, Francis Power 188–90, 201
Collini, Stefan 53, 55
commemoration *see* monuments; murals
Contagious Diseases Acts 187–8
Cowman, Krista 168
Crane, Walter 20, 23, 68, 199
  Ideals in Art 69
Crimean War 15–16
Cromwell, Oliver 2, 8
Cross, F. J.
  Beneath the Banner 5, 25
  Everyday Heroes: Stories of Bravery
    during the Queen's Reign 5, 25
Cubitt, Geoffrey 6, 90

Darling, Grace 90, 168
Davidoff, Leonore 174
Dawson, Graham 27
D' Cruze, Shani 182
Deed, Percy 112
Delap, Lucy 186, 193
De Morgan, William 87
Denman, Alice Maud 95, 208–9
Digby, Kenelm Henry
  The Broad Stone of Honour 56
Dodd, Abraham 27–8

Edward Medal 125
Edwards, John Passmore 87

Febvre, Lucien 10
Froude, J. A.
  Short Studies on Great Subjects 89
Fry, Elizabeth 7, 168

George Cross 32–4
George Medal 32–3
Gillis, John 64
Girouard, Mark 56
Gordon, Charles George 1, 5
Gordon, Percy Henry 96, 107, 113, 115,
    117–18, 209
'Great Men of History' 2, 8, 60
Greenoff, Edward 28
Greg, W. R. 171

Halinstrom, Norah 177, 180
Hall, Catherine 174
Hamilton, C. I. 3–4
Hampden, John 2
Hansard 4
Harrison, Ethel 95, 98–9, 102, 106–8,
    111, 115, 117–18, 123, 200,
    209–10
Harrison, Frederic
  Calendar of Great Men 8
Havelock, Henry 1, 5
Heathorn, Stephen 60, 148, 150, 162–3
heroism
  civilian 4, 31–2, 51, 198, 202–3
  and exemplarity 6, 25
  female 84, 194–5, 201
    domestic ideology 174, 180–4
    compared to male heroism 176–9

marital status   171
occupations   171–4
separate spheres   174–5
Stella disaster   184–7
military   3, 5, 15–16, 202
recognition of   14
and risk to life   3, 11, 49, 168, 197, 199
and the working-classes   11, 15, 18, 22,
    64, 80–1, 83, 91–2, 121, 149, 162,
    168, 172, 175, 191, 198–201, 203
Hill, Christopher   204
Hill, Octavia   20, 24, 65–6, 199
Hird, Barbra   28
history from below   12
Hobsbawm, Eric   12–13, 15
Hodder, Edwin
Heroes of Britain in Peace and
    War   170
Hodges, James   43
Holland, William J.   126
Hoole, Elijah   67
Horncastle, George
Heroes of Everyday Life   26
Hudson, Rock   202
Hunter, Robert   67, 85
Hunter, William   95, 100, 115, 210
Hynd, John   149

Jefferies, Robert   28
Jones, Max   8, 13, 202

Karsten, Peter   2, 13, 199
Keswick School of Industrial Arts
    (KSIA)   85
King, Alex
Memorials to the Great War in
    Britain   97
Kitchener, Horatio   1
Kyrle society   66–7

Lane, Laura M.   20
Heroes of Every-day Life   23, 25, 82
Lawrence, Thomas Edward   1
Layard, Austen   16
Lee, Albert   95, 108–9, 113, 115, 117–18,
    210–11
Legion d' Honneur medal   16
Leighton, Frederick   68
Lewis, Thomas   38

Lieven, Michael   9
Liverpool Shipwreck and Humane
    Society   125
Livingstone, David   1
Lynch, Frederick
Personal Recollections of Andrew
    Carnegie   160

Macbeth, James   149
MacKenzie, John   9, 60
Married Women's Property Act   188
Martin, William
Heroism of Boyhood   5
Mathewson, George   149
Matrimonial Clauses Act   188
McCandless, John   19
McGlennon, Felix
Heroes of Everyday Life   5, 26
medals   15
Albert   4, 1–18, 31–61, 92, 125, 201
Board of Trade   34–6, 45, 167
Carnegie Hero Fund Trust   154
Edward   125
George   32–3
George Cross   32–4
The King's Police and Fire Brigades
    Medal   142
Legion d 'Honneur   16
RHS   4, 20, 26–8, 83, 125, 134–5, 152,
    193, 198, 203
RNLI   26, 49, 125, 167
SPLF   4, 83, 125, 135–6, 152,
    193, 198
Victoria Cross   4, 16, 27, 47,
    60, 193
memorials *see* monuments; murals
Merrington, Martha   188
Metropolitan Fire Brigade Act   135
Metropolitan Open Spaces Act   66
Metropolitan Public Gardens
    Association   66
Michael, Charles D.   25
Deeds of Daring: Stories of Heroism
    in Every Day Life   5
Heroines: True Tales of Brave
    Women   5, 170
Michelet, Jules
History of the French Revolution   10
Milner-Gibson, Thomas   34–6

Milton, John 161
Monroe, Marilyn 202
monuments 4, 22, 96, 188–90, 200
    Albert Lee 109
    Alice Ayres 116
    drinking fountains 95–7
    Edgar George Wilson 102
    Ethel Harrison 96
    local and national identity 118–20
    location, choices for 114–16
    Mark Addy 104, 121
    Mary Rogers 114
    memorial committees 96, 100–1, 105,
        107, 113, 116–17
    messages of 98, 117, 122
    obelisks 97, 108, 113
    Percy Henry Gordon 107
    subscription funded 105–8, 122–3,
        198
    tablets 113–14
    Timothy Trow 111
    Watts Memorial 19–20, 28–9, 86–91,
        96
    William Hunter 101
    William Walton 103
    World War I 97
Moore, Charles 191
    Noble Deeds of the World's Heroines 5
Mottram, Alderman 118
Mundell, Frank 20, 182
    Heroines of Daily Life 5, 25, 84, 170,
        176
murals 24, 65–7, 73–82
Murrell, Minnie 179–80

Napier, Charles James 1
National Union of Women's Suffrage
    Societies 188
Nelson, Horatio 1
New History 10–12
Nightingale, Florence 7, 168

O' Neill, Morna 69–70
Order of St John of Jerusalem 26, 125
Order of the Bath 16
Outram, James 1

Patmore, Coventry
    The Angel in the House 179, 183

Pellew, Jill 46
Penfold, John 186–7
Perrault, Charles
    Riquet with the Tuft 190
Pitt, Leigh 28
Popplestone, Samuel 31–2
popular imperialism 3
Postman's Park 19, 28, 64, 87, 96, 119
Prochaska, Frank 128
Public Monuments and Sculpture
    Association (PMSA) 95, 117
Pugh, Martin 188
Putnam, Charles 47–8

Rawnsley, Hardwicke 20, 67
    Ballads of Brave Deeds 5, 84
Red Cross Hall murals 65–7, 73–82
    Alice Ayres 73–7
    Jamieson 77–8
Reeks, William 184
Regelous, Arthur 208–9
RHS *see* Royal Humane Society
Richards, Jeffrey 59
Rickards, Charles 19
RNLI *see* Royal National Lifeboat
    Institution
Roberts, Frederick 1
Robertson, William 149
Robinson, Benjamin 121
Rogers, Mary Anne 95, 107, 114–15, 119,
    182–90, 194, 211–12
Rosbotham, Hannah 18, 35, 177–8,
    181, 193
Ross, John 126, 130, 149–50
Rowbotham, Judith 168
Royal Humane Society (RHS) 4, 20,
    26–7, 83, 125, 134–5, 152, 193,
    198, 203
Royal National Lifeboat Institution
    (RNLI) 26, 49, 125, 167
Ruben, Arthur 47–8
Ruskin, John 2
Russell, William Howard 16

Samuel, Raphael 12–13
Scobell, George 16
Scobie, Andrew 149
Scott, Robert F. 1, 13
separate spheres 174–5

Sharples, James
    The Forge 78
Shearer, Andrew   149
Shennan, Hay   149
Smiles, Samuel
    Character   7, 53–4
    Duty   7
    Self-Help   7
Smith, Alfred   28
Smith, Greg   70
Smith, Melvin   27, 47
Smith, Sarah   190, 199
Society for Promoting Christian
        Knowledge (SPCK)   83–4
Society for the Protection of Life from Fire
        (SPLF)   4, 83, 125, 135–6, 152,
        193, 198
    women awardees
        marital status   172
        occupations   173
Spencer, Isobel   70
SPLF *see* Society for the Protection
        of Life from Fire
Sprankling, Charles   46
Stevenson, Robert   149

Thompson, Edward P.   13, 51
Thompson, Louisa   98
Tosh, John   181
Toynbee, Arnold   10
Trevelyan, M.
    *Brave Little Women: Tales of the
        Heroism of Girls*   5
Trow, Timothy   95, 110–11, 113, 115,
        117–19, 212

Tuke, Alan Smith   149
Tweedale, Geoffrey   160
Tynewydd colliery   17–18, 28

Vasseur, Catherine   176–7
Vicinus, Martha   174
Victoria Cross   4, 16, 27, 47, 60, 193

Walker, Robert   149
Wall, Joseph   160
Walton, William   95, 101–2, 109, 117–18,
        120–1, 213
Ward, Francis   50
Watts, George Frederic   19–21, 24, 190–1,
        201
    *Caractacus Led in Triumph through the
        Streets of Rome*   63
    The Happy Warrior   84
    *Love Steering the Boat of
        Humanity*   120
Watts Memorial to Heroic Self-Sacrifice
        19–20, 28–9, 86–91, 96
Weir, John   149–50
Wellesley, Arthur   1
Whyte, Jane   12, 167, 176, 180
Williams, George   100
Willsdon, Clare   69
Wilson, Edgar George   96, 100, 103, 109,
        115, 118, 213
Wolseley, Garnet Joseph   1
women *see* heroism: female
Wootton, William   50

Young Men's Christian Association
        (YMCA)   100